Brilliant

Microsoft®

Windows® 10

Steve Johnson

Perspection, Inc.

Harlow, England • London • New York • Boston • San Francisco • Toronto • Sydney • Auckland • Singapore • Hong Kong
Tokyo • Seoul • Taipei • New Delhi • Cape Town • São Paulo • Mexico City • Madrid • Amsterdam • Munich • Paris • Milan

Pearon Education Limited
Edinburgh Gate
Harlow
Essex CM20 2JE
England

and Associated Companies throughout the world

Visit us on the World Wide Web at:
www.pearson.com/uk

Original edition, entitled WINDOWS 8.1 ON DEMAND, 1st edition, 9780789752284 by JOHNSON, STEVE; PERSPECTION, INC., published by Pearson Eduction, Inc., publishing as Que, Copyright © 2014 by Perspection, Inc.

This UK edition published by PEARSON EDUCATION LTD.

This edition is manufactured in the USA and available for sale only in the United Kingdom, Europe, the Middle East, and Africa.

The right of Steve Johnson to be identified as the author of this work has been asserted by him in accordance with the Copyright, Designs and Patents Act 1988.

ISBN: 978-1-292-11817-8 (print)
ISBN: 978-1-292-11866-6 (pdf)
ISBN: 978-1-292-11865-9 (etext)

British Library Cataloguing-in-Publication Data
A catalogue record for this book is available from the British Library

10 9 8 7 6 5 4 3 2 1
19 18 17 16 15

Printed and bound in Slovakia by Neografia

Brilliant Guides

What you need to know and how to do it

When you're working on your computer and come up against a problem that you're unsure how to solve, or want to accomplish something in an application that you aren't sure how to do, where do you look? Manuals and traditional training guides are usually too big and unwieldy and are intended to be used as an end-to-end training resource, making it hard to get to the info you need right away without having to wade through pages of background information that you just don't need at that moment - and helplines are rarely that helpful!

Brilliant guides have been developed to allow you to find the info you need easily and without fuss and guide you through the task using a highly visual, step-by-step approach - providing exactly what you need to know when you need it!!

Brilliant guides provide the quick easy-to-access information that you need, using a detailed index and troubleshooting guide to help you find exactly what you need to know, and then presenting each task on one or two pages. Numbered steps then guide you through each task or problem, using numerous screenshots to illustrate each step. Added features include "See Also..." boxes that point you to related tasks and information in the book, whilst "Did you know?..." sections alert you to relevant expert tips, tricks and advice to further expand your skills and knowledge.

In addition to covering all major office applications, and related computing subjects, the *Brilliant* series also contains titles will help you in every aspect of your working life, such as writing the perfect CV, answering the toughest interview questions and moving on in your career.

Brilliant guides are the light at the end of the tunnel when you are faced with any minor or major task!

Acknowledgments

Perspection, Inc.

Brilliant Microsoft Windows 10 has been created by the professional trainers and writers at Perspection, Inc. to the standards you've come to expect from Pearson publishing. Together, we are pleased to present this training book.

Perspection, Inc. is a software training company committed to providing information and training to help people use software more effectively in order to communicate, make decisions, and solve problems. Perspection writes and produces software training books, and develops multimedia and web-based training. Since 1991, we have written more than 150 computer books, with several bestsellers to our credit, and sold over 6 million books.

This book incorporates Perspection's training expertise to ensure that you'll receive the maximum return on your time. You'll focus on the tasks and skills that increase productivity while working at your own pace and convenience.

We invite you to visit the Perspection web site at:

www.perspection.com

Acknowledgments

The task of creating any book requires the talents of many hard-working people pulling together to meet impossible deadlines and untold stresses. We'd like to thank the outstanding team responsible for making this book possible: the writer, Steve Johnson; the production editor, James Teyler; the proofreader, Beth Teyler; and the indexer, Kristina Zeller.

Perspection

About The Author

Steve Johnson has written more than 90 books on a variety of computer software, including Adobe Photoshop CC, Adobe InDesign CC, Adobe Illustrator CC, Adobe Dreamweaver CS6, Adobe Edge Animate, Adobe Flash Professional CS5, Microsoft Windows 8, Microsoft Office 2013 and 2010, Microsoft SharePoint 2013, Microsoft Office 2008 for the Macintosh, and Apple OS X Mavericks. In 1991, after working for Apple Computer and Microsoft, Steve founded Perspection, Inc., which writes and produces software training. When he is not staying up late writing, he enjoys coaching baseball, playing golf, gardening, and spending time with his wife, Holly, and three children, JP, Brett, and Hannah. Steve and his family live in Northern California, but can also be found visiting family all over the western United States.

Contents

Introduction

Welcome to *Brilliant Microsoft Windows 10*, a visual quick reference book that shows you how to work efficiently with Windows 10. This book provides complete coverage of basic to advanced Windows skills.

How This Book Works

You don't have to read this book in any particular order. We've designed the book so that you can jump in, get the information you need, and jump out. However, the book does follow a logical progression from simple tasks to more complex ones. Each task is presented on no more than two facing pages, which lets you focus on a single task without having to turn the page. To find the information that you need, just look up the task in the table of contents or index, and turn to the page listed. Read the task introduction, follow the step-by-step instructions in the left column along with screen illustrations in the right column, and you're done.

What's New

If you're searching for what's new in Windows 10, just look for the icon: **New!**. The new icon appears in the table of contents and throughout this book so you can quickly and easily identify a new or improved feature in Windows 10. A complete description of each new feature appears in the New Features guide in the back of this book.

Keyboard Shortcuts

Most menu commands have a keyboard equivalent, such as Ctrl+P, as a quicker alternative to using the mouse. A complete list of keyboard shortcuts is available on the web at *www.perspection.com*.

How You'll Learn

How This Book Works

What's New

Keyboard Shortcuts

Step-by-Step Instructions

Real World Examples

Workshops

Get More on the Web

Get Resources on the Web

Step-by-Step Instructions

This book provides concise step-by-step instructions that show you "how" to accomplish a task. Each set of instructions includes illustrations that directly correspond to the easy-to-read steps. Also included in the text are time-savers, tables, and sidebars to help you work more efficiently or to teach you more in-depth information. A "Did You Know?" provides tips and techniques to help you work smarter, while a "See Also" leads you to other parts of the book containing related information about the task.

Real World Examples

This book uses real world examples files to give you a context in which to use the task. By using the example files, you won't waste time looking for or creating sample files. You get a start file and a result file, so you can compare your work. Not every topic needs an example file, such as changing options, so we provide a complete list of the example files used through out the book. The example files that you need for project tasks along with a complete file list are available on the web at *www.perspection.com.*

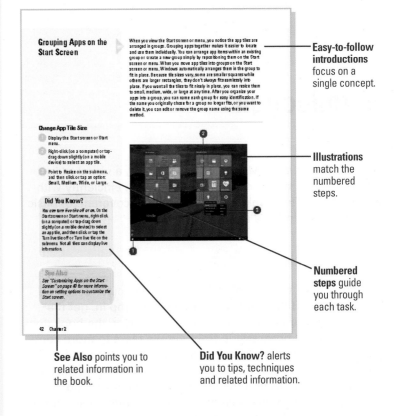

Easy-to-follow introductions focus on a single concept.

Illustrations match the numbered steps.

Numbered steps guide you through each task.

See Also points you to related information in the book.

Did You Know? alerts you to tips, techniques and related information.

Real world examples help you apply what you've learned to other tasks.

Workshops

This book shows you how to put together the individual step-by-step tasks into in-depth projects with the Workshop. You start each project with a sample file, work through the steps, and then compare your results with a project results file at the end. The Workshop projects and associated files are available on the web at *www.perspection.com*.

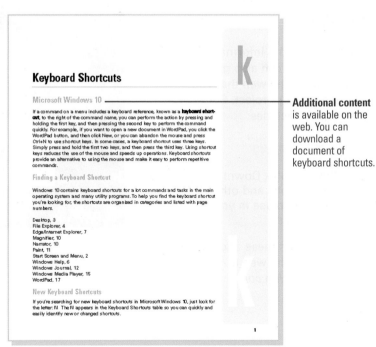

The **Workshops** walks you through in-depth projects to help you put Windows 10 to work.

Get More on the Web

In addition to the information in this book, you can also get more information on the web to help you get up to speed faster with Windows 10. Some of the information includes:

Transition Helpers

◆ **Only New Features.** Download and print the new feature tasks as a quick and easy guide.

Productivity Tools

◆ **Keyboard Shortcuts.** Download a list of keyboard shortcuts to learn faster ways to get the job done.

Additional content is available on the web. You can download a document of keyboard shortcuts.

More Content

- **Windows 10.** Download additional chapters with content to help you get more out of Windows:
  - Administering Windows.
  - Maintaining and Optimizing Windows.

- **Office 2016.** Download more content to learn about new content in Office 2016.

You can access these additional resources on the web at www.perspection.com.

Get Resources on the Web

In addition to the information in this book, you can also get some resources on the web that you can use in your project. Some of the content includes:

More Resources

- **Photographs.** Download photographs and other graphics to use in your documents.

You can access these additional resources on the web at www.perspection.com.

Administering Your Computer 18

Introduction

If you have purchased a personal computer and set it up in your home, you are that PC's administrator. Computers on a network in a company or an institution, such as at a university, are called clients. The clients are managed by one or more system or network administrators, who have the task of ensuring that the network and its services are reliable, fast, and secure. Although most network administration takes place on the server (host, as described in earlier chapters), clients must also be administered. Windows 10 includes administrative tools that make it easy to ensure that client PCs are operating as they should.

You can use the administrative tools to track and view the activity on your PC. You can set up criteria for gathering event information, and then Windows automatically gathers that information for you. In the event of a problem, you can view that data to help you find and fix the problem.

When you open an administrative tool, Windows uses a two-pane view that is similar to File Explorer. The hierarchy of tools in the left pane of the window is called a **console tree**, and each main category of tools is called a **node**. The nodes in the console tree allow you to manage and monitor system events and performance, and make adjustments as necessary.

What You'll Do

Explore Windows Administrative Tools

Schedule Tasks

Monitor Activity with Event Viewer

Manage an Event Log

Manage All Printers

Check Memory for Problems

View and Create Performance Charts

Monitor Local Security Settings

View Computer Management Tools

Manage Disks

Manage Local Users and Groups

View and Save System Information

Set System Configuration Options

483

The additional **Content** helps you get more out of Windows 10.

Download and use **Photographs** to help you add impact to your documents.

Getting Started with Windows 10

1

Introduction

Microsoft Windows 10 introduces a breakthrough user experience that is designed to help you intuitively view, find, and organize information on your PC whether it's a desktop computer, tablet, or mobile device. Windows 10 delivers better personal productivity and digital entertainment with a new touch-based interface to go along with the traditional Windows desktop. Before you get started with Windows 10, check out the new features, which includes Windows Hello for easy sign in, a Start menu (it's back and better than ever), Cortana (your digital personal assistant), a web browser with an Edge, and optimization for PCs and mobile devices, as well as improvements to the standard and full-screen apps, the Store to purchase, download, and update apps, OneDrive to sync data to the cloud, the Start screen, desktop and taskbar, File Explorer, and Settings. A complete description of each new feature appears in the New Features guide in the back of this book.

Microsoft Windows 10 is an **operating system**, a program that controls the basic operation of your PC or mobile device and the programs you run. A **program**, also known as an **application** or **app** (for short), is task-oriented software you use to accomplish a specific task, such as word processing, performing calculations, or managing files on your device. Windows 10 displays programs on your device within windows (thus the name of the operating system). A **window** can contain an app, the contents of a file, or other usable data. A **file** is a collection of information (such as a letter or list of addresses) that has a unique name, distinguishing it from other files. Windows 10 uses tiles, icons, and thumbnails to provide information or meaningful symbols for the items they represent. This use of tiles, icons, thumbnails, and windows is called a **graphical user interface** (GUI, pronounced "gooey"), meaning that you ("user") interact ("interface") with your device through the use of graphics.

Introducing Windows 10

Windows 10 Editions

Windows 10 comes in four editions: the Windows 10 Home Edition for consumers; the Windows 10 Professional Edition for business and power users; the Windows 10 Enterprise Edition for corporations, and the Windows 10 Mobile and Mobile Enterprise Edition for Windows-based touch-optimized devices.

The **Windows 10 Home** Edition provides a basic secure entry point for using Windows 10 with PC computers, 2-in-1s, and tablets.

The **Windows 10 Professional** Edition adds to the basic Windows 10 experience by providing features for encryption, virtualization, PC computer management, and domain and remote desktop connectivity.

The **Windows 10 Enterprise** Edition is for IT-based corporations with advanced data protection, compatibility, and international support needs.

The **Windows 10 Education** Edition (**New!**) is an Enterprise Edition designed for use in schools, colleges and universities.

The **Windows 10 Mobile** Edition provides an entry point for optimizing Windows 10 on smartphones and tablets. It's the successor to Windows RT.

The **Windows 10 Mobile Enterprise** Edition is optimized for smartphones and tablets for use in IT-based corporations.

The **Windows 10 IoT Core** Edition (**New!**) provides an entry point for use in small footprint, low-cost devices and IoT scenarios.

Windows 10 User Experience

Windows 10 provides two distinct user interface experiences: one using touch gestures and the other using a keyboard and mouse.

Both offer a new and intuitive navigation experience that help you more easily find, organize, and use your apps and files on PC computers, 2-in-1s, tablets, and mobile phones.

With Windows 10, you can optimize your experience for a PC computer with a mouse or mobile device with a touch screen or pad by turning Tablet mode (**New!**) on or off (available in the Actions center on the taskbar).

The touch gesture experience provides controls for touch screens or pads to work with and navigate within Windows and applications. For example, you can use a single-finger slide to move the mouse cursor or a single or two finder tap or double tap to click or double-click at the cursor location. You can also use a two finder slide to scroll horizontally or vertically, or a two finger pinch in or out or a three finder slide up or down to zoom in or out.

In addition to simulating mouse features, you can also use swipe gestures to navigate and display commands. For example (**New!**), you can swipe in from the right edge to open the Action Center, swipe in from the top edge to view title bars for full screened apps (where you can close it), swipe in from the bottom to view the taskbar in full screened apps, or swipe in from the left edge to open apps in task view.

The keyboard and mouse experience provides a traditional way to use Windows 10 on a PC computer. Windows 10 comes with keyboard shortcuts to help you navigate the operating system on a PC. For example, you can press Ctrl+Plus Sign to zoom in or Ctrl+Minus Sign to zoom out, or press Win+D to open the desktop. The Win key appears on most keyboards in the lower-left corner as ⊞.

Starting Windows 10

Windows 10 automatically starts when you turn on your PC computer or mobile device. When you first start Windows 10, you see a Lock screen, a full screen image with the time, date and notification icons (with app status), or the Sign in screen, a secure way to identify yourself on your device. With a simple drag of a mouse, press of a key, movement of your finger, you can dismiss the Lock screen to display the Sign in screen. After you sign in by selecting a user and entering a password, gesturing on a picture or using Windows Hello (**New!**) with a look or fingerprint touch, you see the Start (in Tablet mode) or Desktop (**New!**) screen, which you can use to work with apps. If you sign in with a Microsoft account, such as live.com, your device becomes connected to the OneDrive cloud, which allows you to share information with others.

Start Windows 10

1. Turn on your PC computer or mobile device, and wait for Windows 10 to start.

2. If the Lock screen appears, click anywhere on the screen or press a key or move your finger sideways from the edge.

3. Click or tap your username, type your password, and then click or tap the **Submit arrow**, or press Enter. For other options & setup, click or tap **Sign-in options**, or under Accounts in Settings.

   ◆ **Picture password.** Drag a sequence of gestures.

   ◆ **Windows Hello.** Use fingerprint or other reader (**New!**), and then swipe the screen.

   The Windows 10 desktop and taskbar appears (**New!**).

4. On first use, follow the screens or get started with help (depending on your installation):

   ◆ **On-screen help.** Follow the on-screen instructions to show you how to get started.

   ◆ **Get Started with help.** Click or tap the **Get Started** tile (**New!**) on the Start menu to open it.

Start menu   Taskbar   Desktop

For Your Information

Activating or Displaying System Information

If you need to activate Windows or find out your Windows version, system details, or computer or workgroup name, you can quickly display System Information from any screen. Click or tap Settings on the Start menu (**New!**). For activating, click or tap Update & security, and then click or tap Activation. For system information, click System, and then click or tap About. You can also right-click or tap-hold the lower-left corner of the screen, and then click or tap System or press Win+Pause/Break. In the System window, you can view information, change settings, or activate your Windows version.

Using the Mouse or Touch

The user interface for Windows 10 is designed to work on PC computers, 2-in-1s, and mobile devices, including smartphones and tablets. You can switch between PC and tablet mode for optimum use. simply, select the **Action Center** button on the taskbar, and then select **Tablet mode** (New!) (toggles on/off). You can control Windows by using a pointing device on your PC computer or gestures with your finger on a mobile device. A **pointing device** is hardware connected to or built into the PC computer you use to position the **pointer**, the small symbol on the screen that indicates the pointer's position. The most common pointing devices are a **mouse** for desktop computers and a **touch pad** for laptop or notebook computers. When you move the mouse across a flat surface (such as a desk or a mouse pad), or place your finger on the touch pad and drag it across, the pointer on the screen moves in the same direction. The shape of the pointer changes to indicate different activities. Once you move the pointer to a desired position on the screen, you use the buttons on the mouse or touch pad to access the PC computer's functions, "tell" your system what you want it to do. Other available pointing devices include **trackballs**, which function similarly to the mouse, and stylus pens, which work with a tablet pad or mobile device to move the pointer and enter handwritten information. For a mobile device or PC computer touch screen or pad, all you need is your finger to make gestures. A **gesture** (New!) is the movement of one or more fingers on a touch screen or pad. For example, dragging your finger with a flicking motion at the end of the movement is called **swiping** or **sliding**. Some mobile devices also include a **stylus pen** which you can use like on a PC computer.

Positioning the mouse pointer over an item on the screen is called **pointing**. When you point to an item, Windows often displays a **ScreenTip**, identifying the item or displaying status information. A typical mouse has two mouse buttons, however, some models include a third button or wheel in the middle. The act of pressing the left mouse button once and releasing it is called **clicking**, also known as single-clicking, and the act of touching and removing your finger is called **tapping**. The act of clicking or tapping an item, such as a tile or icon, indicates that you have selected it. To perform an operation on a tile or icon, such as opening or moving it, you must first select it. In some instances, such as working with the desktop, you need to click the left mouse button twice in a row, known as **double-clicking** or tap twice, known as **double-tapping**, to open a window, program, or file. Holding down the left mouse and moving is known as **dragging**.

Clicking the right mouse button is known as **right-clicking**. Right-clicking an item displays a shortcut menu. When a step tells you to "click," it means to click the left mouse button. If you are supposed to click the right mouse button, the step will instruct you to "right-click." If you press and hold your finger on a mobile device it does the same thing as right-clicking an item. Anytime you click or tap anywhere outside a selected item, Windows cancels the operation and deselects the item.

When you cannot see all of the items available on a screen, scroll bars appear (when you move your mouse) on the right and bottom edges of the screen or within a window. Scroll bars allow you to display the additional contents of the window by dragging or swiping left or right or up and down. If your mouse has a wheel between the two mouse buttons, you can roll it to quickly scroll a few lines or an entire screen at a time.

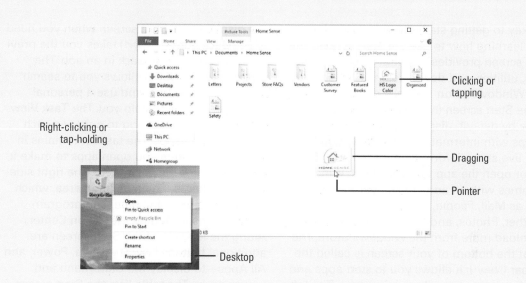

Right-clicking or tap-holding

Clicking or tapping

Dragging

Pointer

Desktop

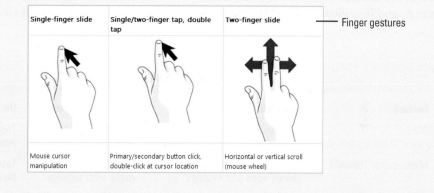

Single-finger slide	Single/two-finger tap, double tap	Two-finger slide
Mouse cursor manipulation	Primary/secondary button click, double-click at cursor location	Horizontal or vertical scroll (mouse wheel)

Finger gestures

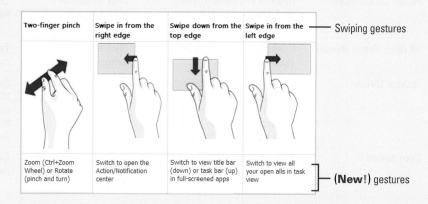

Two-finger pinch	Swipe in from the right edge	Swipe down from the top edge	Swipe in from the left edge
Zoom (Ctrl+Zoom Wheel) or Rotate (pinch and turn)	Switch to open the Action/Notification center	Switch to view title bar (down) or task bar (up) in full-screened apps	Switch to view all your open alls in task view

Swiping gestures

(New!) gestures

Exploring the Start Screen

The key to getting started with the Windows 10 is learning how to use the **Start screen**. The Start screen provides a central place to access apps, utilities, and device settings. When you start Windows 10 on a mobile device and sign in, the Start screen (**New!**) appears in Tablet mode by default, displaying app tiles in groups with information. **Tiles** allow you to view live status information for the specific app or open the app to work with it. Windows 10 comes with an array of standard apps, such as Mail, People, Music, Calendar, Weather, Photos, and Games, and you can download more from the Windows Store. The bar at the bottom of your screen is called the **taskbar** (**New!**); it allows you to start apps and switch among currently running apps. The left side of the taskbar displays the Start, Back, Search, and Task View buttons. The **Start but-**

ton displays the Start screen when you need it. The **Back button** (**New!**) takes you the previously opened app or back in an app. The **Search button** (**New!**) allows you to search your PC and the web and use a personal assistant Cortana to help you. The **Task View button** (**New!**) allows you to quickly switch between open apps. The taskbar remains in place (**New!**) when you open apps to make it easer to switch between them. The right side of the taskbar is the **notification area**, which displays the time, the date, and program related icons, including the Action Center. Along the left side of the Start screen are additional buttons (**New!**)—Menu, Power, and All Apps—to display the Start menu and power down. The table lists the Start screen features, and describes how to access them using either a mobile device or PC computer.

Start Screen

Feature	Description	On a PC computer	On a mobile device
Tiles	Displays program specific information or opens the app	Click to open the app	Tap to open the app
Menu button (**New!**)	Opens the Start menu with pinned apps and settings	Click to display a menu with settings	Tap to display a menu with settings
Power button (**New!**)	Opens a submenu to sleep shut down, or restart your system	Click to display a submenu with options	Tap to display a submenu with options
All Apps button (**New!**)	Opens the Start menu with all installed apps	Click to display a menu with all apps	Tap to display a menu with all apps
Taskbar (**New!**)	Provides buttons to switch to the Start screen,switch back to or in the app, search for information, switch between apps and get notifications.	Remains in place	Swipe in from the left to view all your open apps; swipe in from the right to open the Action Center.
Start button	Displays the Start screen	Click or press the Win key to display the Start screen	Swipe to switch between apps

Start Screen Options

You can customize the way the Start screen appears by changing options in Settings. In the Start screen, tap the **Menu** button, tap **Settings**, tap **Personalization**, and then tap **Start** in the dialog. You can set options (**New!**) to show most used apps, show recently added apps, use Start full screen, and show recently opened items in Jump Lists on Start or the taskbar. You can also set options to choose which folders appear on Start. You can also change taskbar options (**New!**). In the Start screen, tap-hold the taskbar, and then select an option to turn it on or off: Show app icons, Show all notification icons, and Show touch keyboard buttons.

Tablet Mode Options

You can switch tablet mode on and off depending on your needs. simply, select the **Action Center** button on the taskbar, and then select **Tablet mode** (**New!**). In addition, you can set Tablet mode options in Settings. In the Start screen, tap the **Menu** button, tap **Settings**, tap **System**, and then tap **Tablet mode** in the dialog. You can set options (**New!**) to automatically switch tablet mode on or off when you sign in or based on the type of device, as well as make Windows more touch-friendly using your device as a tablet and show or hide app icons on the taskbar in tablet mode.

Menu button   Start screen

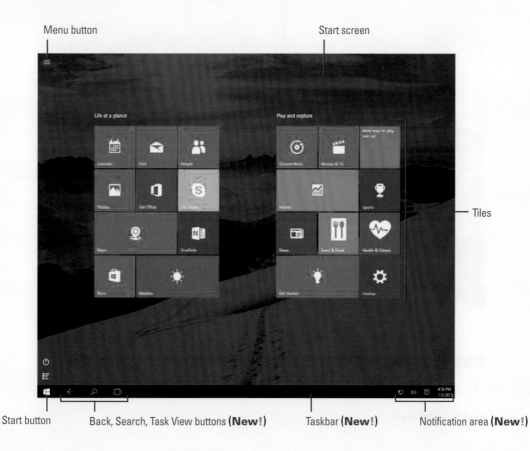

Tiles

Start button   Back, Search, Task View buttons (**New!**)   Taskbar (**New!**)   Notification area (**New!**)

Exploring the Desktop

The traditional desktop from Windows 7 is back (**New!**) in Windows 10 with some improvements. When you start Windows 10 on a PC computer and sign in, the Windows desktop appears by default, which you can turn on and off in the Action Center or Settings. The **desktop** is an on-screen version of an actual desk, containing windows, icons, files, and programs. You can use the desktop to access, store, organize, modify, share, and explore information (such as a letter, the news, or a list of addresses), whether it resides on your PC computer or mobile device, a network, a Homegroup (shared home network), or the Internet. The bar at the bottom of your screen is called the **taskbar**; it allows you to start programs and switch among currently running programs, which appears on the taskbar with a line under the icon for easy identification. The left side of the taskbar displays the Start button, Search box, Task View button and pinned programs. The **Start button** displays the Start menu—it's back—(**New!**) where you can quickly start programs. The **Search box** (**New!**) allows you to search your PC and the web and use a personal assistant Cortana (**New!**) to help you. The **Task View button** (**New!**) allows you to

Desktop icon

Background picture on desktop

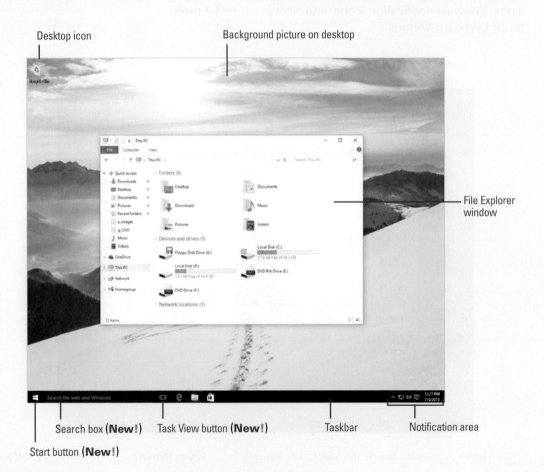

File Explorer window

Search box (**New!**)   Task View button (**New!**)   Taskbar   Notification area

Start button (**New!**)

quickly switch between open programs, close them, and group programs on one or more desktops (**New!**). The default programs pinned to the taskbar include Microsoft Edge (**New!**), File Explorer, and Store, however, you can customize it with other programs. The right side of the taskbar is the **notification area**, which displays the time, date, Action Center (**New!**) with notifications, system icons, such as Network and Volume, and program related icons. You can click or tap an icon to display a window of options. For example, when you click or tap the Volume icon, a window appears where you can adjust or mute the

volume. If icons in the notification area are not used for a while, an arrow appears to hide the icons and reduce clutter. You can click or tap the arrow to display hidden icons. You can quickly drag a hidden icon on or displayed icon off the notification area to add or remove it from the taskbar. Next to the notification area is the Show desktop button (the blank button at the right end of the taskbar), which allows you to quickly show the desktop. If you upgraded your PC computer to Windows 10 from a previous version of Windows, your desktop might contain additional desktop icons and toolbars.

Open program window   Active program window

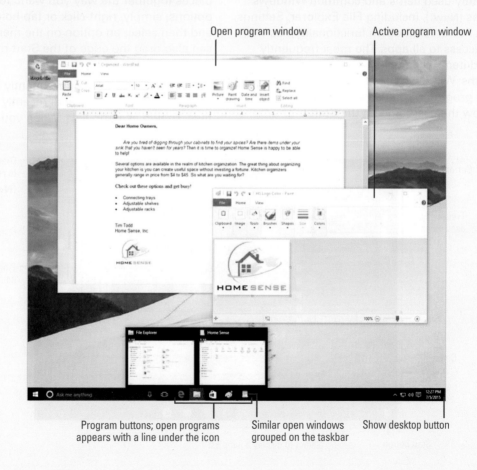

Program buttons; open programs appears with a line under the icon

Similar open windows grouped on the taskbar

Show desktop button

Using the Start Menu

An important part of working with the Start screen and Windows desktop is using the Start menu. Clicking the Menu button (**New!**) (upper-right corner) on the Start screen or the Start button (**New!**) on the taskbar displays the Start menu, a list of commands that allow you to start an app or program, open and manage files, change a Windows setting, power down your device, or sign/log out. The top (left) of the Start menu indicates who is currently using the computer, which you can also click or tap to change account settings, lock Windows, and sign/log out. The (left) column is separated into two lists: most frequently used items and common Windows items (**New!**), including File Explorer, Settings, and Power (shut down functionality), as well as access to all apps. The most frequently used items change as you use apps and programs: Windows keeps track of which apps and programs you use and displays them below the username on the Start menu for

easy access. For the desktop, the Start menu includes a right column with groups of tiles (**New!**), like those on the Start screen, as **pinned** items. The pinned items remain on the Start menu, like a push pin holds paper on a bulletin board, until you unpin it. Tiles allow you to view live status information, such as a photo or text, for a specific app (which you can toggle on and off) or open a app to work with it. You can quickly customize the tiles on the Start menu by dragging them to a new location. If the size of a tile is not quite right to fit in a specific spot, you can resize it to small, medium, wide or large to put the tile pieces together the way you want. To set tile options, simply, right-click or tap-hold a tile, and then select an option on the menu. You can also drag the edge of the Start menu to resize it (**New!**).

In addition to tracking frequently used programs, Windows also tracks recently opened files, known as **jump lists**. When you point to

Current user

Frequently used items

Common Windows items

Start button

Drag edge to resize (**New!**)

Pinned items

Select to display a jump list

a program—such as File Explorer—on the Start menu with a arrow next to it, a list of recently opened files or folders and related tasks appear for easy access. The arrow next to a menu item indicates a cascading menu, or submenu, which is a list of commands for that menu item. You can also pin recently opened files to the Start menu that you want to use on a regular basis.

As you continue to install apps and programs on your computer, finding them on the Start menu can sometimes be difficult. Windows 10 makes it easy with a quick text search or voice search with Cortana (**New!**)—a personal assistant you can talk to get things done—and the Search box (**New!**), which allows you to search the web and your PC,

including apps, programs, and other Windows items, such as favorites, files, contacts, messages, appointments, reminders, and alerts. To perform a search, click the Search button (Start screen only), click in the Search box on the taskbar, and then type the search or say it. If you'd like to say it to Cortana, select the microphone (**New!**), and then say it; you can also turn on an option to have Cortana respond to you anytime you say "Hey Cortana" (**New!**). Otherwise, start typing the search text you want. As you type, the results appear by categories. The search results continue to narrow as you continue to type. If you don't find what you are looking for, you can click My Stuff or Web (**New!**) to change the listing of highlighted results.

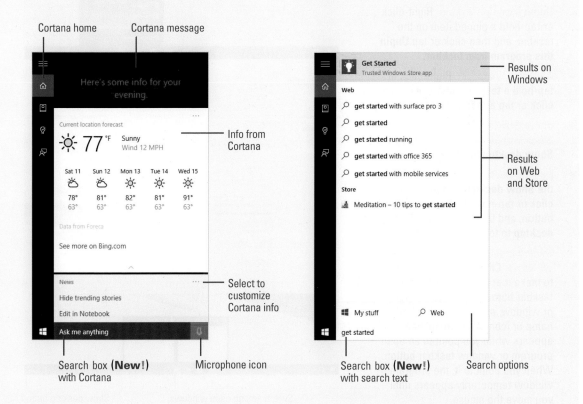

Cortana home   Cortana message

Info from Cortana

Select to customize Cortana info

Search box (**New!**) with Cortana   Microphone icon

Results on Windows

Results on Web and Store

Search box (**New!**) with search text   Search options

Using the Taskbar

The horizontal bar at the bottom of the Start screen (**New!**) and desktop is called the taskbar; it contains several important items: Start button, Search box (**New!**), Task View button (**New!**), program and taskbar buttons, notification area, and Show desktop button (desktop). The taskbar allows you to start apps and programs, files, and windows, as well as switch among currently running or open ones or to the desktop or Start screen. For easy access, you can pin programs and windows to the taskbar. The default programs pinned to the taskbar include Microsoft Edge, File Explorer, and Store, however, you can customize it. The Show desktop button (desktop) minimizes all open windows to display the desktop. With the Peak at desktop option, you can quickly see the desktop. In addition to tracking frequently used programs, Windows also tracks recently opened files, known as jump lists, which you can open from the taskbar. You can also show or hide options, such as display a touch screen keyboard for use on PC and mobile devices.

Use the Taskbar

◆ **Pin to the Taskbar.** Right-click or tap-hold an open program or taskbar button, and then click or tap **Pin this program to taskbar**.

◆ **Unpin from the Taskbar.** Right-click or tap-hold a pinned item on the taskbar, and then click or tap **Unpin this program from taskbar**.

◆ **Access a Jump List.** Right-click or tap-hold a taskbar button, and then click or tap a recently opened item.

◆ **Show desktop (minimize all windows) (desktop).** Click or tap the **Show desktop** button on the taskbar.

◆ **Peek at desktop (desktop).** Point to the **Show desktop** button. Right-click or tap-hold the **Show desktop** button, and then click or tap **Peek at desktop** to toggle on and off.

◆ **Switch among open programs or windows.** Click or tap in a window to make it active, or point to a taskbar button for an open program or window, and then click or tap a name or icon. A live thumbnail appears when you point to an open program or window taskbar button. When you point to it, the program or window temporarily appears until you move the mouse.

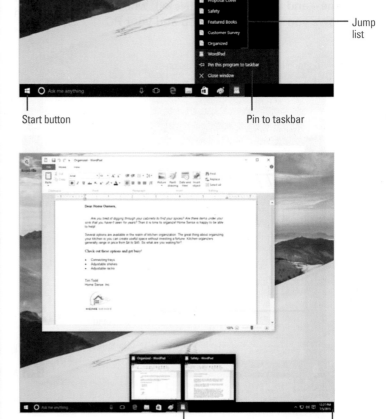

Jump list

Start button

Pin to taskbar

Switch among open windows

Show desktop button

Set Taskbar Options

◆ **Show or hide toolbars (desktop).**
Right-click or tap-hold a blank
area of the taskbar, point to
Toolbars, and then click or tap a
toolbar: **Address**, **Links**, or
Desktop.

◆ **Show or hide buttons.** Right-click
or tap-hold a blank area of the
taskbar, and then click or tap an
option to toggle on or off.

  ◆ **Show app icons (Start screen).**
  Use to show/hide pinned apps
  on taskbar (**New!**).

  ◆ **Show all notification icons
  (Start screen).** Use to
  show/hide notification icons on
  the taskbar (**New!**).

  ◆ **Show touch keyboard button
  (Start screen).** Use to show/hide
  the Touch Keyboard button on
  the taskbar.

  ◆ **Show Task View button
  (desktop).** Use to show/hide the
  Task View button on the taskbar
  (**New!**).

◆ **Arrange windows.** Open the
windows you want to arrange,
right-click or tap-hold a blank area
of the taskbar, and then click or
tap **Cascade windows, Show
windows stacked**, or **Show
windows side by side**.

◆ **Show Task Manager.** Right-click
or tap-hold a blank area of the
taskbar, and then click or tap **Task
Manager**.

◆ **Lock or Unlock the Taskbar.** Right-
click or tap-hold a blank area of
the taskbar, and then click or tap
Lock the taskbar.

◆ **Customize the Taskbar.** Right-click
or tap-hold a blank area of the
taskbar, and then click or tap
Properties.

Touch keyboard

Emoji icons   Right-click or tap-hold the taskbar to access commands   Touch Keyboard button

---

For Your Information

Using to a Touch Keyboard

When you type on a touch keyboard on a touch-sensitive screen, the
keyboard tries to learn and guess the current and next word you're
typing, and shows suggestions above the keyboard. You can choose
a suggestion by tapping it, or using a gesture to slide your thumb left
and right across the Spacebar to cycle through the them so you
don't have to take your fingers off the keyboard. You can quickly
insert numbers with a swipe on the top row of the touch keyboard.
In addition, emoji character symbols are in color for easier viewing.

The touch keyboard supports long-press gestures, which allows you
to access other keys on the keyboard. For example, you can long
press the question mark key to reveal an exclamation mark. Once,
you know a key is available under another one, you can perform a
short swipe up on the question mark key to quickly use the exclamation mark key.

Managing Windows

One of the most powerful things about Windows is that you can open more than one window or program at once from the desktop. This means, however, that the desktop can get cluttered with many open windows for the various programs. Windows groups similar types of windows under a program button on the taskbar or in Task View (**New!**), which you can use to switch among open windows and programs, close them, or create multiple desktops (**New!**). You can identify a window by its name on the title bar at the top of the window, which you can also use to move or resize it. Each window is surrounded by a border and resize buttons that you can use to resize the window.

Switch Among Open Windows

◆ Click or tap anywhere in a window to make it active, or point to a taskbar button for an open program or window, and then click or tap a name or icon.

   ◆ A live thumbnail appears when you point to an open program or window taskbar button. When you point to the thumbnail, the program or window temporally appears until you move the mouse.

◆ Click the **Task View** button (**New!**) on the taskbar, and then click or tap an open program or window. You can also press Alt-Tab to switch windows and other Windows apps.

Task View button (**New!**)   Switch open program window

Move or Resize a Window

1 In the desktop, point to the window's title bar.

2 Drag the window to a new location.

   ◆ **Maximize active window.** Drag the title bar to the top edge of the desktop or double-click or double-tap the title bar.

   ◆ **Resize active window for side by side use.** Drag the title bar to the left or right edge of the desktop.

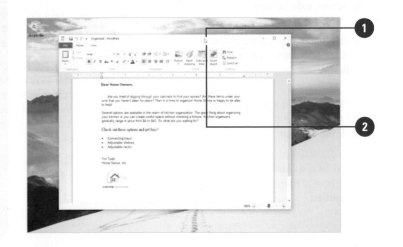

Use Buttons to Resize and Close a Window

In the desktop, all windows contain the same sizing and close buttons:

◆ **Maximize button.** Click or tap to make a window fill the entire screen.

◆ **Restore Down button.** Click or tap to reduce a maximized window.

◆ **Minimize button.** Click or tap to shrink a window to a taskbar button.

◆ **Close button.** Click or tap to close the window.

◆ **Show desktop button.** Click or tap to minimize or restore all windows.

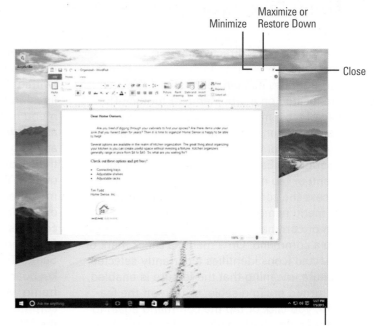

Minimize

Maximize or Restore Down

Close

Show desktop

Use the Pointer to Resize a Window

◆ **Resize a window using a border.** Move the pointer over a border in a non-maximized window until the pointer changes into a two-headed arrow, and then drag to the size you want.

◆ **Resize all open windows on the desktop.** Right-click or tap-hold a blank area of the taskbar, and then click or tap a command:

 ◆ **Cascade windows.**

 ◆ **Show window stacked.**

 ◆ **Show windows side by side.**

◆ **Minimize or restore all open windows except active one.** Drag the title bar back and forth (shake) to minimize or restore all open windows except the active one.

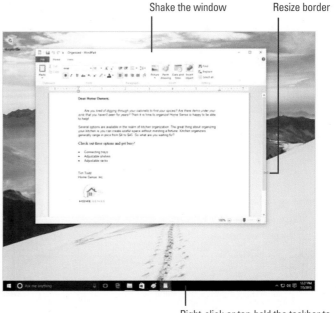

Shake the window

Resize border

Right-click or tap-hold the taskbar to resize all open windows

Using Tabs, Menus, and Toolbars

A **command** is a directive that provides access to a program's features. Each Windows program has its own set of commands, which are located on a tab, menu, or toolbar. The use of tabs, menus, and toolbars vary depending on the program. A **tab** or **menu** organizes commands into groups of related operations. Each group is listed under the menu or tab name, such as File or Home. To access the commands, you click or tap the tab or menu name, and then click or tap the button or command. If a menu appears, click or tap a command. On a menu, a check mark or selected icons identifies a currently selected feature, meaning that the feature is enabled, or turned on. To disable, or turn off the feature, you click or tap the command again to remove the check mark. A bullet mark also indicates that an option is enabled. To disable

a command with a bullet mark next to it, however, you must select another command (within the menu section, separated by gray lines) in its place. If a command on a tab or menu includes a keyboard reference, known as a **keyboard shortcut**, you can perform the action by pressing the first key, then pressing the second key to perform the command quickly. You can also carry out some of the most frequently used commands by clicking or tapping a button on a toolbar. A **toolbar** contains buttons that are convenient shortcuts for commands. When you point to a button, a ScreenTip appears with a description and the keyboard shortcut, if available. A **pane** is a frame within a window where you can access commands and navigation controls, such as the Navigation pane in File Explorer.

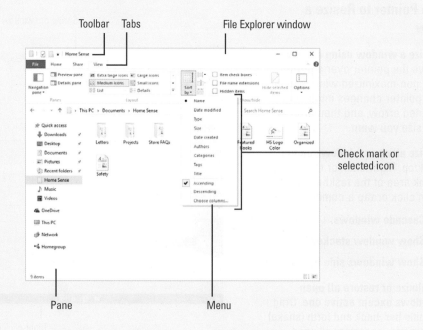

Toolbar   Tabs   File Explorer window

                                                      Check mark or
                                                      selected icon

Pane   Menu

Choosing Dialog Box Options

A **dialog box** is a window that opens when you choose a command followed by an ellipsis (. . .). The ellipsis indicates that you must supply more information before the program can carry out the command you selected. Dialog boxes open in other situations as well, such as when you open a program in the Control Panel. In a dialog box, you choose various options and provide information for completing the command.

Choose Dialog Box Options

All dialog boxes contain the same types of options, including the following:

- **Tabs.** Click or tap a tab to display its options. Each tab groups a related set of options.

- **Option buttons.** Click or tap an option button to select it. You can usually select only one.

- **Up and down arrows.** Click or tap the up or down arrow to increase or decrease the number, or type a number in the box.

- **Check box.** Click or tap the box to turn on or off the option. A checked box means the option is selected; a cleared box means it's not.

- **List box.** Click or tap the list arrow to display a list of options, and then click or tap the option you want.

- **Text box.** Click or tap in the box and type the requested information.

- **Command buttons.** Click or tap a button to perform a specific action or command. A button name followed by an ellipsis (...) opens another dialog box. OK executes the options and closes the dialog box. Cancel ignores the options and closes the dialog box. Apply executes the options and leaves the dialog box open.

- **Preview box.** Many dialog boxes show an image that reflects the options you select.

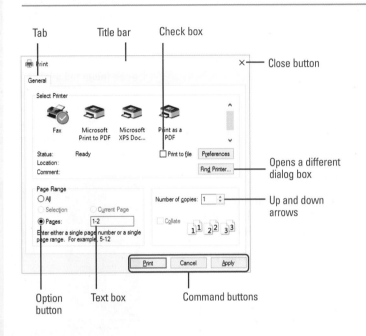

For Your Information

Navigating a Dialog Box

Rather than clicking or tapping to move around a dialog box, you can press the Tab key to move from one box or button to the next. You can also use Shift+Tab to move backward, or Ctrl+Tab and Ctrl+Shift+Tab to move between dialog box tabs.

Getting Help and Personal Assistance

When you have a question about how to do something in Windows 10, you can usually find the answer with a few clicks of your mouse or taps of your finger, or a simple voice command with a microphone. If you want to find out what's new or quickly get to know Windows 10, use Get Started, which includes text, pictures, and videos (**New!**). If you want to get help from a personal assistant, you can talk to Cortana. With Cortana (**New!**), you can search the web and your PC, including apps and programs and other items, such as favorites, files, contacts, messages, appointments, reminders, and alerts. As you use Cortana's Notebook, it gets to know your needs—such as favorite places, news, food & drink, music, weather, or travel—for a more personalized experience (even tell a joke). You can access Cortana from the taskbar or with a voice command, "Hey Cortana" (**New!**), which shows you today's trending stories from the web (**New!**). You can also have Cortana give you tidbits (**New!**) with thoughts and greetings. You can adjust Cortana's options or turn it off in Notebook Settings.

Get Started with Help

1. Click or tap the Start button on the taskbar (desktop), and then click or tap the **Get Started** tile.

2. Click or tap a help category in the left column.

   TIMESAVER *Click or tap the Menu button to collapse/expand the left column.*

3. Click or tap a tile for a help topic.

4. Read the help information, play a video, or click or tap any links to access other information.

5. To go back to the previous page, click or tap the **Back** button or swipe.

6. To close Get Started, use the following:

   ◆ *From Deskop.* Click or tap the **Close** button.

   ◆ *From Start screen.* Point to the top of the screen (Title bar appears), and then click or tap the **Close** button or swipe to the bottom.

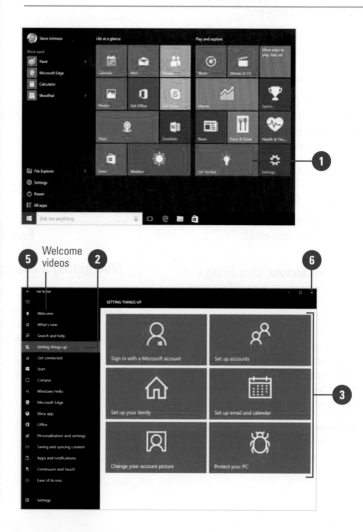

Use Cortana

① Say "Hey Cortana," or click or tap the Search box on the taskbar, and then click the **Microphone** icon.

TROUBLE? *If Cortana doesn't respond to "Hey Cortana," you need to turn it on in Settings.*

The Cortana home appears with today's stories from the web.

② Say or type a command or question, such as "Tell me a joke," or "What's happening today?".

③ Respond or click or tap an item—click or tap **My Stuff** or **Web** to change the results.

④ Click or tap off Cortana home to close it.

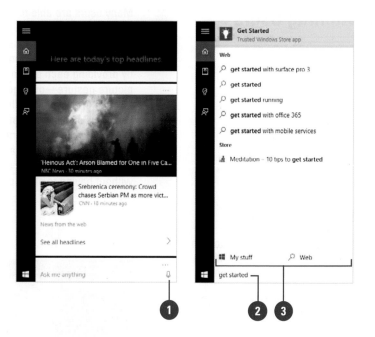

Set Cortana Options

① Click or tap the **Search** box (desktop) or **Cortana** button (Start screen) on the taskbar.

② Click or tap the **Notebook** icon.

③ Click or tap the **Settings** button.

④ Click or drag options on or off.

◆ **Cortana can give you suggestions, ideas, reminders, alerts and more**. Use to enable or disable Cortana.

◆ **Hey Cortana.** Use for voice response.

◆ **Find flights and more.** Use for tracking information.

◆ **Taskbar tidbits.** Use to get thoughts from Cortana.

⑤ Click or tap off Cortana home to close it.

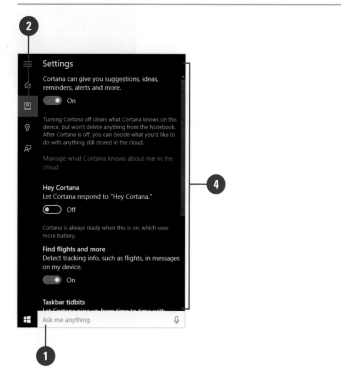

Switching Users

Many users are able to share the same PC computer or mobile device. Their individual Windows identities allow them to keep their files completely private and to customize the operating system with their own preferences. Windows manages these separate identities, or accounts, by providing each user a unique username and password—either text, picture gesture—or fingerprint touch or scan with Windows Hello (**New!**) (if available). When a user selects an account and signs in, Windows starts with that user's configuration settings and network permissions. When you want to change users, you can sign out, (which closes all running programs, saves your settings, and signs you off the PC computer) or switch users, which quickly switches between users without having to close programs and saves your current settings.

Switch Users Quickly

1. Click or tap the **Start** button on the taskbar (desktop) or **Menu** button on the Start screen.

2. Click or tap the **User Account** (username and picture).

3. Click or tap the name of the user to which you want to switch.

4. Use any of the following to sign in or click or tap **Sign-in options**.

   ◆ Type password. Type your password, and then click or tap the **Submit arrow**, or press Enter.

   ◆ Picture password. Drag a sequence of gestures.

   ◆ Windows Hello. Use fingerprint or other reader (**New!**), and then swipe the screen.

   The desktop or Start screen appears for the user.

1 Start button

Did You Know?

You can change user account options. Click or tap Settings on the Start menu, click or tap Accounts, click or tap Family & other users, select a user, click or tap Change account type, and then select the options you want.

Sign Out and Sign In

1 Click or tap the **Start** button on the taskbar (desktop) or **Menu** button on the Start screen.

2 Click or tap the **User Account** (username and picture).

3 Click or tap **Sign out** to close all your programs, save your settings, and sign off.

4 If the Lock screen appears, drag your mouse anywhere on the screen, move your finger sideways from the edge, or press a key to dismiss it.

5 Use any of the following to sign in or click or tap **Sign-in options**.

◆ **Type password.** Type your password, and then click or tap the **Submit arrow**, or press Enter.

◆ **Picture password.** Drag a sequence of gestures.

◆ **Windows Hello.** Use fingerprint or other reader (**New!**), and then swipe the screen.

The desktop or Start screen appears for the user.

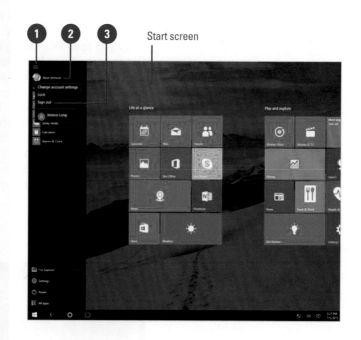

Start screen

Powering Down

When you finish working on your device, you need to make sure to turn off, or shut down, it properly. This involves several steps: saving and closing all open files, exiting all running programs, shutting down Windows itself, and finally, turning off the device. However, if you shut down your device before or while installing Windows updates (download must be complete), Windows will automatically complete the install before shutting down, so you don't have to wait around. Shutting down your device makes sure Windows and all its related programs are properly closed and avoid potential problems in the future. In addition to the Shut down option, you can put your PC in sleep (useful for short periods) or hibernate (useful for longer periods) mode, or restart to reset your device if problems occur.

Power Down Your Device

1 Click or tap the **Start** button on the taskbar (desktop) or **Menu** button on the Start screen.

2 Click or tap the **Power** button on the Start menu.

TIMESAVER *The Power button* (**New!**) *is also available on the Sign in screen on the Start screen.*

3 Click or tap the option on the menu you want (confirm as prompted):

◆ **Sleep.** Saves your session to memory and switches to low-power mode; you can press the hardware power button to wake.

◆ **Hibernate.** Saves your session to memory and hard disk, and then exits Windows. Press the hardware power button to restore your session.

◆ **Shut down.** Exits Windows 10 and prepares the PC to be turned off.

◆ **Restart.** Exits Windows 10 and restarts the PC.

IMPORTANT *Options vary depending on Windows settings.*

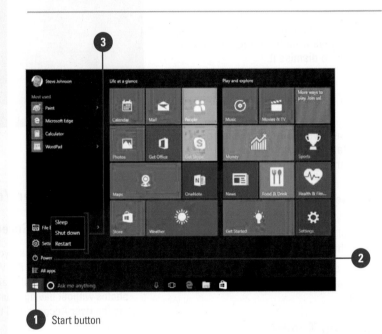

1 Start button

For Your Information

Setting Power and Sleep Options

You can specify how long your screen waits before it turns off or goes to sleep to save power. To set these options, click or tap the Settings button on the Start menu, click or tap System, click or tap Power & Sleep, and then specify the timing you want. To set more custom options, including what options show in the Power button, click or tap the Additional power settings link to open Power Options in the Control Panel.

Working with Windows Apps

2

Introduction

Now that you know how to work with the graphical elements that make Windows 10 work, you're ready to work with apps. An **app** (short for application), also known as a program, is software you use to accomplish specific tasks, such as browsing the web using the Microsoft Edge app or communicating with others using the Skype app. When you display the Start screen or Start menu (**New!**) on Windows 10, you will notice live tiles, which you can use to get quick status information for apps or open them in full screen view. The apps on the Start screen or Start menu with a tile are a new generation of full screen apps, known as **Windows apps**, that were primarily designed for use on Windows 8, yet enhanced in Windows 10.

The apps available on the Start screen are not all the apps installed on your PC computer or mobile device. Windows 10 comes with additional built-in Windows Accessories and System tools, known as **Desktop apps**, that—although not as feature-rich as many apps sold separately—are extremely useful for completing basic tasks. For those who are familiar with Windows 7, you'll recognize them. They include Paint, WordPad, Windows Media Player, File Explorer, Internet Explorer, Sticky Notes, Calculator, Character Map, and Command Prompt to name a few.

This chapter shows you how to locate and access your Windows apps (and to customize this access). It also shows you how to work with multiple apps at the same time, share information between apps, and install or update apps from the Windows Store.

Displaying All Your Apps

When you display the Start screen or Start menu (**New!**) on Windows 10, you will notice live tiles, which you can use to get quick status information for apps, like text or photos, or open them in full screen view. The apps available on the Start screen and menu are not all the apps installed on your PC computer or mobile device. Windows 10 comes with additional built-in Windows Accessories and System tools that are extremely useful for completing basic tasks. For those who are familiar with Windows 7, you'll recognize them. They include Paint, WordPad, Windows Media Player, File Explorer, Internet Explorer, Sticky Notes, Calculator, Character Map, and Command Prompt to name a few. When you install an app, it appears in All apps on the Start menu, not the Start screen unless you choose to pin it to the Start screen and menu. You can display all the available apps on your device by accessing All apps from the Start menu (**New!**). You can scroll through the list or find apps by category, such as numbers and letters.

Display All Your Apps

1. Click or tap the **Start** button on the taskbar (desktop) or **Menu** button on the Start screen.

   The Start menu appears displaying frequently used and pinned apps.

2. Click or tap the **All apps** button (**New!**) or swipe up from the bottom of the Start screen.

   TIMESAVER *Click or tap the All apps button on the Start screen (above the Start button) to display all your apps.*

   A list of all your apps appear.

3. To scroll through your apps, drag the scroll bar in the list with your mouse, roll a mouse wheel, or swipe up or down.

4. To exit All apps, click or tap the **Back** button (**New!**).

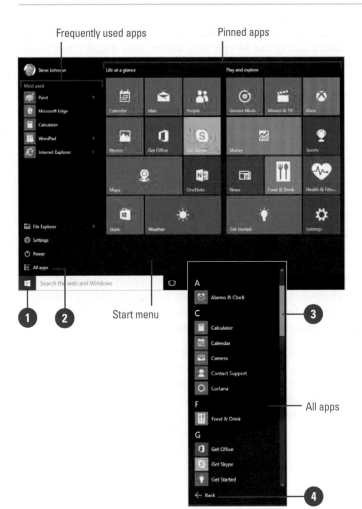

Frequently used apps

Pinned apps

Start menu

All apps

Display All Your Apps by Categories

1. Click or tap the **Start** button on the taskbar (desktop) or **Menu** button on the Start screen.

   The Start menu appears displaying frequently used and pinned apps.

2. Click or tap the **All apps** button (**New!**) or swipe up from the bottom of the Start screen.

   TIMESAVER *Click or tap the All apps button on the Start screen (above the Start button) to display all your apps.*

   A list of all your apps appear.

3. Click or tap a number or letter in the All apps list.

   A display of categories by number and letter appears. Items in white have apps while those in grey don't have apps.

4. Click or tap a number or letter in the All apps list.

   Apps in the selected category appear in the list.

5. To exit All apps, click or tap the **Back** button (**New!**).

Did You Know?

You can choose default apps. If you like a certain browser, you can choose a default app for it. In the Start screen or menu, click or tap Settings, click or tap System, click or tap Default apps, and then click the Add button (+) to select an app or click an existing app button to change it to a different one.

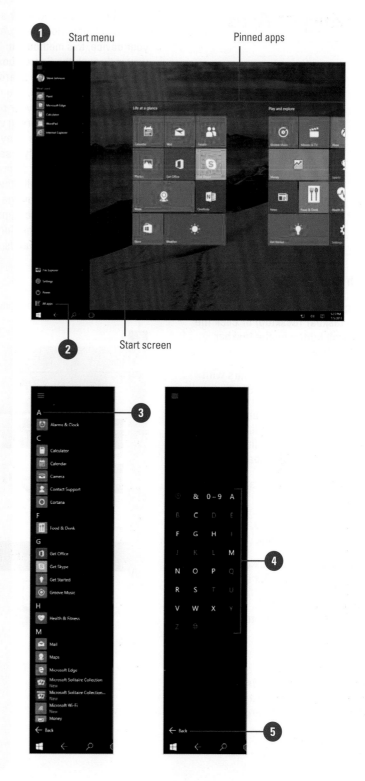

Start menu   Pinned apps

Start screen

Searching for Apps

The simplest way to look for a specific app is to scroll through the Start screen or menu. However, when you have a lot of apps installed on your device, this method can be too time consuming. A more direct way is through the Search box (**New!**) on the taskbar. The Search box is a centralized place to search for apps, settings, and files in Windows 10. With the Search box, you can simply type text or use a microphone with Cortana (**New!**)—your personal assistant—to use voice commands. If you prefer starting with a voice command, you can set an option in Settings to use "Hey Cortana" (**New!**) to make it easier to get started. After you specify a search, Windows narrows down and displays the search results from your PC and the web in categories, which you can narrow more with the options My Stuff or Web. Windows starts by default with Cortana turned off (**New!**), which you can see by the Cortana button in the Apps bar, so only search with text is available. When you click or tap the Cortana button to turn it on, you can search with text or voice commands.

Search for Apps

1 Click or tap the **Search** box on the taskbar (desktop) or click the **Search** button on the taskbar (Start screen).

The Search home appears with today's new from the Bing.

2 Type the first few characters for the app you want to find. You can continue typing or edit the text to narrow down your search.

The Search displays a list of results.

3 To narrow the results, click or tap **My Stuff** or **Web**.

4 To open an app, click or tap the app's name in the list of results.

5 To cancel the search, click or tap off the Search panel to close it.

See Also

See "Setting Search Options for Apps" on page 45 for more information on customizing the use of Search.

Home   Content from Bing

Click or tap to enable Cortana (**New!**)

Search for Apps with Cortana

1. Say "Hey Cortana," or click or tap the **Search** box on the taskbar, and then click the **Microphone** icon.

   TROUBLE? *If Cortana doesn't respond to "Hey Cortana," you need to turn it on in Settings.*

   The Cortana home appears with today's stories from the web.

2. Say or type the name of the app you want to find.

   The Search displays a list of results.

3. To narrow the results, say or click or tap **My Stuff** or **Web**, if available.

4. To open an app, click or tap the app's tile in the list of results.

5. To cancel the search, click or tap off Cortana home to close it.

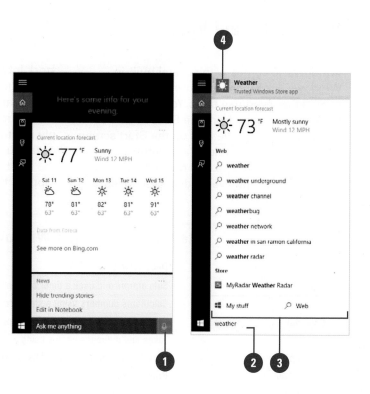

Did You Know?

You can set options for Cortana. Click or tap the Search box, click or tap the Notebook button on the Apps bar, and then click or tap Settings, where you can turn on "Hey Cortana," other options, or turn off Cortana altogether.

You may not be able to use Cortana. Cortana is only available in certain countries/regions and some Cortana features might not be available everywhere. If Cortana isn't available or is turned off, you can still use search.

Touchpad Gestures

Action	Result
Select an item	Tap on the touchpad
Scroll	Place two fingers on the touchpad and slide horizontally or vertically
Zoom in or out	Place two fingers on the touchpad and pinch in or stretch out
Show more commands	Tap the touchpad with two fingers or press in the lower-right corner
See all open windows (**New!**)	Place three fingers on the touchpad and swipe them away from you
Show the desktop (**New!**)	Place three fingers on the touchpad and swipe them towards yourself
Switch between open windows (**New!**)	Place three fingers on the touchpad and swipe right or left

Using Different Apps

Windows 10 comes with several built-in Windows apps that are extremely useful for completing everyday tasks. You can access the Windows apps from the Start screen or menu (New!). The live tiles on the Start screen and menu provide quick status information that relates to the app. For example, the tile for the Money app (New!) displays current stock information from the different exchanges. The information on the live tiles continually changes. If you prefer to not view live tile information, you can turn it off; simply right-click or hold-tap a tile, and then click or tap Turn live tile off. You can start an app on the Start screen or menu by simply clicking or tapping the app's tile.

Start Screen Default Windows Apps	
Program	**Description**
Alarms	Sets alarms and uses a timer or stopwatch
Calculator	Calculates numbers using a standard, scientific, or converter calculator
Calendar	Creates and manages events and appointments in a calendar
Camera	Takes and manages photos using a camera
Desktop	Provides access to the Windows desktop
Edge (New!)	Browses the web
Food & Drink	Provides food and drink information from popular services
Games	Provides access to games and online services
Get Started (New!)	Provides quick help, tips, and what's new for Windows 10
Groove Music (New!)	Provides access to music and online services
Health & Fitness	Provides health and fitness information from popular services
Mail	Sends and receives electronic messages to contacts
Maps	Provides maps and directions
Money (New!)	Provides financial information from popular services
Movies & TV (New!)	Provides access to movies & TV and online services
News	Provides news information from popular services
OneDrive (New!)	Stores and manages files on a Microsoft cloud service
People	Creates and manages contact information
Photos	Works with pictures and photos
Reader	Displays PDF and XPS documents
Reading List	Keeps track of articles you want to read on the web or in apps
Scan	Scans pages and information from a connected scanner
Skype	Sends and receives online calls and messages to contacts
Sports	Provides sports information from popular services
Store	Purchases, installs, and updates apps
Travel	Provides travel information from popular services
Weather	Provides weather information

Starting and Closing Apps

Starting an app is pretty straight forward in Windows 10. You can start a Windows app from the Start screen, Start menu (**New!**), or search results with a simple click of a mouse or tap of your finger. When you click or tap an app tile, the app opens in full screen view, where you can start using it. Some apps even allow you to start multiple instances. As you work with an app in full screen view, you'll notice it doesn't display a visual way to close it. You can close an app when you point to the top edge of the screen to display a title bar where you can click or tap the Close button or drag from the top edge of the screen to the bottom edge of the screen. Unlike Windows 8, when you close an app, it is closed for good (like Windows 7) (**New!**).

Start and Close an App

1. Display the Start screen or Start menu.

2. Search as needed to locate the tile for the app you want to start; click or tap the **Search** button, and then type search criteria or use Cortana.

3. To open an app in full screen view, click or tap the app's tile.

   IMPORTANT *When you open a desktop app from the desktop, it opens in a window with a title bar, which includes Minimize, Maximize, and Close button.*

4. To close the app, use the following:

   ◆ Close button. Point to the top edge of the screen (title bar appears), and then click or tap the **Close** button.

   The Close button turns red when you point to it.

   ◆ Close drag. Point to the top edge of the screen (title bar appears), and then drag down to the bottom of the screen.

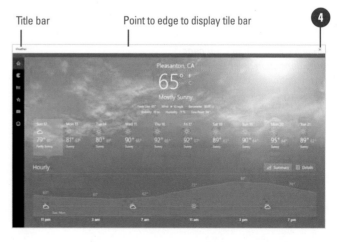

Title bar   Point to edge to display tile bar

Using the App Bar

When you're working with many Windows apps and programs—such as the Search/Cortana window—in Windows 10, you can access commands and other options from the App bar (**New!**). The App bar appears on the left side of the window with buttons. The top button is typically the Menu button (**New!**), and the bottom one is typically the Settings button. The Menu button shows or hides the button names, while the Settings button opens a screen with app specific options, such as General, Privacy statement, Terms of use, Credits, and About (where you can get app specific help0. The other buttons on the App bar are specific to the app or program.

Use the App Bar

1. Open an app or program with an App bar.

   NOTE *Not all apps, such as the Windows Store or Settings, have an App bar.*

2. To show or hide button names on the App bar, click or tap the **Menu** button.

3. Click or tap a button on the App bar.

   ◆ **Settings.** Click or tap to set app specific options.

4. If available, click or tap a command or option.

5. To exit, click or tap the **Back** button in the upper-left corner or on the taskbar (Start screen).

> ### See Also
>
> *See "Changing Apps Settings" on page 31 for more information on changing Windows app options.*

② Back button   Weather app

③

⑤ App bar

Changing App Settings

In addition to changing Windows options in Settings, you can also change app specific settings by using the Settings button on the App bar. With an app open, the Settings button appears at the bottom of the App bar. When you select the Settings button on the App bar, a Settings screen appears displaying app specific options. The typical options include General, Privacy statement, Terms of use, Credits, and About. When you select an option, the panel displays app specific settings. When you're done, you can use the Back button in the upper-left corner of the window or on the taskbar (Start screen) to exit.

Change App Settings

1. Open an app or program with an App bar.

2. To show or hide button names on the App bar, click or tap the **Menu** button.

3. Click or tap the **Settings** button on the App bar.

4. Click or tap a tab at the top of the screen:

   ◆ **General.** Click or tap to set app specific options.

   ◆ **Privacy statement.** Click or tap to display app privacy and cookie usage information.

   ◆ **Terms of use.** Click or tap to display app terms of use.

   ◆ **Credits.** Click or tap to display app credits.

   ◆ **About.** Click or tap to display links to get app information or app help.

5. Click or tap an option on the Settings screen for the open app.

6. To exit, click or tap the **Back** button in the upper-left corner or on the taskbar (Start screen).

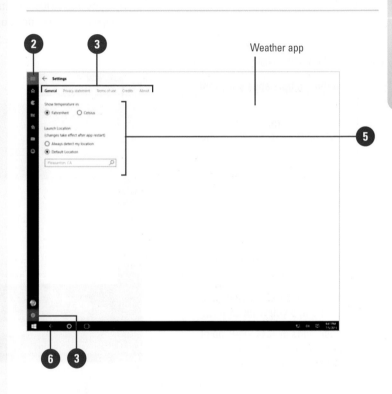

Weather app

Working with Multiple Apps and Desktops

Windows 10 is designed to work with multiple apps at the same time, so switching between apps is a common part of using Windows. After you open multiple apps, you can quickly switch between open apps with a click or tap, swipe, or keyboard shortcut. With the Task View button (**New!**) on the taskbar, you can view all your open apps and click or tap the one you want to view. In Task view, you can also click or tap the Close button (**New!**) for an open app to close it. If you prefer a gesture, you can swipe right from the left edge in Tablet mode to switch between open apps. In addition to switching between multiple apps, you can also group apps into virtual desktops (**New!**), so you can work and multitask with apps on multiple desktops.

Switch Between Apps

① Open the multiple apps you want to use.

② Click or tap the **Task View** button (**New!**) on the taskbar or use any of the following:

◆ Swipe. Swipe right from the left edge in Tablet mode to switch between apps.

◆ Keyboard Shortcut. Press Alt+Tab to cycle through open apps or press Alt+Shift+Tab to reverse the order.

③ To switch apps in Task view, click or tap the app you want to view.

④ To close apps in Task view, point to the app, and then click or tap the **Close** button.

Did You Know?

You can change multitasking options.
Click or tap the Settings button on the Start menu, click or tap the Systems icon, click or tap Multitasking, and then turn snap options on or off, such as automatically arrange windows, adjust the size of windows, or show what I can snap next to it.

Task view

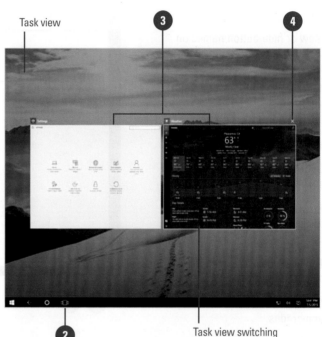

Task view switching

Keyboard shortcut switching

Create and Work with Virtual Desktops

1. In the desktop, click or tap the **Task View** button on the taskbar.

2. Click or tap the **New desktop** button (**New!**).

   TIMESAVER *Drag an app to the New desktop button to create a virtual desktop with an app.*

   A desktop thumbnail appears at the bottom of the screen.

3. Point to a desktop thumbnail to peek at it, or click or tap the thumbnail to display it.

4. To move apps between virtual desktops, drag the app from one desktop to another.

5. To remove a desktop, point to the desktop thumbnail, and then click or tap the **Close** button.

Change Virtual Desktop Options

1. Click or tap the **Settings** button on the Start menu.

2. Click or tap the **System** icon.

3. Click or tap **Multitasking** (**New!**).

4. Click or tap the list arrow, and then select an option to filter the list.

   ◆ **On the taskbar, show windows that are open on.**

   ◆ **Pressing Alt + Tab shows windows that are open on.**

5. Select an option from the list.

   ◆ **Only the desktop I'm using.**

   ◆ **All desktops.**

6. Click or tap the **Close** button to exit Settings.

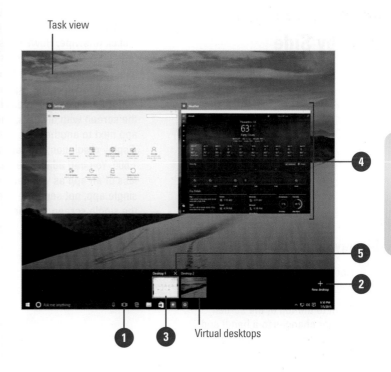

Task view

Virtual desktops

Working with Apps Side by Side

Windows 10 was designed to work with multiple full screen Windows apps at the same time. You can quickly switch between open apps with a click or swipe. However, sometimes you want to display more than one full screen app on the screen at the same time. For example, you might want to view your Weather on one part of the screen while you work with files in File Explorer on another part of the screen. The snap feature enables you to display up to four apps side by side by splitting the screen with dividers, known as Separation bars, as you drag one app next to another. The number of apps you can use, depends on your display resolution; four apps need a large screen resolution of 2,560 x 1,600. You can adjust the position of the Separation bar to show more or less of an app as you need it. The screen with multiple apps acts like a single app, not separate ones. For example, when you switch apps, only the single screen appears.

Display Apps Side by Side

1 Open one of the apps that you want to use from the Start screen.

2 Point to the top of the screen (cursor changes to a hand) and drag down (on a computer) or swipe in slowly from the left edge (on a mobile device), and then drag to the right or left edge.

A Separation bar appears to indicate a split screen. The app displays on one side while the Start screen displays on the other.

3 Open another app from the Start screen to fill in the split screen; you can repeat for up to four apps, and drag app to place.

4 To adjust the size of a side, point to the Separation bar, and then drag left or right to adjust it.

5 To remove an app from the split screen, point to the Separation bar, and then drag left or right to the edge towards the app you want to remove.

Sharing Between Apps

Windows 10 makes it easy to share information, either text or pictures, using other apps. For example, you can select text or pictures on a page in WordPad or on a web page in Microsoft Edge, and then share it with others in an email using Mail. The typical sharing apps are Mail and OneNote (in most cases; depends on the app), however, you can also install and use other online services, such as Twitter and Facebook. The process is pretty simple. Open an app with the content you want to share, display or select the information or item, open the Share panel, and then select the sharing app you want to use.

Share Between Apps

1 Open the app with the content you want to share.

2 Display or select the information or item you want to share.

3 Point to the lower- or upper-right corner and move up or down (on a computer) or swipe left from the right edge of the screen (on a mobile device).

4 Press Win+H to display the Share panel or swipe left from the right edge (on a mobile device).

5 Click or tap the app that you want to use.

TROUBLE? *If a sharing app is not available, make sure it is installed using the Windows Store.*

6 Use the app to send the information to another person.

1 WordPad

Did You Know?

You can use a keyboard shortcut to take a screenshot. In any app, press Win+PrtScn (Print Screen) to take a screenshot and automatically save it in the Pictures folder in the Screenshots folder as a PNG file.

Installing Apps from the Store

Windows 10 comes with a default set of apps, such as Edge, Mail, Skype, Photos, Movies & TV, and Groove Music, developed by Microsoft. However, there are a lot more apps available for almost any need developed by third parties. You can purchase and install apps quickly and easily from the Windows Store. The Windows Store organizes apps by the main categories, such as Home, Apps, Games, Music, and Movies & TV, and then further breaks them down into Apps we picked for you, Top free apps, Top paid apps, Best-rated apps, to make apps easy to find and discover. If you're looking for a specific app, you can use the Search box. The Windows Store uses your Microsoft email (the one used to Sign-in to Windows 10) as the account to purchase apps. If you have multiple devices with Windows 10, you can install a purchased app on up to five of them using your Microsoft account. You can display a list of the apps you own in My Library. This doesn't include any Windows 10 apps installed along with operating system. From the Store, you can install or reinstall an app or an app update.

Use the Windows Store

1. Click or tap the **Store** tile on the Start screen or Start menu.

   ◆ You can also click or tap the **Store** button on the taskbar (desktop).

2. Click or tap the App (or Games) category.

3. To search for an app, click or tap in the Search box, and then type an app name to find it.

4. Scroll through the categories, such as **Apps we picked for you**, **Top free apps**, **Top paid apps**, **Best-rated apps**, as desired.

5. Click or tap a specific app tile.

6. Click or tap the **Install** button, and then follow any on-screen instructions as needed.

   Windows starts installing the selected apps.

View App Downloads and My Library Apps from the Store

1. Click or tap the **Store** tile on the Start screen or Start menu.

   ◆ You can also click or tap the **Store** button on the taskbar (desktop).

2. Click or tap the **Downloads** icon or click or tap the **User Account** icon, and then click or tap **Downloads**.

   A list of apps in process appear in the download and install queue. Windows automatically starts downloading and installing the specified apps.

3. To pause a download and install app, click or tap the **Pause** button to the right of the progress meter.

4. To remove an app, click or tap the **Close** button to the right of the progress meter.

5. To view your installed apps, click the **User Account** icon, and then click or tap **My Library**.

6. To set options for App updates, click the **User Account** icon, and then click or tap **Settings**.

   ◆ **Update apps automatically.**

   ◆ **Show products on tile.**

   ◆ **Only update the tile when I'm on Wi-Fi.**

7. To go back to the main Store screen, click or tap **Home**.

Did You Know?

You can view app disk space usage. Click or tap the Settings button on the Start menu, click or tap the System icon, and then click or tap Apps & features to display app sizes.

For Your Information

Viewing Your Account Information

Before you can purchase an app, you need to add a payment method to your Microsoft account. You can do this from your account in the Windows Store. Click or tap the Store tile on the Start menu, click or tap the User Account icon, click or tap the Purchased, click or tap Payment & billing, and then use the tabs and follow the on-screen instructions to specify payment information. If you have a gift card or promotional code you can redeem it. From your account, you can also change your user account and remove your user account from your device.

Changing Windows Store Settings

You can change Windows Store preferences to make it easier to find certain types of apps when you browse categories or view list of apps in the Store. You can set options to make it easier to find apps in my preferred languages or that include accessibility features. You can also set an option to have the Store recommend apps for you. In Windows Store, click or tap the User Account icon, and then click or tap Settings.

Updating Apps

Developers, including Microsoft, continually update apps to provide additional features. If a new version of an app you have installed is available, Windows automatically generates an update icon for you in the Windows Store. The Downloads and installs screen automatically displays a list of apps with an available update. The updates appear by title with options to download and install. You can use the buttons next to the app to download and install updates or remove the app. Windows starts installing the app updates in the background by default, however you can set options to change it.

Update an App from the Store

1. Click or tap the **Store** tile on the Start screen or Start menu.

   ◆ You can also click or tap the **Store** button on the taskbar (desktop).

2. Click or tap the **Downloads** icon or click or tap the **User Account** icon, and then click or tap **Downloads**.

3. Click or tap the **Check for updates** button.

   If the Check for updates button is not available, it means that all the apps you have installed on your device are up-to-date with the latest version.

   Windows checks for available updates for your apps.

4. To download an update an app, click or tap the **Download** button.

5. To delete an app, click or tap the **Delete** button.

6. To go back to the main Store screen, click or tap **Home**.

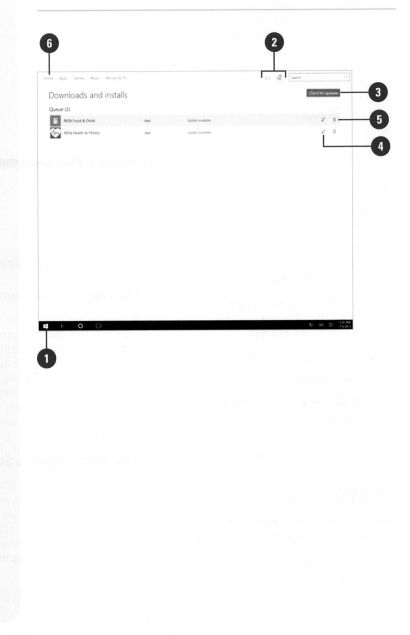

Uninstalling Apps

When you install an app, including the ones that come by default with Windows 10, it takes up storage space on your PC computer or mobile device. If space becomes limited or you just don't use an app anymore, you can uninstall it to free up storage space. You can uninstall one or more apps at the same time from the Start screen and menu. Simply select the app you want to uninstall, then use the Uninstall command on the submenu. After an alert message to confirm the uninstall, Windows 10 uninstalls the app. If you want to uninstall Windows accessories and system tools, you need to turn the Windows features off under Programs within the Control Panel from the desktop, which you'll learn about in a later in this book.

Uninstall an App from the Store

1 Display the Start screen or Start menu with tiles.

2 Right-click (on a computer) or tap-drag down slightly (on a mobile device) to select or deselect an app tile.

3 Click or tap **Uninstall** on the submenu.

4 Click or tap **Uninstall** to confirm the uninstall.

The app tile is removed from the Start screen and menu, and Windows uninstalls the app from your device. However, as a purchased app, you can install it again in this or any other Windows 10 device.

Did You Know?

You can uninstall an app from Settings. Click or tap the Settings button on the Start menu, click or tap the System icon, click or tap Apps & features and apps, click or tap an app, click or tap Uninstall button, and then click or tap Uninstall.

Customizing Apps on the Start Screen

The Start screen or menu is the beginning point for accessing apps and features in Windows 10. Customizing the Start screen and menu can save you time and effort by making it easier to find the Windows apps or accessories you use most often. You can add apps or accessories to the Start screen and menu, or customize the way the Start screen and menu looks and functions. The Start screen and menu contains pinned items from All apps, which is the default location for installed apps. Pinned items are shortcuts to make it easier to open an app or accessory. The Start screen and menu come with a default set of pinned items when you install Windows 10, however you can add your own. The pinned items remain on the Start screen and menu, like a push pin holds paper on a bulletin board, until you unpin them. When you unpin an item, Windows removes the shortcut from the Start screen and menu, however, it doesn't remove the app or accessory from your device. You can also change a few display options using Settings, such as personalizing the Start background, showing accessories on the Start screen and clearing live tile information to maintain privacy.

Customize Apps on the Start Screen and Menu

1. Display the Start screen, Start menu, or All apps.

2. Right-click (on a computer) or tap-drag down slightly (on a mobile device) to select an app tile.

3. Click **Pin to Start** or **Unpin from Start** on the submenu.

Did You Know?

You can pin to or unpin from taskbar. Display the Start screen, Start menu or All apps, right-click (on a computer) or tap-drag down slightly (on a mobile device) to select an app tile, and then click or tap Pin to taskbar or Unpin from taskbar on the submenu.

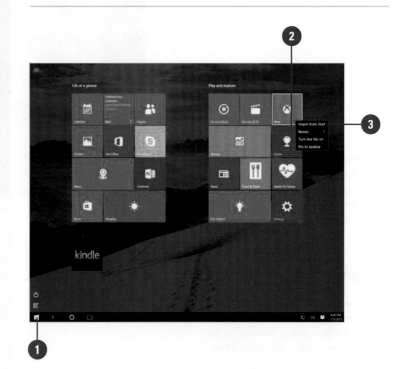

Change Start Settings

1. Click or tap the **Settings** button on the Start screen or Start menu.

2. Click or tap **Personalization**.

3. Click or tap **Background (New!)** under Personalization.

4. Click or tap the **Background** list arrow, and then select **Picture**, **Solid color**, or **Slideshow**.

5. Select options based on your Background selection.

6. Click or tap **Colors**.

7. Click or tap any of the following options:

   ◆ **Automatically pick an accent color from my background.**

   ◆ **Show color on Start, taskbar, and action center.**

   ◆ **Make Start, taskbar, and action center transparent.**

8. Click or tap **Start**.

9. Click or tap any of the following options:

   ◆ **Show most used apps.**

   ◆ **Show recently added apps.**

   ◆ **Use Start full screen.**

   ◆ **Show recently opened items in Jump List on Start or the taskbar.**

10. Click or tap the **Close** button to exit Settings.

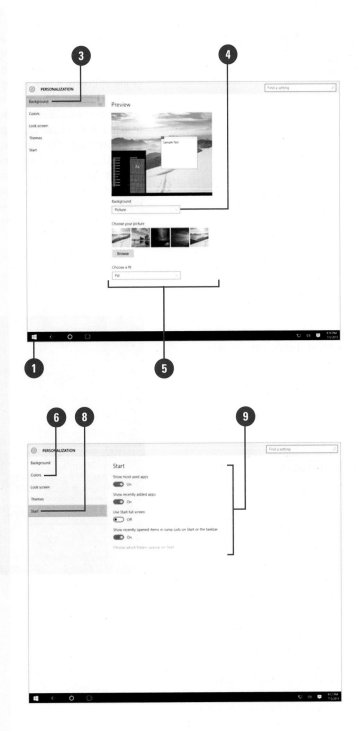

Grouping Apps on the Start Screen

When you view the Start screen or menu, you notice the app tiles are arranged in groups. Grouping apps together makes it easier to locate and use them individually. You can arrange app items within an existing group or create a new group simply by repositioning them on the Start screen or menu. When you move app tiles into groups on the Start screen or menu, Windows automatically arranges them in the group to fit in place. Because tile sizes vary, some are smaller squares while others are larger rectangles, they don't always fit seamlessly into place. If you want all the tiles to fit nicely in place, you can resize them to small, medium, wide, or large at any time. After you organize your apps into a group, you can name each group for easy identification. If the name you originally chose for a group no longer fits, or you want to delete it, you can edit or remove the group name using the same method.

Change App Tile Size

1. Display the Start screen or Start menu.

2. Right-click (on a computer) or tap-drag down slightly (on a mobile device) to select an app tile.

3. Point to **Resize** on the submenu, and then click or tap an option: **Small**, **Medium**, **Wide**, or **Large**.

Did You Know?

You can turn live tile off or on. On the Start screen or Start menu, right-click (on a computer) or tap-drag down slightly (on a mobile device) to select an app tile, and then click or tap the Turn live tile off or Turn live tile on the submenu. Not all tiles can display live information.

See Also

See "Customizing Apps on the Start Screen" on page 40 for more information on setting options to customize the Start screen.

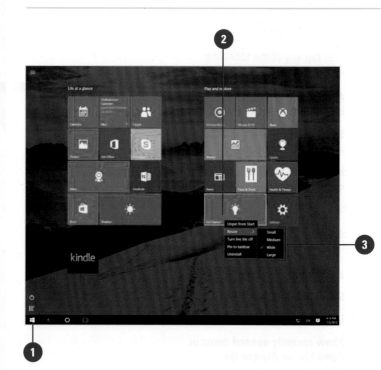

Group Apps on the Start Screen or Start Menu

1. Display the Start screen or Start menu.

2. Drag a tile to another existing group of tiles, or drag a tile to the blank area on the side of the screen to create a new group.

3. Point above the group you want to name, if no name exist.

4. Click or tap in the Group Name box or **Edit** button (=), and then enter or edit the group name.

   ◆ **Remove group name.** Point to a group name, click or tap the Group Name box or **Edit** button (=), and then click the **Delete** button (x).

5. Click or tap outside the Group Name box in a blank area to exit edit mode.

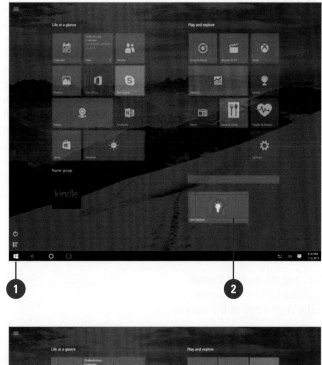

Edit button

Setting Notification Options for Apps

Notifications are a way for Windows 10 and apps to communicate with you. When new information is available within an app or an action is requested by Windows, a notification appears on your screen or in the Action center (**New!**) on the taskbar. There are several types of notifications: a pop-up, start screen tile or badge, and lock screen icon. You can open the Action center to read a notification or clear or close it. You can change notifications settings under Notifications or Lock screen to customize the way it works. You can enable or disable app notifications for all apps or just specific ones and play sounds. You can also specify a quiet time to stop notifications and calls when you're away. You can quickly turn all notifications on and off with the Quiet hours button (**New!**) on the Action center. For the Lock screen, you can specify up to seven apps to show notifications and status.

Set Notification Options for Apps

1. Display the Start screen or desktop.

2. Click or tap the **Action Center** icon on the taskbar or swipe left from the right edge of the screen.

   TIMESAVER *Press Win+A to open the Action center.*

   The Action Center panel appears.

3. Point to a notification, and then click or tap the down arrow to view more information or click or tap the **Close** button to remove it.

4. To turn all notifications on and off, click **Quiet hours** (**New!**) on the Action Center panel.

5. Click or tap **All Settings** on the Action center panel or **Settings** on the Start screen or menu.

6. Click or tap the **System** icon, and then click or tap **Notifications & actions**.

7. Set options to stop notifications and receive calls during quiet times.

8. Drag the slider to turn notification options and apps on or off.

9. Click or tap the **Close** button (x) to exit Settings.

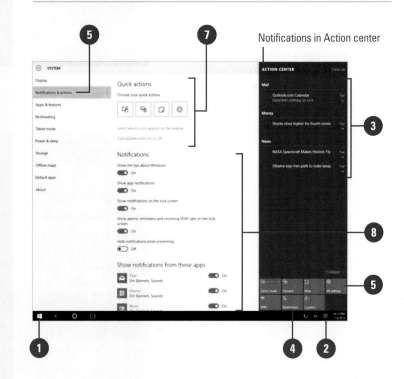

Notifications in Action center

Setting Search Options for Apps

When you use the Search box (**New!**) or Search/Cortana button (**New!**) on the taskbar to locate information on the web or your PC, you can set options under Settings to customize the way it works. With Windows 10, you can search by typing text criteria or voicing commands with Cortana, your personal assistant. When Windows starts for the first time, it defaults to Search with Cortana turned off. You can set options to use Bing to search online. With Cortana turned on, you can access Cortana from the taskbar or with a voice command, "Hey Cortana" (**New!**). You can also have Cortana give you tidbits (**New!**) from time to time with thoughts and greetings. You can adjust Cortana's options or turn it off in Notebook Settings.

Set Search Options for Apps

1. Click or tap the **Search** box (desktop) or **Search/Cortana** button (Start screen) on the taskbar.

2. Click or tap the **Settings** icon (Search) or click or tap the **Notebook** icon (Cortana), and then click or tap **Settings**.

3. Click or drag the **Cortana can give you sug-gestions, ideas, reminders, alerts and more** slider to turn the Cortana on or off (enables Search only).

4. Click or drag options on or off.

   ◆ **Search online and include web results (Search)**. Use to enable or disable search online.

   ◆ **Hey Cortana (Cortana)**. Use for voice response.

   ◆ **Find flights and more (Cortana)**. Use for tracking information.

   ◆ **Taskbar tidbits (Cortana)**. Use to get thoughts from Cortana.

5. Click or tap off Cortana home to close it.

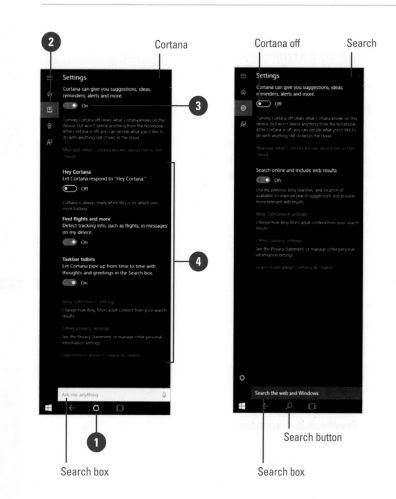

Cortana

Cortana off   Search

Search box

Search button

Search box

Setting Privacy Options for Apps

When you use apps (which you can specify), such as Maps or Skype, the app includes functionality that uses information from Windows, such as my name and account picture, my location, my webcam, my microphone, and other devices. For example, the Maps app uses your current location (my location) to pin point it on a map, and the Skype app displays your name (my name) and account picture and uses a webcam and microphone during calls and conversations. You can set privacy settings to enable or disable these and other options to specify the level of protection you want and the apps you want to use.

Set Privacy Options for Apps

1. Click or tap the **Settings** button on the Start menu.

2. Click or tap the **Privacy** icon, and then click or tap **General**, if needed.

3. Drag the slider to turn general privacy options on or off.

4. Click or tap a category, and then drag the Slider **On** or **Off** to let Windows and apps use it for the specified function.

   - ◆ **Location.**
   - ◆ **Camera.**
   - ◆ **Microphone.**
   - ◆ **Speech, inking, & typing.** (New!)
   - ◆ **Account info.** (New!)
   - ◆ **Contacts.** (New!)
   - ◆ **Calendar.** (New!)
   - ◆ **Messaging.** (New!)
   - ◆ **Radios.** (New!)
   - ◆ **Other devices.**
   - ◆ **Feedback & diagnostics.** (New!)
   - ◆ **Background apps.** (New!)

5. When turned on, drag the slider as needed for the app you want to enable or disable the use.

6. To close Settings, click or tap the **Close** button (x).

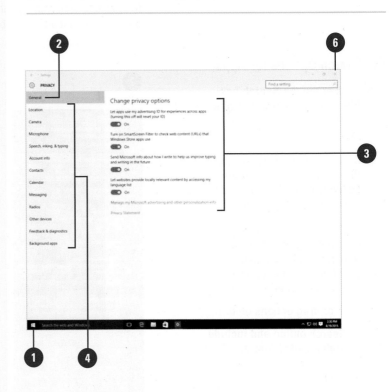

Managing Files and Folders

3

Introduction

File management is organizing and keeping track of files and folders, helping you stay organized, so information is easily located. A **folder** is a container for storing programs and files, similar to a folder in a file cabinet. As with a file cabinet, working with poorly managed files is like looking for a needle in a haystack—it is frustrating and time-consuming to search through irrelevant, misnamed, and out-of-date files to find the one you want. Windows allows you to organize folders and files in a file hierarchy, imitating the way you store paper documents in real folders. Just as a file cabinet contains several folders, each containing related documents with dividers grouping related folders together, so the Windows file hierarchy allows you to organize your files in folders, and then place folders in other folders. File Explorer comes with four libraries: Documents, Music, Pictures, and Videos. Libraries are special folders that catalog folders and files in a central location. A library includes and displays folders that are stored in different locations on your PC computer, Homegroup, or network.

Using the file management tools, you can save files in folders with appropriate names for easy identification, quickly and easily create new folders so you can reorganize information and delete files and folders that you no longer need. You can also search for a file when you cannot remember where you stored it, create shortcuts to files and folders for quick and easy access, and even compress files and folders to save space.

A folder can hold different types of files, such as text, spreadsheets, and presentations. The Documents folder is the main location in File Explorer where you store your files. However, there are some special folders, such as Pictures and Music, designed with specialized features to store specific types of files.

Using the Explorer Window

Explorer windows, such as File Explorer, are powerful easy-to-use tools for working with files in Windows 10. Explorers give you more information and control while simplifying how you work with your files. The experience is easy and consistent, whether you're browsing documents or photos or even using Settings or the Control Panel. Key elements of the Explorer windows in the desktop are designed to help you get to the information you need, when you need it. Each Explorer window includes the following elements:

◆ **Toolbar.** Use to access frequently used commands, known as the Quick Access Toolbar.

◆ **Ribbon.** Use to access buttons or options organized in groups on tabs.

◆ **Back, Forward, and Up buttons.** Use to navigate between previously viewed folders.

◆ **Address bar.** Use to navigate directly to a different location, including local and network disks, folders, and web locations.

◆ **Search box.** Use to perform instant searches, which show only those files that match what you typed in the Search box for the current folder and any of its subfolders.

◆ **Navigation pane.** Use to display common folders, such as Quick access (**New!**), OneDrive, Homegroup (a shared network), This PC, and Network, using a Folder list tree structure.

◆ **OneDrive, This PC, or Libraries.** Use to access common folders, such as Documents, Music, Pictures, and Videos located on your OneDrive on the Microsoft cloud, or local PC. A library is a collection of files and folders linked from different locations—such as a OneDrive or This PC by default—into a central place. A file or folder can be stored in one location, yet linked to a library for easy access in one place.

◆ **Status bar.** Displays number of items and selected items in a folder, and Details and Icons view buttons.

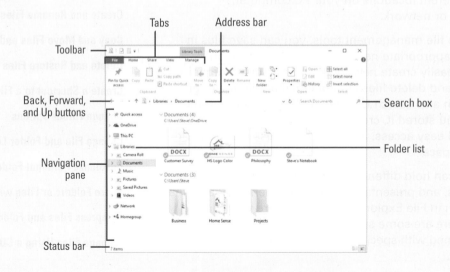

Tabs

Address bar

Toolbar

Back, Forward, and Up buttons

Navigation pane

Status bar

Search box

Folder list

Changing the Explorer Window View

The Explorer window displays the contents of a drive or folder in different ways to help you find the information you are looking for about a file or folder. The available views on the View tab of an Explorer window include Extra Large, Large, Medium and Small Icons, List, Details, Tiles, and Content.

Icons view displays icons in different sizes (Extra Large, Large, Medium, and Small), sorted alphabetically in horizontal rows with the name of the file or folder below each icon. When you view files using one of the Icon views, Live icons—thumbnails—display the first page of documents, the image of a photo, or the album art for individual songs, making it easier to find exactly what you are looking for.

List view displays small icons, sorted alphabetically into vertical columns with the name of the file or folder next to each icon.

Details view displays small icons, sorted alphabetically in a vertical column with the name of the file or folder and additional infor-mation, such as file size, type, and date, in columns to the right.

Tiles view displays icons, sorted alphabetically into vertical columns, with information about the file next to each icon.

Content view displays medium icons in a vertical column with date modified information.

Switching Between Views

You use the Layout options on the View tab in an Explorer window to quickly switch between window views. When you point to a Layout option—such as Extra large icon, Large icon, Medium icons, Small icons, List, Details, Tiles or Content—on the View tab, File Explorer displays a live preview of the option change so that you can see exactly what your change will look like before committing to it. You can also quickly change between Details and the current icons view by using the Details View and Icons View buttons on the Status bar.

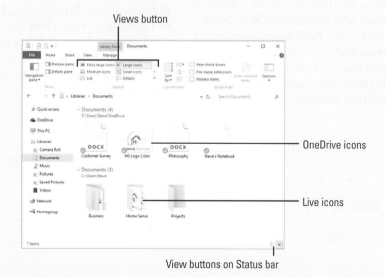

Views button

OneDrive icons

Live icons

View buttons on Status bar

Using the Ribbon

The **Ribbon** is a results oriented way of working in File Explorer. The Ribbon is located at the top of the window and is comprised of **tabs** that are organized by task or objects. The controls on each tab are organized into **groups**, or subtasks. The controls, or **command buttons**, in each group execute a command, or display a menu of commands or a drop-down gallery. Controls in each group provide a visual way to quickly make document changes. The File tab on the left side of the Ribbon displays a menu of files related commands.

> **TIMESAVER** *To minimize the Ribbon, click or tap the Minimize the Ribbon button (Ctrl+F1) or double-click or double-tap the current tab. Click or tap a tab to auto display it (Ribbon remains minimized). Click or tap the Expand the Ribbon button (Ctrl+F1) or double-click or double-tap a tab to maximize it.*

If you prefer using the keyboard instead of the mouse to access commands on the Ribbon, File Explorer provides easy to use shortcuts. Simply press and release the [Alt] or [F10] key to display **KeyTips** over each feature in the current view, and then continue to press the letter shown in the KeyTip until you press the one that you want to use. To cancel an action and hide the KeyTips, press and release the [Alt] or [F10] key again. If you prefer using the keyboard shortcuts found in previous versions of Windows, such as Ctrl+C (for Copy) and Ctrl+V (for Paste), all the keyboard shortcuts and keyboard accelerators work exactly the same in File Explorer.

Tabs

File Explorer provides three types of tabs on the Ribbon. The first type is called a **standard** tab—such as File, Home, Share, and View—that you see whenever you use File Explorer. The second type is called a **contextual** tab—such as Library Tools, Picture Tools, or Video Tools—that appears only when they are needed based on the type of task you are doing. File Explorer recognizes what you're doing and provides the right set of tabs and tools to use when you need them. The third type is called a **program** tab that replaces the standard set of tabs when you switch to certain views or modes, such as Homegroup, This PC, or Network.

Live Preview

When you point to some options, such as a Layout option—Extra large icon, Large icon, Medium icons, Small icons, List, Details, Tiles or Content—on the View tab on the Ribbon, File Explorer displays a live preview of the option change so that you can see exactly what your change will look like before committing to it.

Choosing Commands

File Explorer commands are organized in groups on the Ribbon and Quick Access Toolbar. Commands are available as buttons or options on the Ribbon, or as menus on button or option arrows or the File tab. The Quick Access Toolbar displays frequently used buttons that you may be already familiar with from other Microsoft programs, while the File tab on the Ribbon displays file related menu commands. In addition to the File tab, you can also open a shortcut menu with a group of related commands by right-clicking or tap holding an element.

Choose a Menu Command Using the File Tab

1. In File Explorer, click or tap the **File** tab on the Ribbon.

2. If the command is followed by an arrow, point to the command to see a list of related options.

3. Click or tap a command.

    TIMESAVER *You can use a shortcut key to choose a command. Press and hold down the first key and then press the second key. For example, press and hold the Ctrl key and then press W (or Ctrl+W) to select the Close command.*

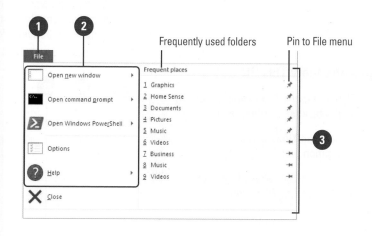

Frequently used folders   Pin to File menu

Choose a Menu Command from a Shortcut Menu

1. In the desktop or File Explorer, right-click or tap-hold an icon.

    TIMESAVER *Press Shift+F10 to display the shortcut menu for a selected command.*

2. Click or tap a command on the shortcut menu. If the command is followed by an arrow, point to the command to see a list of related options, and then click or tap the option you want.

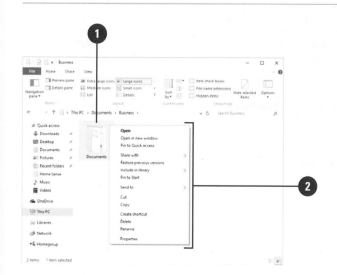

Opening and Viewing This PC

The This PC window is the starting point to access every disk, folder, and file on your PC computer. You can access the This PC window from File Explorer. The This PC window displays local folders and several types of local, removable (like a USB drive), and network drives. Drives and folders are represented by icons. Each drive is assigned a drive letter, denoted with parentheses and a colon, such as Local Disk (C:), to make it easier to identify. Typically, the floppy is drive A (normally found on old computers), the hard (also known as local) disk is drive C, and the CD or DVD is drive D. If your PC computer includes additional drives, your PC computer assigns them letters in alphabetical order. Once you open more than one drive or folder, you can use buttons on the Ribbon to help you move between folders.

Open and View This PC

1 Click or tap the **File Explorer** icon on the taskbar or Start menu.

2 Click or tap **This PC** in the Navigation pane.

> **TIMESAVER** *Press Win+E to display the This PC window.*

3 Click or tap a drive to select it.

4 To review the drive details, click or tap the **Details pane** button on the View tab.

5 Double-click or double-tap the drive to open it.

6 Click or tap the **Back** or **Forward** button or the **Up** button on the toolbar to return or move to a previously visited window.

> **TIMESAVER** *You can press the Backspace key to go back to a previous folder you visited.*

7 When you're done, click or tap the **Close** button.

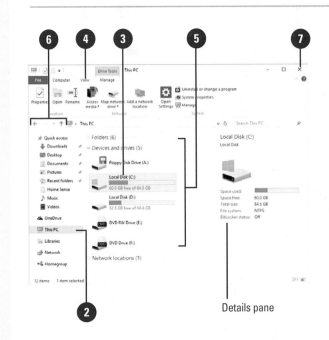

Details pane

Typical Disk Drives on a Computer

Icon	Type Description
Local	A hard magnetic disk (or hard disk) on which you can store large amounts of data. The Local Disk (C:) stores all the files on your PC computer.
Floppy	A soft removable magnetic disk that comes in a 3½-inch size, which stores up to 1.44 MB of data. Floppy disks are slower to access than a hard disk, but are portable and much less expensive.
Removable	A removable magnetic disk on which you can store PC computer data, such as a Zip disk (requires software). Another is a Flash memory card the size of a large stamp that holds128, 256, 512 MB or greater. Flash drives connect directly into a USB plug without software.
CD-ROM	**Compact Disc-Read-Only Memory** An optical disk on which you can stamp, or burn, up to 1 GB (typical size is 650 MB) of data in only one session. The disc cannot be erased or burned again with additional new data.
CD-R	**Compact Disc-Recordable** A type of CD-ROM on which you can burn up to 1 GB of data in multiple sessions. The disc can be burned again with new data, but cannot be erased.
CD-RW	**Compact Disc-Rewriteable** A type of CD-ROM on which you can read, write, and erase data, just like a hard disk.
DVD	**Digital Video Disc** A type of DVD-ROM that holds a minimum of 4.7 GB, enough for a full-length movie.
DVD-R	**Digital Video Disc-Recordable** A type of DVD-ROM on which you can burn up to 4.7 GB of data in multiple sessions. The disc can be burned again with new data, but cannot be erased.
DVD-RW	**Digital Video Disc-Rewriteable** A type of DVD-ROM on which you can read, write, and erase data, just like a hard disk.
HD-DVD DVD-ROM	**High Density Digital Video Disc** A type of high density on which you can read data; the disc appears as a high density drive.
Blu-ray	**High Density Blu-ray Disc** A type of high density DVD-ROM on which you can read data; the disc appears as a high density drive.

Viewing and Opening Documents

Windows makes it easy to manage the personal and business files and folders you work with every day. You can access your Documents folder from File Explorer, which displays the Documents library folder. The Documents library folder links and displays files and folders from different locations on your PC computer and OneDrive in a central place, which includes your Documents folder located in your personal folder. In the folder, you can view file information, organize files and folders, and open files and folders. Once you open more than one folder, you can use buttons to help you move quickly between folders. Depending on previous installation, devices installed, or other users, your personal folders might differ.

View and Open Documents

1. Click or tap the **File Explorer** icon on the taskbar or Start menu.

2. Click or tap **Documents** in the Navigation pane.

3. Double-click or double-tap a folder to navigate to the document location.

4. Click or tap the document file to select it.

5. To review document details, click or tap the **Details pane** button on the View tab.

6. To open the document file, double-click or double-tap the file icon.

7. When you're done, click or tap the **Close** button.

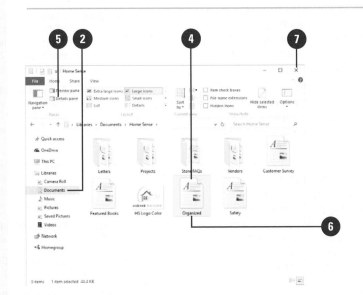

Did You Know?

Windows creates a separate Documents folder for each user.
When you share a PC, Windows creates a separate Documents folder and stores personalized settings for each user. Each user's Documents folder is located in the Documents And Settings folder under the user's name on the local hard disk.

For Your Information

Viewing Frequently Used Folders and Files

In File Explorer, you can display frequently used folders and recently used files with Quick access in the Navigation pane. In File Explorer, click or tap Quick acess (**New!**) n the Navigation pane, which displays Frequent folders and Recent files.

If you want to clear File Explorer history (**New!**), click or tap the Options button on the View tab, click or tap Change folder and search options, and then click or tap Clear. If you only want to hide a few specific frequently used folders or recented used files, click or tap Quick access, and then right-click or tap-hold, and then click or tap Clear recent items list.

Open Any Folder and Switch Between Folders

① Click or tap the **File Explorer** icon on the taskbar or Start menu.

② Click or tap any other Explorer window, such as **Documents**, **Videos**, **Pictures**, or **Music**, in the Navigation pane.

③ Double-click or double-tap the folder to open it.

④ Click or tap the **Back** or **Forward** button or the **Up** button on the toolbar to return or move to a previously visited window.

⑤ When you're done, click or tap the **Close** button.

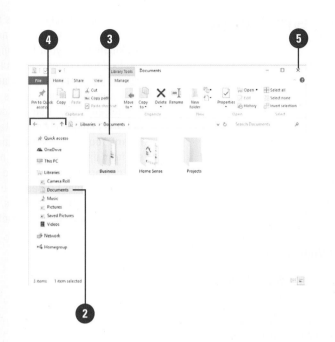

Did You Know?

Windows stores music and picture files in separate folders in your personal folder. Windows stores music files in the Music folder and pictures in the Pictures folder in your personal folder, which you can access from the Music and Pictures libraries.

See Also

See "Changing the Explorer Window View" on page 49 for information on changing the display of a folder's contents.

See "Working with Libraries" on page 56 for information on using and creating libraries.

For Your Information

Opening a Document with a Different Program

Most documents on your desktop are associated with a specific program. For example, if you double-click or double-tap a document whose file name ends with the three-letter extension ".txt," Windows automatically opens the document with Notepad, a text-only editor. There are situations, though, when you need to open a document with a program other than the one Windows chooses, or when you want to choose a different default program. For example, you might want to open a text document in WordPad rather than Notepad so that you can add formatting and graphics. To do this, right-click or tap-hold the document icon you want to open, point to Open With, and then click or tap the application you want to use to open the document, or click or tap Choose Program to access more program options. Once you open a text file using WordPad, this option is automatically added to the Open With menu.

Working with Libraries

Libraries are special folders that catalog folders and files in a central location. A library includes and displays folders that are stored in different locations on your PC computer, OneDrive, Homegroup, or network. File Explorer comes with four libraries: Documents, Music, Pictures, and Videos. The Documents library, for example, includes files and folders from your Documents—This PC and OneDrive—folders, which are actually stored in your Users folder. Instead of navigating to separate folders, you can quickly navigate to one central place, the Documents library. You can create additional libraries at any time and include folders from different locations or remove them. After you open a library, you can arrange all files and folders included in a library by folder (the default) or other properties based on the library type (General Items, Documents, Music, Pictures, or Videos). When you save a file to a library, you can specify which folder it actually gets stored in.

Open and View a Library

1. Click or tap the **File Explorer** icon on the taskbar or Start menu.

2. To show libraries, click or tap the **Navigation pane** button on the View tab, and then click or tap **Show libraries**.

3. Click or tap a library folder in the Navigation pane or double-click or double-tap a library folder.

4. To change the library display, right-click or tap-hold a blank area, point to **Arrange by**, and then click or tap an option.

    ◆ Folder. File and folders.

    ◆ General Items. Date modified, Tag, Type, or Name.

    ◆ Documents. Author, Date modified, Tag, Type, or Name.

    ◆ Pictures. Month, Day, Rating, or Tag.

    ◆ Music. Album, Artist, Song, Genre, or Rating.

    ◆ Video. Year, Type, Length, or Name.

    ◆ Clear changes. Clears any arrange by modifications.

5. To sort or group items, click or tap the **Sort by** or **Group by** button on the View tab, and then click or tap an option.

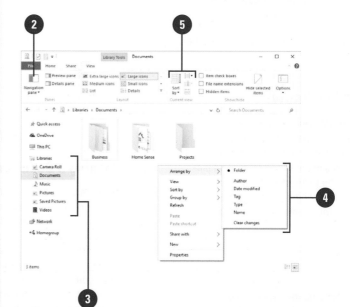

Create a New Library and Include or Remove Folders

1 Click or tap the **File Explorer** icon on the taskbar or Start menu.

2 Click or tap the **Libraries** in the Navigation pane.

3 Click or tap the **New item** button on the Home tab, click or tap **Library**, type a library name, and then press Enter.

◆ To delete a library, select it, click or tap the **Delete** button on the Home tab, click or tap **Permanently delete**, and then click or tap **Yes**.

4 To include a folder in a library, navigate to the folder location, click or tap the **Easy access** button on the Home tab, point to **Include in library**, and then select the library you want.

5 To remove a folder from a library, open the library, click or tap the **Manage library** button on the Manage tab, select the folder you want to remove, click or tap **Remove**, and then click or tap **OK**.

Did You Know?

You can change the save location. Open the folder you want to change the save location, click or tap the Manage tab, click or tap the Set save location button, and then select a folder location. A check mark appears to the left of the selected folder location.

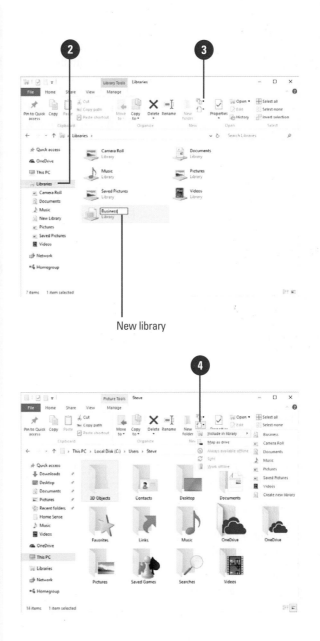

New library

Working with Personal Folders

File Explorer comes with a personal folder that stores your most frequently used folders in one location. The personal folder appears in File Explorer with the name of the person logged on to the PC computer. The personal folder only contains files and folders associated with a user account and are unique for each user. The personal folder includes a variety of folders: 3D Objects (**New!**), Contacts, Desktop, Documents, Downloads, Favorites, Links, Music, OneDrive, Pictures, Saved Games, Searches, and Videos. You can access these folders using the personal folder from File Explorer under This PC, hard drive (with Windows 10) in the Users (user name account) folder. The Documents, Pictures, Music, and Videos folders are included in the Documents, Pictures, Music, and Videos libraries respectively, so you can also access them by name in File Explorer.

View and Open a Personal Folder

1. Click or tap the **File Explorer** icon on the taskbar or Start menu.

2. Click or tap the **This PC** in the Navigation pane.

3. Double-click or double-tap the hard drive (with Windows 10), and then double-click or double-tap the Users folder to open it.

   TIMESAVER *To show your personal folder in the Navigation pane, click or tap the Navigation pane button on the View tab, and then click or tap Show all folders.*

4. Double-click or double-tap the folder with the user account's name to open it.

5. Double-click or double-tap a folder to open it.

6. When you're done, click or tap the **Close** button.

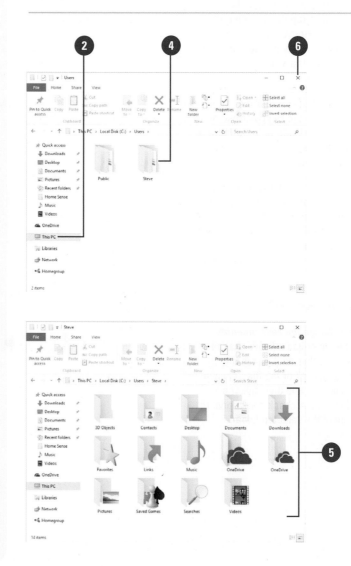

Navigating Between Folders

The Address bar appears at the top of every Explorer window and displays the current location on your PC computer, OneDrive, or network. The location appears as a series of links separated by arrows. You can change your current location by either typing a new location—even a web address on the Internet—or selecting one using the Address bar. You can also use the Back and Forward buttons to the left of the Address bar to switch between locations you have previously visited.

Navigate to a Location

- **Click or tap a location**. Use either of the following methods:

  - ◆ Visible folder location. To go directly to a location visible in the Address bar, click or tap the location name.

  - ◆ Visible subfolder location. To go to a subfolder of a location visible in the Address bar, click or tap the arrow to the right, and then click or tap the location name.

- **Type a location**. Click or tap a blank space (to the right of text) in the Address bar, and then type the complete folder name or path to the location, and then press Enter.

  You can type common locations and then press Enter. The common locations include: This PC, Contacts, Control Panel, Documents, Favorites, Games, Music, Pictures, Recycle Bin, and Videos.

  If you type a web address (URL) in the Address bar, the Explorer window switches to Microsoft Edge (**New!**).

Click a location   Address bar

Navigation pane

Viewing the Folders List

Windows offers a useful feature for managing files and folders, called the **Folders list**, which is integrated under categories—Quick access (similar to favorites) (**New!**), OneDrive, Homegroup, This PC, Libraries, and Network—into the Navigation pane. The Folders list displays the window in two panes, or frames, which allows you to view information from two different locations. The Navigation pane displays the file hierarchy of all the drives and folders on the PC computer, and the right pane displays the contents of the selected drive or folder. This arrangement enables you to view the file hierarchy of your PC computer and the contents of a folder simultaneously making it easy to copy, move, delete, and rename files and folders. Using the non filled arrow and the filled arrow to the left of an icon in the Folders list allows you to display different levels of the drives and folders on your PC computer without opening and displaying the contents of each folder.

View the Folders List

1 Click or tap the **File Explorer** icon on the taskbar or Start menu.

2 Open any folder window.

3 In the Navigation pane, point to an item to display the navigation arrows.

4 Perform the commands you want to display folder structure and contents:

◆ To show the file and folder structure, click or tap the non filled arrow.

◆ To hide the file and folder structure, click or tap the filled arrow.

◆ To display the contents of a folder, click or tap the folder icon.

Did You Know?

You can quickly determine if a folder contains folders. When an arrow doesn't appear next to an icon in the Folders list, the item has no folders in it.

Folder list tree structure

Changing the Explorer Layout

File Explorer gives you the option to customize the layout for each Explorer window depending on the information the window contains. The layout for each Explorer window includes a Preview pane, Details pane, and Navigation pane. The Preview pane provides a preview of the selected item, such as a picture. The Details pane a thumbnail pre-view and information about the selected item, such as the file name, type, date modified, dimensions, size, and date created. The Navigation pane provides a tree structure to navigate folders and drives on your OneDrive, This PC, Network, Homegroup, or libraries. The Details and Navigation panes appear by default. The Panes group on the View tab provides options to show or hide the Explorer layout elements.

Change the Explorer Layout

1. Click or tap the **File Explorer** icon on the taskbar or Start menu.

2. Open the folder window you want to change.

3. Click or tap the **View** tab.

4. Select the layout pane button you want to show or hide: **Preview Pane**, **Details Pane**, or **Navigation Pane** (and then click or tap **Navigation pane**).

5. Click or tap the **Navigation Pane** button, and then click or tap an option to show or hide items in the Navigation pane: **Show all folders** or **Show libraries**.

   The Show all folders options displays your personal folder (with your account name), Control Panel, and Recycle.

   Layout options vary depending on the type of Explorer window.

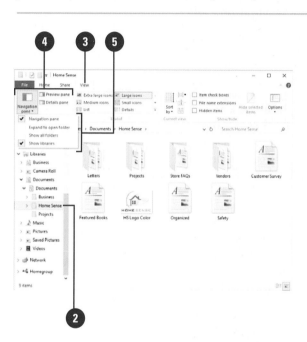

Customizing the Navigation Pane

The Navigation pane provides links to commonly used drives and folders to reduce the number of clicks or taps it takes to locate a file or folder. File Explorer provides a default list of quick access (**New!**), libraries, homegroups, and networks in the Navigation pane. You can customize the list of quick access—such as pin or unpin items (**New!**), like the Start menu—for your own purposes. You can move links, add or rename folders, or remove an item. If the Navigation pane gets cluttered, you can restore it back to the original default items. You can also set Navigation pane options to show recently used files in Quick access (**New!**) and show frequently used folders in Quick access (**New!**).

Customize the Navigation Pane

◆ **Pin or unpin a link.** Select the item item, and then click or tap the **Pin to Quick access** button (**New!**) on the Home tab, or click or tap right-click or tap-hold the item, and then click or tap **Pin to Quick access** or **Unpin from Quick access** (**New!**).

◆ **Add or Move a link.** Drag an item from its original location (add) to a position in Quick access or drag an item (Move) in Quick access.

◆ **Rename a link.** Right-click or tap-hold the original item, click or tap **Rename**, type a new name, and then press Enter. The link is renamed with the folder (**New!**).

◆ **Remove a link.** Right-click or tap-hold the link in Quick access, and then click or tap **Remove** or **Don't show in navigation pane** (**New!**). The original folder or search is not removed, only the Navigation link.

◆ **Show recently used files in Quick access or Show frequently used folders in Quick access.** Click or tap the **Options** button on the View tab, click or tap **Change folder and search options**, select check boxes on the General tab, and then click or tap **OK**.

   ◆ **Show recently used files in Quick access. (New!)**

   ◆ **Show frequently used folders in Quick access. (New!)**

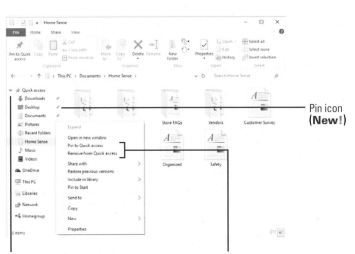

Pin icon (**New!**)

Quick access (**New!**) in the Navigation pane   Pin (**New!**) or Remove a link

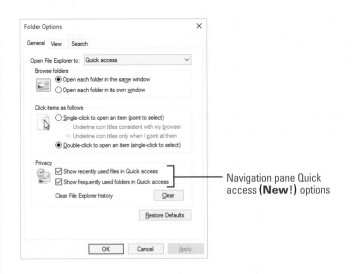

Navigation pane Quick access (**New!**) options

Organizing Files by Headings

In Explorer windows, files and folders appear in lists with headings at the top in Details view. You can use the headings to change how files are displayed in the window. You can use filtering and sorting to display the files and folders you want. Filtering displays only files and folders with the properties you select by heading type. For example, the A - H filter for file and folder names displays only files and folder that start with A - H. Sorting displays the files and folders in ascending or descending order by heading type. For example, the sort by name displays files and folders from A to Z or Z to A. You can apply a filter and sort a column to achieve the results you want.

Organize Files Using Filtering or Sorting

1. Click or tap the **File Explorer** icon on the taskbar or Start menu.

2. Open the folder that contains the files you want to sort or filter.

3. Click or tap **Details** on the View tab, or click or tap the **Details** button.

4. To sort files by headings, click or tap the heading title you want to sort by. An arrow in the middle of the heading indicates the sort direction, ascending and descending.

5. Point to the heading you want to filter by.

6. Click or tap the arrow to the right of the heading you want to filter by.

7. Select the property check boxes you want to filter by.

8. Click or tap in a blank area to close the search menu.

   A check mark replaces the arrow to indicates a filter is in place.

   ◆ To cancel the search, you can also press Esc.

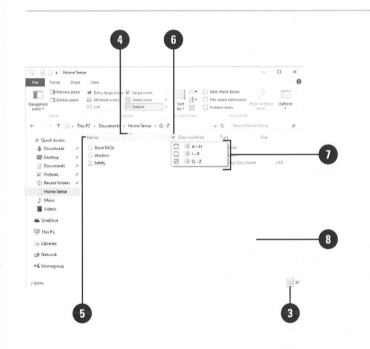

Sorting and Grouping Files

In Explorer windows, files and folders appear sorted or grouped by different attributes, such as name or type, in the different views, such as Icons (Extra large, Large, Medium, or Small), List, Details, Tiles, and Content. You can select the attributes you want to use and then select whether to display the files and folders in ascending (A-Z) or descending (Z-A) order. You can use the Sort by or Group by buttons on the View tab to specify the options you want to apply to the current folder. The Sort by and Group by options are the same. However, the available options vary depending on the selected folder type, such as a Documents or Pictures folder.

Sort Files and Folders

1. Click or tap the **File Explorer** icon on the taskbar or Start menu.

2. Open the folder that contains the files you want to group.

3. Click or tap the **Sort by** button on the View tab.

4. Select a sort by option on the menu.

   ◆ **Options.** Select an option, such as name, Date, Size, Type, Date modified, and Dimensions.

   The available options vary depending on the selected folder type.

   ◆ **Ascending.** Select to sort items in ascending order A-Z.

   ◆ **Descending.** Select to sort items in descending order Z-A.

   ◆ **Choose columns.** Select to customize the columns shown in Details view.

See Also

See "Changing File and Folder List Views" on page 80 for more information on setting options for customizing the columns shown in Details view.

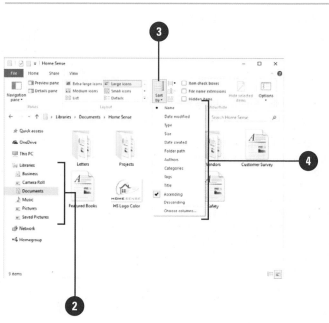

Group Files and Folders

1. Click or tap the **File Explorer** icon on the taskbar or Start menu.

2. Open the folder that contains the files you want to group.

3. Click or tap the **Group by** button on the View tab.

4. Select a group by option on the menu.

   ◆ **Options.** Select an option, such as Name, Date, Size, Type, Date modified, and Dimensions.

   The available options vary depending on the selected folder type.

   ◆ **(None).** Select to remove the group by option.

   ◆ **Ascending.** Select to group items in ascending order A-Z.

   ◆ **Descending.** Select to group items in descending order Z-A.

   ◆ **Choose columns.** Select to customize the columns shown in Details view.

5. Click the **Collapse** or **Expand** arrow next to the heading to collapse or expand the grouping.

Did You Know?

You can size all columns to fit their contents in Details view. In File Explorer, open the folder you want to size columns, click or tap Details on the View tab, and then click or tap the Size All Columns To Fit button on the View tab.

Searching for Files and Folders

Sometimes remembering precisely where you stored a file can be difficult. File Explorer allows you to use Windows Search Explorer (by default) to help you find and view all of your files or folders in one place. You start a search by using the Search box. As you type in a Search box, the search looks for matches in the file name, contents, and property tags, and displays the highlighted results in a Search Results folder. If you don't find the file or folders you're looking for, you can perform an advanced search using a menu from the Search box. An advanced search gives you the option to find files or folders by type, name, title, location, date (taken, modified, or created), size, or property tag. The search locates files and programs stored anywhere in indexed locations, which includes personal folders, e-mail, offline files, and web sites in your History list.

Create a Simple Search

1. Click or tap the **File Explorer** icon on the taskbar or Start menu.

2. Open an Explorer window in the location where you want to search.

3. Click or tap in the Search box.

   A search tab appears. Disregard the tab for a simple search.

4. Type a word or part of a word.

   As you type, programs and files that match your text appear highlighted in the Search Results window. You don't have to press Enter.

   TROUBLE? *In the Search box, you must press Enter to start a search for non-indexed files.*

5. To clear and close the search, click or tap the **Close** button (x) on the Search tab or in the Search box.

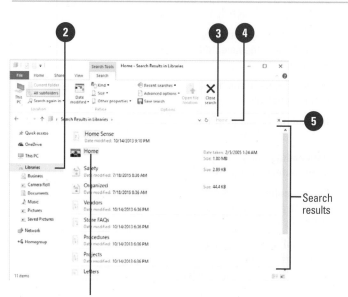

Highlighted search results

Search results

Create an Advanced Search

1. Click or tap the **File Explorer** icon on the taskbar or Start menu.

2. Open an Explorer window in the location where you want to search.

3. Click or tap in the Search box.

   A Search tab appears with advanced options.

4. Click or tap the **This PC**, **Current folder**, or **All subfolders** to specify a search location.

5. Click or tap the Refine buttons you want on the Search tab, and then select an option.

   ◆ **Date modified.** Searches by date modified.

   ◆ **Kind.** Searches by kind of file, such as Document, E-mail, Video, or Instant Message.

   ◆ **Size.** Searches by file size.

   ◆ **Other properties.** Searches by file type, name, folder path, or property tag.

6. To set additional options, click or tap the **Advanced options** button, and then click or tap **Partial matches**, **File contents**, **System files**, or **Zipped (compressed folders)** to enable or disable.

7. Type in search criteria in the Search box or select from the available criteria.

8. To search again in other locations, click or tap the **Search again in** button, and then click or tap **Homegroup**, **Libraries**, or **Internet**.

9. To clear and close the search, click or tap the **Close** button (x) on the Search tab or in the Search box.

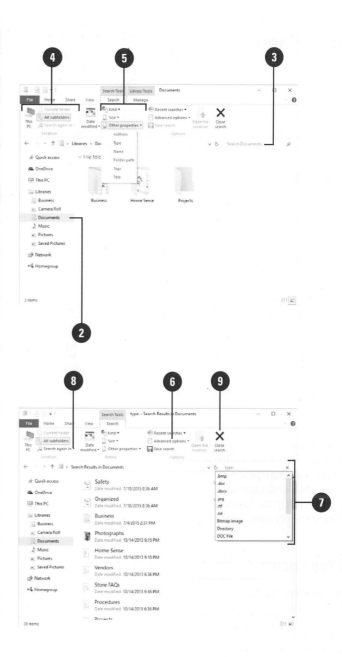

Saving a Search

If you frequently perform the same search, you can save your search results like any file and perform or modify the search again later. When you save a search, the search is saved by default with Window Search Explorer in the Searches folder in your personal folder and added to the Quick access folder in the Navigation pane. Like any link, you can move a saved search from the Searches folder to the Quick access category in the Navigation pane to make it more accessible. To run a saved search, display the saved search link, and then click or tap it.

Save a Search

1. Click or tap the **File Explorer** icon on the taskbar or Start menu.

2. Open an Explorer window in the location where you want to search.

3. Click or tap in the Search box, specify the criteria you want, and then perform the search.

4. Click or tap the **Save search** button on the Search tab.

5. Type a name for the search.

6. Click or tap **Save**.

7. To use a saved search, click or tap the saved search link in Quick access in the Navigation pane or double-click or double-tap the saved search in the Searches folder in the personal folder.

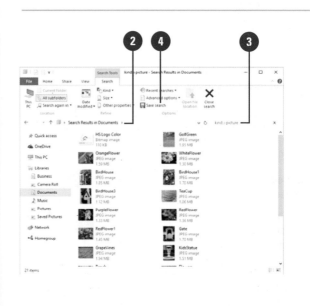

Did You Know?

You can quickly perform a recent search. Click in the Search box to the display the Search tab. Click or tap the Recent Searches button, and then select a recent search. If the list gets cluttered, you can clear items. Click or tap the Recent Searches button, and then click or tap Clear Search History.

Changing Search Options

When you perform a search for files or folders, File Explorer uses the search options to help customize the search results. You can specify whether you want to search for file names and content or just for file names and whether to include subfolders. For non-indexed searches, you can set options to include system directories or compressed files (ZIP, CAB...), or always search file names and contents. The search options are available in the Folder Options dialog box under the Search tab.

Change Search Options

1 Click or tap the **File Explorer** icon on the taskbar or Start menu.

2 Click or tap the **Options** button on the View tab, and then click or tap **Folder and search options**.

3 Click or tap the **Search** tab.

4 Select or clear the check boxes under How to search:

- ◆ **Don't use the index when searching in file folders for system files (searches might take longer).**

5 Select or clear the check boxes under When searching non-indexed locations:

- ◆ **Include system directories.**

- ◆ **Include compressed files (ZIP, CAB, ...)**

- ◆ **Always search file names and contents (this might take several minutes)**

6 Click or tap **OK**.

Modifying the Index to Improve Searches

Windows keeps track of files in indexed locations and stores information about them in the background using an index, like the one found in the back of this book, to make locating files faster and easier. You can use Indexing Options in the Control Panel to view, pause, add, remove, and modify indexed locations, indexed file types, and other advanced index settings. For example, if a file type is not recognized by the index, you can add it; if you want to stop indexing new content for 15 minutes to specify options, you can pause it; or if you're having problems with the search index, you can rebuild or restore it.

View, Pause, Add, or Remove Indexed Locations

1. Click or tap **All apps** on the Start menu.

2. Click or tap the down arrow next to **Windows System** to expand it, and then click or tap **Control Panel**.

   ◆ You can also right-click or tap-hold the **Start** button on the taskbar, and then click or tap **Control Panel** on the submenu.

3. Click or tap the **Indexing Options** icon in Small icons or Large icons view.

4. To pause new indexing for 15 minutes, click or tap **Pause**.

5. Click or tap **Modify**.

6. If you don't see all the locations, click or tap **Show all locations**.

7. If a folder location contains subfolders, click or tap the Expand arrow to expand it.

8. Select or clear the check box next to the folder locations you want to add or remove from the index.

9. Click or tap **OK**.

10. Click or tap **Close**.

Set Advanced Indexing Options

1. Click or tap **All apps** on the Start menu.

2. Click or tap the down arrow next to **Windows System** to expand it, and then click or tap **Control Panel**.

3. Click or tap the **Indexing Options** icon in Small icons or Large icons view.

4. Click or tap **Advanced**.

5. Click or tap the **Index Settings** tab.

6. Select or clear the following check boxes:

   ◆ **Index encrypted files.**

   ◆ **Treat similar words with diacritics as different words.**

7. For index troubleshooting, use either of these buttons:

   ◆ To re-index selected locations, click or tap **Rebuild**.

   ◆ To restore your index to its original settings, click or tap **Restore Defaults**.

8. If you need to change the Index Location, specify a new location or click or tap **Select new**.

9. Click or tap the **File Types** tab.

10. Select or clear the check boxes with the file types you want to include or exclude in the index.

11. For each selected file type, click or tap the option to specify how the file should be indexed.

12. Click or tap **OK**.

13. Click or tap **Close**.

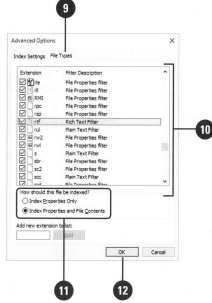

Adding Properties and Tags to Files

When you create a file, Windows automatically adds properties to the files, such as name, creation date, modified date, and size. These properties are important to Windows, however, they may not be useful when you are searching for a file. You can add or modify common file properties and create or modify custom tag properties to make it faster and easier to locate files in the future. You can add or modify properties for most files. However, there are some exceptions, such as plain text (.txt) or rich text format (.rtf) files. You can add or modify properties using the Details pane in an Explorer window, the Details tab in the Properties dialog box, or in some Save As dialog boxes. If you want to remove some or all of the property information in a file, you can quickly remove it using the Properties dialog box.

Add or Modify Properties

1. Click or tap the **File Explorer** icon on the taskbar or Start menu.

2. Click or tap the file you want to add or modify properties.

3. In the Details pane, click or tap the tag you want to change, and then type the new tag.

   ◆ To display the Details pane, click or tap the **Details pane** on the View tab.

   ◆ If you want to work with more properties and tags, right-click or tap-hold the file, click or tap **Properties**, and then click or tap the **Details** tab. When you're done, click or tap **Apply**.

4. To add more than one tag, separate each entry with a semicolon.

5. To rate a file using the rating property, click or tap the star that represents the rating you want to give the file.

6. Click or tap **Save**.

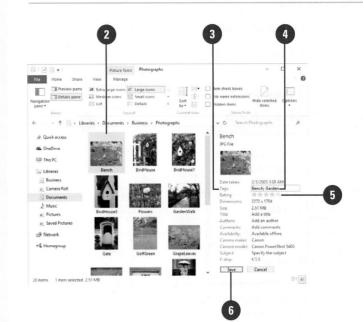

Remove Properties

1 Click or tap the **File Explorer** icon on the taskbar or Start menu, and then locate the file in which you want to change.

2 Select the file you want to remove properties.

3 Click or tap the **Properties** button on the Home tab, and then click or tap **Remove properties**.

4 Click or tap the **Create a copy with all possible properties removed** option or click or tap the **Remove the following properties from this file:** option.

5 Select or clear the check boxes for each property.

6 Click or tap **OK**.

Did You Know?

You can add properties while you save a file. In some Save As dialog boxes, such as Microsoft Word, you can specify properties, such as Author and Tags.

Creating and Renaming Files and Folders

The keys to organizing files and folders effectively within a hierarchy are to store related items together and to name folders informatively. Creating a new folder can help you organize and keep track of files and other folders. In order to create a folder, you select the location where you want the new folder, create the folder, and then lastly, name the folder. You should name each folder meaningfully so that just by reading the folder's name you know its contents. After you name a folder or file, you can rename it at any time.

Create a Folder

1. Click or tap the **File Explorer** icon on the taskbar or Start menu.

2. Open the drive or folder where you want to create a folder.

3. Click or tap the **New Folder** button on the Home tab.

   TIMESAVER *Right-click or tap-hold a blank area of the window, point to New, and then click or tap New folder.*

4. With the New Folder name selected, type a new name.

5. Press Enter or tap in a blank area.

Did You Know?

File names can be up to 255 characters. You can use spaces and underscores in names, but you can't use the following characters: @ * : < > | ? " \ or /. Remember the best way to keep your files organized is with a consistent naming convention.

Rename a File or Folder

① Click or tap the **File Explorer** icon on the taskbar or Start menu.

② Select the file or folder you want to rename.

③ Click or tap the **Rename** button on the Home tab.

④ With the name selected, type a new name, or click or tap to position the insertion point, and then edit the name.

⑤ Press Enter or tap in a blank area.

TIMESAVER *Right-click or tap-hold the file or folder you want to rename, click or tap Rename, type a name, and then press Enter or tap in a bland area. You can also select the file, click or tap the file name, type a name, and then press Enter or tap in a blank area.*

Did You Know?

You can rename a group of files. In File Explorer, select all the files you want to rename, right-click or tap-hold one of the selected files, click or tap Rename from the shortcut menu, type a name, and then press Enter or tap in a blank area. The group name appears with numbers in consecutive order.

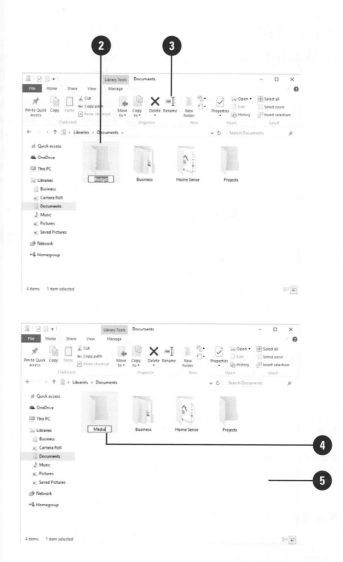

Copying and Moving Files and Folders

Sometimes you will need to move a file from one folder to another, or copy a file from one folder to another, leaving the file in the first location and placing a copy of it in the second. You can move or copy a file or folder using a variety of methods. If the file or folder and the location where you want to move it are visible in a window or on the desktop, you can simply drag the item from one location to the other. Moving a file or folder on the same disk relocates it whereas dragging it from one disk to another copies it so that it appears in both locations. When the destination folder or drive is not visible, you can use the Move to or Copy to commands or the Cut (to move), Copy, and Paste commands on the Home tab to move or copy the items.

Copy or Move a File or Folder

1. Click or tap the **File Explorer** icon on the taskbar or Start menu.

2. Open the drive or folder containing the file or folder you want to copy.

3. Select the files or folders you want to copy or move.

4. Click or tap the **Copy** or **Cut** (to move) button on the Home tab.

5. Display the destination folder where you want to copy or move the files or folder.

6. Click or tap the **Paste** button on the Home tab.

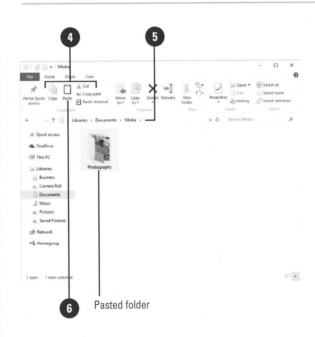

Pasted folder

Did You Know?

You can copy or move directly to a folder or drive. In File Explorer, select the files or folder you want to copy or move, click or tap the Copy to or Move to button on the Home tab, and then select a destination or click or tap Choose location to select the one you want.

Copy or Move a File or Folder Using Drag and Drop

1. Click or tap the **File Explorer** icon on the taskbar or Start menu.

2. Open the drive or folder containing the file or folder you want to copy or move.

3. Select the files or folders you want to copy or move.

4. In the Navigation pane, point to a folder list to display the expand and collapse arrows.

5. Click or tap the arrows to display the destination folder.

6. Right-click or tap-hold the selected files or folders, drag to the destination folder, and then click or tap **Copy Here** or **Move Here**.

   TIMESAVER *To move the selected items, drag them to the destination folder. To copy the items, hold down the Ctrl key while you drag.*

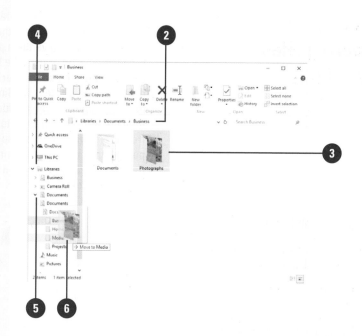

Did You Know?

You can transfer files using a disk. You can copy files from your PC computer to a disk if you need to either transfer files from one stand-alone PC computer to another. You can also save a copy of important files to prevent losing them in the event of a power failure or a problem. You can use several methods: copy and paste, drag and drop, and the Send To command.

For Your Information

Sending Files and Folders

When you right-click or tap-hold most objects on the desktop or in This PC or File Explorer, the Send To command, located on the shortcut menu, lets you send, or move, a file or folder to a new location on your PC computer. For example, you can send a file or folder to a removable disk to make a quick backup copy of the file or folder, to a mail recipient as an electronic message, or to the desktop to create a shortcut. You can also use the Send To command to move a file or folder from one folder to another. To send a file or folder, right-click or tap-hold the file or folder you want to send, point to Send To on the shortcut menu, and then click or tap the destination you want.

Deleting and Restoring Files and Folders

When you organize the contents of a folder, disk, or the desktop, you might find files and folders that you no longer need. You can delete these items or remove them permanently. If you delete a file or folder from the desktop or from the hard disk, it goes into the Recycle Bin. The **Recycle Bin**, located on your desktop, is a temporary storage area for deleted files. The Recycle Bin stores all the items you delete from your hard disk so that if you accidentally delete an item, you can remove it from the Recycle Bin to restore it. Be aware that if you delete a file from a removable disk or use the Permanently delete command, it is permanently deleted, not stored in the Recycle Bin. The files in the Recycle Bin do occupy room on your PC computer, so you need to empty it to free up space.

Delete Files and Folders

1. Click or tap the **File Explorer** icon on the taskbar or Start menu.

2. Select the files and folders you want to delete.

3. Click or tap the **Delete** button arrow on the Home tab, and then click **Recycle** or **Permanently delete**.

   TIMESAVER *Press the Delete key to recycle the items or press Shift+Delete to permanently delete the items.*

4. If prompted, click or tap **Yes** to confirm the deletion and place the items in the Recycle Bin.

   ◆ **Enable delete confirmation.** Click or tap the **Delete** button arrow on the Home tab, and then click or tap **Show recycle confirmation**.

5. In the desktop, right-click or tap-hold the **Recycle Bin** icon, and then click or tap **Empty Recycle Bin**.

   Your device permanently removes the items.

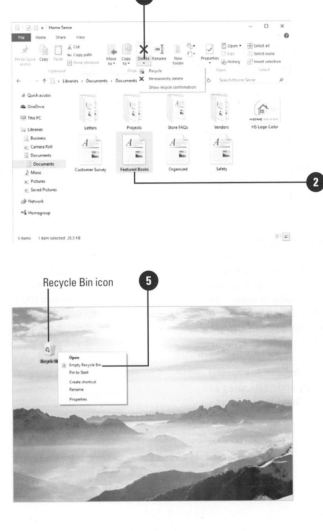

Recycle Bin icon

Restore Files and Folders

1 In the desktop, double-click or double-tap the **Recycle Bin** icon on the desktop.

2 Select the item or items you want to restore.

3 Click or tap the **Restore this item** or **Restore all items** button on the Manage tab.

◆ Empty Recycle Bin. Click or tap the **Empty Recycle Bin** button on the Manage tab, and then click or tap **Yes** to confirm.

4 If prompted, click or tap **Yes** to confirm the restore or click or tap **No** to cancel it.

Did You Know?

You can undo a deletion. If you accidentally delete a file, click or tap the Undo button on the Quick Access toolbar. Windows remembers your last three actions.

You can't open a deleted folder and restore selected items. When you've deleted a folder, you have to restore the entire folder.

Changing File and Folder List Views

You can display files and folders in a variety of different ways, depending on what you want to see and do. When you view files and folders in Details view, a default list of file and folder information appears, which consists of Name, Size, Type, and Date Modified. If the default list of file and folder details doesn't provide you with the information you need, you can add and remove any file and folder information from the Details view. If you need to change the way Windows sorts your files and folders, you can use the column indicator buttons in the right pane of Details view. Clicking or tapping one of the column indicator buttons, such as Name, Size, Type, or Date Modified, in Details view sorts the files and folders by the type of information listed in the column.

Change File Details to List

1. Click or tap the **File Explorer** icon on the taskbar or Start menu.

2. Open the folder you want to change in Details view.

3. Click or tap the **Add column** button on the View tab, and then click or tap a column (select or clear check mark) or click or tap **Choose columns**.

4. Select the check boxes with the details you want to include and clear the ones you don't.

5. Click or tap the **Move Up** or **Move Down** buttons to change the order of the selected items.

6. Click or tap the **Show** or **Hide** buttons to show or hide the selected items.

7. Specify the width in pixels of the column for the selected items.

8. Click or tap **OK**.

Did You Know?

An ellipsis indicates information is hidden. To show the information, drag the edge of the column indicator button to resize the column.

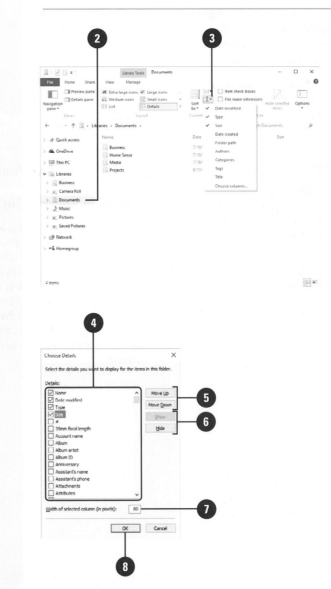

Hiding Files and Folders

If you want to hide files and folders for added privacy purposes, you can do it by setting two separate options: one to set the option to hide specific files and folders, and the other to set a general folder option to show or hide files and folders. If you set the option to hide specific files and folders and the Show hidden files and folders option is set, the hidden files and folders appear transparent. If the general option is set to Do not show hidden files and folders, the hidden files and folders are actually hidden. The only way to view them again is to set the general option to Show hidden files and folders again. Anyone can show hidden files and folders, so it shouldn't be used for security purposes.

Show or Hide Hidden Files and Folders

1. Click or tap the **File Explorer** icon on the taskbar or Start menu.

2. Select the files or folders you want to hide or unhide.

3. Click or tap the **Hide selected items** button on the View tab.

4. Select the **Hidden items** check box on the View tab to show hidden files or folders. To hide hidden items, clear the check box.

   The hidden files or folders appear transparent.

5. To unhide hidden files or folders, select them, and then click or tap the **Hide selected items** button on the View tab.

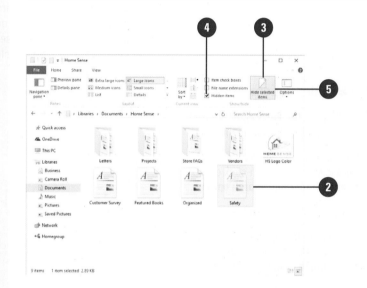

Did You Know?

You can set options to show or hide files and folders. In File Explorer, click or tap the Options button on the View tab, click or tap Change folder and search options, click or tap the Do Not Show Hidden Files And Folders or Show Hidden Files And Folders option, click or tap Apply to Folders, and then click or tap OK.

Changing Folder Options

When you work with files and folders, Windows displays folder contents in a standard way, known as the **default**. The default folder view settings are as follows: Tiles view displays files and folders as icons; common task links appear in the Navigation pane; folders open in the same window; and items open when you double-click or double-tap them. Instead of changing the folder view to your preferred view—Icons, List, or Details—each time you open a folder, you can change the view permanently to the one you prefer, including what shows when you open File Explorer (**New!**)—Quick access or This PC. In addition to the defaults, you can change options such as folder settings to show or hide file extensions, show or hide hidden files and folders, show or hide protected operating system files, and show pop-up descriptions of folders and desktop items. You can also set Privacy options to show recently used files and frequently used folders in Quick access (**New!**) as well as clear File Explorer history (**New!**).

Change Folder Options

1. Click or tap the **File Explorer** icon on the taskbar or Start menu.

2. Click or tap the **Options** button on the View tab, and then click or tap **Change folder and search options**.

3. Click or tap the **General** tab.

4. Click or tap the **Open File Explorer** list arrow (**New!**), and then click or tap **Quick access** or **This PC**.

5. Select a Browse folders option to display each folder in the same window or its own window.

6. Select a Click items as follows option to single-click or double-click items.

7. Select the Navigation pane check boxes option to **Show recently used files in Quick access (New!)** or **Show frequently used folders in Quick access (New!)**.

   ◆ **Clear File Explorer history.** Click or tap **Clear (New!)**.

8. To restore all folder options to default Windows settings, click or tap **Restore Defaults**.

9. Click or tap **OK**.

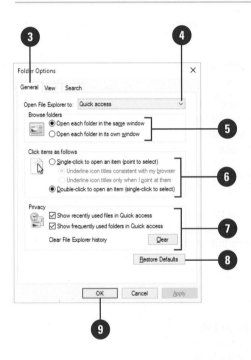

Change the Folder View

1. Click or tap the **File Explorer** icon on the taskbar or Start menu.

2. Click or tap the **Options** button on the View, and then click **Change folder and search options**.

3. Click or tap the **View** tab.

4. To set the current view to all folders, click or tap **Apply to Folders**.

5. Select the check boxes for the options you want, and clear the check boxes for the ones you don't. Some common options include:

   ◆ **Always show menus.**

   ◆ **Hidden files and folders.**

   ◆ **Hide extensions for known file types.**

   ◆ **Hide protected operating system files (Recommended).**

   ◆ **Show encrypted or compressed NTFS files in color.**

   ◆ **Show pop-up description for folder and desktop items.**

6. Click or tap **OK**.

Did You Know?

You can reset folder views to original Windows settings. On the View tab in the Folder Options dialog box, click or tap Reset Folders.

For Your Information

Understanding File Extensions

The program Windows uses to open a document depends on a three-letter extension to the document's file name, called a **file extension**. You might have never seen a document's file extension because your system might be set up to hide it. The file extension for simple text files is ".txt" (pronounced "dot t-x-t"), and many graphic files have the extension ".bmp". This means that the full name for a text file named Memo is Memo.txt. If you double-click or double-tap a document whose file name ends with the three-letter extension ".txt," Windows automatically opens the document with Notepad, a text-only editor. If you want to display file extensions in dialog boxes and windows, select or clear the File Name Extensions check box on the View tab in File Explorer. If you want to change the program Windows automatically starts with a given file extension, open the Control Panel (locate with the Search box), click or tap Default Programs in Small or Large icons view, click or tap Default Programs, click or tap Associate A File Type Or Protocol With A Program, select the file type, and then click or tap Change Program to see the list of the file extensions Windows recognizes and the programs associated with each of them, and then make changes as appropriate.

Customizing Library Folders

In your library folders, you can customize view options based on the contents. In the tab of the Pictures and Music library folders, Windows provides buttons with file management activities specifically related to the contents of the folder, such as Slide Show in the Pictures library, or Play All in the Music library. The Arrange by options are also related to the folder contents, such as Rating in the Pictures library, or Artist in the Music library. When you create a new library folder, you can customize it for documents, pictures, music, and videos by applying a folder template, which is a collection of folder tasks and viewing options. When you apply a template to a folder, you apply specific features to the folder, such as specialized tasks and viewing options for working with documents, pictures, music, and videos.

Customize a Library Folder

1. Click or tap the **File Explorer** icon on the taskbar or Start menu.

2. Open the library folder you want to change.

3. Click or tap the **Properties** button on the Home tab.

4. Click or tap the **Optimize this library for** list arrow, and then select the type of folder you want: **General Items, Documents, Music Pictures**, or **Videos**.

   TIMESAVER *Click or tap the Optimize library for button on the Manage tab, and then select an option.*

5. To show or hide the library in the Navigation pane, select or clear the **Shown in navigation pane** check box.

6. To restore library default settings for this folder, click or tap **Restore Defaults**.

7. Click or tap **OK**.

Customizing Personal Folders

In your personal folders, you can create your own folders and customize view options based on the contents. In the toolbar of the Pictures and Music folders, Windows provides buttons with file management activities specifically related to the contents of the folder, such as Slide Show in the Pictures folder, or Play All in the Music folders. When you create a new folder, you can customize it for documents, pictures, music, and videos by applying a folder template, which is a collection of folder tasks and viewing options. When you apply a template to a folder, you apply specific features to the folder, such as specialized tasks and viewing options for working with documents, pictures, music, and videos.

Customize a Folder

1. Click or tap the **File Explorer** icon on the taskbar or Start menu.

2. Open the folder you want to change.

3. Click or tap the **Properties** button on the Home tab.

4. Click or tap the **Customize** tab for a folder.

5. Click or tap the **Optimize this folder for** list arrow, and then select the type of folder you want: **General Items, Documents, Pictures, Videos**, or **Music**.

6. Select the **Also apply this template to all subfolders** check box to apply the option.

7. To select a picture for display on the folder icon, click or tap **Choose File.**

8. To restore the default picture for the folder, click or tap **Restore Default**.

9. Click or tap **OK**.

Sharing Folders or Files with Others

File Explorer maintains a set of personal folders and options for everyone on your PC computer to make sure the contents of each user's personal folders remain private. The contents of your personal folders are private, unless you decide to share the contents with others who use your PC computer or OneDrive. If you want the other users to have access to shared files, you can place those files in a shared folder on your OneDrive called the Public folder that users can access online. If you're connected online, the files in the public folder are available to users. You can also share files from any folder on your PC computer that you want to designate as a shared folder to those connected to your network or Homegroup, a shared network. When you specify a shared folder, you can also set access permission levels for a person or group. If you no longer want to share a folder, you can stop sharing.

Share a File or Folders from the Public Folder on OneDrive

1. Click or tap the **File Explorer** icon on the taskbar or Start menu.

2. Open the drive or folder containing the files or folders you want to share.

3. Select the files or folders you want to share.

4. In the Navigation pane, point to a folder list to display the expand and collapse arrows.

5. Click or tap the arrow next to the **OneDrive** to display the Public folder, and then click or tap the arrow next to the **Public** folder (if available) to display the Public subfolders.

6. Drag the selected items onto the Public folder or subfolder where you want to share files.

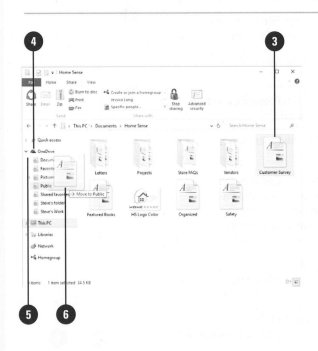

Share or Unshare a Folder

1 Click or tap the **File Explorer** icon on the taskbar or Start menu.

2 Select the folders you want to share or unshare.

3 Click or tap **Specific people** on the Share tab to set multiple options.

◆ *Share with options.* Click or tap Homegroup (view) or Homegroup (view and edit) or a contact.

◆ *Unshare a folder.* Click or tap the **Stop sharing** button.

4 Do any of the following:

◆ Type the name of the person with whom you want to share files, and then click or tap **Add**.

◆ Click or tap the arrow to the right of the text box, click or tap the person's name, and then click or tap **Add**.

5 Click or tap the arrow next to the permission level for the person or group, and then select a sharing permission:

◆ **Read.** Allows viewing only.

◆ **Read/Write.** Allows viewing, adding, changing, and deleting all files.

◆ **Remove.** Deletes the current permission setting.

6 Click or tap **Share**, and then wait while Windows sets up sharing.

7 If you want, click or tap the e-mail or copy link to notify people you have shared this folder and files.

8 Otherwise, click or tap **Done**.

Use to stop sharing

Compressing Files and Folders

You can compress files in special folders that use compressing software to decrease the size of the files they contain. Compressed folders are useful for reducing the file size of one or more large files, thus freeing disk space and reducing the time it takes to transfer files to another PC computer over the Internet or network. A compressed folder is denoted by a zippered folder icon. You can compress one or more files in a compressed folder by simply dragging them onto the compressed folder icon. When a file is compressed, a copy is used in the compression, and the original remains intact. You can uncompress, or extract, a file from the compressed folder and open it as you normally would, or you can open a file directly from the compressed folder by double-clicking or double-tapping it. When you open a file directly, Windows extracts the file when it opens and compresses it again when it closes.

Compress Files and Folders

1. Click or tap the **File Explorer** icon on the taskbar or Start menu.

2. Select the files and folders you want to copy to a compressed folder.

3. Click or tap the **Zip** button on the Share tab.

   ◆ Right-click or tap-hold one of the selected items, point to **Send to**, and then click or tap **Compressed (zipped) folder**.

4. If you want, rename the compressed folder, and then press Enter or tap a blank area.

5. To copy additional files or folders to the compressed folder, drag the files onto the compressed folder.

Did You Know?

You can Share files from File Explorer. In File Explorer, elect the files, click or tap the Share tab, click or tap the Share button (**New!**), and then select the share app you want to use in the Share panel.

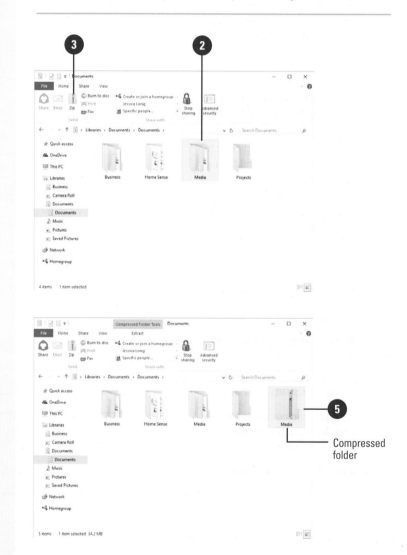

Compressed folder

View Compressed Files

1. Click or tap the **File Explorer** icon on the taskbar or Start menu.

2. Double-click or double-tap the compressed folder to open it.

3. Double-click or double-tap an item in the folder to open it using its associated program.

Uncompress Files and Folders

◆ **Individual files or folders.** In File Explorer, double-click or double-tap the compressed folder to open it, select the files and folders you want to uncompress, and then drag the selection from the compressed folder to a new location in an uncompressed folder.

◆ **All files.** In File Explorer, double-click or double-tap the compressed folder, and then click or tap the **Extract all** button on the Extract tab, and then step through the Extraction Wizard.

Extract all button

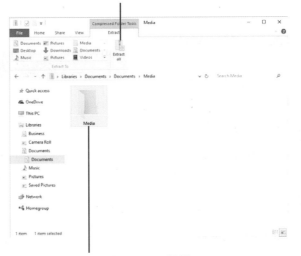

Opened compressed folder

Did You Know?

You can also compress file attributes in a folder. Select the folder, click or tap the Properties button on the Home tab, click or tap Properties, click or tap the General tab, click or tap Advanced, select the Compress Contents To Save Disk Space check box, and then click or tap OK twice.

Managing Files Using a CD or DVD

The low cost and large storage size of discs makes creating and using CDs or DVDs an effective way to back up information or transfer large amounts of data to another PC computer without a network. Before you can create a CD or DVD, you must have a blank writable disc and a recorder (also known as a writer or burner) installed on your PC computer. You can copy, or write, files and folders to either a writable disc (CD-R or DVD-R) or a rewriteable disc (CD-RW or DVD-RW). With writable discs, you can read and write files and folders many times, but you can't erase them. With rewriteable discs, you can read, write, and erase files and folders many times, just like a hard disk. When you burn a disc, Windows needs disk space on your hard disk equal to the capacity of the disc. For a typical CD, this is between 650 and 740 megabytes (MB) and for a DVD, this is about 4.7 gigabytes (GB). Do not copy more files and folders to the CD or DVD than it will hold; anything beyond the limit will not copy. You can burn a disc using one of two formats: Live File System or Mastered. The **Live File System** format (*Like a USB flash drive* option) allows you to copy files to a disc at any time, while the **Mastered** format (*With a CD/DVD player* option) needs to copy them all at once. If you need a disc and want the convenience of copying files at any time, the Live File System is the best choice. When you need a compatible disc for older PC computers, the Mastered format is the better choice.

Burn a Disc Using the Mastered Format

1. Insert a writable CD or DVD into your CD or DVD recorder.

2. Click or tap the notification, and then click or tap **Burn files to disc** or click or tap the **Finish burning** button on the Share tab in File Explorer.

3. Type a name for the disc.

4. Click or tap the **With a CD/DVD player** option.

5. Click or tap **Next** to continue.

6. Open the folder that contains the files you want to burn, and then drag the files onto the empty disc folder.

7. Click or tap **Finish burning** button on the Manage tab, and then follow the wizard steps.

   The disc recorder tray opens when the disc is complete.

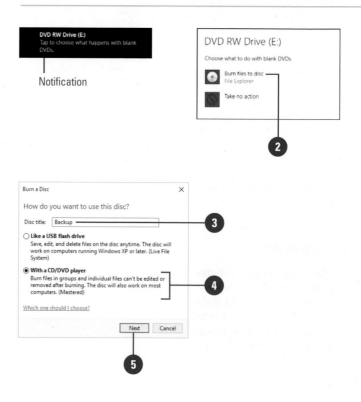

Notification

Burn a Disc Using the Live System Format

① Insert a writable CD or DVD into your CD or DVD recorder.

② Click or tap the notification, and then click or tap **Burn files to disc** or click or tap the **Finish burning** button on the Share tab in File Explorer.

③ Type a name for the disc.

④ Click or tap the **Like a USB flash drive** option.

⑤ Click or tap **Next** to continue.

Windows names, formats, and prepares the disc for use.

⑥ Upon completion, open the folder with the files you want to burn.

⑦ Drag the files into the disc folder.

As you drag files, they are copied automatically to the disc.

⑧ To close the session and prepare the disc for use, display the disc folder, click or tap the **Eject** button on the Manage tab.

After you close a session, you can still add files to the disc. However, you need to close the session.

Did You Know?

You can erase some or all of the files on a disc. Insert the writable disc with the Live File System format, click or tap This PC in File Explorer, click or tap the writable drive, and then click or tap Erase This Disc on the Manage tab to erase all the files. Double-click or double-tap the writable drive, select the files you want to delete, and then click or tap the Delete button on the Home tab.

Creating a Shortcut to a File or Folder

It could take you a while to access a file or folder buried several levels down in a file hierarchy. To save some time, you can create shortcuts to the items you use frequently. A **shortcut** is a link that you can place in any location to gain instant access to a particular file, folder, or program on your hard disk or on a network just by double-clicking or double-tapping. The actual file, folder, or program remains stored in its original location, and you place an icon representing the shortcut in a convenient location, such as in a folder or on the desktop.

Create a Shortcut to a File or Folder

1. Click or tap the **File Explorer** icon on the taskbar or Start menu.

2. Select the file or folder in which you want to create a shortcut.

3. Right-click or tap-hold the selection, and then click or tap **Create shortcut**.

   - To use a wizard, click or tap the **New item** button on the Home tab, and then click or tap **Shortcut**.

4. To change the shortcut's name, select it, click or tap the **Rename** button on the Home tab, type a new name, and then press Enter or tap in a blank area.

5. Drag the shortcut to the desired location.

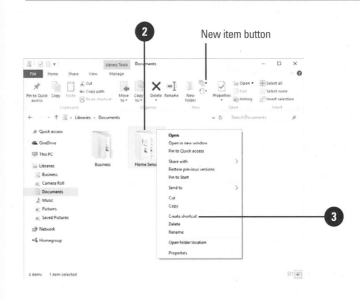

New item button

For Your Information

Placing Shortcuts on the Desktop or Taskbar

You can place shortcuts to frequently used files, folders, and programs on the desktop or toolbar on the taskbar. To do this, simply drag the shortcut file, folder, or program to the desktop. You can also drag a shortcut to a toolbar on the taskbar using the same method. When you release the mouse or finger, the item appears on the desktop or toolbar. In addition, you can right-click or tap-hold a file selection, point to Send To, and then click or tap Desktop (create shortcut).

Exploring the Internet

Introduction

The **Internet** is a global collection of more than a billion computers (and growing) linked together to share information. The Internet's physical structure includes telephone lines, cables, satellites, and other telecommunications media. Using the Internet, users can share many types of information, including text, graphics, sounds, videos, and programs. The **World Wide Web** (also known as the web) is a part of the Internet that consists of web sites located on different computers around the world.

A **web site** contains web pages linked together to make searching for information on the Internet easier. **Web pages** are documents that contain highlighted words, phrases, and graphics, called **hyperlinks** (or simply **links**) that open other web pages when you click or tap them. Some web pages contain frames. A frame is a separate window within a web page that lets you see more than one web page at a time. **Web browsers** are software programs that you use to "browse the web," or access and display web pages. Browsers make the web easy to navigate by providing a graphical, point-and-click or tap environment.

With a web browser, you can display web pages from all over the world, display web content on the desktop, view web feeds, use links to move from one web page to another, play audio and video clips, search the web for information, make favorite web pages available offline (when you're not connected to the Internet), and print text and graphics on web pages. Windows 10 comes with two browsers: Microsoft Edge and Internet Explorer. Microsoft Edge (**New!**) is a new generation browser from Microsoft while Internet Explorer (IE) is a transitional browser.

What You'll Do

Start Microsoft Edge

View the Edge Window

Navigate the Web with Edge

Search the Web with Edge & Bing

Change Edge Settings

Start Internet Explorer

View the Internet Explorer Window

Change Your Home Page

Browse the Web

Use Compatibility View

Add a Web Page to the Favorites List

View and Maintain a History List

Read and Subscribe to Feeds

Search the Web

Preview and Print a Web Page

Save Pictures or Text from a Web Page

Save a Web Page

Get Suggestions for Web Sites

Download Files from the Web

Connect to the Internet

Create an Internet Connection

Set Up Windows Firewall

Starting Microsoft Edge

Windows 10 comes with two browsers: Microsoft Edge and Internet Explorer (version 11). Microsoft Edge (**New!**) is a new generation browser from Microsoft while Internet Explorer (IE) is a transitional browser. You can start either app from the Start menu (**New!**) under All apps as well as Edge from the taskbar (**New!**). After you start the Edge (or IE for that matter), you might need to establish a connection to the Internet by entering a username and password. Edge starts in full screen view and loads your home page, which is a page that you set to display when you start the app. The elements of the Edge window allow you to view and search for information on the Internet.

Start Microsoft Edge

1 Click or tap **Microsoft Edge** on the taskbar (desktop) or on the Start menu under All apps.

2 If necessary, click or tap **Connect** to dial your ISP. You might need to type your username and password before Edge will connect to the Internet.

The Edge window opens with the Address bar at the top, and a default Start page with a Search box and My news feed from MSN.

Microsoft Edge on the Start menu under All apps

> ## Did You Know?
>
> **You can pin a web page to the Start screen and menu.** In Edge, display the web page you want to pin, click or tap the More button on the toolbar, and then click or tap Pin to Start.
>
> **You can view downloads from the web in Edge.** In Edge, click or tap the Hub button on the toolbar, and then click or tap the Downloads button on the panel.
>
> **You can open an page in Edge with Internet Explorer.** In Edge, display the web page you want to pin, click or tap the More button on the toolbar, and then click or tap Open with Internet Explorer.

Microsoft Internet Explorer

Viewing the Edge Window

The Edge window (**New!**) provides a stream-line interface with tabs and an Address bar with toolbar buttons (Reading view, Add Favorites or Reading List, Hub, Web Notes, Share, and More). The Hub button displays a panel, where you can work with Favorites, Reading List, History, and Downloads. The More button displays a menu with commands to create a new window, zoom, find on the page, print, and settings. Besides web addresses, you can also search for content on the web directly in the Address bar as well as ask Cortana (**New!**), your personal assistant, to hear about the content. With Edge, you can not just view information, but take notes, draw, and highlight directly on webpages, then share the results.

Tabs
Displays multiple web sites in a single browser window.

Address bar
Displays the address of the current web page or document you are viewing and allows you to search.

Reading view
Toggles a web page in reading view.

Browser pane
Displays the current web page, document, or folder contents.

Tools and menus
Tools and menus to work with favorites, reading list, history, and downloads.

Navigating the Web with Edge

With Edge (**New!**), you can navigate the web by clicking or tapping a web page link, such as a picture or colored, underlined text, or use the Address bar to enter a web address. When you use the Address bar, Edge displays frequently-used web sites. When you enter a web address, Edge provides suggestions and tries to complete the address for you using AutoComplete. If you have recently entered the web page address, AutoComplete remembers it and tries to complete the address for you. The smart Address bar searches your history, favorites, and offers up suggestions. The suggested matches are highlighted in blue in the Address bar. You can click or tap a suggestion, the correct address or continue to type until the address you want appears in the bar, or select an item from the drop-down list. If you like a web page, you can add it to your favorites for easy access in the future. If a web page contains article, you can switch to Reading view, which displays the page article for easy reading, or add it to your reading list.

Navigate the Web Pages with Edge

1. Click or tap **Microsoft Edge** on the taskbar (desktop) or on the Start menu under All apps.

2. Click or tap any link on the web page, such as a picture or colored, underlined text.

   The pointer changes to a hand when it is over a link.

3. To navigate back or forward to web pages you already visited, click or tap the **Back** button or **Forward** button on the Address bar.

   ◆ Use arrows. Move your pointer on the right or left side of the screen to display an arrow, and then click or tap the arrow to navigate back or forward.

   ◆ Use gestures. Swipe left or right to navigate back or forward.

4. To view pages in Reading view, click or tap the **Reading view** button. Click or tap the button again to exit.

Navigate the Web Addresses with Edge

1. Click or tap **Microsoft Edge** on the taskbar (desktop) or on the Start menu under All apps.

2. Click or tap in the Address bar, and then type the web address.

   As you type, the app displays suggestions and tries to complete the address using AutoComplete.

3. Click or tap a suggestion from the drop-down list, the correct address or continue to type until the address you want appears in the bar, and then press Enter.

4. To add this page as a Favorite web address, click or tap the **Add Favorites or Reading List** button on the Address bar, click or tap **Favorites**, use or edit the title, select a Create in folder location, and then click or tap **Add**.

   ◆ **Create new folder**. In the Favorites panel, click or tap the **Create new folder** link, enter a folder name, and then click or tap **Add**.

   ◆ **Remove a favorite**. Go to the favorite, click the **Add Favorites or Reading List** button, and then click or tap **Remove**.

5. To add this page to a Reading List, click or tap the **Add Favorites or Reading List** button on the Address bar, click or tap **Reading List**, use or edit the title, select a Create in folder location, and then click or tap **Add**.

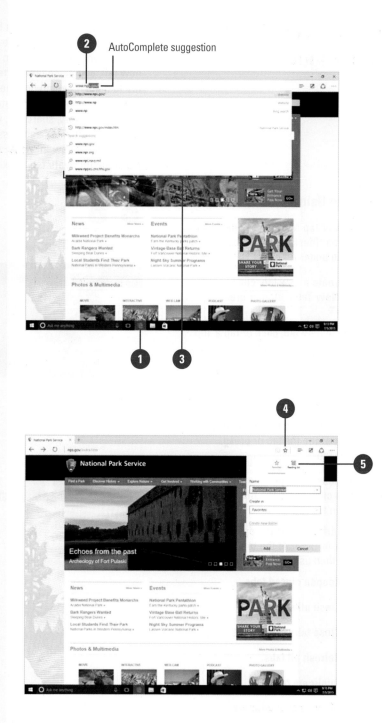

AutoComplete suggestion

Navigating Using Tabs with Edge

As you open web sites with Edge (**New!**), you can use separate tabs for each one, so you can view multiple web sites in a single window. You can open web pages on new tabs, use InPrivate browsing on a new tab, and close tabs. After you open a tab, you can click or tap a tab to quickly switch between them or click or tap the Close button on the tab to remove it. InPrivate browsing doesn't retain or keep track of browsing history, searches, temporary Internet files, form data, cookies, and usernames and passwords. You can start InPrivate browsing by creating a new InPrivate tab. When you're done InPrivate browsing, close the InPrivate tab to exit it.

Navigate Using Tabs with Edge

1. Click or tap **Microsoft Edge** on the taskbar (desktop) or on the Start menu under All apps.

2. To create a new tab, click or tap the **New Tab** button or press Ctrl+T.

    On the new tab, click or tap a Top Site tile or navigate to a web page.

    TIMESAVER *In the Address bar, type a URL and then press Alt+Enter to open it in a new tab.*

3. To switch between open tabs, click or tap the tab or press Ctrl+Tab.

4. To close a tab, point to the tab, and then click or tap the **Close** button (x) on the tab.

5. To perform other tab options, right-click or tap-hold the tab you want, and then use any of the following:

    ◆ **Reopen closed tabs**.

    ◆ **Close other tabs**.

    ◆ **Close tabs to the right**.

    ◆ **Refresh all tabs**.

    ◆ **Duplicate tab**.

    ◆ **Move to new window**.

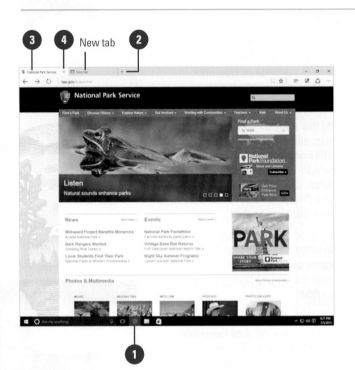

New tab

Navigate Privately with Edge

1. Click or tap **Microsoft Edge** on the taskbar (desktop) or on the Start menu under All apps.

2. Click or tap the **More** button on the Address bar, and then click or tap **New InPrivate window**.

   The InPrivate tab opens, displaying information about the tab. An InPrivate icon appears in the Address bar to indicate InPrivate browsing is active.

3. Click or tap in the Address bar, type the web address, and then click or tap the **Go** button or press Enter.

   ◆ You can also perform a search in the Address bar.

4. To close a tab, click or tap the **Close** button (x) on the tab.

Did You Know?

You can open a new window instead of a tab. In Edge, click or tap the More button on the Address bar, click or tap New Window.

You can open a new tab or window from a link. In Edge, right-click or hold-tap the link you want, and then click or tap Open In New Tab or Open In New Window.

More button

InPrivate browsing

Searching the Web with Edge & Bing

With Edge (**New!**), you can find text on the current web page or search the web with the Microsoft Bing search engine using the bing.com web site. In the Address or Search box, you can enter the criteria you want to find, where you can narrow down a search, and display a list of suggestions and sites in a drop-down. As you type the search criteria in the Address or Search box, Windows narrows down and displays the search results. The Search results from Bing display a list of matches found on the web from the search engine. If you need to find information on the current web page, you can use the Find on page command to highlight it. If you want to share your results, you can use the Share button on the Address bar.

Find Information on a Web Page with Edge

1. Click or tap **Microsoft Edge** on the taskbar (desktop) or on the Start menu under All apps.

2. Click or tap the **More** button on the Address bar, and then click or tap **Find on page**.

3. In the Find box, type the text you want to find.

   As you type, the information is highlighted on the page and the number of occurrences.

   ◆ To clear the Find box, click or tap **Close** button (x).

   ◆ To change match options, click or tap **Options**, and then click or tap **Match whole word** or **Match case**.

4. Click or tap the **Previous** or **Next** button on the Find bar to move back and forward to the occurrences of the text.

5. To exit, click or tap the **Close** button (x) on the Find bar.

Match options

Search the Web with Edge & Bing

1. Click or tap **Microsoft Edge** on the taskbar (desktop) or on the Start menu under All apps.

   The default Start page with a Search box and My news feed from MSN.

2. Click or tap the **Search** box on the default Start page or the **Address** box on the Address bar.

3. Type the first few characters for the information or item you want to find.

4. Click or tap a suggestion, or continue typing, and then click or tap the **Search** button or press Enter.

5. To cancel the search, delete the search text in the Search box.

6. In the Bing search results, click or tap the links to the items you want to view.

See Also

See "Setting Search Options for Apps" on page 45 for information on setting Bing and safe search options.

See "Protecting Privacy with Edge" on page 374 for information on setting privacy and web services options.

Default Start page

Suggestions and sites

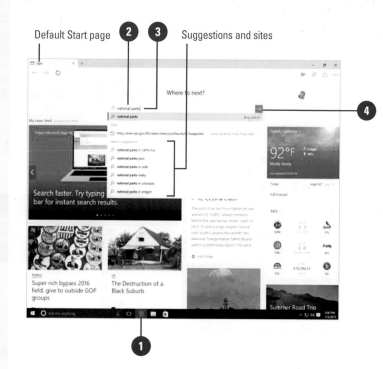

Bing search results

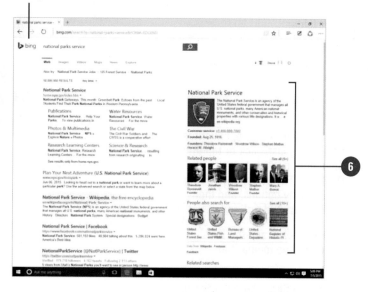

Writing on the Web with Edge

With Edge (**New!**), you can take notes, write, highlight, and draw directly on web pages. You can use the Make a web note button on the Address bar to start adding to the web page, where you can use the Pen to write using your touchscreen or mouse, the Highlighter to emphasize content, the Type to create a note, the Eraser to remove content, or the Clip to cut and copy content. After you add content to a web page, you can save and share it with others.

Write on a Web Page with Edge

1. Click or tap **Microsoft Edge** on the taskbar (desktop) or on the Start menu under All apps.

2. Go to a web page.

3. Click or tap the **Make a Web Note** button on the Address bar.

4. Click or tap any of the following tabs (click or tap again to view options):

   - **Pen.** Select a pen color and size, and then draw.

   - **Highlighter.** Select a pen color and size, and then draw.

   - **Eraser.** Click or tap a favorite or folder.

   - **Note.** Click or tap, and then type a note. Use **Delete** icon to remove it.

   - **Cut.** Drag to select the copy area.

5. To save it to OneNote, Favorites, or Reading List, click or tap the **Save** button, click or tap **OneNote**, **Favorites**, or **Reading List**, specify options, and then click or tap **Add** or **Send**.

6. To exit, click or tap the **Exit** button on the toolbar bar.

   - To share the content, click or tap the **Share** button, click or tap an app on the Share panel, and then use the app options to send it.

Highlighter   Note

Pen options; click or tap button again

Pen

Managing Web Content with Edge

Edge (**New!**) comes with a Hub (**New!**), which is a centralized place with work with favorites, reading list, history, and downloads. You can access the Hub from the Address bar. With Favorites, you can open, organize, rename, and remove them. With Reading List, you can view, organize, and remove articles. With History, you can view your browsing history to find past sites or clear it altogether. With Downloads, you can view current and past downloads and open the downloads folder.

Use the Hub to Manage Web Content with Edge

1. Click or tap **Microsoft Edge** on the taskbar (desktop) or on the Start menu under All apps.

2. Click or tap the **Hub** button on the Address bar.

   ◆ You can click or tap the **Pin** to keep the panel in place.

3. Click or tap any of the following tabs:

   ◆ **Favorites.** Click or tap a favorite or folder.

      ◆ Manage. Right-click or tap-hold an item to **Create new folder, Rename**, or **Remove**.

   ◆ **Reading List.** Click or tap an article to open it.

      ◆ Manage. Right-click or tap-hold an item to **Remove**.

   ◆ **History.** Click or tap arrows to expand or collapse history, or click or tap **Delete** button (x).

      ◆ Manage. Right-click or tap-hold an item to **Open in new tab, Open in new window, Delete**, or **Delete all visits**.

   ◆ **Downloads.** Click or tap an item to open it click or tap the **Delete** button (x) or **Clear all** to remove it.

4. To exit, click or tap off the panel or click the **Close** button (x).

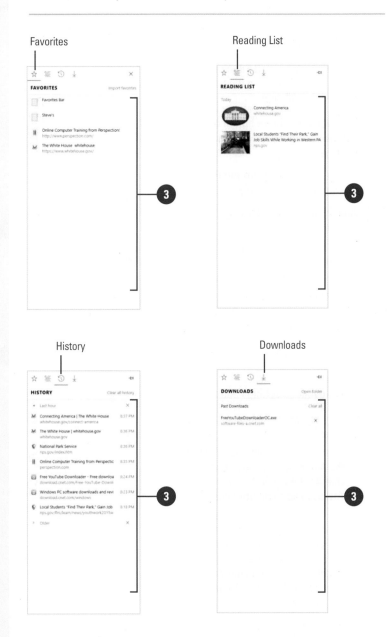

Favorites

Reading List

History

Downloads

Changing Edge Settings

With Edge (**New!**), you can set basic as well as advanced level options by using the Settings panel. You can set basic options to set start pages, specify new tabs, clear browsing data, and customize reading view. In addition, you can set advanced options to show the home button, block pop-ups, use Adobe Flash Player, always use caret browsing (select text with keyboard, F7), save passwords or form entries, track requests, use Cortana (**New!**), select search engine, use search suggestions, block cookies, and protect from malware.

Change Edge Settings

1. Click or tap **Microsoft Edge** on the taskbar (desktop) or on the Start menu under All apps.

2. Click or tap the **More** button on the Address bar, and then click or tap **Settings**.

   ◆ You can click or tap the **Pin** to keep the panel in place.

3. Specify any of the following options:

   ◆ **Open with**. Select a page option.

   ◆ **Open new tabs with**. Select a site option.

   ◆ **Clear browsing data**. Select **Choose what to clear**.

   ◆ **Reading**. Select a style and font size.

4. For more options, click or tap the **View advanced settings** button.

5. Specify any of the following options:

   ◆ **General**. Select options to **Show the home button**, **Block pop-ups**, **Use Adobe Flash Player**, or **Always use caret browsing**.

   ◆ **Privacy and services**. Select options to save passwords or form entries, track requests, use Cortana (**New!**), select search engine, use search suggestions, block cookies, and protect from malware.

6. To exit, click or tap off the panel or click the **Close** button (x).

Edge app settings

Back button to Settings panel

Pin panel in place

Starting Internet Explorer

Windows 10 comes with two web browsers: Microsoft Edge, a new generation, and Internet Explorer (version 11), a transitional more compatible one. You can start Internet Explorer from the Start menu under All apps. Internet Explorer starts and loads your home page, which is a page that you set to display when you start the program. After you start Internet Explorer (or Edge for that matter), you might need to establish a connection to the Internet by entering a username and password. If you have problems running Internet Explorer—sudden crash—due to add-on programs, only that tab is affected while the other tabs remain stable. The affected tab is automatically reloaded.

Start Internet Explorer

1. Click or tap **All apps** on the Start screen or menu.

2. Click or tap **Windows Accessories** to expand the sublist of apps.

3. Click or tap **Internet Explorer**.

4. If necessary, click or tap **Connect** to dial your ISP. You might need to type your username and password before Internet Explorer will connect to the Internet.

   The Internet Explorer window opens.

Did You Know?

You can turn off the alert asking to make Internet Explorer the default. Click or tap the Tools button, and then click or tap Internet Options. Click or tap the Advanced tab, clear the Tell Me If Internet Explorer Is Not The Default Web Browser check box, and then click or tap OK.

You can start Internet Explorer with tabs from the last session. Click or tap the Tools button, and then click or tap Internet Options. Click or tap the General tab, click or tap the Start With Tabs From The Last Session option, and then click or tap OK.

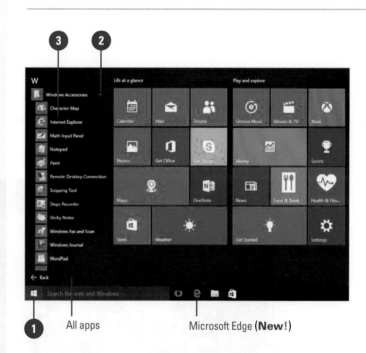

All apps

Microsoft Edge (**New!**)

For Your Information

Browsing with Protected Mode

Internet Explorer includes protected mode, which makes it difficult for hackers using a web site to install malicious software, yet makes it easy for you to install wanted software using the Standard user account (with security enabled) instead of the Administrator user account (with security disabled). When a web page tries to install unwanted software, a warning message appears on the Status bar. If you need to disable or enable it (on by default), click or tap the Tools button, click or tap Internet Options, click or tap the Security tab, clear or select the Enable Protected Mode (requires restarting Internet Explorer) check box, and then click or tap OK.

Viewing the Internet Explorer Window

The Internet Explorer window for the desktop provides a streamline interface with an Address bar, tabs, and toolbar buttons (Home, Favorites, and Tools). You can access frequently used menu commands using the toolbar buttons. However, you can access these and additional commands by using the Menu bar, Favorites bar, Command bar, or Status bar. You can show or hide these bars by right-clicking or tap-holding the title bar, and then choosing the command from the context menu. A check mark appears on the menu when the element is shown. The elements of the Internet Explorer window allow you to view, print, and search for information on the web.

Address bar
Displays the address of the current web page or document you are viewing or trying to access.

Tabs
Displays multiple web sites in a single browser window.

Favorites bar
Displays favorite sites, RSS feeds, and web slices.

Browser pane
Displays the current web page, document, or folder contents.

Status bar
Indicates the progress of loading a web page, as well as other messages about selected actions.

Changing Your Home Page

Your **home page** in Internet Explorer is the page that opens when you start the program. When you first install Internet Explorer, the default home page is the Microsoft Network (MSN) web site. If you want a different page to appear when you start Internet Explorer and whenever you click or tap the Home button, you can change your home page. With the introduction of tabbed browsing, you can display multiple home pages in tab sets. You can choose one of the millions of web pages available through the Internet, or you can select a particular file on your hard drive.

Change the Home Page

1. In Internet Explorer, open the web page or multiple web pages you want to be the new home page.

2. Click or tap the **Tools** button, and then click or tap **Internet options**.

3. Click or tap the **General** tab.

4. Use any of the following options:

   ◆ **Enter or edit addresses.** Type or edit each address on its own line to create home page tabs.

   ◆ **Use current.** Sets the current web page as the home page.

   ◆ **Use default.** Sets the default MSN web page as the home page.

   ◆ **Use new tab.** Sets a new tab as the home page. Select the default tab, and then enter an address.

5. Click or tap the **Start with home page** option.

6. To remove a web page as one of your home pages, select it, and then press Delete or clear it.

7. Click or tap **OK**.

Browsing the Web

A **web address** (also known as a URL, which stands for Uniform Resource Locator) is a unique place on the Internet where you can locate a web page. With Edge (**New!**) or Internet Explorer, you can browse sites on the web with ease by entering a web address or by clicking or tapping a link. Each method is better at different times. For example, you might type an address in the Address bar to start your session. Then you might click or tap a link on that web page to access a new site. When you type an Internet address in the Address bar, Edge or Internet Explorer uses **AutoComplete** to search for a recently visited page, favorite, and RSS feed that matches what you've typed so far. If Edge or Internet Explorer finds one or more matches, it displays a drop-down menu and highlights them in blue. You can also use AutoComplete to fill out forms on the web, including single-line edits, and usernames and passwords.

View a Web Page

In Edge (**New!**) or Internet Explorer, use any of the following methods to display a web page:

- In the Address bar, type the web address, and then click or tap the **Go** button or press Enter.

  If you have recently entered the web page address, AutoComplete remembers it and tries to complete the address for you. The smart Address bar searches your history, favorites, displaying a drop-down menu with matches from any part of the web site address. The suggested matches are highlighted in blue. Click or tap the correct address or continue to type until the address you want appears in the Address list.

  If you want to get rid of suggestions in the drop-down menu, you can delete them. Point to a menu item, and then click or tap the **Delete** button (red X).

- Click or tap any link on the web page, such as a picture or colored, underlined text. The pointer changes to a hand when it is over a link.

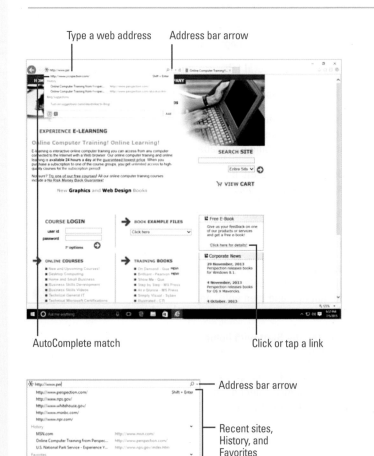

Type a web address   Address bar arrow

AutoComplete match   Click or tap a link

Address bar arrow

Recent sites, History, and Favorites

Change AutoComplete Options

1. In Internet Explorer, click or tap the **Tools** button, and then click or tap **Internet options**.

2. Click or tap the **Content** tab.

3. Click or tap **Settings**.

4. Select or clear the AutoComplete options you want to turn on or off.

5. To delete AutoComplete history, click or tap **Delete AutoComplete history**, select the check boxes with the options you want, and then click or tap **Delete**.

6. Click or tap **OK**.

7. Click or tap **OK**.

Did You Know?

You can have AutoComplete quickly complete a web address. In the Address bar, type the name of the web site, such as *perspection*, and then press Ctrl+Enter. AutoComplete adds the "www." and ".com".

You can use the Address bar to search for information. In the Address bar, type a word or phrase, and then click or tap the Go button or press Enter.

You can browse using your keyboard. With caret browsing, you can use the navigation keys—Home, End, Page Up, Page Down, and the arrow keys. Press F7 or click or tap the Tools button, point to File, click or tap Caret Browsing, and then click or tap Yes.

For Your Information

Understanding a Web Address

The address for a web page is called a URL. Each web page has a unique URL that is typically composed of four parts: the protocol (a set of rules that allow systems to exchange information), the location of the web site, the name that maintains the web site, and a suffix that identifies the type of site. A URL begins with a protocol, followed by a colon, two slashes, the location of the web site, a dot, the name of the web site, a dot, and a suffix. The web site is the system where the web pages are located. At the end of the web site name, another slash may appear, followed by one or more folder names and a file name. For example, in the web site address, http://*www*.perspection.com/ downloads/main.htm, the protocol is *http* (HyperText Transfer Protocol), the location of the web site is *www* (World Wide Web), the name of the web site is *perspection*, and the suffix is *com* (a commercial organization); a folder at that site is called */downloads*; and within the folder is a file called *main.htm*.

Browsing with Tabs

As you open web sites, you can use separate tabs for each one, so you can view multiple web sites in a single window. You can open web pages on new tabs by using the redesigned New Tab page with links—use an Accelerator (IE), use InPrivate browsing, reopen closed tabs, and reopen your last browsing session—to help you get started quickly. After you open a tab, you can click or tap a tab to quickly switch between them or click or tap the Close button on the tab to exit it. When you open a new tab from another tab, the new tab is grouped together and color coded, which you can always ungroup later. You can right-click or tap-hold a tab to quickly perform a variety of operations, such as close a tab or tab group, ungroup a tab, refresh tabs, open a new tab, reopen the last tab closed, or see a list of all recently closed tabs and reopen any or all of them.

Use Tabbed Browsing

In Edge (**New!**) or Internet Explorer, use any of the following methods to use tabbed browsing:

◆ **Open a blank tab.** Click or tap the **New Tab** button, or press Ctrl+T.

On the new tab, click or tap a Frequent tile to open the page.

TIMESAVER *In the Address bar, type a URL and then press Alt+Enter to open it in a new tab.*

◆ **Switch between tabs.** Click or tap a tab, or press Ctrl+Tab.

◆ **Close a tab.** Click or tap the **Close** button on the tab, or press Ctrl+W.

◆ **Close other tabs.** Right-click or tap-hold the tab you want open, and then click or tap **Close other tabs**.

◆ **Reopen closes tabs.** Right-click or tap-hold the **New Tab** button, click or tap the **Reopen Closed tabs** arrow, and then click or tap a site or **Open all closed tabs**.

◆ **Reopen last session.** Right-click or tap-hold the **New Tab** button, and then click or tap the **Reopen last session** link to reopen all tabs when the browser was last closed.

Open tabs   New Tab button

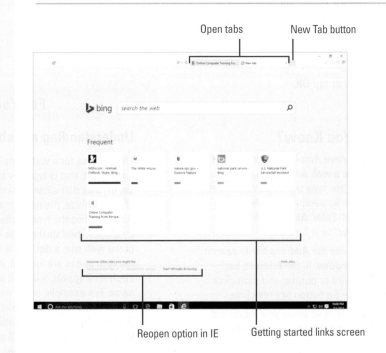

Reopen option in IE   Getting started links screen

Group or Ungroup Tabs

◆ **Open a new tab in a group (in background).** Press Ctrl+click a link or right-click or tap-hold a link, and then click or tap **Open in new tab**.

◆ **Open a new tab in a group (in foreground).** Press Ctrl+Shift+click a link.

◆ **Ungroup a tab.** Right-click or tap-hold a tab in a group, and then click or tap **Ungroup this tab**.

Click or tap to close this tab group   Tabbed group in color

Set Tabbing Options

1. In Internet Explorer, click or tap the **Tools** button, and then click or tap **Internet options**.

2. Click or tap **Tabs** on the General tab.

3. If enabled, select the options that you want. Some options require you to restart Internet Explorer. Some common ones include:

   ◆ **Warn me when closing multiple tabs.**

   ◆ **When a pop-up is encountered.**

   ◆ **Open links from other programs in.**

4. To restore default settings, click or tap **Restore defaults**.

5. Click or tap **OK**.

6. Click or tap **OK**.

Navigating Basics

As you browse the web or your local hard disk, you may want to retrace your steps and return to a web page, document, or hard disk you've recently visited. You can move backward or forward one location at a time. When you go back, sometimes it takes you to the start of an application, such as a map. Now Edge (**New!**) and Internet Explorer take you back to the right page. After you start to load a web page, you can stop if the page opens too slowly or if you decide not to access it. If a web page loads incorrectly or you want to update the information it contains, you can reload, or **refresh**, the page. If you get lost on the web, you can start over with a single click or tap of the Home button.

Move Back or Forward

◆ To move back or forward one web page or document at a time, click or tap the **Back** button or the **Forward** button on the Address bar.

TIMESAVER *To move back, press Alt+left arrow. To move forward, press Alt+right arrow.*

Back button

Forward button

Stop, Refresh, or Go Home

◆ Click or tap the **Stop** button on the Address bar.

TIMESAVER *Press Esc.*

◆ Click or tap the **Refresh** button on the Address bar.

TIMESAVER *Press F5.*

◆ Click or tap the **Home** button on the toolbar.

  ◆ Show Home Button. In Edge (**New!**), click or tap **More** button, click or tap **Settings**, click or tap **View advanced settings**, and then turn on **Show the home.**

TIMESAVER *Press Alt+Home.*

Refresh button

Stop button

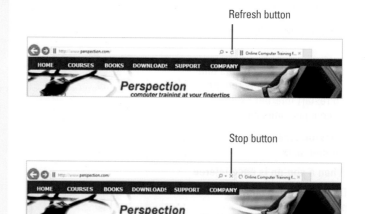

Browsing Privately

If you're using a system at a friend's house, another office, hotel, or an Internet cafe and you don't want to leave any trace or evidence of your web activity, you can use InPrivate browsing. InPrivate browsing doesn't retain or keep track of browsing history, searches, temporary Internet files, form data, cookies, and usernames and passwords. You can start InPrivate browsing from a new tab or use the Tools button on the toolbar. When you start InPrivate browsing, Internet Explorer opens a new browser window. An InPrivate indicator icon appears in the Address bar when the feature is turned on. When you're done, simply close the browser window to end the InPrivate browsing session.

Browse the Web Privately

1. In Internet Explorer, start an InPrivate browsing session using any of the following:

   ◆ **Tools button.** Click or tap the **Tools** button, point to **Safety**, and then click or tap **InPrivate Browsing**.

   ◆ **New tab.** Click or tap the **New Tab** button to open a new tab, and then click or tap **InPrivate Browsing**.

   ◆ **Shortcut.** Press Ctrl+Shift+P.

   A new window opens, where you can browse the web.

2. Browse the web.

   The InPrivate indicator appears in the Address bar.

3. To end InPrivate browsing, click or tap the **Close** button to close the browser window.

See Also

See "Navigating Using Tabs with Edge" on page 98 for more information on InPrivate browsing in Edge.

New tab or inPrivate browsing   **1** New tab

Click or tap to start InPrivate browsing

2   **3**

Using Compatibility View

If you visit an older web site that doesn't display correctly—misaligned text, images, and text boxes—in Internet Explorer, you can quickly fix it, in most cases, with Compatibility view. When you open an older site that Internet Explorer recognizes, the Compatibility View button appears in the Address bar, near the Refresh button. The button appears on a per site basis. However, once you click or tap the button for a site, you don't have to do it again. Internet Explorer maintains a list of sites with Compatibility view, which you can customize.

Fix the Display of Older Web Sites

1. In Internet Explorer, open the older web page with the display you want to fix.

   If the Compatibility View button appears in the Address bar next to the Refresh button, the option is available.

2. To fix the display of an older web site, click or tap the **Compatibility View** button in the Address bar.

3. To change Compatibility view settings, click or tap the **Tools** button on the Command bar, and then click or tap **Compatibility View Settings**.

4. To remove a site, select the site, and then click or tap **Remove**.

5. To enable other options, select the check boxes you want.

6. Click or tap **Close**.

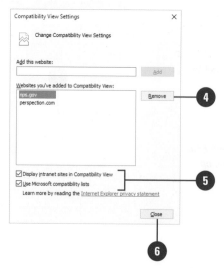

Did You Know?

You can show or hide toolbars the Internet Explorer window. Right-click or tap-hold a blank area on the title bar, and then select Menu bar, Favorites bar, Command bar, or Status bar to show or hide it.

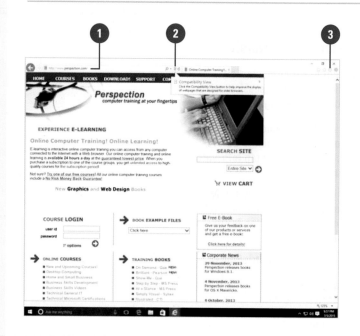

Zooming the View In and Out

Working with the Zoom tools gives you one more way to control exactly what you see in a web page. Edge (**New!**) and Internet Explorer uses Adaptive Page Zoom tools that allow you to enlarge or reduce everything on the page, including text and images, by relaying out the page. You can adjust the zoom from 10% to 1000%. The Zoom tools are located on the More menu (Edge) or on the Status bar or on the Zoom submenu on the Tools button (IE). If you have a mouse with a wheel, hold down the Ctrl key, and then scroll the wheel to zoom in or out.

Change the View

1. In Edge or Internet Explorer, use any of the following zoom options:

   ◆ **Zoom Level (Edge).** Click or tap the **More** button, and then click or tap **Minus** (-) or **Plus** (+).

   ◆ **Zoom Level (IE).** Click or tap the **Change Zoom Level** button on the Status bar to cycle through 100%, 125%, and 150% or the button arrow , and then click or tap a percentage.

   TIMESAVER *Press Ctrl+(+) to zoom in by increments of 10%, or press Ctrl+(-) to zoom out by increments of 10%. Press Ctrl+0 to restore the zoom to 100%.*

   ◆ **Zoom Custom (IE).** Click or tap the **Change Zoom Level** button arrow on the Status bar, click or tap **Custom**, type a zoom value, and then click or tap **OK**.

2. To toggle the view to full screen (IE), click or tap the **Tools** button, point to **File**, and then click or tap **Full Screen**, or press F11.

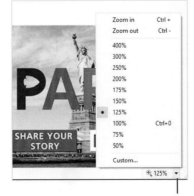

Change Zoom Level button arrow on the Status bar

Did You Know?

You can change web page text size to make it easier to read. In IE, click or tap the Page button on the Command bar, point to Text Size, and then click or tap the size you want. When you change the text size, graphics and controls remain unchanged.

Adding a Web Page to the Favorites List

Rather than memorizing URLs or keeping a handwritten list of web pages you want to visit, you can use the Favorites Center or Favorites bar to store and organize the addresses. The Favorites Center provides easy access to favorites, RSS feeds, and browsing history. When you display a web page that you want to display again at a later time, you can add the web page to the Favorites bar with one click or tap or to the Favorites Center. Once you add the web page to the Favorites bar or Center, you can quickly return to the page. To open all the favorites in a folder at the same time, click or tap the blue arrow to the right of the folder. If your list of favorites grows long, you can delete favorites you don't visit anymore or move favorites into folders.

Add and Delete Favorites

1 In Internet Explorer, open the web site you want to add to your Favorites list.

2 Click or tap the **Favorites Center** button, and then click or tap **Add to Favorites**.

◆ You can also click or tap the **Add to Favorites** button on the Favorites bar.

3 Type the name for the site, or use the default name supplied.

4 Click or tap **Create In** arrow, and then select a location.

5 To create a new folder, click or tap **New Folder**, type a folder name, and then click or tap **OK**.

6 Click or tap **Add**.

7 To remove an item from the Favorites bar or Favorites Center, right-click or tap-hold it, and then click or tap **Delete**.

Did You Know?

You can import favorites. Click or tap the Favorites Center button, click or tap the Add to Favorites button arrow, click or tap Import and Export, and then follow the wizard steps.

Favorites bar

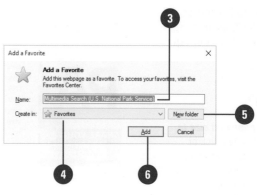

Access Favorites

 In Internet Explorer, click or tap the **Favorites Center** button.

The Favorites Center pane appears with the Favorites tab. The pane is not pinned (locked) to the window.

2. To pin the pane to the window, click or tap the **Pin the Favorites Center** button (green arrow).

When the pane is pinned, the Close button appears on the pane.

3. Click or tap a folder, if necessary.

4. To open all the favorites in a folder at the same time, click or tap the blue arrow next to the folder.

5. Click or tap the page you want.

6. Click or tap off the pane or click or tap the **Close** button.

Organize Favorites

1. In Internet Explorer, click or tap the **Favorites Center** button, click or tap the **Add to Favorites** button arrow, and then click or tap **Organize Favorites**.

2. Select one or more favorites.

3. Do any of the following:

   ◆ New Folder. Click or tap **New Folder**, type the new folder name, and then press Enter.

   ◆ Move. Click or tap **Move**, select a folder, and then click or tap **OK**.

   ◆ Rename. Click or tap **Rename**, type a new name, and then press Enter.

   ◆ Delete. Click or tap **Delete**.

4. When you're done, click or tap the **Close** button.

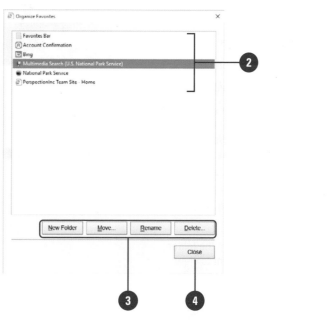

Viewing and Maintaining a History List

Sometimes you run across a great web site and simply forget to add it to your Favorites list. With Internet Explorer there's no need to try to remember all the sites you visit. The History feature keeps track of where you've been by date, site, most visited, or order visited today, which you can now sort by. To view the History list, click or tap the History button in the Favorites Center, select a sort option, and then click or tap a link (if necessary) in the pane to expand the list of web sites visited. You can also search for pages in the History list by typing keywords. Because the History list can grow to occupy a large amount of space on your hard drive, it's important to control the length of time you retain web sites in the list. Internet Explorer deletes the History list periodically, based on the settings you specify. When you delete your History list, you can now protect and preserve your related data for trusted sites in your favorites list.

View and Change the History List

1. In Internet Explorer, click or tap the **Favorites Center** button.

2. Click or tap the **History** tab.

3. To change the history view, click or tap the **Sort** button, and then select the view option you want.

   ◆ **View By Date.**

   ◆ **View By Site.**

   ◆ **View By Most Visited.**

   ◆ **View By Order Visited Today.**

   ◆ **Search History.** Type a keyword to search for a page, and then click or tap **Search Now**. Click or tap **Stop** to end the search.

4. If view By Date, click or tap a week or day to expand or compress the list of web sites visited.

5. If necessary, click or tap the folder for the web site you want to view, and then click or tap a page within the web site.

6. Click or tap off the pane or click or tap the **Close** button.

Change the Number of Days Pages Are Saved

1 In Internet Explorer, click or tap the **Tools** button, and then click or tap **Internet options**.

2 Click or tap the **General** tab.

3 In the Browsing history section, click or tap **Settings**.

4 Click or tap the **History** tab.

5 Specify the total number of days you want to keep links listed in history.

6 Click or tap **OK**.

7 Click or tap **OK**.

Clear the History List

1 In Internet Explorer, click or tap the **Tools** button, point to **Safety**, and then click or tap **Delete Browsing History.**

◆ You can also open this dialog by clicking or tapping **Delete** on the **General** tab in the Internet Options dialog box.

◆ To delete browsing history on exit, click or tap the **Tools** button, click or tap **Internet options**, select the **Delete browsing history on exit** check box, and then click or tap **OK**.

2 To preserve cookies and temporary Internet files for sites in your Favorites folder, which are trusted sites, select the **Preserve Favorites website data** check box.

3 Select the **History** check box to clear the history list.

4 Click or tap **Delete**.

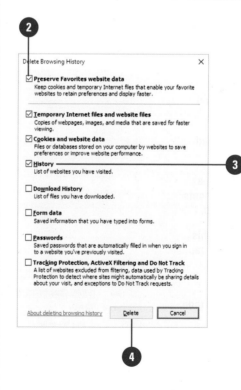

Reading and Subscribing to Feeds

A **feed** delivers frequently updated web content to your browser on a continuous basis. A feed, also known as RSS (Really Simple Syndication) feed, XML feed, syndicated content, or web feed, is usually offered on a subscription basis and typically free of charge. A feed can deliver text content in the form of news headlines or blogs, or digital content in the form of pictures, audio, and video. When audio content is delivered usually in the MP3 format, it's referred to as a podcast. When you visit a web site, Internet Explorer checks for available feeds. If it discovers a feed, the orange Feeds button appears on the Command bar. You can view an individual feed or subscribe to one to get content automatically. When you subscribe to a feed, Internet Explorer checks the web site and downloads new content so you always stay updated with the latest site content. You can also add an RSS feed to your Favorites Center, making it easy to view updates. Internet Explorer manages a common feeds list, which allows other programs, such as e-mail, to use them.

View and Subscribe to a Feed

1. In Internet Explorer, visit a web site with a feed.

   The Feeds button changes color and plays a sound.

   TIMESAVER *You can also press Alt+J to check for feeds.*

2. Click or tap the **Feeds** button arrow on the Command bar, and then select an available feed.

3. If available, click or tap the feed you want to see.

   A web page opens, displaying a lists of articles and other elements you can read and subscribe to.

4. Click or tap the **Subscribe to this Feed** button, and then click or tap **Subscribe to this Feed**, if necessary.

5. Type a name for the feed, and then select a location for the feed.

6. To add the feed to the Favorites bar, select the **Add to Favorites Bar** check box.

7. Click or tap **Subscribe**.

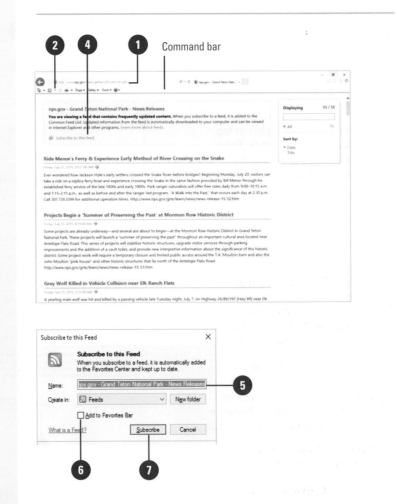

Command bar

View Subscribed Feeds

1 In Internet Explorer, if available, click or tap the **Feed** button on the Favorites bar, and then click or tap a specific feed.

◆ If the feed button on the Favorites button is bold, the feed has been updated.

2 Click or tap the **Favorites Center** button.

3 Click or tap the **Feeds** tab.

4 If needed, click or tap a folder to display related feeds.

5 Click or tap the feed to visit the web site for the feed.

6 Click or tap off the pane or click or tap the **Close** button.

Did You Know?

What formats are feeds available in?
The most common formats are RSS and Atom. All web feed formats are based on XML. XML (Extensible Markup Language) is a platform-independent language that enables you to create documents in which data is stored independently of the format. XML is a markup language just like HTML. You mark up a document to define the structure, meaning, and visual appearance of the information.

You can change feed settings. Click or tap the Tools button, click or tap Internet Options, click or tap the Content tab, click or tap Settings in the Feeds and Web Slices section, specify the options you want, and then click or tap OK twice.

For Your Information

Resetting Internet Explorer Settings

If you installed another web browser after installing Internet Explorer, some of your Internet Explorer settings may have changed. You can reset your Internet Explorer settings to their original defaults, including your home page and search pages, and choice of default browser, without changing your other browser's settings. To reset Internet Explorer settings, click or tap the Tools button, click or tap Internet Options, click or tap the Advanced tab, click or tap Reset, read the dialog box carefully, and then click or tap Reset again.

Searching the Web

You can find all kinds of information on the web using the Address box on the Address bar. The best way to find information is to use a search engine. A **search engine** is a program you access through a web site and use to search through a collection of Internet information to find what you want. Many search engines are available on the web, such as Bing, Wikipedia, Google, and Yahoo, which you can add-on to Internet Explorer. When performing a search, the search engine compares keywords with words that if finds on various Internet web sites. **Keywords** are words or phrases that best describe the information you want to retrieve. As you type in the Address box, the search engine displays a menu list of text and visual suggestions for the matched sites. These matched sites are sometimes called **hits**. The search results of different search engines vary. If you're looking for information on a page, you can use the Find toolbar to help highlight the text you want to find.

Search the Web

1. In Internet Explorer, click or tap in the Address box.

   TIMESAVER *Press Ctrl+E to go to the address box.*

2. To use a specific search provider for this session only, click or tap the **Address** box arrow, and then click or tap the provider you want.

3. Type the information you want to find. Use specific words, eliminate common words, such as "a" or "the", and use quotation marks for specific phrases.

   As you type, a drop-down menu appears with text and visual suggestions.

4. Click or tap a suggestion or continue to type. Click or tap the **Go** button. You can also press Enter or press Alt+Enter to display the search results in a new tab.

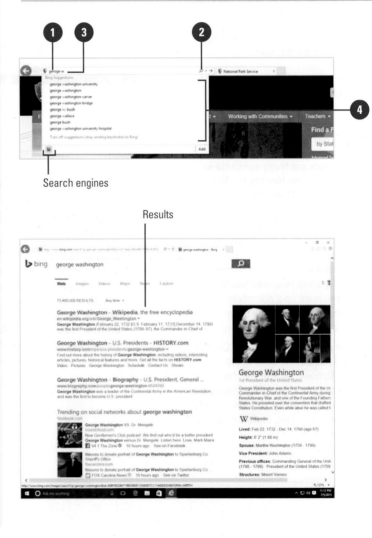

Search engines

Results

Add or Change Search Providers

1 In Internet Explorer, click or tap the **Address** box arrow, and then click or tap the Search Provider's icon.

◆ To add search providers, click or tap the Address box arrow, click or tap **Add**, and then follow the web site instructions.

2 To set search provider options, click or tap the **Tools** button, click or tap **Manage add-ons**, click or tap **Search Providers**, select a search provider, click or tap **Set as default** or **Remove**, and then click or tap **Close**.

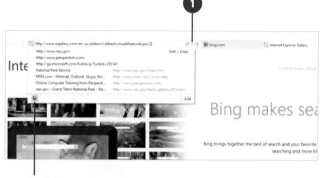

Available search providers

Find Text on a Page

1 In Internet Explorer, click or tap the **Tools** button, point to **File**, and then click or tap **Find on this page** to display the toolbar.

TIMESAVER *Press Ctrl+F to find text on this page.*

2 Click or tap the **Highlight all matches** button to turn highlighting in yellow on or off.

3 Click or tap the **Options** button, and then click or tap **Match whole word only** or **Match case** to turn them on or off.

4 Type text in the Find box. As you type, the search displays the results on the page.

5 Click or tap the **Previous** or **Next** button to go to the results.

6 Click or tap the **Close** button on the toolbar.

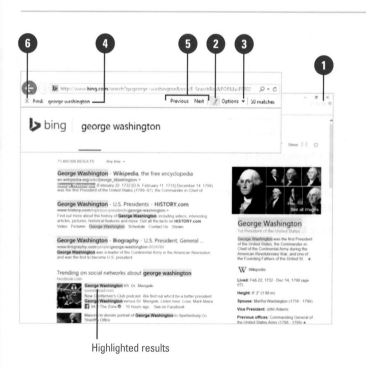

Highlighted results

Previewing and Printing a Web Page

Web pages are designed for viewing on a screen, but you can also print all or part of one. Before you print, you should verify that the page looks the way you want. You save time, money, and paper by avoiding duplicate or wasteful printing. Printing now scales web pages to fit the paper you're using. Print Preview shows you exactly how the web page will look on the printed page, and gives you more control over margins and scaling. This is especially helpful when you have multiple pages to print. When you are ready to print, Edge (**New!**) or Internet Explorer provides many options for previewing and printing web pages. For web pages with frames, you can print the page just as you see it, or you can elect to print a particular frame or all frames. You can even use special Page Setup options to include the date, time, or window title on the printed page. You can also choose to print the web addresses from the links contained on a web page.

Preview a Web Page

1. In Internet Explorer, click or tap the **Tools** button, point to **Print**, and then click or tap **Print Preview**.

2. Use the Print Preview toolbar buttons to preview or print the web page:

   ◆ **Print the document.**

   ◆ **Portrait** or **Landscape**.

   ◆ **Page Setup.** Opens the Page Setup dialog box.

   ◆ **Turn headers and footers on and off.**

   ◆ **View Full Width** or **View Full Page.**

   ◆ **Show Multiple Pages.**

   ◆ **Change the Print Size.**

3. Use options at the bottom of the Print Preview to specify the page to display or switch between pages.

4. Drag a margin adjust handle to fine tune the page margins.

5. When you're done, click or tap the **Close** button.

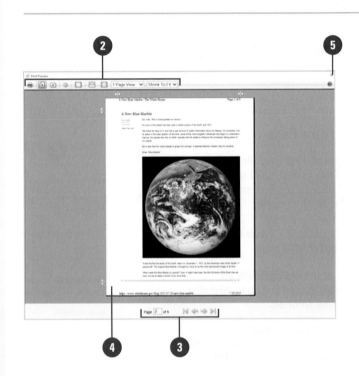

Print a Web Page

1. In Edge (**New!**), click or tap the **More** button, and then click or tap **Print**.

   In Internet Explorer, click or tap the **Tools** button, point to **Print**, and then click or tap **Print**.

   TIMESAVER *To print the current page with the current print settings (IE), click or tap the Print button on the Command bar.*

2. Click or tap a printer to select it for use.

3. Specify the available options you want to print.

4. For additional options (IE), click or tap the **Options** tab, and then specify settings for frames and linked or table links.

5. Click or tap **Print**.

Did You Know?

You can set up the page format. To control the printing of text and graphics on a page in Internet Explorer, click or tap the Tools button (IE), point to Print, and then click or tap Page Setup. The Page Setup dialog box specifies the printer properties for page size, orientation, and paper source; in most cases, you won't want to change them. From the Page Setup dialog box, you can also change header and footer information. In the Headers and Footers text boxes, you can use variables to substitute information about the current page, and you can combine text and codes. Check IE Help for a complete list of header and footer codes.

Saving Pictures or Text from a Web Page

If you find information on a web page that you want to save for future reference or share with others, you can copy and paste it to another document or save it on your system. When you copy information from a web page, make sure you're not violating any copyright laws.

Save a Picture from a Web Page

1. In Edge (**New!**) or Internet Explorer, open the web page with the picture you want to save.

2. Right-click or tap-hold the picture, and then click or tap **Save picture** (Edge) or **Save picture as** (IE).

3. Select the drive and folder in which you want to save the file.

4. Type a name for the file, or use the suggested name.

5. To change the format of a file, click or tap the **Save as type** arrow, and then click or tap a file format.

6. Click or tap **Save**.

Did You Know?

You can save a page or picture without opening it. In IE, right-click or tap-hold the link for the item you want to save, and then click or tap Save Target As.

You can create a desktop shortcut to the current web page. In IE, right-click or tap-hold in the web page, click or tap Create Shortcut, and then click or tap Yes.

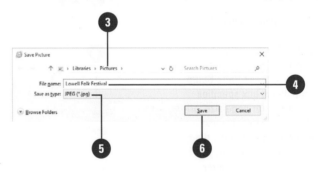

Set a Picture from a Web Page as the Background Picture

1. In Internet Explorer, open the web page with the picture you want to use.

2. Right-click or tap-hold the picture, and then click or tap **Set As Background**.

Copy Text from a Web Page

1. In Internet Explorer, open the web page with the text you want to copy.

2. Select the text you want to copy.

   TROUBLE? *The I-beam cursor may or may not appear. You can still select the text.*

3. Right-click or tap the selected text, and then click or tap **Copy**, or press Ctrl+C.

   ◆ You can also access an Accelerator from the shortcut menu where you can use the selected text in an e-mail, blog, search, or translate.

4. Switch to where you want to paste the text.

5. Click or tap the **Edit** menu, and then click or tap **Paste**, or press Ctrl+V.

Available Accelerators

Saving a Web Page

You can save a web page you want to view offline even if you don't need to share it with others or update its content, such as a published article whose content will not change. There are several ways you can save the web page, from saving just the text to saving all of the graphics and text needed to display that page as it appears on the web. When you save a complete web page, Internet Explorer saves all the graphic and text elements in a folder. If you need to send a web page to a friend or co-worker, you can save all the elements of the web page in a single file to make the process easier.

Save a Web Page

1. In Internet Explorer, open the web page you want to save.

2. Click or tap the **Tools** button, point to **File**, and then click or tap **Save as**.

3. Select the drive and folder in which you want to save the file.

4. Type a name for the file, or use the suggested name.

5. Click or tap the **Save as type** arrow, and then click or tap one of the following:

   ◆ **Web Page, complete** to save the formatted text and layout with all the linked information, such as pictures, in a folder.

   ◆ **Web Archive, single file** to save all the elements of the web page in a single file.

   ◆ **Web Page, HTML only** to save the formatted text and layout without the linked information.

   ◆ **Text File** to save only the text.

6. Click or tap **Save**.

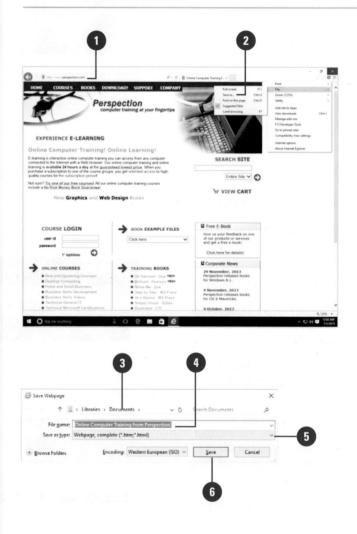

Getting Suggestions for Web Sites

If you're not sure what good sites are out there based on your own browsing history, then you might want to try Suggested Sites, a free online service from Microsoft. When enabled, Microsoft uses your browsing history to give you suggestions. Simply, click or tap the See Suggested Sites the Favorites Center to see a list of suggestions. The more places you visit, the better the suggested sites. You can also delete sites from your history. If you no longer want the service, you can choose to turn it off at any time.

Use Suggested Sites

1. In Internet Explorer, click or tap the **Tools** button, point to **File**, click or tap **Suggested Sites,** and then click or tap **Yes**.

   ◆ You can also click or tap **Turn on Suggested Sites** in the Favorites Center.

   Suggested Sites is enabled.

2. Click or tap the **Favorites Center** button.

3. Click or tap the **See Suggested Sites**.

   A web site opens, displaying suggested sites based on your browsing history.

4. View the suggested sites that you want.

5. To turn off Suggested Sites, click or tap the **Tools** button, point to **File**, click or tap **Suggested Sites**.

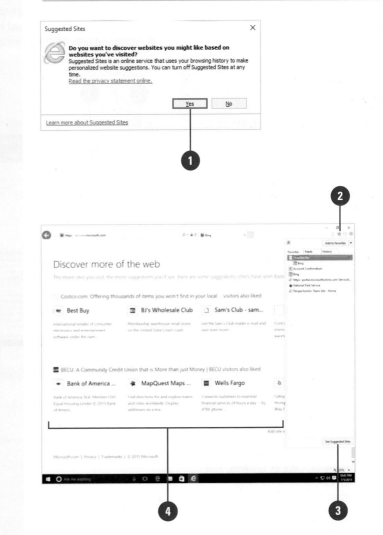

Downloading Files from the Web

There are tons of sites on the web offering all sorts of files you can download to your system. You can download files from any web site by finding the file you want, right-clicking or tap-holding the link, and telling Internet Explorer where you want to save the file. Some web sites are designed with specific links to make it easier to download files. When you click or tap a download link, a Message bar appears, asking you to run or don't run the file from the Internet or save the file. Internet Explorer checks to see whether there are any irregularities with the file or a potential for harm based on the file type, and provides strong warning and guidance to help you understand more about the file you are downloading. Just beware of viruses which can come from downloaded files off the Internet.

Download a File from a Web Page

1. In Internet Explorer, open the web page from which you want to download a file.

   IMPORTANT *Before you download files, make sure your antivirus software is up-to-date.*

2. Click or tap the download link.

   A Message bar appears at the bottom of the screen.

   ◆ You can also right-click or tap-hold the link pointing to the actual file, and then click or tap **Save target as**.

3. Click or tap **Save**.

   ◆ To specify a download location, click or tap **Save** arrow, click or tap **Save as**, specify a location, and then click or tap **Save**.

   ◆ To execute the file after the download, click or tap **Run**, and then follow the on-screen instructions.

   The Message bar displays the estimated time to download the file, along with the estimated transfer time.

4. To view the downloaded item, click or tap **View download**.

View Downloads

① In Internet Explorer, click or tap the **Tools** button, and then click or tap **View Downloads**.

TIMESAVER *Press Ctrl+J to view downloads.*

② To execute a downloaded file, click or tap **Run**, and then follow the on-screen instructions.

IMPORTANT *Before you download files, make sure your antivirus software is up-to-date.*

③ To open the folder where the downloaded file is stored, click or tap the **Downloads** link.

④ To change the default download location, click or tap the **Options** link, specify a location, and then click or tap **OK**.

⑤ To clear the downloads list, click or tap **Clear list**.

⑥ Click or tap **Close**.

Did You Know?

You can access a site with lots of files to download. Try these sites to find plenty of files to download: *http://www.download.com* and *http://www.shareware.com*.

See Also

See "Managing Web Content with Edge" on page 103 for more information on working with downloads in Edge.

Download options

Connecting to the Internet

Universities and large companies are most likely connected to the Internet via high-speed wiring that transmits data very quickly. As the Internet continues to explode around the world, several high-speed connection options are becoming more available and affordable for business and home use: DSL (Digital Subscriber Lines), wires that provide a completely digital connection; and cable modems, which use cable television lines. DSL and cable modems, also known as broadband connections, are continually turned on and connected and use a network setup. If a broadband connection is not available, you need to establish a connection over a phone line using a dial-up modem. Data travels more slowly over phone lines than over digital lines and cable modems. Whether you use a phone line, a DSL line, or a cable modem, Windows can help you establish a connection between your system and the Internet using the Connect to the Internet wizard. First, you need to select an ISP (Internet Service Provider), which is a company that sets up an Internet account for you and provides Internet access. ISPs maintain servers connected directly to the Internet 24 hours a day. You pay a fee, sometimes by the hour, but more often a flat monthly rate. To connect to the Internet, you need to obtain an Internet account and connection information from your ISP or your system administrator. For details, see "Creating an Internet Connection" on page 133. If you are working on a network, you can also share one Internet connection with everyone.

Protecting your System with a Firewall

When you connect to the Internet, you can access web sites on the Internet, but other users on the Internet can also access information on your system and potentially infect it with harmful viruses and worms. For more information, see "Avoiding Viruses and Other Harmful Attacks" on page 360.

You can prevent this by activating Windows Firewall, another security layer of protection. A **firewall** is a security system that creates a protective barrier between your system or network and others on the Internet. Windows Firewall monitors all communication between your system and the Internet and prevents unsolicited inbound traffic from the Internet from entering your system. Windows Firewall blocks all unsolicited communication from reaching your system unless you specifically allow it (unblock) to come through, known as an exception. For example, if you run a program that needs to receive information from the Internet or a network, Windows Firewall asks if you want to block or unblock the connection. If you choose to unblock it, Windows Firewall creates an exception so the program can receive information. For details, see "Setting Up Windows Firewall" on page 134.

If you send and receive e-mail, Windows Firewall doesn't block spam or unsolicited e-mail or stop you from opening e-mail with harmful attachments. Windows Firewall helps block viruses and worms from reaching your system, but it doesn't detect or disable them if they are already on your system or come through e-mail. To protect your system, you need to install antivirus software.

Creating an Internet Connection

Sometimes connecting your system to the Internet can be the most difficult part of getting started. The Connect to the Internet wizard simplifies the process, whether you want to set up a new connection using an existing account or select an Internet Service Provider (ISP) to set up a new account. In either case, you will need to obtain connection information from your ISP or your system administrator.

Create an Internet Connection

1. Click or tap the **Network** icon on the taskbar, and then click or tap the **Network settings** link.

2. Click or tap **Network and Sharing Center**.

3. Click or tap **Set up a connection or network**, click or tap **Connect to the Internet**, and then click or tap **Next**.

4. Click or tap **Set up a new a connection**, or **Set up a new connection anyway** to set up a second connection.

5. Click or tap the option with the way you want to connect: **Wireless, Broadband (PPPoE)**, or **Dial-up**.

   ◆ For the wireless option, select a network, and then go to Step 10.

6. Type the name and password from your ISP. For a dial-up connection, type a dial-up phone number.

7. For the password, select or clear the **Show characters** or **Remember this password** check boxes.

8. Type a connection name.

9. Select or clear the **Allow other people to use this connection** check box.

10. Click or tap **Connect**.

Setting Up Windows Firewall

If your system is directly connected to the Internet, you need Windows Firewall to protect it from unauthorized access from others on the Internet for each network location you use. Windows Firewall is enabled by default for all Internet and network connections. However, some manufacturers and administrators might turn it off, so you need to check it. When Windows Firewall is enabled, you might not be able to use some communication features, such as sending files with a messaging program or playing an Internet game, unless the program is listed on the Exceptions list in Windows Firewall. If you use multiple Internet and networking connections, you can enable or disable individual connections.

Set Up Windows Firewall

1. Click or tap the **Network** icon on the taskbar, and then click or tap the **Network settings** link.

2. Click or tap **Windows Firewall**.

3. In the left pane, click or tap **Turn Windows Firewall on or off**.

4. Select the **Turn on Windows Firewall** check box for each networks.

5. To set maximum protection, select the **Block all incoming connections, including those in the list of allowed programs** check box or clear it to make exceptions for each network.

6. Click or tap **OK**.

7. To make program exceptions, click or tap the **Allow a program or feature through Windows Firewall** in the left pane, select the check boxes with the exceptions you want; if necessary, click or tap **Allow another app** to add it, and then click or tap **OK**.

8. To restore default settings, click **Restore defaults** in the left pane, click or tap **Restore defaults**, and then click or tap **Yes**.

9. Click or tap the **Close** button.

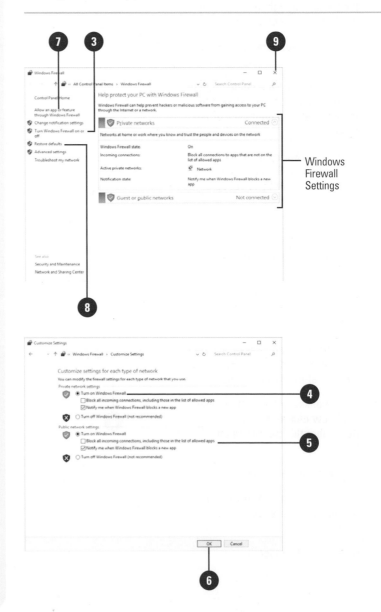

Windows Firewall Settings

Working with Contacts and Calendars

Introduction

A contact is a person or company with whom you communicate. Windows 10 uses the People app as a centralized place to add and manage contact information, including a person's name, address, phone, and email, which you can use in other apps, including Mail and Skype, to communicate with others. You can create and manage contacts in the People app and add contacts from other online service accounts, such as Facebook, Outlook.com (Hotmail, Live or MSN), Twitter, Microsoft Exchange, LinkedIn, and Google. When you setup Windows 10, you also setup or specify a Microsoft account, which becomes your default account and profile in the People app.

In addition to the People app, Windows 10 includes a Calendar app, an electronic version of the familiar paper daily planner. The Calendar app allows you to update the appearance and organization of events on your calendar in order to make things less cluttered and easier to read. You can use the Calendar app to schedule time for completing specific tasks, appointments, meetings, vacations, holidays, or for any other activity. You can adjust the Calendar Home screen to show events using the What's Next, Day, Work Week, Week, or Month view. The Calendar app comes with multiple calendars for different purposes, which include Main (with the username), Birthday, Personal, Holidays, and Work. When you create a calendar event, you can specify a specific calendar, where and when the event takes place, how long the event will last, how often the event occurs, whether you want to a reminder notice, your status, and whether to make the event private.

What You'll Do

Start the People App

View the People App Window

Add Contacts from Online Accounts

View and Find Contacts

Filter Contacts

Share Contacts

Add or Edit Contacts

Delete Contacts

Link Contacts

Start the Calendar App

Change Calendar Views

Schedule Events

Schedule Recurring Events

Schedule Events with Reminders

Edit or Delete Events

Work with Calendars

Change Calendar Options

Starting the People App

Windows 10 comes with a built-in app that allows you to work with contacts. The People app (**New!**) is a centralized place to add and manage contact information, including a person's name, address, phone, and email, which you can use in other apps, including Mail and Skype, to communicate with others. You can create and manage contacts in the People app and add contacts from other online social media accounts, such as Outlook.com (including Hotmail.com, Live.com, or MSN), Facebook, Twitter, Exchange (including Microsoft Exchange, Office 365, or Outlook.com), Google, and LinkedIn. When you setup Windows 10, you also setup or specified a Microsoft account, which becomes your default account and profile in People. Like other windows apps, you can start it from the Start screen or Start menu.

Start the People App

1. Click or tap the **People** tile on the Start screen or Start menu.

   The People app window opens in full screen view.

   On first use, a list of social media accounts appear on the left side of the Home screen.

2. If you want to add contacts from an online social media account, click or tap the **More** button on the Contact list, click or tap **Settings**, and then click or tap **Get social apps** to display a list of accounts.

See Also

See "Adding Contacts from Online Accounts" on page 138 for information on adding contacts to the People app from social media accounts.

Start menu

Viewing the People App Window

Contact List Tools
Displays tools to create new contacts, search & filter contacts, and add accounts.

Contact Tools
Displays buttons and menus for the selected contact.

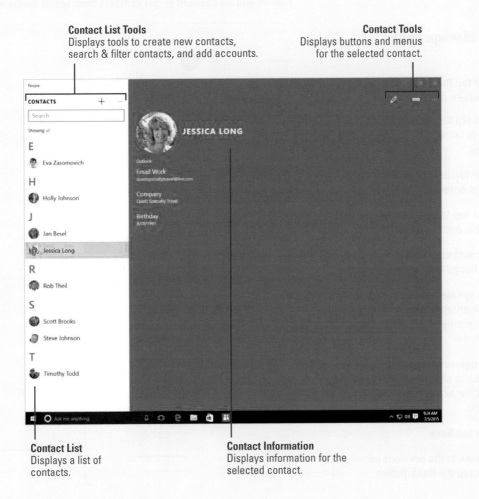

Contact List
Displays a list of contacts.

Contact Information
Displays information for the selected contact.

Adding Contacts from Online Accounts

With the People app, you can add contacts from online media accounts, such as Outlook.com (including Hotmail.com, Live.com, or MSN), Exchange (including Microsoft Exchange, or Office 365), Google, and iCloud, as well as social media apps, such as LinkedIn, Facebook, or Twitter (which you can add from the Windows Store). When you setup Windows 10, you also setup or specified a Microsoft account, which becomes your default account and profile in People. In the People app, you can access a list of accounts from Settings on the More menu, as well as add an account or get contacts from social media apps.

View and Manage Online Accounts

1. Click or tap the **People** tile on the Start screen or Start menu.

2. Click or tap the **More** button in the Contacts list, and then click or tap **Settings**.

3. Click or tap an account on the Settings screen.

4. Click or tap to change the available options.

   ◆ **Account name.** Edit the text box to change the account name.

   ◆ **Change mailbox sync settings.** Click or tap to change options for syncing email, contacts, and calendar.

   ◆ **Change account settings.** Click or tap to change your password or other account settings online.

5. Click or tap **Save**.

6. To go back to the previous panel, click or tap the **Back** button.

Add Contacts from Online Accounts

1 Click or tap the **People** tile on the Start screen or Start menu.

2 Click or tap the **More** button on the Contacts list, and then click or tap **Settings**.

3 Click or tap **Add an account** on the Settings screen.

4 Click or tap the account from which you want to add contacts:

◆ **Outlook.com.** Outlook.com, Live.com, Hotmail, or Hotmail.

◆ **Exchange.** Exchange or Office 365.

◆ **Google.** Sign in to your Google account.

◆ **iCloud.** Enter your iCloud email address and password.

◆ **Advanced setup.** Use to setup an Exchange ActiveSync account, or an Internet email account for POP or IMAP.

5 Follow the on-screen instructions to connect to the online account; steps vary depending on the account you select.

6 To go back to the previous panel, click or tap the **Back** button.

Did You Know?

You can add social media apps to get contacts. In the People app, click or tap the More button, click or tap Settings, click or tap Get Social Apps, and then follow the online instructions to install the app from the Windows Store or select the app.

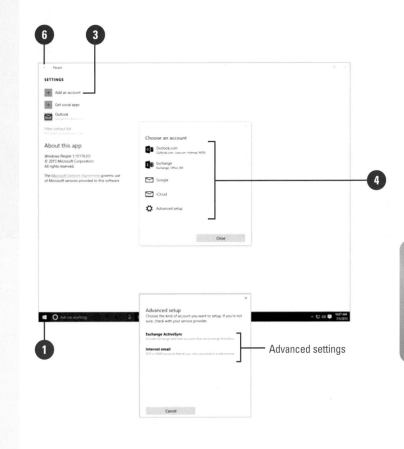

Advanced settings

Viewing and Finding Contacts

A **contact** is a person or company that you communicate with. One contact can often have several mailing addresses, phone numbers, or e-mail addresses. You can store this information in the People app along with other detailed information, such as job title, cell phone number, and web page addresses. You can add contacts directly within the People app for local use or from online media accounts, such as Facebook, Hotmail, Twitter, Outlook, LinkedIn, and Google. You can view all contacts or only the ones organized by A to Z. If you don't see the contact you want, you can use the Search box to find it. The list of contacts also includes your contact, which displays contact information for the current user account for Windows 10.

View Contacts

1. Click or tap the **People** tile on the Start screen or Start menu.

2. Scroll as needed, and then click or tap the contact icon or name you want to view in the Contacts list.

   The contact information appears in the Contact information pane.

3. To make a call, send an email, map a location, click or tap an item in the Contact information pane.

4. To edit the contact information, click or tap the **Edit** button.

See Also

See "Adding or Editing Contacts" on page 144 for more information on adding or editing contacts.

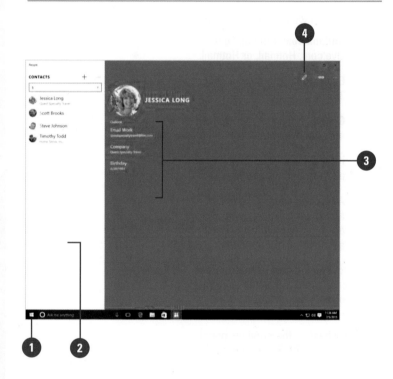

Find and View a Contact

1 Click or tap the **People** tile on the Start screen or Start menu.

2 To search for a contact, click in the Search box, and then enter a search contact name.

As you type, the search narrows down in the Contacts list.

3 To access contact by letter, click or tap **A** to **Z** in the Contacts list, and then click or tap a letter.

4 Click or tap the contact icon or name you want to view in the Contacts list.

The contact information appears in the Contact information pane.

5 To make a call, send an email, map a location, click or tap an item in the Contact information pane.

Did You Know?

You can remove a contact. In the People app, right-click or tap-hold a contact in the Contacts list, and then click or tap Delete.

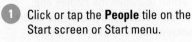

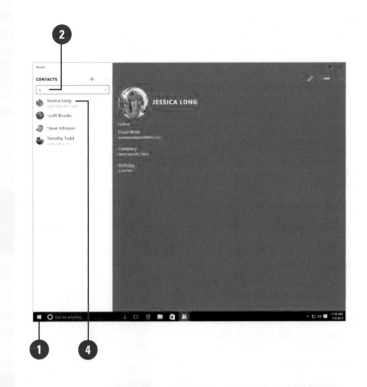

Filtering Contacts

With the Filter contracts dialog box (**New!**) in the People app, you can filter contacts on the Contacts list. When you open the People app, contacts are sort by first name by default. When you add online media accounts to the People app, the Contacts list can become cluttered with a lot of contacts. With the Filter option, you can show or hide contacts for a specific type of account to work with the ones you want. In addition, you can show or hide contacts without phone numbers.

Set Options to Filter Contacts

1 Click or tap the **People** tile on the Start screen or Start menu.

2 Click or tap the Showing **all** link in the Contacts list.

◆ You can also click or tap the **More** button, click or tap **Settings**, and then click or tap the **Filter contact list** link.

3 To hide contacts without phone numbers, drag the slider to **On**. To show all contacts, drag the slider to **Off**, the default.

You can still find contacts by searching.

4 To filter contacts by specific accounts, select or clear the account check boxes.

5 Click or tap **Done**.

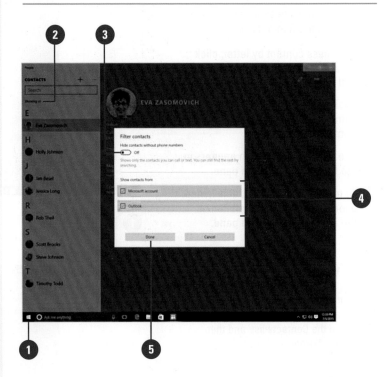

Sharing Contacts

Windows 10 makes it easy to share contacts (**New!**) with the People app. For example, you can select a contact in the People app, and then share it with others in an email using Mail. The typical sharing apps are Mail and OneNote (in most cases; depends on the app), however, you can also install and use other online services, such as Twitter and Facebook. The process is pretty simple. Open the People app, select the contact you want to share, select the Share contact command to open the Share panel, and then select the sharing app you want to use.

Share a Contact

1. Click or tap the **People** tile on the Start screen or Start menu.

2. Click or tap the contact icon or name you want to share in the Contacts list.

3. Click or tap the **More** button in the Contact information pane, and then click **Share contact** (**New!**).

4. Click or tap the **Apply** button.

   The Share panel appears with available sharing apps.

5. Click or tap the app in the Share panel that you want to use.

   TROUBLE? *If a sharing app is not available, make sure it is installed using the Windows Store.*

6. Use the app to send the information to another person.

> ### See Also
>
> *See "Sharing Between Apps" on page 35 for more information on sharing content with others.*

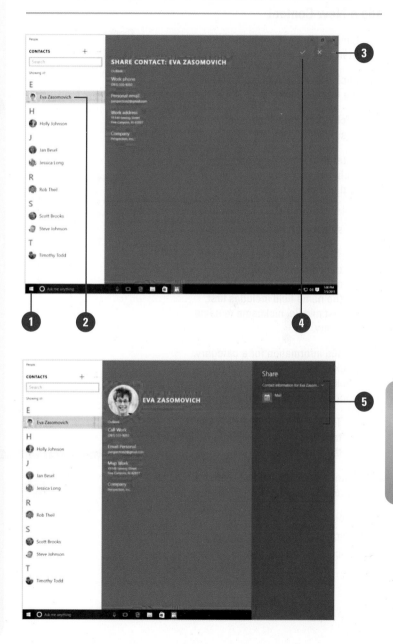

Adding or Editing Contacts

A **contact** is a person or company that you communicate with. One contact can often have several mailing addresses, phone numbers, or e-mail addresses. You can store this information in the People app along with other detailed information, such as job title, mobile phone number, web page addresses, and other notes. This information can be used to send emails and instant messages. You can use the Add or Edit button to quickly add a new contact or change an existing one.

Add a New Contact

1. Click or tap the **People** tile on the Start screen or Start menu.

2. Click or tap the **Add** button (+) in the Contacts list.

3. Click or tap the account you want to save new contacts.

4. Enter the contact's information, including name, company, e-mail, and phone.

   ◆ Photo. Click or tap **Add photo** to select a photo for the contact.

   ◆ Add/Edit Content. Click or tap the **Edit** icon to add or edit additional content. For example, the name field includes first, last middle, nickname to name a few.

5. To add information for a category, click or tap the **Add** button (+), click or tap an option for the specified type of information.

   ◆ To remove a category, click or tap the category, and then click the **Remove** button (x).

6. Enter any additional information for a new category.

7. Click or tap the **Save** button.

   ◆ To cancel the new contact, click or tap the **Cancel** button.

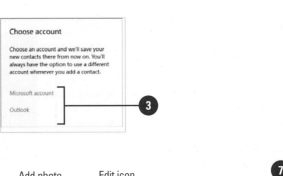

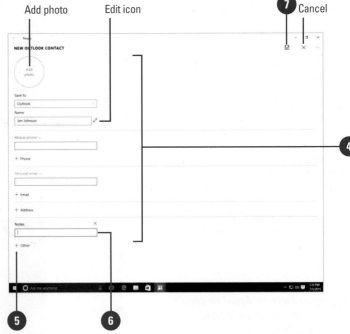

Add photo   Edit icon   Cancel

Edit a Contact

1. Click or tap the **People** tile on the Start screen or Start menu.

2. Click or tap the contact that you want to edit.

3. Click or tap the **Edit** button in the Contact Information pane.

4. Edit the contact's information as desired.

   ◆ **Change photo.** Click or tap the photo to select another one.

   ◆ **Add/Edit Content.** Click or tap the **Edit** icon to add or edit additional content. For example, the name field includes first, last middle, nickname to name a few.

5. To add information for a category, click or tap the **Add** button (+), click or tap an option for the specified type of information.

   ◆ To remove a category, click or tap the category, and then click the **Remove** button (x).

6. Enter any additional information for a new category.

7. Click or tap the **Save** button.

   ◆ To cancel the operation, click or tap the **Cancel** button.

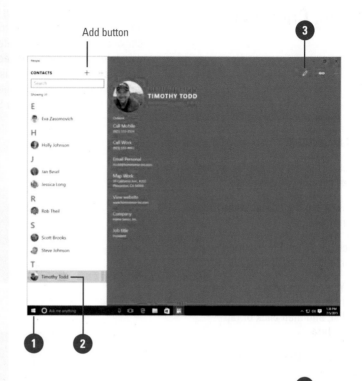

Add button

Change photo   Edit icon   Cancel

Deleting Contacts

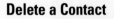

If you contacts list is getting to large or you no longer need a contact anymore, you can delete it from the People app. With a few simple clicks or taps, you can delete a contact using the More menu. When you delete a contact, the People app asks for a confirmation, so you don't delete a contact by mistake. Since, your user account is linked to your contact, you cannot delete it in the People app. You would need to remove the user account in Settings for Windows 10.

Delete a Contact

1 Click or tap the **People** tile on the Start screen or Start menu.

2 Click or tap the contact that you want to delete.

3 Click or tap the **More** button, and then click or tap **Delete**.

◆ You can also right-click or tap-hold a contact in the Contacts list, and then click or tap **Delete**.

4 Click or tap **Delete** to confirm the deletion.

Linking Contacts

A contact can be linked with other profiles and contacts in the People app. With a few simple clicks or taps, you can link a contact with other information. You can view your current links as well as add new ones by using the Link button for a specific contact. For those of you using Messenger, friends can't be linked to each other.

Link a Contact

1 Click or tap the **People** tile on the Start screen or Start menu.

2 Click or tap the contact that you want to link.

3 Click or tap the **Link** button.

The People app displays the linked profiles for the contact.

4 Click or tap the **Choose a contact to link** button.

The People app displays contacts to which you want to link.

5 Select the contacts you want to link.

6 To unlink a profile, click the linked profile you want to unlink, and then click or tap **Unlink**.

7 To go back to the previous screen, click or tap the **Back** button.

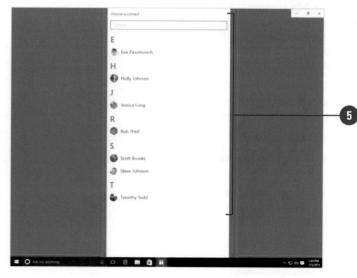

Starting the Calendar App

Windows 10 comes with a built-in calendar app that allows you to manage your schedule. The Calendar app (**New!**) is an electronic version of the familiar paper daily planner that allows you to schedule time for completing specific tasks, appointments, meetings, vacations, holidays, or for any other activity. You can add or modify calendars from other online accounts, such as Hotmail (Hotmail.com, Live.com, or MSN), Outlook (Microsoft Exchange, Office 365, or Outlook.com), and Google. Each calendar appears in a different color to make things less cluttered and easier to read. Like other Windows apps, you can start it from the Start screen or Start menu.

Start the Calendar App

1 Click or tap the **Calendar** tile on the Start screen or Start menu.

The Calendar app window opens in full screen view, displaying the current month's calendar.

The current day is highlighted in blue (default) for easy viewing.

◆ **On first use.** Click or tap **Get started**, select an account or add one, and then click or tap **Ready to go.**

2 To add or modify accounts for calendar, click or tap the **Settings** button, click **Accounts**, and then do any of the following:

◆ **Add an Account.** Click or tap the **Add account** link (+), click or tap the account you want to add, and then follow the on-screen instructions; steps vary depending on the account.

◆ **Modify an Account.** Click or tap an account, and then specify or select the options you want:

◆ **Account name.**

◆ **Change mailbox sync settings.**

◆ **Change account settings.**

Start menu

On first use, Get started

Changing the Calendar View

With the Calendar app, you can adjust the display to show events using the Day, Work Week, Week, Month, or Today view. When you display events using the Day view, you can view events for the current day and up to 6 days afterwards (**New!**). After viewing other dates in the calendar, you can use the Today button to quickly display today's date in the current view. The current day is highlighted in blue for easy viewing. You can switch between the different views by using buttons at the top of the screen. You can also select a day in the Mini Calendar in the Navigation pane, use the Up or Down arrow or swipe left or right to navigate the calendar. If you want more working room, you can use the Collapse/Expand button to show or hide the Navigation pane.

Change the Calendar View

1. Click or tap the **Calendar** tile on the Start screen or Start menu.

2. Click or tap one of the View buttons.

    ◆ **Day.** Displays an hourly schedule for the selected day and 1-6 days after (**New!**).

        ◆ Today. Click or tap the **Day** button (**New!**).

        ◆ Today & Days. Point to the **Day** button, click or tap the button arrow (**New!**), and then click or tap **1 day - 6 day**.

    ◆ **Work Week.** Displays an hourly schedule for the 5-day work week.

    ◆ **Week.** Displays an hourly schedule for the 7-day week.

    ◆ **Month.** Displays a monthly schedule.

    ◆ **Today.** Displays the current day.

3. To navigate backward and forward in the calendar, click or tap the **Up** or **Down** arrow, or swipe left or right.

        ◆ You can also select a day or today in the Mini-Calendar in the Navigation pane.

Collapse/Expand button

Mini-Calendar   Current day

Settings button   Month view

Scheduling Events

The Calendar app comes with multiple calendars for different purposes, which include Main (with the username), Birthday, Personal, Holidays, and Work. When you create a calendar event, you can specify a specific calendar, where and when the event takes place, how long the event will last, how often the event occurs, whether you want to a reminder notice, your calendar status (Free, Tentative, Busy, or Out of office), and whether to make the event private. If an event recurs on a regular basis, such as a meeting, you can set Repeat options. If you need a reminder, you can also set the amount of time you need. If you don't want others to see an event, you can make it private.

Schedule a New Quick Event

① Click or tap the **Calendar** tile on the Start screen or Start menu.

② Click or tap the day you want.

③ Specify any of the following:

◆ **Name.** Type a name for the event.

◆ **Start.** Specify the start date and time for the event. If it's an all day event, select or tap the **All day** check box.

◆ **End.** Specify the end date and time for the event.

◆ **Location.** Type a location for the event.

◆ **Calendar.** Select the calendar for the event.

④ Click or tap **Done** or **More details** (go to the next page).

◆ To cancel, click the **Close** button (x).

◆ More details. Specify more event details, and then click or tap the **Save and close** button.

Collaspe/Expand the Navigation pane   Add a quick event

Close button

Schedule a New Detailed Event

1 Click or tap the **Calendar** tile on the Start screen or Start menu.

2 Click or tap the **New event** button.

3 Type a name and location for the event.

4 Specify any of the following:

◆ **Start.** Specify the start date and time for the event. If it's an all day event, select or tap the **All day** check box.

◆ **End.** Specify the end date and time for the event.

◆ **Location.** Type a location for the event.

◆ **Calendar.** Select the calendar for the event.

◆ **Description.** Enter details or notes about the event.

◆ **People.** Select the people you want at the event. You can also invite others; enter email addresses (separated by a semi-colon).

5 Specify any of the following:

◆ **Show as.** Specify your status (Free, Tentative, Busy, or Out of office).

◆ **Reminder.** Select None for no reminder, or an option for when you want a reminder.

◆ **Repeat.** Specify the available options for a recurring event.

◆ **Private.** Select to create a private event.

6 Click or tap the **Save this event** button.

◆ To cancel, click or tap the **Back** button. If prompted, click or tap **Save** or **Discard changes**.

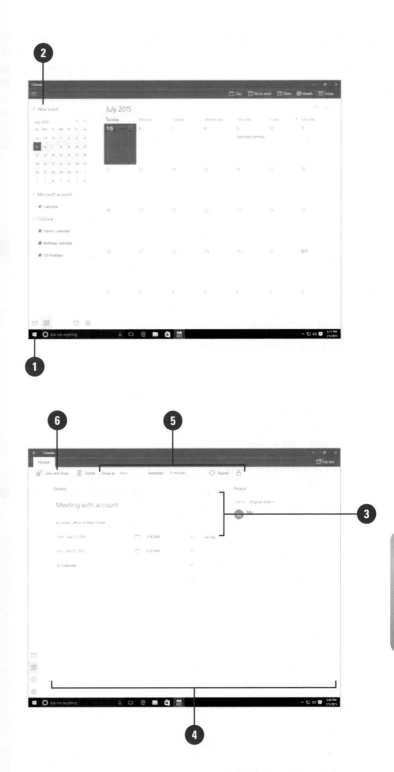

Scheduling Recurring Events

If an event recurs on a regular basis, such as a meeting, you can set Repeat options to specify the interval in which you want to schedule it. You can specify the following intervals—Daily, Weekly, Monthly, or Yearly—with start and end dates. You can set Repeat options when you create a new event or edit an existing one. If you want to change a recurring event to an individual event, you can select the Repeat button to toggle it off. If you need a reminder, you can also set the amount of time you need. As you create an event, you can also show calendar status as Free, Tentative, Busy, or Out of office.

Schedule a Recurring Event

1. Click or tap the **Calendar** tile on the Start screen or Start menu.

2. Click or tap the **New event** button.

3. Specify any of the following information:

   ◆ **Name** and **Location**.

   ◆ **Start**, **End**, **Location**, **Calendar**, **Description**, and **People**.

   ◆ **Show as**, **Reminder**, or **Private**.

4. Click or tap the **Repeat** button.

   The Repeat button turns on and the Repeat pane opens.

5. Specify any of the following information:

   ◆ **Start.** Specify the start date for the repeating event.

   ◆ **Interval.** Specify an interval and options for the repeating event: Daily, Weekly, Monthly, or Yearly.

   ◆ **Every on.** Specify an every interval.

   ◆ **End.** Specify the end date for the repeating event.

6. To turn off a repeating event, click or tap the **Repeat** button.

7. Click or tap the **Save and close** button.

   ◆ To cancel, click or tap the **Back** button. If prompted, click or tap **Save** or **Discard changes**.

Toggles on and off

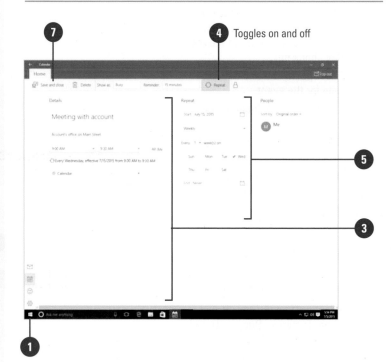

Scheduling Events with a Reminder

If you have an event, such as a meeting, in the Calendar app, you can invite others to attend and provide a reminder. When you create a new event or edit an existing one, you can set the amount of time you need for a reminder and enter email addresses or select contacts from the People app in order to send email invitations. When the timing for the reminder takes place, a notification appears in the upper-right corner of the screen, where you can click or tap the notification to view the event. If you need a recurring event, you can also set the Repeat option. As you create an event, you can also show calendar status as Free, Tentative, Busy, or Out of office.

Schedule an Event with a Reminder

1. Click or tap the **Calendar** tile on the Start screen or Start menu.

2. Click or tap the **New event** button.

3. Specify any of the following information:

   ◆ **Name** and **Location**.

   ◆ **Start**, **End**, **Location**, **Calendar**, **Description**, and **People**.

   ◆ **Show as**, **Repeat**, or **Private**.

4. Click or tap the **Reminder** button.

5. Click or tap the **Save and close** button.

   ◆ To cancel, click or tap the **Back** button. If prompted, click or tap **Save** or **Discard changes**.

Did You Know?

You can show an event as Free, Tentative, Busy, or Out of office. In the Calendar app, create a new event or edit an existing one, click or tap the Show as list arrow, and then click or tap Free, Tentative, Busy, or Out of office.

Editing or Deleting Events

After you create an event, you edit it at any time. With a simple click or tap, you can open an event and make any changes that you want or delete it from the calendar. When you open an recurring event, the Calendar app asks you whether you want to open the individual event or the entire series. After you make changes to an individual or recurring event, you simply save it. If you no longer need an individual or recurring event, you can delete it from the calendar.

Edit or Delete an Event

1. Click or tap the **Calendar** tile on the Start screen or Start menu.

2. Navigate to the event you want to edit or delete.

    ◆ To navigate backward and forward in the calendar, click or tap the **Up** or **Down** arrow, or swipe left or right.

3. Point to the event, and then click or tap **Edit series** or **Edit occurrence.**

4. Make the changes you want for the event.

5. Click or tap the **Save and close** button to save the edited event or click or tap the **Delete** button to remove the event.

    ◆ To cancel, click or tap the **Back** button. If prompted, click or tap **Save** or **Discard changes**.

Point to event

Working with Calendars

You can work with multiple accounts with the Calendar app. The Microsoft account comes by default when you sign in to the account for Windows 10. However, you can add other accounts, such as Outlook.com. You can add accounts using the Settings button. You can view calendar accounts in the Navigation pane, where you can collapse and expand individual calendars (which you can show and hide in Calendar Settings). To reduce clutter, you can select or clear the check boxes for individual calendars.

Work with Calendars and Accounts

1. Click or tap the **Calendar** tile on the Start screen or Start menu.

2. To add or modify accounts for calendar, click or tap the **Settings** button, click **Accounts**, and then do any of the following:

   ◆ Add an Account. Click or tap the **Add account** link (+), click or tap the account you want to add, and then follow the on-screen instructions; steps vary depending on the account.

   ◆ Modify an Account. Click or tap an account, and then specify or select the options you want:

      ◆ **Account name.**

      ◆ **Change mailbox sync settings.**

      ◆ **Change account settings.**

3. To collapse or expand calendars, click or tap the **Collapse** or **Expand** arrow in the Navigation pane.

4. To show or hide items on a calendar, select or clear the calendar items under the Calendar.

See Also

See "Adding Contacts from Online Accounts" on page 138 for more information on working with accounts.

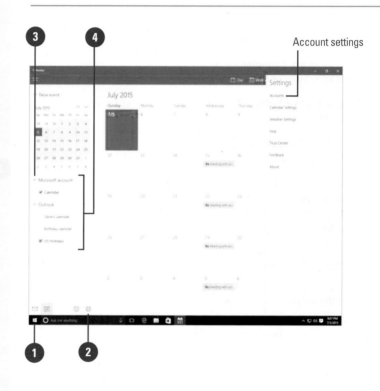

Account settings

Changing Calendar Options

With the Settings panel in the Calendar app , you can set options for Accounts, Calendar Settings, Weather Settings (connect to weather content), Help, Trust Center (let Office connect to online services from Microsoft), Feedback (online comments about Windows), or About. In Calendar Settings, you can set options for the First Day of Week, Days in Work Week, Working Hours, Week Numbers, and Calendar Color. When you hide a calendar, the color option is disabled. If you want to go back to the previous panel, click the Back button. If you want to exit, press Esc.

Change Calendar Options

1. Click or tap the **Calendar** tile on the Start screen or Start menu.

2. Click or tap the **Settings** button on the Navigation pane.

3. Click or tap **Calendar Settings** on the Settings panel.

   ◆ You can also click or tap **Accounts, Weather Settings, Help, Trust Center, Feedback,** or **About** to set other options.

4. Specify the following calendar options for the available accounts:

   ◆ First Day of Week. Select a day of the week.

   ◆ Days in Work Week. Select the check boxes for the days you want.

   ◆ Working Hours. Select a start and end time.

   ◆ Week Numbers. Select **First Day of Year, First Full Week,** or **Off.**

   ◆ Calendar Color Options. Select the **Light Colors** or **Bright Colors** option.

5. To go back to the previous panel, click or tap the **Back** button.

   To exit the panel, click or tap off the panel, or press Esc.

Exchanging Mail

Introduction

If you're like many people today who are using the Internet to communicate with friends and business associates, you probably have piles of information (names, email addresses, phone numbers, etc.) that you need often. Unless this information is in one convenient place, and can be accessed immediately, the information becomes ineffective and you become unproductive. The Mail app that comes with Windows 10 solves these problems by integrating management and organization tools into one simple system. The Mail app is a powerful program for managing **electronic mail** (known as email), and accessing contact information like names, and email addresses.

Using the Mail app with an Internet connection allows you to accomplish several tasks:

- Create and send email messages

- Manage multiple email accounts

- Use contacts from the People app to address emails messages

- Format email messages with emoticons

- Add signatures to email messages

- Attach a file to an email message

- Manage email messages with folders and favorites

- Remove unwanted email messages with delete, sweep, or junk

- Search for content within email messages

Starting the Mail App

Whether you want to exchange email with colleagues or friends, the Mail app (**New!**) that comes with Windows 10 provides you with the tools you need. When you setup Windows 10, you also setup or specified a Microsoft account, which becomes your default email account in the Mail app. So, when you start the Mail app, you are ready to go. Like other Windows apps, you can start the Mail app from the Start screen or menu. You can also add more email accounts, such as Hotmail (Hotmail.com, Live.com, or MSN), Outlook (Microsoft Exchange, Office 365, or Outlook.com), and Google.

Start the Mail App

1. Click or tap the **Mail** tile on the Start screen or Start menu.

   The Mail app window opens in full screen view.

   When you setup Windows 10, you also setup or specified a Microsoft account, which becomes your default email account in the Mail app.

   ◆ **On first use.** Click or tap **Get started**, select an account or add one, and then click or tap **Ready to go.**

Start menu

Did You Know?

You can get Help in the Mail app. In the Mail app, click or tap the Settings button on the Navigation panel, click or tap Help, click or tap Open Help, and then view the content in your browser.

You can enable online services from Microsoft in the Mail app. In the Mail app, click or tap the Settings button on the Navigation panel, click or tap Trust Center, and then drag to turn on the option, which lets Office connect to online services from Microsoft to provide functionality that's relevant to your usage and preferences.

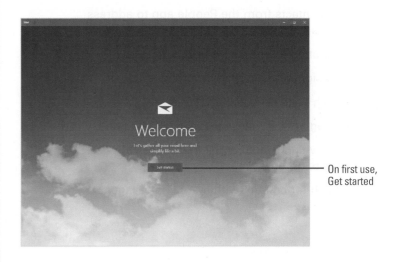

On first use, Get started

Getting Around the Mail Window

After you start the Mail app, you can use the full-screen window to work with email messages. Along the left side of the window is the **Folders pane**, which contains folders to store and manage messages. The Folders pane provides easy access to the Inbox with new messages, Favorites sent from a person, Flagged messages, and More folders (Outbox, Inbox, Drafts, Junk, Sent, and Trash). At the top of the Folders pane is a list of active email accounts you can use to switch between them. The **Messages pane** to the right of the Folders pane displays a list email messages. You can click or tap or use check boxes in the Messages pane to select and work with messages. The **Reading pane** displays the contents of the selected message in the Messages pane. If you want more room, you can use the Collapse/Expand button to show or hide the Folders pane.

Get Around the Map Window

1 Click or tap the **Mail** tile on the Start screen or Start menu.

2 To switch email accounts, click or tap the current account on the Folders pane, and then click or tap an account.

3 Click or tap a folder in the Folders pane. Click or tap the **More** link to access more folders.

   ◆ Add/Remove Favorites. On the Folders pane, right-click or tap-hold a folder, and then click or tap **Add to Favorites** or **Remove from Favorites**.

   ◆ Pin/Unpin Start. On the More panel, right-click or tap-hold a folder, and then click or tap **Pin to Start** or **Unpin from Start**.

4 Click or tap a message in the Messages pane.

   ◆ Options. When you point to a message, you can click or tap an icon to **Mark Read/Unread**, **Add/Remove Flag**, or **Delete**.

5 Read the selected message in the Reading pane.

Collaspe/Expand button

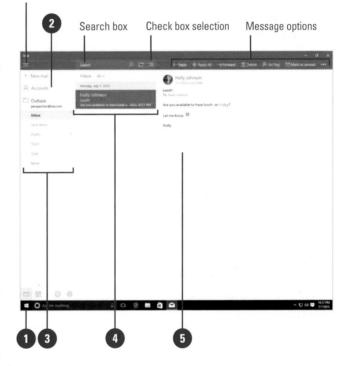

Search box   Check box selection   Message options

Adding Mail Accounts

When you setup Windows 10, you also setup or specified a Microsoft account, which becomes your default email account in the Mail app. So, when you start the Mail app, you are ready to go. However, if you have other email accounts, you can set up multiple accounts in the Mail app. You can add email accounts, such as Outlook.com (Outlook.com Live.com, Hotmail, or MSN), Exchange (Exchange or Office 365), Google, Yahoo! Mail, and iCloud. When you add an email account, the Mail app does all the work for you, unless it needs your help with additional information. For some account types, such as Exchange, you need additional information, such as your account name, password, email server type, and the names of your incoming and outgoing email servers from your ISP or network administrator. The Mail app allows you to send and retrieve email messages from different types of email servers, which are the locations where your email is stored before you access it.

Add a Mail Account

1. Click or tap the **Mail** tile on the Start screen or Start menu.

2. Click or tap the **Settings** button.

3. Click or tap **Accounts** on the Settings panel.

4. Click or tap **Add account** on the Accounts panel.

   ◆ To go back to the previous panel, click or tap the **Back** button.

   ◆ To exit the panel, click or tap off the panel, or press Esc.

   A Choose an account dialog box opens.

5. Click or tap an account type, such as Outlook.com (Outlook.com, Live.com, Hotmail, or MSN), Exchange (Exchange or Office 365), Google, Yahoo! Mail, and iCloud.

   ◆ To exit the dialog box, click or tap the **Close** button.

6 Enter the email address and password for the account.

7 Click or tap **Sign in** or **Next** to continue.

8 Enter the information requested for the account; the information varies depending on the account type.

◆ **Username.** Enter the username associated with the account.

◆ **Incoming (IMAP) email server.** Specify the incoming web address and port number; see host administrator.

◆ **Incoming server requires SSL.** Select if security is required by the host administrator.

◆ **Outgoing (SMTP) email server.** Specify the outcoming web address and port number; see host administrator.

◆ **Outgoing server requires SSL.** Select if security is required by the host administrator.

◆ **Outgoing server requires authentication.** Select if security authentication is required by the host administrator.

◆ **Use the same username and password to send and receive email.** Select to use the same user authentication for the incoming and outgoing server.

9 Click or tap **Done** or **Connect**.

For Your Information

How Do I Choose an Email Server?

The Mail app supports three types of incoming email servers: **POP3** (Post Office Protocol), **IMAP** (Internet Message Access Protocol), and **HTTP** (Hypertext Transfer Protocol). A protocol is a set of rules and standards that control the transmission of content, format, sequencing, and error management for information over the Internet or network much like rules of the road govern the way you drive. POP3 servers allow you to access email messages from a single Inbox folder, while IMAP servers allow you to access multiple folders. HTTP servers are used on web sites, and allow you to send and receive email messages on a web site. When you use POP3 or IMAP email servers, you also need to provide an outgoing email server. **SMTP** (Simple Mail Transfer Protocol) is generally used to send messages between email servers.

Modifying Account Settings

With the Mail app, you want to change options for the default Microsoft account or for any ones that you have added. You can change email account options by using an accounts panel, which you can access from the Settings panel. In an accounts panel, you can change the account name, specify how and when to download email, specify whether to synchronize content—such as email, contacts, or calendar—with this account, whether to show newsletters or social updates in the folders pane, how to show email notifications, specify whether to use an email signature at the end of a message, show or hide email notifications for this account, or remove this account.

Modify Account Settings

1. Click or tap the **Mail** tile on the Start screen or Start menu.

2. Click or tap the **Settings** button.

3. Click or tap **Accounts** on the Settings panel.

4. Click or tap the account that you want to change.

   ◆ To go back to the previous panel, click or tap the **Back** button.

   ◆ To exit the panel, click or tap off the panel, or press Esc.

   An account settings dialog box opens.

5. Specify a name for the account in the Mail app.

6. Enter the information requested for the account; the information varies depending on the account type.

   ◆ **Change mailbox sync settings.** Click or tap to change sync settings.

   ◆ **Change account settings.** Click or tap to change account settings on the web in your browser.

   ◆ **Delete account.** Click or tap to remove this account, and then click or tap **Delete** to confirm.

7 For Change mailbox sync settings, specify any of the following (scroll as needed), and then click or tap **Done**.

- ◆ **Download new content.** Select an option when to download content.

- ◆ **Always download full message and Internet images.** Select to specify options where to download email and server address.

- ◆ **Server requires encrypted (SSL) connection.** Select to require.

- ◆ **Sync options.** Drag to turn on or off sync to email, calendar, or contacts.

8 For Change account settings, specify any of the following (scroll as needed), and then click or tap **Close** button to exit the browser.

- ◆ **Home.** Use to access quick links.

- ◆ **Your info.** Use to change your personal information.

- ◆ **Services & subscriptions.** Use to change OneDrive, and other services, like Office 365 or Xbox Live.

- ◆ **Payment & billing.** Use to change payment & billing options.

- ◆ **Devices.** Use to work with devices.

- ◆ **Family.** Use to set Internet safety options for kids.

- ◆ **Security & privacy.** Use to change passwords and set safety settings.

9 To exit the dialog box, click or tap the **Save** or **Close** button.

- ◆ To exit the panel, click or tap off the panel, or press Esc.

Change mailbox sync settings

Change account settings

Composing and Sending Email

Email is becoming the primary form of written communication for many people. Email messages in the Mail app follow a standard memo format, with fields for the sender, recipient, and subject of the message. To send an email, you need to enter the recipient's email address, type a subject, then type the message itself. The subject is the first information the recipient sees about the email, so it should provide a short, concise summary of the message content. For an added touch, you can add a signature at the end of a new email. You can send the same email to more than one individual. Before you send the email, you can set a priority level (high or low) to convey the message's importance. When you create a new message, Mail designates it as a draft (which you can save) until you send it.

Compose and Send an Email

1. Click or tap the **Mail** tile on the Start screen or Start menu.

2. If you have multiple accounts, click or tap **Accounts**, and then select an account.

3. Click or tap the **New mail** button.

   TIMESAVER *Press Ctrl+ N to create a new email message.*

4. Enter an email address (separate by a semi-colon) or name. As you type, any address or name matches appear in a drop-down menu.

   Click or tap the **Cc & Bcc** link to add the Cc, or Bcc fields where you can enter addresses or select contacts from the People app.

   ◆ To. Use if you want the recipient to receive the message.

   ◆ Cc (Carbon Copy). Use if you want the recipient to receive a copy of the message.

   ◆ Bcc (Blind Carbon Copy). Use if you want the recipient to receive a copy of the message but not be listed as a recipient on any copy of the message.

5. Click or tap in the **Subject** box, and then enter a brief description of your message.

Cc & Bcc link

Contacts from People app

6 Click or tap in the Message box below the subject box, and then type the text of your message.

◆ If a red line appears under a word, right-click or tap-hold the misspelled word, and then click or tap a suggested word, **+word** (add to dictionary), **Ignore**, or **Ignore All**.

7 If you want, select the text you want to format and then use the commands on the **Format** tab to customize your message.

◆ Save draft. The Mail app automatically saves the message as a draft until you send it.

◆ Delete draft. Click or tap the **Discard** button.

8 Use tabs to modify the message:

◆ Insert Media. Click or tap the **Insert** tab, and then click or tap a button (**Attach**, **Table**, **Pictures**, or **Link**).

◆ Options. Click or tap the **Options** tab, and then click or tap a button (**High Priority**, **Low Priority**, **Language**, **Spelling**, or **Proofing and Language Options**).

9 Click or tap the **Send** button.

The email message is sent.

Did You Know?

You can view or delete a saved draft message to finish and send later. In the Mail app, click or tap Folders in the Folders pane, and then click or tap the Drafts folder. Select the email message to edit it, and then click or tap the Send button or Delete icon in the message.

Discard message

For Your Information

Checking the Spelling in Email

Before you send an email message, you should spell check the text and read through the content to make sure your spelling is accurate and your content conveys the message you want to the recipient(s). The Mail app automatically checks your email message as you type it. When a red line appears under a word or phrase, the app dictionary doesn't recognize it. You can correct the word or phrase spelling, add the word or phrase to the dictionary, or ignore it. To manually check spelling, click or tap the Options tab (**New!**) in a message, and then click or tap the Spelling button. Next to the Spelling button on the Options tab is a list arrow with proofing and language options **New!**), which include Hide All Proofing Marks and Hide Proofing Marks in Selected Text.

Formatting Email Messages

When you create an email message, you can quickly enter the text you want to send. However, if you want to add some emphasis to your message, you can format it with the Format tab above the message. The formatting options include font, highlight, bold, italic, underline, color, styles, bulleted or numbered list, alignment, and spacing. Before you can format text, you need to select it or click or tap to place the insertion point first. If you don't like the formatting changes, you can undo (reverse) it or clear formatting. In addition, you can use the Insert tab to insert media, such as file attachments, tables, pictures, and hyperlinks. If you want to multitask, you can open a message in a side by side window.

Format an Email Message

1. Click or tap the **Mail** tile on the Start screen or Start menu.

2. Click or tap **New mail**.

3. Address the email message, and then enter a subject.

4. In the Message box, select the text you want to format or click or tap the place the insertion point.

5. Click or tap the **Format** tab, and the use the formatting button you want.

   ◆ **Bold**, **Italic**, or **Underline.** Formats text in bold, italic, or underline.

   ◆ **Font Formatting.** Select a font type, font size, Strikethrough, Subscript, Superscript, Highlight, Font Color, or Clear Formatting.

   ◆ **Paragraph Formatting.** Creates a bulleted or numbered list, adjust indents, alignment, and spacing.

   ◆ **Styles.** Select a text style from the list.

   ◆ **Undo.** Undos the previous command.

6. Click or tap the **Insert** tab, and then click or tap a button (**Attach**, **Table**, **Pictures**, or **Link**).

7. Type any text, as desired.

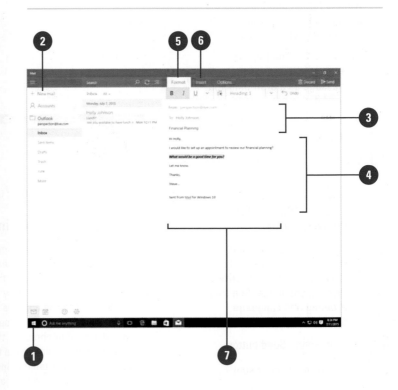

Creating Email Signatures

Instead of typing the same ending signature and other personal or business card information, such as address, phone number, or web site, at the end of your email messages, you can have the Mail app automatically insert it for you. You can enable and create a signature for each email account used in the Mail app. You can enable and create a signature by using an Options panel, which you can access from the Settings panel.

Use an Email Signature

1 Click or tap the **Mail** tile on the Start screen or Start menu.

2 Click or tap the **Settings** button.

3 Click or tap **Options** on the Settings panel.

4 Click or tap the **Account** list arrow, and then select the account that you want to change.

5 Drag the Use an email signature slider to **On**.

6 Enter the signature you want to use for this account.

7 To go back to the previous panel, click or tap the **Back** button.

To exit the panel, click or tap off the panel, or press Esc.

Turn on to automatically send replies

Did You Know?

You can create automatic replies If you're not available to reply to email, such as Out of Office, you can create an automatic reply. In the Options panel, drag the Send Automatic Replies slider to On, and then enter a message, and select or clear the check box to send replies only to my contacts.

Reading and Replying to Email

You can receive email anytime—even when your PC is turned off. You can retrieve your email manually or set the Mail app to do so automatically. When you start the Mail app, the program checks for new email. It continues to check periodically while the app is open. New messages appear in boldface in the Inbox along with any messages you haven't moved or deleted. Message flags may appear next to a message, which indicate a priority, the need for follow up, or an attachment. The Mail app blocks images and other potentially harmful content from automatically downloading in an email message from unknown people. Blocked items are replaced with a red "x". Any email messages identified as junk mail is automatically moved to the Junk folder. You can respond to a message in two ways: reply to it, which creates a new message addressed to the sender(s) and other recipients; or forward it, which creates a new message you can send to someone else. In either case, the original message appears in the response and all related messages are grouped together in a conversation. When you reply to a message that had an attachment, the attachment isn't returned to the original sender. You can forward the message to the original sender if you need to send the attachment back.

Open and Read an Email

1. Click or tap the **Mail** tile on the Start screen or Start menu.

2. If you have multiple accounts, click or tap **Accounts**, and then select an account.

3. To manually check for email messages, click or tap the **Sync** button.

4. Click or tap the **Inbox** folder for the mail account you want.

5. Click or tap an email message to read it in the Reading pane. If you select a conversation, it expands or collapses to display or hide the conversation email messages.

6. To mark an email message as unread, click or tap the **Mark unread** button.

7. To flag a message for action, click or tap the **Set Flag** button.

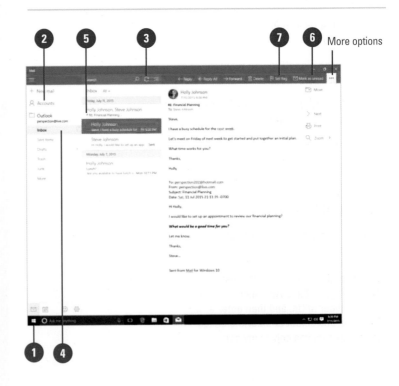

More options

Reply to an Email

1. In the Mail app, click or tap the email message you want to reply to.

2. If you have multiple accounts, click or tap **Accounts**, and then select an account.

3. Click or tap the **Reply** to respond to the sender only, or click the **Reply all** to respond to the sender and to all recipients.

   TIMESAVER *Press Ctrl+R to reply to the message author.*

4. Click or tap the To, Cc, or Bcc box, and then add or delete names as desired.

5. Type your message.

6. Click the **Send** button.

Reply email (RE:)

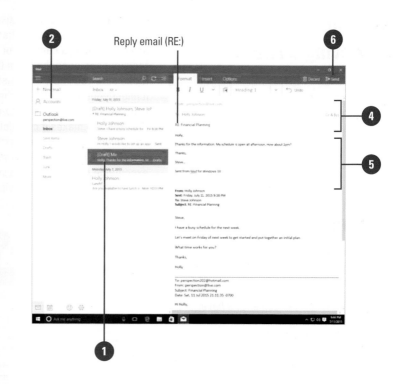

Forward an Email

1. In the Mail app, click or tap the email message you want to forward.

2. If you have multiple accounts, click or tap **Accounts**, and then select an account.

3. Click or tap the **Forward** button.

4. Click or tap the To, Cc, or Bcc box, and then type the name(s) of the recipient(s).

5. Type your message.

6. Click the **Send** button.

Forward email (FW:)

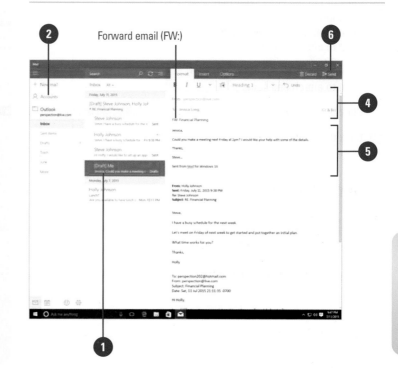

Sending and Retrieving a File

With the Mail app, you can use email to easily share a file, such as a picture or a document by attaching it to an email from a folder, network, device (such as a camera), or OneDrive. Upon receiving the email, the recipient can open the file in the program that created it or save it. Make sure you know and trust the sender before you open it, because it might contain a virus or other security threat. It's important to keep your antivirus software up-to-date. If an attachment is considered safe, the Mail app makes it completely available to you. Examples of safe attachments are text files (.txt) and graphic files, such as JPEGs (.jpg) and GIFs (.gif). Beware of potentially unsafe attachments, such as an executable program (.exe), screensavers (.scr) or script files (including .vbs) that could put your device at risk of problems.

Send a File in an Email

1. In the Mail app, compose a new message or reply to an existing message.

   IMPORTANT *Some ISPs have trouble sending large attachments; check with your ISP.*

2. Click the **Insert** tab.

3. Click the **Attach** button.

4. Click or tap the **Files** list arrow, and then select the drive and folder that contains the file you want to attach.

5. Click or tap to select the files you want to attach and send.

6. Click or tap **Open**.

7. Click the **Send** button.

Attached file

Did You Know?

You can print an email. In the Mail app, click or tap the the message you want to print, click or tap the More button, click or tap Print, select the print options you want, and then click or tap Print.

Download a File in an Email

1. In the Mail app, select the message with the attached file.

   IMPORTANT *If you're not sure of the source of an attachment, don't open it, because it might contain a virus or worm. Be sure to use anti-virus software.*

2. Click or tap the **Download** link, if available.

   The file is downloaded to your device.

See Also

See "Avoiding Viruses and Other Harmful Attacks" on page 360 for information on how to avoid getting a virus and other harmful threats.

Open or Save Files in an Email

1. In the Mail app, select the message with the attached and downloaded file.

2. To open the file with the default app, click or tap the attached file.

3. To open with or save, right-click or tap-hold the attached file, and then select any of the following:

   ◆ **Open.** Select an option to specify how to open the attached file.

   ◆ **Save.** Enter a name for the file or use the existing one, use the Files list arrow to specify a location, and then click or tap Save.

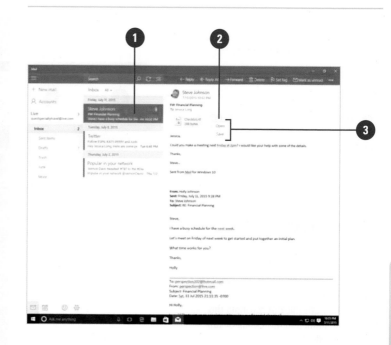

Managing Email

A common problem with using email is an overcrowded Inbox. To keep your Inbox organized, you can move the messages you want to the folders or delete messages you no longer want. Storing incoming messages in folders and deleting unwanted messages make it easier to see the new messages you receive and to keep track of important messages. If you frequently use a folder, you can make it a favorite so you can easily view them from the Folders pane. You can also do the same for folders, so you can access them more easily. For easy access, you can also pin a folder to the Start screen or menu. If you need to work with multiple messages, yo can use Selection Mode to easily select them.

Move Emails to a Folder

1. In the Mail app, click or tap a folder in the Folders pane. Click or tap the **More** link to access more folders.

2. Select the email messages that you want to move.

3. Click or tap the **More** button, and then click or tap **Move**.

   ◆ You can also drag the selected messages to a folder.

4. Click or tap the folder in the Folders pane where you want to move the email messages.

See Also

See "Removing Unwanted Email" on page 174 for more information on deleting, sweeping, or junking email messages.

Did You Know?

You can pint a folder to the Start screen or menu. In the Mail app, right-click or tap-hold the folder you want to pin, and then click or tap Pin to Start. To unpin it, right-click or tap-hold the the pinned item, and then click or tap Unpin from Start.

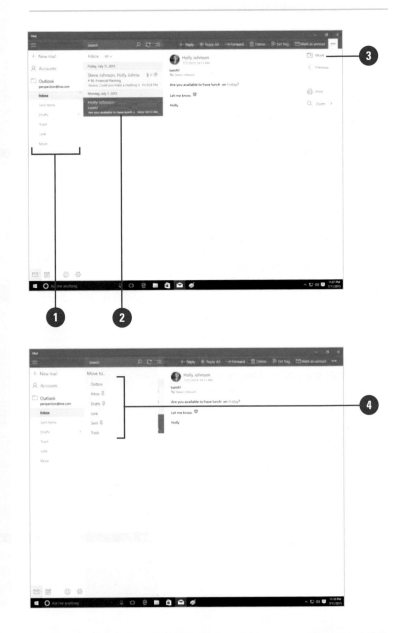

Make a Folder a Favorite

1. In the Mail app, click or tap the **More** link to access more folders.

2. Right-click or tap-hold the folder (one without a Pin) you want to make a favorite, and then click or tap **Add to Favorites**.

   The folder appears on the Folders pane where you can quickly access it.

3. To remove a favorite, right-click or tap-hold the favorite folder (one with a Pin) , and then click or tap **Remove from Favorites**.

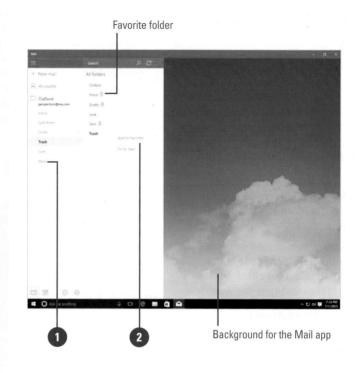

Favorite folder

Background for the Mail app

Work with Multiple Messages

1. In the Mail app, click or tap a folder in the Folders pane. Click or tap the **More** link to access more folders.

2. Click the **Selection Mode** button.

   Check boxes appear next to messages.

3. Select the check boxes next to the ones you want to change.

4. Click or tap any of the following buttons (some accessible from the **More** button):

   ◆ **Delete** or **Move**.

   ◆ **Set** or **Clear Flag**.

   ◆ **Mark** or **Unmark Message**.

Removing Unwanted Email

The Mail app provides three ways to remove unwanted email messages: Delete or Junk. When you delete an email message, the Mail app simply moves it into the Trash folder. If you want to recover a deleted message, you just have to retrieve it from the Trash folder. To get rid of a message permanently, you need to open the Trash folder, select the message, and then click Delete. If you receive junk mail, you can move it to the Junk folder, which marks it as junk. You can delete the junk messages just like you delete messages in the Trash folder.

Delete or Junk Unwanted Email

1. In the Mail app, click or tap a folder in the Folders pane. Click or tap the **More** link to access more folders.

2. To work with multiple messages, click the **Selection Mode** button, and then select the check boxes next to the messages you want.

3. Do any of the following:

   ◆ Delete. Click or tap the **Delete** button.

   TIMESAVER *Press Delete or Ctrl+D to delete the message(s).*

   ◆ Junk. Click or tap the **Move** button, and then click or tap the **Junk** folder.

   ◆ You can also drag the selected messages to a folder.

4. Click or tap **Trash** or **Junk** folder on the All Folders pane.

5. Do any of the following to permanently delete messages:

   ◆ Delete Selected. Select the email messages, and then click or tap the **Delete** button.

Searching for Email

If you can't find a message, you can use the Search box in the Mail app to quickly find it. You can access the Search box by clicking or tapping the Search button at the top of the Messages pane. You can search a specific folder or all folders. When you perform an email search, the results appear in the Messages pane. If you searched a specific folder and want to search all the folders, you can easily use the Search in all folders link. When you're finished working with the search results, you can click or tap the Close button (x) in the Search box to cancel the search.

Search for Email

1. In the Mail app, navigate to the folder you want to search. If you want to search all folders, you can use the Inbox.

2. Click or tap the **Search** button in the Messages pane.

3. Type the text you want to search for in the Search box.

4. Click or tap the **Search** button or press Enter.

   The results for the search appears in the Messages pane.

5. Click or tap the **All folders** list arrow, and then click or tap **Search folder name** or **Search all folders**.

6. To cancel the search, click or tap the **Close** button (x) in the Search box.

Setting Mail Options

The Mail app provides a Settings panel with options you can customize the way the app works. In the Settings panel, you can work with accounts, change the background picture, and specify options for reading messages. In addition app specific options, you can set account specific options, such as custom quick actions when you swipe or hover, use an email signature, send automatic replies, and show notifications as a banner or play a sound.

Set Options in Mail

1. Click or tap the **Mail** tile on the Start screen or Start menu.

2. Click or tap the **Settings** button.

3. Click or tap **Options** on the Settings panel, select an account, and then select the options you want.

   - **Quick Actions.** Select the options you want when you swipe (left/right) or hover.

   - **Signature.** Drag to turn the option on (and enter a message) or off.

   - **Automatic Replies.** Drag to turn the option on (and enter a message) or off.

   - **Notifications.** Drag to turn the option on (select options to show notifications)or off.

4. Click or tap **Reading** on the Settings panel, and then select the options you want.

   - **Auto-open next item.** Drag to turn the option on or off.

   - **Mark item as read.** Click or tap an option when to mark items.

   - **Caret Browsing.** Drag to turn the caret to navigate the reading pane on or off.

5. Click or tap **Background** on the Settings panel, and then click or tap **Browse** to select a graphic.

6. To go back to the previous panel, click or tap the **Back** button.

   To exit the panel, click or tap off the panel, or press Esc.

6

< Options

Outlook

Quick Actions
Your most frequently used actions are just a swipe away.

Swipe actions
On

Swipe right / hover
Set flag/Clear flag

Swipe left / hover
Delete

Signature

Use an email signature
On

Sent from Mail for Windows 10

Automatic Replies

Send Automatic Replies
On

✓ Send replies only to my contacts

Notifications

Show in action center
On

Show a notification banner

Play a sound

3

< Reading

Auto-open next item
Off

Mark item as read
● When selection changes

Don't automatically mark item as read

When viewed in the reading pane

Seconds to wait:

Caret Browsing

Use the caret to navigate the reading pane.
Off

4

< Background Picture

Select a background picture.

Browse...

5

Exchanging Calls and Instant Messages

7

Introduction

Windows makes communicating with others over the Internet easier than ever with the Skype app. You can talk to others over the Internet (like you do on a telephone) and exchange instant messages. An instant message is an online typewritten conversation in real time between two or more contacts. Unlike an email message, instant messages require both parties to be online (like a phone call), and the communication is instantaneous. With the Skype app, you can send instant messages to any of your contacts from the People app or Skype who are online and have conversations with friends.

Using the Skype app with an Internet connection allows you to accomplish several tasks:

- ◆ Manage messaging accounts
- ◆ Make audio and video phone calls
- ◆ Use contacts to address instant messages
- ◆ Create and send instant messages
- ◆ Add emoticons to instant messages
- ◆ Invite others to instant messages
- ◆ Send files in instant messages

Before you can use Skype, you need to get it first (download and install). You can quickly download it with the Get Skype app (**New!**) available on the Start screen or Start menu. You can download Skype for Windows desktop, Skype for Mobile, Skype for Tablet, or Skype for Xbox One. This chapter describes how to use Skype for Windows desktop (version 7.7).

Starting the Skype App

Whether you want to exchange calls (audio and video) or instant messages with colleagues and friends, the Skype app that comes with Windows 10 provides you with the tools you need. Before you can use Skype, you need to get it (download and install) for your device first. You can start the Get Skype app (**New!**) from the Start screen or Start menu to do it. If you have not signed in to Skype, you'll be prompted to enter an existing Skype account or specify your Microsoft account as a new user. During the process, an existing Skype account gets merged with your Microsoft account, which is what you'll use in the future to sign in.

Start the Skype App and Sign In or Out

1 In the Start screen or Start menu, click or tap **All apps**, and then click or tap **Skype for desktop** under Skype.

   ◆ Download Skype. Click or tap the **Get Skype** tile on the Start screen or Start menu to download the Skype app for your device, and then follow the online instructions.

2 If you're not signed into Skype, click or tap **Skype name**, **Microsoft account**, or **Create an account**, and then follow the on-screen instructions to enter a username and password to complete the process to sign and merge accounts.

3 On first use, follow the on-screen instructions to set up sound, video, and profile picture. Upon completion, click or tap **Start using Skype**.

   The Skype app window opens and a shortcut icon appears on the desktop.

4 To sign out, click or tap the **Skype menu**, and then click or tap **Sign out**.

5 To quit Skype, right-click or tap-hold the **Skype** icon on the taskbar, and then click or tap **Quit Skype**. If prompted, click or tap **Quit**.

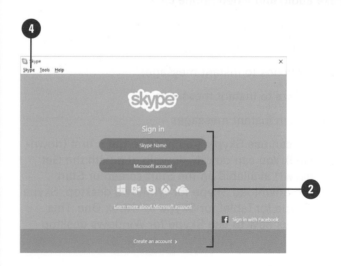

Start menu

1 Get Skype app

4

2

Viewing the Skype App Window

Status
Displays status for the signed in user.

Home
Displays the Skype Home page with quick access content.

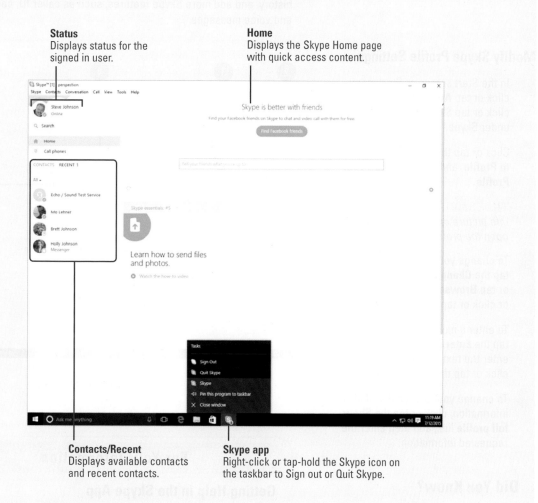

Contacts/Recent
Displays available contacts and recent contacts.

Skype app
Right-click or tap-hold the Skype icon on the taskbar to Sign out or Quit Skype.

Modifying Skype Profile Settings

With the Skype app, you want to change Skype profile options and online account settings. You can change profile options by using the Profile panel, which you can access from the Settings panel. In a Profile panel, you can change your Skype picture, enter a mood message, change your profile information and access your account settings online with your web browser. With your online account, you can change personal and contact details, link and unlink accounts (such as Microsoft or Facebook), set notifications, change billing & payments, view usage history, and add more Skype features, such as caller ID, call forwarding, and voice messages.

Modify Skype Profile Settings

1. In the Start screen or Start menu, click or tap **All apps**, and then click or tap **Skype for desktop** under Skype.

2. Click or tap the **Skype** menu, point to **Profile**, and then click **Edit Your Profile**.

   TIMESAVER *Click the Status info picture on the Home screen to open the profile.*

3. To change your picture, click or tap the **Change picture** link, click or tap **Browse** to select a picture or click or tap **Take a picture**.

4. To enter a mood message, click or tap the **Enter mode message** link, enter the text in the box, and then click or tap the **Apply** button.

5. To change your personal profile information, click or tap the **Show full profile** link, and then enter the requested information.

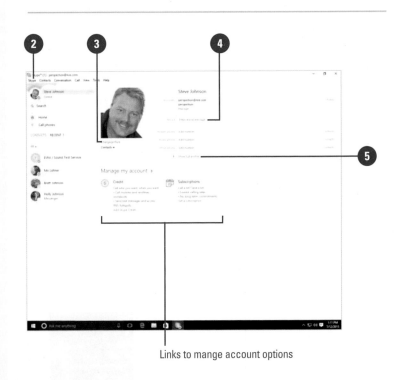

Links to mange account options

For Your Information

Getting Help in the Skype App

Sometimes setting up Skype can be a challenge depending on accounts and connections. If so, you can help more help in Skype. In the Skype app, click or tap the Help menu, and then select a command to learn about Skype and get help, support, or tips from the Skype Community.

Modify Skype Account Settings

1. In the Start screen or Start menu, click or tap **All apps**, and then click or tap **Skype for desktop** under Skype.

2. Click or tap the **Skype** menu, and then click **My account**.

   Your default web browser opens, displaying your Skype account.

3. Click or tap any of the following links or tiles:

   ◆ **Caller ID.** Set up for caller ID.

   ◆ **Skype Number.** Get a Skype number to use from mobile or landline phones.

   ◆ **Skype To Go.** Call from mobile or landline numbers.

   ◆ **Voice messages.** Activate voice messages.

   ◆ **Call forwarding.** Use call forwarding for a low fee.

4. Scroll down, and then click or tap any of the following links or tiles:

   ◆ **Edit profile.** Enter personal information and contact details.

   ◆ **Change password.** Change account password to sign in.

   TIMESAVER *Click or tap the Skype menu, and then click or tap Change Password.*

   ◆ **Account settings.** Change account information and notification settings.

5. Click or tap the **Close** button to exit your browser.

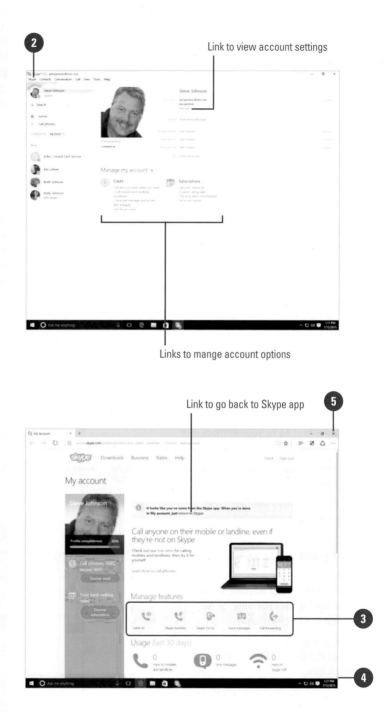

Link to view account settings

Links to mange account options

Link to go back to Skype app

Changing Skype Options

Before you get started with the Skype app it's a good idea to select options for settings audio and video hardware, use of WiFi, display of notifications, as well as making calls and sending instant messages while maintaining your privacy. You can use the Options dialog box in the Skype app to select the options you want. For audio, you can select an attached microphone and speakers and for video, you can select an attached camera.

Change Audio, Video, and WiFi Options

1 In the Start screen or Start menu, click or tap **All apps**, and then click or tap **Skype for desktop** under Skype.

2 Click or tap the **Tools** menu, and then click **Options**.

3 Click or tap **General**, and then specify the following options:

◆ Start. Specify settings to start Skype and show elements.

4 Click or tap **Audio settings**, and then specify the following options:

◆ Microphone. Select a specific one attached to your system.

◆ Speakers and Ringing. Select a specific one attached to your system.

5 Click or tap **Video settings**, and then specify the following options:

◆ Camera. Select a camera attached to your system.

◆ Receive video and screen sharing. Select **anyone**, **people in my Contact list only**, or **no one** to start sharing.

6 Click or tap **Skype WiFi**, and then select the **Enable Skype WiFi** check box.

7 To save option changes, click or tap the **Save** button.

Start and app options

Microphone and audio options

Change Notification, Privacy, Call, and IM & SMS Options

1. In the Start screen or Start menu, click or tap **All apps**, and then click or tap **Skype for desktop** under Skype.

2. Click or tap the **Tools** menu, and then click **Options**.

3. Click or tap **Notifications**, and then select settings to display notifications in the Windows tray.

4. Click or tap **Privacy**, and then specify the following options:

    ◆ Allow calls or IMs from. Select **anyone** or **people in my Contacts list only**.

    ◆ Automatically receive video and share screens with. Select **anyone, people in my Contacts list only**, or **no one**.

5. Click or tap **Calls**, and then specify the following options:

    ◆ Allow calls from. Select **anyone** or **only allow people in my Contacts list only**.

    ◆ Advanced. Click or tap **Show advanced options** to show call controls, and answer incoming calls automatically.

6. Click or tap **IM & SMS**, and then specify the following options:

    ◆ Allow calls from. Select **anyone** or **only allow people in my Contacts list only**.

7. Click or tap **IM appearance** (under IM & SMS), and then select settings to show or hide IM elements.

8. To save option changes, click or tap the **Save** button.

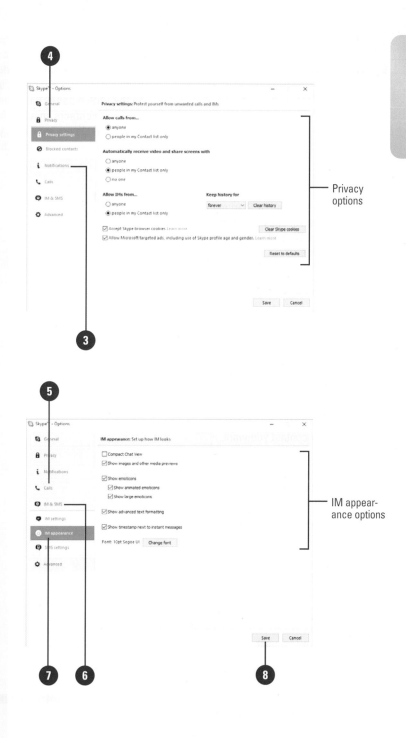

Privacy options

IM appearance options

Adding Skype Contacts

When you sign in to the Skype app with your Microsoft account, your Messenger buddies (the ones used with the Messaging app and Windows platforms) are added to your Skype contact list automatically. If you linked your Facebook account to Skype using the account option on the Profile panel, your contacts are added to your Skype contact list too. Your contacts show up in the People list on the Skype Home screen. If a contact is not available, you can search the Skype directory to find it. You can always enter a name and phone number to create a contact.

Add Skype Contacts

1 In the Start screen or Start menu, click or tap **All apps**, and then click or tap **Skype for desktop** under Skype.

2 Click or tap the Search box, and then enter the name or email address.

As you type, the search narrows down the search.

◆ You can also click or tap the **Contacts** menu, point to **Add Contact**, and then click or tap **Search Skype Directory**.

3 Select the contact you want to add.

◆ If you don't see the contact you want, click or tap **Search Skype** to find it in the Skype directory.

4 Click or tap the **Add to contacts** button.

5 Enter a send request message, and then click or tap **Send** to send a request to the contact.

The contact is added to your contacts as offline until the person accepts your request.

6 To accept a contact request, go to the Home screen, select the contact request under Recent on the Home screen, and then click or tap **Accept**.

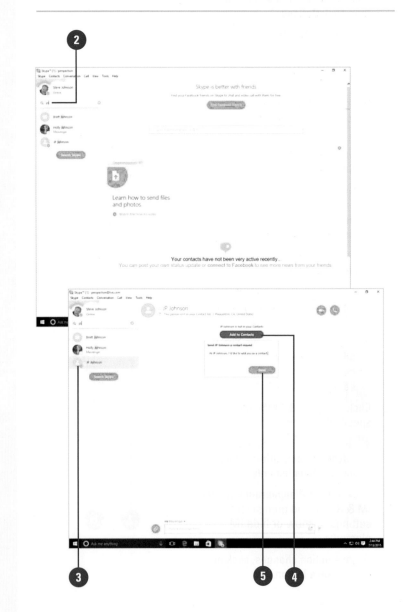

Add a Mobile or Landline Contact

1. In the Start screen or Start menu, click or tap **All apps**, and then click or tap **Skype for desktop** under Skype.

2. Click or tap the **Contacts** menu, point to **Add Contact**, and then click or tap **Save a Phone Number**.

3. Enter your contact's name.

4. To change the country code, click or tap the **Code** list arrow, and then select a country code.

5. Enter the number (without the country code).

6. Click or tap the **Type** list arrow, and then select a type: **Mobile**, **Home**, **Office**, or **Other**.

7. Click or tap **Add number**.

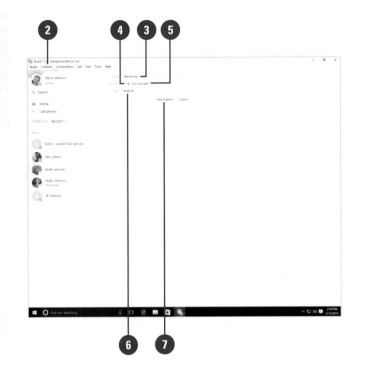

Did You Know?

You can search for contacts. In the Skype for desktop app (Home screen), click or tap the Search box, type the contact name to display a list of matches. If you don't see the contact you want, click or tap Search Skype to find it.

You can remove a contact. In the Skype for desktop app, select the contact, click or tap the Contacts menu, click or tap Remove from Contacts, and then click or tap Remove to confirm it.

You can backup contacts. In the Skype for desktop app, click or tap the Contact menu, point to Advanced, click or tap Backup Contacts to File, specify a name and location, and then click or tap Save.

For Your Information

Creating and Filtering Contact Lists

When you have a lot of contacts, it can be hard to find them. To create a contact list, click or tap the Contacts menu, point to Contact Lists, click or tap Create New List, enter a name, and then press Enter. To add a contact to a list, right-click or tap-hold the contact, point to Add to List, and then select a list. To filter contacts, click or tap the Contacts menu, point to Contact Lists, and then select a contact list or messaging type to filter by: All, Skype, Online, or Messenger. You can also click the list arrow (above the contacts) to select a filter.

Making Phone Calls

In the Skype app, you can quickly make calls to available Skype contacts or use the dial pad to manually make them. A contact is available if a green circle icon status indicator appears next to their name. You can make an audio or video call to a Skype contact, mobile phone or landline phone. When you call a mobile or landline phone, there is a low rate fee, which you can pay for with Skype Credit or a subscription. As you make a call, you can also select options to start an instant message, open the dial pad, add participants, or send files.

Make a Call with the Dial Pad

1. In the Start screen or Start menu, click or tap **All apps**, and then click or tap **Skype for desktop** under Skype.

2. Click or tap the **Call phones** button on the Skype Home screen.

   TIMESAVER *To redial a recent call, click or tap the call button under recent calls on the Home or Dial Pad screen.*

3. To change the country code, click or tap the **Code** list arrow, and then select a country code.

4. Click or tap the dial pad number to dial the phone number.

5. Click or tap the **Call** button.

   Skype dials the call to the contact; wait for the receiver to accept or decline the call.

6. Use any of the following options:

   ◆ **Webcam.** Turns it on and off.

   ◆ **Microphone.** Turns it on and off.

   ◆ **Options.** Show options to start an instant message, open the dial pad, add participants, or send files.

7. To end the call, click the **End call** button.

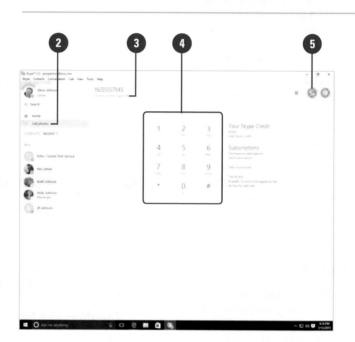

For Your Information

Changing My Status

When you sign in with the Skype for desktop app, the program notifies your contacts that you are available to call or chat. In the Skype window, your status appears in the upper-left corner along with your picture. A green circle (Status) icon also appears to the left of your status to indicate your available status. While you're signed in, you might need to leave for a meeting or lunch. Instead of closing the Skype app, you can change your online status to let your contacts know that you're not available at the moment. To change your status, click or tap the Status icon next to your picture, and then click or tap Online, Aways, Do Not Disturb, Invisible or Offline.

Make Audio or Video Calls to Contacts

1. In the Start screen or Start menu, click or tap **All apps**, and then click or tap **Skype for desktop** under Skype.

2. Click or tap an available contact (one with a green icon) under Contacts.

3. Click or tap the **Call** (audio) or **Video** button in the window, and then click or tap any of the following on the menu:

   ◆ **Call Skype.** Use to call a contact with Skype.

   ◆ **Mobile.** Select the mobile number to call the phone (requires a fee).

   ◆ **Landline.** Select the landline number to call the phone (requires a fee).

   Skype dials the call to the contact; wait for the receiver to accept or decline the call.

4. Use any of the following options:

   ◆ **Webcam.** Turns it on and off.

   ◆ **Microphone.** Turns it on and off.

   ◆ **Options.** Show options to start an instant message, open the dial pad, add participants, or send files.

5. To end the call, click the **End call** button.

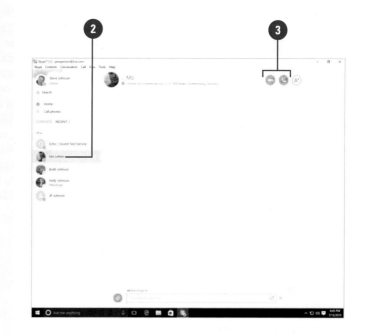

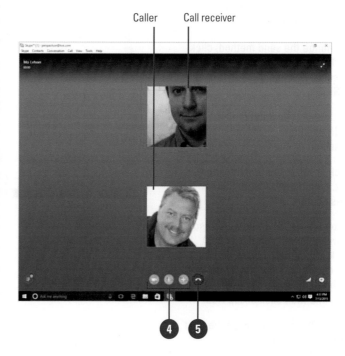

Caller   Call receiver

Sending and Receiving Instant Messages

An instant message is an online typewritten conversation in real-time between contacts. You can select contacts directly from the Skype Home screen. As you type an instant message, you can format your messages by adding graphical symbols called **emoticons**, such as a happy face, which help convey your emotions. In addition to text and symbols, you can also send one or more files in a message. When you send a message, Skype uses an instant messaging service, such as Messenger, Skype, or SMS (Short Message Service—a standard for mobile and landline phones, which requires a fee with Skype Credit or a subscription). You cannot send an instant message to more than one person with the Messenger service, however you can with the Skype service using the Add people button (+) in the contact. This is also the case for sending files and video messages.

Start a New Instant Message

1. In the Start screen or Start menu, click or tap **All apps**, and then click or tap **Skype for desktop** under Skype.

2. Click or tap an available contact (one with a green icon) under people or favorites.

3. To change the send method, click the **Method** list arrow, and then select **Messenger**, **Skype** (default) or **SMS**.

   ◆ **Default.** The default method (Messenger or Skype) changes based on the type of contact.

4. Click or tap in the Conversation box, type a message, and then press Enter.

5. If you want to add another person to the conversation (for Skype), click or tap the **Add people** button (+), click or tap the check box next to the participants you want to add, and then click or tap **Add**.

6. Follow the instructions on the next page for send and receiving instant messages.

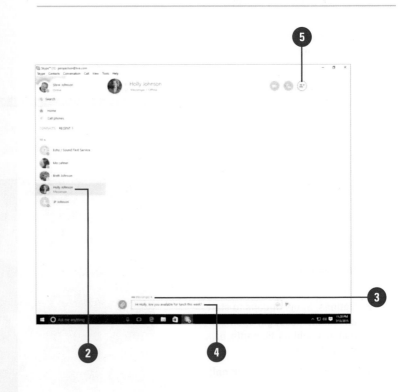

Send and Receive Instant Messages

1 In a conversation for a contact in the Skype app, click or tap the conversation thread that you want to use.

◆ **Open existing conversation.** Click or tap the contact with the instant message.

◆ **Another conversation.** If you receive a message or call from someone else, an orange dot icon with the number of unread messages appears, which you can click or tap to view it.

2 Click or tap in the box at the bottom of the screen.

3 Type your message. When you get to the end of the first line, keep typing. The text will automatically wrap to the next line.

To start a new line while typing, press Shift+Enter.

4 Press Enter, and then wait for a reply.

5 If you want to add an emoticon, click or tap the **Emoticon** button, and then click or tap an icon.

6 To send one or more files, click the **Add** button (+) click or tap **Send file**, select the files you want, and then click or tap **Open**.

◆ The instant messaging service needs to be Skype to send files.

7 To exit a conversation, change your status to invisible or click or tap the **Close** button (x) to close the Skype app.

Instant message conversation

Working with Contacts

As you make phone call or send and receive instant messages in the Skype app to more and more people, you many need to filter down the contact list to a more manageable size, remove contacts you no longer use or block contacts you don't want. If you like a contact, you can make it a favorite for easy access on the Skype Home screen. You can manage a contact by opening it and using options.

Work with Contacts

1. In the Start screen or Start menu, click or tap **All apps**, and then click or tap **Skype for desktop** under Skype.

2. To filter down contacts, click or tap the **Contact List** list arrow, and then click or tap **All**, **Skype**, **Online**, or **Messenger**.

    ◆ Create list. Click or tap the **Contacts** menu, point to **Contact Lists**, and then click or tap **Create New List**.

3. Click or tap the contact you want to manage.

4. To make a contact a favorite, click or tap the **Add to favorites** button (star) next to the contact name. To remove the favorite, click or tap the star again.

5. Click or tap the **Conversation** menu, and then click or tap any of the following:

    ◆ **Add to Favorites** or **Remove from Favorites**. Adds or removes the contact to your favorites on the Home screen.

    ◆ **Block**. Select or clear options to remove from your Contact list or report abuse, and then click or tap **Block**.

6. To remove the contact, click or tap the **Contacts** menu, click or tap **Remove from Contacts**, and then click or tap **Remove** to confirm it.

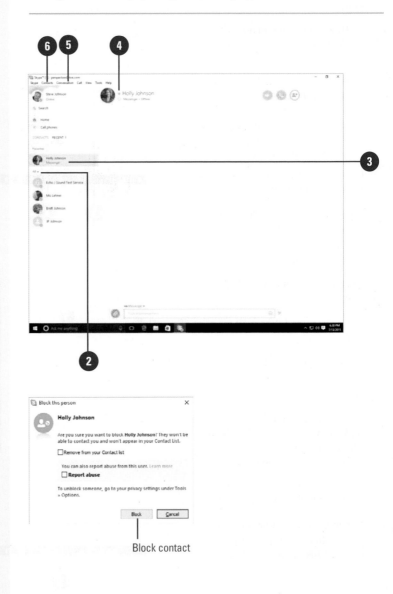

Block contact

Working with Photos and Pictures

8

Introduction

Windows 10 comes with two main ways to work with photos and pictures. One is with the Photos app, available on the Start screen or Start menu, and the other is with the Pictures folder in File Explorer, available on the desktop.

With the Photos app, you can display photos and pictures stored in the Pictures library, OneDrive, and any attached devices, such as a camera. The Pictures library is stored locally on your device; you can manage photos and pictures in the Pictures library from File Explorer in the desktop. The OneDrive is a cloud-based storage device where you can share photos and other documents; you can access and manage files on the OneDrive from the OneDrive app.

With the Pictures folder, you can view, organize, and share pictures with others. When you download and save pictures from your digital camera or scanner, Windows stores the digital images in the Pictures folder by default, however, you can specify an alternative location. You can view your picture files as a slide show or in the Extra-Large view, which displays a larger image above thumbnail images of the pictures. The Pictures folder also contains links to specialized picture tasks that help you share pictures with others, such as sending pictures in an email. You can also create your own pictures or edit existing ones in Paint, a Windows accessory program designed for drawing and painting. Paint is useful for making simple changes to a picture, adding a text caption, or saving a picture in another file format.

What You'll Do

Start and View the Photos App

Navigate in the Photos App

Import Photos

Delete Photos

Edit Photos

Set a Photo as a Lock or Background Screen

Set Photos App Options

Draw or Edit a Picture

View Pictures

Format and Print Photos

Share Pictures

Email Pictures

Install a Scanner or Digital Camera

Download Digital Camera Pictures

Use Pictures as a Screen Saver

Use a Picture as a Background

Understand Picture File Formats

Starting and Viewing the Photos App

The Photos app that comes with Windows 10 is a centralized place (**New!**) to view all your photos, pictures, and videos. You can display photos and pictures stored in the Pictures library, OneDrive, and any attached devices, such as a camera. The Pictures library is stored locally on your device; you can manage photos and pictures in the Pictures library from File Explorer. OneDrive is a cloud-based storage device where you can share photos and other documents; you can access and manage files on the OneDrive from the OneDrive app. Like other Windows apps, you can start the Photos app from the Start screen or Start menu. After you start the app, you can change the view to display details (name, modify date, and size) or thumbnails with previews.

Start the Photos App

1. Click or tap the **Photos** tile on the Start screen or Start menu.

   The Photos app window opens.

2. To change the photo display (**New!**), click or tap **Collection** or **Albums**.

3. To show photos and videos from OneDrive, click or tap **Sign In**.

   The Photo apps uses the current sign in to access OneDrive. The Sign In command changes to the User Account name.

   When you click the User Account name, a dialog box opens, displaying the Microsoft account.

Did You Know?

You can specify the sources for photos. In the Photos app, click or tap the Settings button, click or tap the Add a folder, select the folder you want, and then click Add This Folder To Pictures.

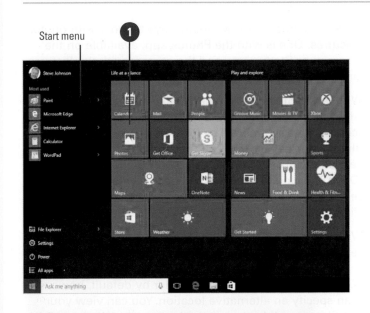

Start menu

Navigating in the Photos App

The Photos app allows you to view photos from your Pictures library, OneDrive, or Devices in a central location in a full screen view. When you start the Photos app, you can select the stored location of the photos in a Collection (**New!**) or Albums (**New!**)—a series of related photos in your Pictures folder—you want to view. You can navigate in the Photos app by simply clicking or tapping a photo to display it. Within a a collection or album, you can scroll left or right or zoom in or out. When you display a photo, you can use the Back or Forward arrow or a swipe left or right to quickly display each photo in the folder. To move back to the previous screen, you can use the Back button.

Navigate in the Photos App

1. Click or tap the **Photos** tile on the Start screen or Start menu.

2. Click or tap **Collection** (**New!**) or **Albums** (**New!**).

   The photos in the Collection or Albums appear for display.

3. Move the pointer to display the scroll bar, and then click or tap the **Scroll** arrows or bar, or swipe left or right.

4. To find photos by date, click or tap any date (**New!**), and then click or tap the date you want.

5. Click or tap a photo to display it.

6. To navigate through photos, move the pointer, and then click or tap the **Back** or **Forward** arrows, or swipe right or left.

7. To zoom, move the pointer to display the button, and then click or tap the **Zoom in** or **Zoom out** buttons or pinch in or out to gesture zoom.

8. To go back to previous screen, click or tap the screen, if needed to display the button, and then click or tap the **Back** button.

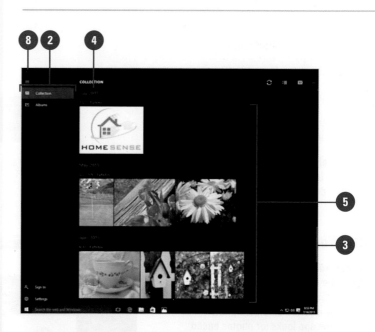

Importing Photos

When you connect a digital camera or other device with digital images, you can import them into a folder using the Photos app. After you connect the device and start the Photos app, you can use the Import button to import the photos from the connected device. The photos appear based on the creation date of the photos.

Import Photos

1. Connect your device with the photos to your PC computer or mobile device, and then turn it on.

2. Click or tap the **Photos** tile on the Start screen or Start menu.

3. Click or tap the **Import** button.

4. Click or tap **Import**.

5. Look for the import done notification.

   The selected photos are imported into a folder with today's date in the Pictures folder.

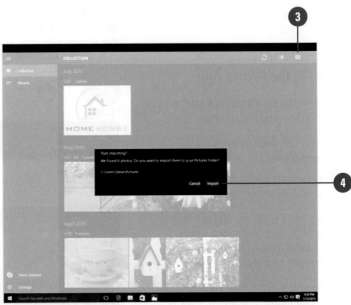

Did You Know?

You can add an album to the Photos app. In the File Explorer, open the Pictures folder, create a folder, and then copy a series of related photos (the Photos app looks for photos based on date) into the folder.

You can copy photos. In the Photos app, point to a photo, select the check box, select more photos, and then click or tap the Copy button. Now, you can paste the photos where you want.

You can share photos. In the Photos app, point to a photo, select the check box, select more photos, click or tap the Share button or press Win+H, click or tap the app you want to use for sharing, and then use the selected app to share the photos.

Deleting Photos

If you no longer need some photos, you can use the Photos app to delete them. It's quick and easy to do. Simply, navigate to the folder location where the photos are stored, select the ones that you want to delete with the Selection option, and then click or tap the Delete button. After a confirmation, the photo files are permanently removed from their location.

Delete Photos

1 Click or tap the **Photos** tile on the Start screen or Start menu.

2 Click or tap **Collection** or **Albums**.

The photos in the Collection or Albums appear for display.

3 Click or tap to navigate to where you want to delete photos.

◆ Move the pointer to display the scroll bar, and then click or tap the **Scroll** arrows or bar, or swipe left or right.

4 Click or tap the **Select** button.

5 Click or tap each photo you want to delete to select it.

A check mark appears in the selected photo.

To select the entire group, click or tap the **Select** link.

6 To clear an individual selection, click or tap the selected photo.

To clear the entire selection, click or tap the **Clear** link (appears when a collection is selected).

7 Click or tap the **Delete** button.

8 Click or tap **Delete** to confirm the deletion.

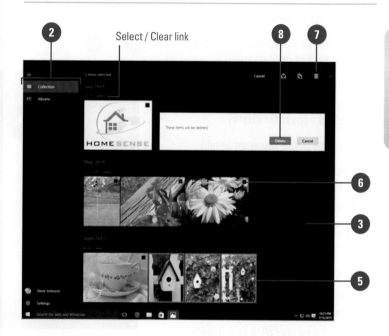

Select / Clear link

For Your Information

Using Windows Live Photo Gallery

Windows Live Photo Gallery allows you to view, locate, organize, open, and edit photos and pictures. Windows Live Photo Gallery shows all the pictures and videos located in the Pictures folder. In Windows Live Photo Gallery, you can also print photos, order photos through an online service, email photos and pictures using your email program, create CDs or DVDs, and make a movie using Windows Live Movie Maker. Windows Live Photo Gallery and Windows Live Movie Maker don't come installed with Windows 10; they are available for free online from Microsoft. You can download the programs from Windows Live at *http://download.live.com*.

Editing Photos

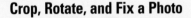

In addition to viewing photos, you can also use the Photos app to edit and enhance a photo. You can use photo related options to automatically fix images or apply basic fixes like rotate, crop, remove red eye, or retouch. If you have an eye for editing photos, you can also apply brightness, contrast, highlights, shadows, temperature, tint, saturation, color enhance, vignette or selective focus.

Crop, Rotate, and Fix a Photo

1 Click or tap the **Photos** tile on the Start screen or Start menu.

2 Click or tap **Collection** or **Albums**.

The photos in the Collection or Albums appear for display.

3 Click the photo you want to edit.

4 Click or tap the **Edit** button or press Ctrl+E.

5 Click or tap the **Crop** button.

6 Drag the corner point to the area you want to crop.

7 Click or tap the **Apply** button.

8 Click or tap the **Save a copy** or **Save** button.

◆ You can also click or tap the **Undo** button, and then click or tap **Cancel** to cancel it.

9 To rotate the photo, click or tap the **Rotate** button.

10 To further fix the photo, click or tap the **Enhance**, **Straighten**, **Red Eye**, or **Retouch** button.

11 To go back to previous screen, click or tap the screen, if needed to display the button, and then click or tap the **Back** button.

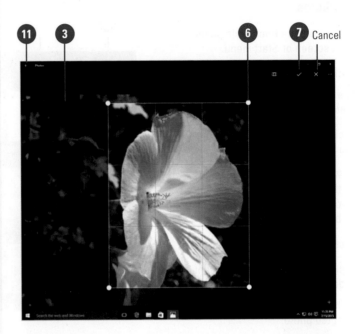

Edit and Enhance a Photo

1. Click or tap the **Photos** tile on the Start screen or Start menu.

2. Click or tap **Collection** (**New!**) or **Albums** (**New!**).

   The photos in the Collection or Albums appear for display.

3. Click the photo you want to edit.

4. Click or tap the **Edit** button or press Ctrl+E.

5. Click or tap the editing options on the left pane.

   ◆ **Basic fixes.** Use buttons to rotate, crop, remove red eye, or retouch.

   ◆ **Filters.** Use buttons to apply a filter (thumbnail).

   ◆ **Light.** Use buttons to apply brightness, contrast, highlights, and shadows.

   ◆ **Color.** Use button to apply temperature, tint, saturation, or color enhance.

   ◆ **Effects.** Use buttons to apply a vignette or selective focus.

6. Click or tap the available editing options for the selected editing option.

7. Click or tap the **Save a copy** or **Save** button.

   ◆ You can also click or tap the **Undo** button, and then click or tap **Cancel** to cancel it.

8. To go back to previous screen, click or tap the screen, if needed to display the button, and then click or tap the **Back** button.

Setting a Photo as the Lock or Background Screen

Instead of using one of the photos provided by Windows, you can select a photo in the Photos app as the lock screen or background screen for the Start screen and desktop. The lock screen is the security screen that appears when you start Windows 10 or return to Windows 10 after signing out or going to sleep. So, the Lock screen option allows you to change the lock screen to a photo of your choice. The Background screen option allows you to customized the background on the Start screen and desktop.

Set a Photo as the Lock or Background Screen

1. Click or tap the **Photos** tile on the Start screen or Start menu.

2. Click or tap **Collection** or **Albums**.

   The photos in the Collection or Albums appear for display.

3. Click or tap the photo you want to set as the lock or background screen.

4. Click or tap the **More** button.

5. Click or tap one of the following options on the menu:

   ◆ **Set as lock screen.** Changes the photo of the lock screen.

   ◆ **Set as background.** Changes the photo of the background of the Start screen and desktop (**New!**).

6. To go back to previous screen, click or tap the screen, if needed to display the button, and then click or tap the **Back** button.

For Your Information

Displaying a Slide Show

Instead of manually navigating through a set of photos in a folder, you can also display the photos as a slide show in the Photos app. That way, you don't need to manually scroll through each photo. The Photos app displays the photos for you every 3 to 4 seconds. The Photos apps uses the open folder for the contents of the slide show. However, you can start the slide show from any photo in the folder. The slide show continue to run until you stop it with a click or tap or press Esc. In the Photo app, click or tap the photo you want to use as the start image, click or tap the Slide Show button. To stop the show, click or tap the screen or press Esc.

Setting Photo App Options

The Photo app shows you photos from different folder sources, such as those on your device, network, or OneDrive. You can specify these folders as well as turn OneDrive on and off in Settings (**New!**). Along with these options, you can also set options to view photos, show exact duplicates as a single file, and automatically enhance photos.

Set Photo App Options

① Click or tap the **Photos** tile on the Start screen or Start menu.

② Click or tap **Settings** (**New!**).

③ Click or tap any of the following options (**New!**):

◆ **Automatically enhance my photos.** Drag to turn on auto enhancements shown only in the Photos app.

◆ **Linked duplicates.** Drag to turn on (exact duplicates shown as a single file).

◆ **Tile.** Select **Recent photos** or **A single photo** to specify what to show on the Photos file.

◆ **Sources.** Use to add or remove a folder to show in the Photos app.

◆ **Add folder.** Click or tap **Add a folder**, select a folder, and then click or tap **Add this folder to Pictures**.

◆ **Remove folder.** Click or tap the **Remove** button (x).

◆ **Show my photos and videos from OneDrive.** Drag to turn on the display of photos and videos stored from your OneDrive.

④ To go back to previous screen, click or tap the screen, if needed to display the button, and then click or tap the **Back** button.

Drawing a Picture

Paint is a Windows accessory you can use to create and work with graphics or pictures. Paint is designed to create and edit bitmap (.bmp or .dib) files, but you can also open and save pictures created in or for other graphics programs and the Internet using several common file formats, such as .jpeg, .gif, .tiff, or .png. A **bitmap** file is a map of a picture created from small black, white, or colored dots, or bits. When you start Paint, a blank canvas appears in the work area, along with a File menu and Ribbon at the top. The Ribbon with two tabs—Home and View—allows you to quickly select document related commands. Paint comes with a File menu with file related commands and a set of tools on the Ribbon that you can use for drawing and manipulating pictures. A tool remains turned on until you select another tool. In addition to the drawing tools, you can also add text to a picture. When you create a text box and type the text, you can edit and format it, but once you deselect the text box, the text becomes part of the picture, which you can't edit.

Draw a Picture

1. In the Start screen or Start menu, click or tap **All apps**, and then click or tap **Paint**.

2. If you want, drag a resize handle on the canvas to resize it.

3. Click or tap a drawing tool.

   ◆ If available, use the **Outline**, **Fill**, and **Size** buttons for the selected tool.

4. Click or tap **Color 1** to select the foreground color or click or tap **Color 2** to select the background color.

5. Drag the shapes you want by holding down one of the following:

   ◆ The left mouse button to draw with the foreground color.

   ◆ The right mouse button to draw with the background color.

   ◆ The Shift key to constrain the drawing to a proportional size, such as a circle or square.

6. Click or tap the **File** menu, and then click or tap **Exit**.

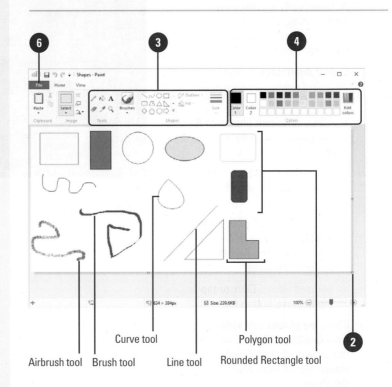

Airbrush tool Brush tool   Curve tool   Line tool   Polygon tool   Rounded Rectangle tool

Add Text to a Picture

1. In Paint, create or open the picture you want to modify.

2. Click or tap the **Text** tool on the Home tab.

3. Drag a text box.

4. Using the **Text** tab, select the font, font size, and any formatting you want to apply to the text.

5. Click or tap in the text box, if necessary, and then type the text.

6. Drag a text box resize handle to enlarge or reduce the text box.

7. Edit and format the text.

8. Click or tap outside the text box to deselect it and change the text to a bitmap.

> **IMPORTANT** *Once you click or tap outside the text box to place the text in the picture, the text becomes part of the picture.*

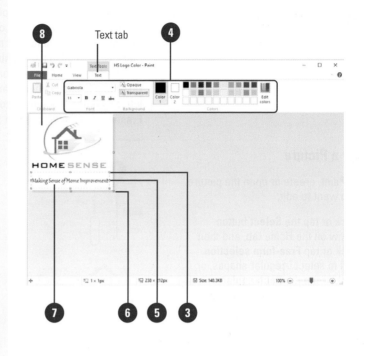

Save a Picture in Different Formats

1. In Paint, create or open the picture you want to save.

2. Click or tap the **File** tap, and then click or tap **Save as**. You can also point to Save as, and then select a format (PNG, JPEG, BMP, or GIF).

3. Select the drive and folder in which you want to save the file.

4. Type a name for the file, or use the suggested name.

5. Click or tap the **Save as type** list arrow, and then click or tap a file format.

6. Click or tap **Save**.

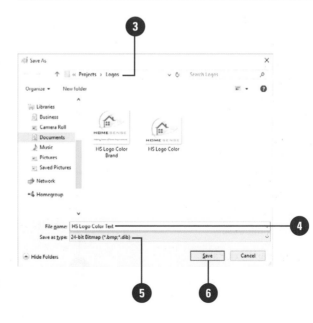

Editing a Picture

After you create or open a picture, you can select all or part of the picture and use commands on the Image menu, such as rotate, stretch, and invert colors, to further modify it in Paint. In addition to the drawing tools, you can also use painting tools, such as Fill With Color, Airbrush, Brush, Pencil, and Pick Color, to transform the picture. The Fill With Color tool is useful if you want to color an entire item or recolor text letter by letter. If you need to remove part of a picture, you can use the Eraser tool, which comes in four different sizes.

Modify a Picture

1. In Paint, create or open the picture you want to edit.

2. Click or tap the **Select** button arrow on the Home tab, and then click or tap **Free-form selection** tool to select irregular shapes, or click or tap the **Rectangular section** tool to select rectangle shapes.

3. Drag the selection area you want.

4. Click or tap the **Select** button arrow, and then click or tap **Transparent selection** to select it to use a transparent background or deselect it to use an opaque background.

   ◆ Copy selection. Hold down the Ctrl key, and then drag the selection.

5. In the Image area of the Home tab, click or tap any of the following buttons:

   ◆ **Rotate or flip.**

   ◆ **Resize and skew.**

   ◆ **Crop.**

   ◆ Invert colors. Right-click or tap-hold the selection, and then click or tap **Invert color**.

6. Click or tap **OK**, if necessary.

7. Save the picture and exit Paint.

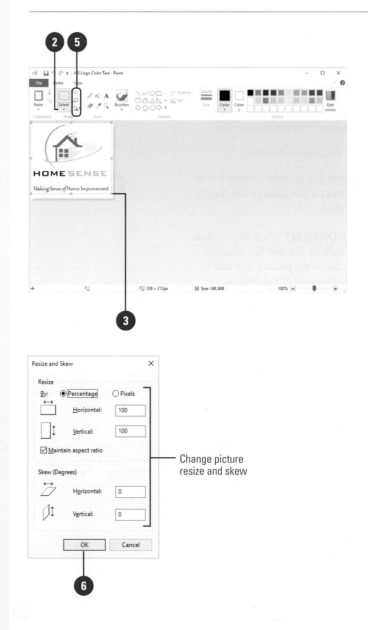

Change picture resize and skew

Fill Part of a Picture

① In Paint, create or open the picture you want to edit.

② Click or tap the color you want to fill, or click or tap the **Color picker** tool and click or tap a color from the picture.

③ Click or tap the **Fill with color** tool.

④ Point the tip of the paint bucket to the area you want to fill, and then click or tap.

Erase Part of a Picture

① In Paint, create or open the picture you want to edit.

② To magnify an area of the screen, click or tap the **Magnifier** tool, and then click or tap the area you want to magnify.

◆ You can also drag the **Zoom** slider to change the view size.

③ Click or tap the **Eraser** tool.

④ Drag the Eraser over the area you want to erase.

⑤ If you make a mistake, click or tap the **Undo** button on the Quick Access toolbar (on title bar) to restore your last action.

⑥ To restore the magnification, click or tap the **Zoom (-)** or **Zoom (+)** buttons.

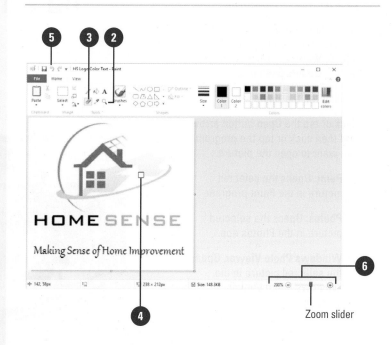

Zoom slider

Viewing Pictures

Windows gives you several ways to view pictures. In a folder with pictures, you can use Extra Large Icons view to see a larger view of the pictures. In the Pictures folder, you can use the slide show feature to display pictures in a full screen slide show. If you want to preview pictures or open a picture to edit, you can double-click or double-tap the file icon to use the default program associated with the picture file type, or select the specific program—such as Paint, Photos app, or Windows Photo Viewer—you want to use to make changes.

View a Picture

1 Click or tap the **File Explorer** icon on the taskbar.

2 Click or tap the **Pictures** folder in the Navigation pane in the Explorer window, and then navigate to the folder you want.

3 Click or tap the picture or photo you want to view.

TIMESAVER *Press Win+ PrtScn to take a screenshot and save it in the Pictures folder.*

4 To display details about the selected picture or photo, click or tap the **View** tab, and then click or tap the **Details pane** button.

5 Click or tap the **Home** tab.

6 Click or tap the **Open** button arrow, and then click or tap the program you want to open the picture.

- ◆ **Paint.** Opens the selected picture in the Paint program.

- ◆ **Photos.** Opens the selected picture in the Photos app.

- ◆ **Windows Photo Viewer.** Opens the selected picture in the Windows Photo Viewer program.

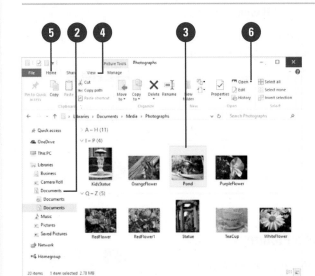

Preview in Windows Photo Viewer

View Pictures as Extra Large Icons

1. In File Explorer, click or tap **Pictures** in the Navigation pane, or open any other folder with pictures you want to view.

2. Click or tap the **View** tab.

3. Click or tap **Extra large icons**.

    ◆ To preview a view change, point to the view.

    ◆ If the pictures are too large, you can also use **Large icons** and **Medium icons** to display pictures.

View Pictures as a Slide Show

1. In File Explorer, click or tap **Pictures** in the Navigation pane, or open any other folder with pictures you want to view.

2. Select the pictures you want in the show, or click or tap one picture to see all the pictures.

3. Click or tap the **Manage** tab under Picture Tools.

4. Click or tap the **Slide show** button, and then watch the show.

5. To manually advance to the next slide, click or tap anywhere in the picture.

6. To control the slide show, right-click or tap the screen, and then click or tap the control you want, including **Shuffle**, **Loop**, or a **Slide Show Speed (Slow, Medium, or Fast)**.

7. To exit the slide show, press Esc or right-click or tap-hold the screen, and then click or tap **Exit**.

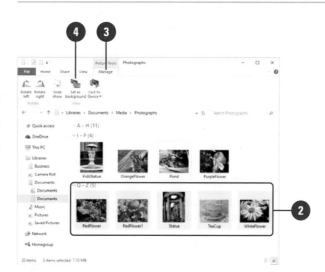

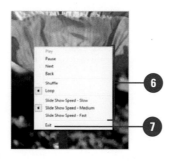

Formatting and Printing Photos

Windows makes it easy to format and print photographs from Windows Photo Viewer, which allows you to print photographs. During the process, you can select the photo(s) to print, the paper type, and a page layout, such as full-page prints, contact-sheet prints, 4 x 6-inch prints, 5 x 7-inch prints, 8 x 10-inch prints, 3.5 x 5-inch prints, and wallet size prints. To print a photo, you need a color printer and special photo paper. In order to get the best results when you print photographs, set your printer resolution to the highest setting for the best quality output, and use high-quality glossy paper designed specifically for printing photographs. Check your printer documentation for the best resolution setting suited to print your photographs. When you print photographs with a high resolution setting, the printing process might take longer. Many printer manufacturers also make paper designed to work best with their printers; check your printer manufacturer's web site for more information.

Format and Print a Photo

1. In File Explorer, click or tap **Pictures** in the Navigation pane, or open any other folder with pictures you want to use.

2. Select the photo you want to format and print.

3. Click or tap the **Print** button on the Share tab.

    ◆ You can also click or tap the **Open** button arrow on the Home tab, and then click or tap **Windows Photo Viewer**.

4. Click or tap the **Print** button on the toolbar, and then click or tap **Print**.

5. Specify the printer options (printer, paper size, quality resolution, or paper type) you want.

6. Specify a number of copies.

7. Select or clear the **Fit picture to frame** check box.

8. Click or tap **Print**, and then follow any printer specify instructions.

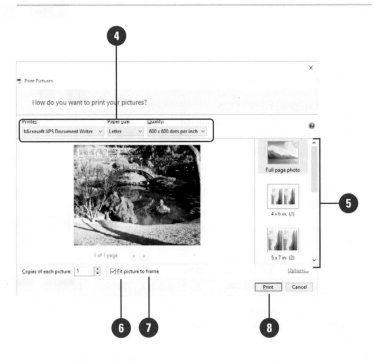

Sharing Pictures

When you are working with pictures or other files in Windows Explorer, you can quickly share them using the Share button (**New!**) on the Share tab. For example, you can pictures, and then share them with others in an email using Mail. The typical sharing apps are Mail and OneNote (in most cases; depends on the app), however, you can also install and use other online services, such as Twitter and Facebook. The process is pretty simple. Open an app with the content you want to share, display or select the information or item, open the Share panel, and then select the sharing app you want to use.

Share Pictures

1 In File Explorer, click or tap **Pictures** in the Navigation pane, or open any other folder with pictures you want to use.

2 Select the pictures or a folder with pictures you want to email.

3 Click or tap the **Share** button on the Share tab.

4 Click or tap the app that you want to use.

> **TROUBLE?** *If a sharing app is not available, make sure it is installed using the Windows Store.*

5 Use the app to send the pictures to another person.

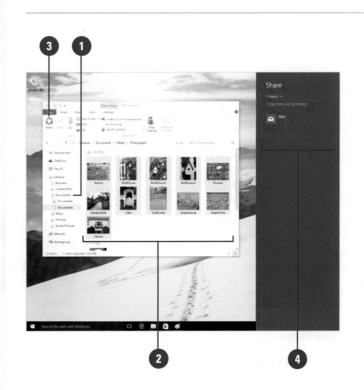

Did You Know?

You can order photo prints from the web. In File Explorer, select the photos you want to print, click or tap the Open button arrow on the Home tab, and then click or tap Windows Photo Viewer, click or tap the Print button on the toolbar, click or tap Order prints, select the printing company, click or tap Send Pictures, and then follow the online instructions.

Emailing Pictures

If you have one or more photos, pictures, or documents that you want to share with others, you can send them in an email as attachments. Before you send photos or pictures in an email as an attachment, you typically need to resize them in a separate graphics program so your recipient can view them with minimal scrolling, open your email program (non-Windows app, such as Windows Live Mail), and then attach the files. You can send a photo or picture in an email message without having to resize it in a separate graphics program, or even open your email program. Using the Email button on the Share tab in any Explorer window or the E-mail button on the toolbar in Windows Photo Viewer, Windows opens an email message window with the attached files from your default email program. All you need to do is address the message, add any message text, and then send it.

Email a Photo or Picture

1. In File Explorer, click or tap **Pictures** in the Navigation pane, or open any other folder with pictures you want to use.

2. Select the pictures or a folder with pictures you want to email.

3. Click or tap the **Email** button on the Share tab, or click or tap the **E-mail** button on the toolbar in Windows Photo Viewer.

   ◆ Click or tap the **Open** button arrow on the Home tab, and then click or tap **Windows Photo Viewer**.

4. Click or tap the **Picture size** list arrow, and then select a size.

5. Click or tap **Attach**.

   Your default email program (non Windows app, such as Windows Live Mail) opens, displaying an email message with a file attachment.

6. Type an email address and a subject.

7. Click or tap **Send** on the toolbar.

Installing a Digital Camera or Scanner

Windows makes it easy to install a scanner or digital camera on your PC computer or mobile device using plug-and-play. In most cases, all you need to do is plug in the hardware device. Windows recognizes the new hardware and installs it. If the hardware provides it's own installation wizard, the program will automatically start. If for some reason Windows doesn't recognize the hardware, you can start a wizard, which walks you through the installation process.

Install a Digital Camera or Scanner

1. Plug your camera or scanner into your PC to start the device installation wizard or the Scanner and Camera wizard.

   If the wizard doesn't open, open the Control Panel, click or tap the **Devices and Printers** icon in Small icons or Large icons view, and then click or tap the **Add a device** button on the toolbar.

2. Click or tap **Next** to continue.

3. Click or tap the device manufacturer you want to install, click or tap the device name, and then click or tap **Next** to continue.

4. Select a port and any device specific options, and then click or tap **Next** to continue.

5. Type a name for the device, or use the suggested one, and then click or tap **Next** to continue.

6. Click or tap **Finish**.

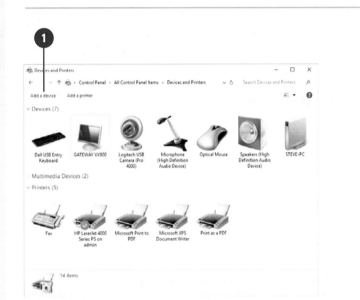

Did You Know?

You can remove a scanner or camera. In the Control Panel, click or tap Devices And Printers in Small icons or Large icons view, select the device icon, and then click or tap the Remove Device button on the toolbar, and then or tap click or tap Yes.

For Your Information

Scanning Pictures

After you connect and install a scanner, you can use the Scanner device in the Devices and Printer window in the Control Panel or start the Scan app on the Start menu (under All apps) to scan pictures. In the Scan app, specify the scan settings (File Type, Color mode, Resolution (DPI), and Save folder), and then click or tap the Scan or Preview button. The Scan button scans and saves, while the Preview scans and previews. After the scan, you can click or tap View to see your scan. If you saved it as an image file, it automatically opens in the Photos app in a split window. If you want to edit the scan, use the Rotate, Crop, or Edit buttons.

Downloading Digital Camera Pictures

A **digital still camera** stores pictures digitally rather than on film. The major advantage of digital still cameras is that making photos is fast and inexpensive. In order to use the digital camera features of Windows, you need to have a digital still or video camera attached and installed on your PC computer or mobile device. When you connect a digital camera to your device, Windows 10 displays the AutoPlay pop-up notification, where you can choose to import files using the Photos app or view files from the device window using File Explorer. If you don't use AutoPlay, you can also use an Import pictures and videos command in the Computer window. You can use the device window to view pictures that you have already taken with the camera and copy them in a folder on your device, or delete pictures from your camera.

Download Pictures from a Camera

1. Connect the digital camera to your device, and follow instructions to install and recognize the camera.

2. If the AutoPlay pop-up notification appears, click or tap the pop-up, click or tap **Open device to view files** (File Explorer) to import the pictures.

   If the AutoPlay pop-up notification doesn't open, open File Explorer, and then click or tap **This PC** in the Navigation pane.

3. Right-click or tap-hold the digital camera icon, and then click or tap **Import pictures and videos**.

4. Click or tap the **Review, organize, and group items to import** or **Import all new items now** option.

5. To more import settings, click or tap the **More options** link, select the options you want, and then click or tap **OK**.

6. Click or tap **Import**.

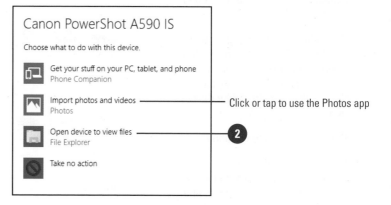

Click or tap to use the Photos app

Manage Pictures on the Camera

1 Connect the digital camera to your PC computer or mobile device.

2 If the AutoPlay pop-up notification appears, click or tap the pop-up, click or tap **Open device to view files** (File Explorer) to import the pictures, and then skip to Step 4.

If the AutoPlay dialog box doesn't open, continue.

3 In File Explorer, click or tap **This PC** in the Navigation pane, and then double-click or double-tap the Camera icon associated with the digital camera.

4 Double-click or double-tap the removable storage icon, and any folders to display the pictures stored on the digital camera.

5 Click or tap a picture to select the one you want to work with.

6 Perform any of the following commands:

◆ Open. Click or tap the **Open** button arrow on the Home tab, and then click or tap **Paint**, **Photos**, or **Windows Photo Viewer**.

◆ Edit. Click or tap the **Edit** button on the Home tab. Opens in the Paint where you can edit it.

◆ Delete. Click or tap the **Delete** button on the Home tab.

◆ Move or Copy. Click or tap the **Move to** or **Copy to** button on the Home tab, and then select a destination folder.

You can also right-click or tap-hold a picture, and then select an option.

Using Pictures as a Screen Saver

Instead of using standard screen savers provided by Windows, you can use your own pictures to create a slide show screen saver. Windows displays all the pictures, which you have designated in a folder, to create as a full screen slide show. You can add or remove pictures from the folder to modify the slide show.

Use Pictures as a Screen Saver

1. In File Explorer, if you want to create a custom folder for pictures, create a folder, and then place the pictures you want to use in the slide show in the folder.

2. Right-click or tap-hold a blank area of the desktop, and then click or tap **Personalize**.

3. Click or tap **Lock screen**, and then click or tap **Screen saver settings**.

4. Click or tap the **Screen Saver** list, and then click or tap **Photos**.

5. Click or tap **Settings**.

6. If necessary, click or tap **Browse**, select the folder with your pictures, and then click or tap **OK**.

7. Click or tap the **Slide show speed** list, select the speed you want, and then select or clear the **Shuffle pictures** check box.

8. Click or tap **Save**.

9. Click or tap **Preview**, and then click or tap the screen to stop it.

10. Click or tap **OK**.

Did You Know?

You can set screen timeout settings. Right-click or tap hold the desktop, click or tap Personalize, click or tap Lock screen, click or tap Screen Timeout Settings, and then set the screen and sleep options you want.

Using a Picture as a Background

Instead of using one of the pictures provided by Windows, you can select a picture on your hard disk or from a web page as the desktop background. You can use Paint or any graphics program to create new background designs or change existing ones. Acceptable formats for background files are Bitmap (the format of a Paint file), JPEG (the format of an Internet graphic file), or HTM (the format of a web page). After you set a picture as the desktop background, Windows adds the picture to the Background list in the Desktop Background dialog box. When you use a picture from a web page, Windows saves it in the Background list as Internet Explorer Background. Each new picture from a web page you set as a background replaces the previous one.

Set a Picture as the Start Screen and Desktop Background

1. In File Explorer, open the folder or the web page with the picture you want to set as the background.

2. Click or tap the picture you want to use.

3. Click or tap the **Set as background** button on the Manage tab under Picture Tools.

   If the picture doesn't appear on your desktop, continue.

4. Right-click or tap-hold a blank area of the desktop, and then click or tap **Personalize**.

5. Click or tap **Background**.

6. Click or tap the picture you set as the background, or click or tap **Browse** to select a picture.

7. Click or tap the **Close** button (x).

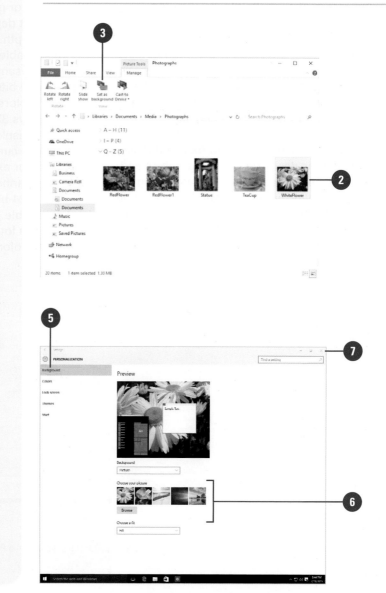

Did You Know?

You can save an web page picture as a background. In your web browser, right-click or tap-hold the picture, click or tap Save as background, and then click or tap Yes.

Understanding Picture File Formats

Each file type has a different format and recommended use. JPG (Joint Photographic Experts Group; also known as JPEG) and PNG (Portable Network Graphics) are graphic file formats commonly used on web pages, while BMP (Bit-mapped) and TIF (Tagged Image File Format, also known as Tiff) are file formats used in documents. The format specifies how the information in the file is organized internally. JPG and PNG formats are compressible, which means that the file size is smaller and transfers over the Internet faster. Each file format uses a different compression method, which produces different results when you display the graphic files. JPG is designed for photographs and supports millions of colors, but loses some image quality by discarding image data to reduce the file size. PNG is designed for web graphics and supports millions of color without losing image quality, but not all web browsers fully support its capabilities without using a plug-in, which is a software add-on installed on your PC computer or mobile device. TIF is designed for all graphics and colors and one of the most widely used graphic formats, but the file size is large. BMP is the standard Windows graphic format and is similar to TIF.

Understanding 8-, 16-, and 32-Bit Images

Along with the file format is a number. Sometimes it's shown and sometimes it's not. The number indicates the colors available for displaying or printing each pixel in an image is called **bit depth**—also known as pixel depth or color depth. A higher bit depth means more available colors and more accurate color representation in an image. A bit depth setting of 2 bits displays 4 colors, 4 bits displays 16 colors, 8 bits displays 256 colors, 16 bits displays 32,768 colors, and 24 bits and 32 bits both display 16.7 million colors. Most digital images currently use 8 bits of data per channel. For example, an RGB image with 8 bits per channel is capable of producing 16.7 million (a 24-bit RGB image: 8 bits x 3 channels) possible colors per pixel. While that may seem like a lot of color information, when it comes to color correction and adjustment, it isn't.

File formats with color depth in Paint

Working with Windows Media

Introduction

You can use Windows Media Player (WMP version 12) to play sounds, music, and digital movies. In addition, you can play and copy CDs, rip music from CDs, create your own CDs, play DVDs or VCDs, and copy music and videos to portable devices, such as portable digital audio players and portable PCs. If you have your media on another PC computer, you can use Remote Media Streaming to play it on your PC computer. Using Windows Media Player requires a sound card, speakers, and an Internet connection to view online content.

Windows also comes with Voice Recorder, a sound recording utility program you can use to create and modify a sound. You can use the sound to indicate a Windows event, such as starting Windows or if an error has occurred. Using Voice Recorder requires a sound card, speakers, and a microphone.

If you want to create movies, you can download and install Windows Live Essentials, which is a set of programs that allows you to create, work with, and share media as well as communicate on the web. The Windows Live programs include Microsoft OneDrive, Mail, Messenger, Photo Gallery, Movie Maker, and Writer. With Movie Maker, you can create, edit, and export movies for use in Windows Media Player.

You can also use the Cast to Devices button in File Explorer to work with devices, such as a printer or second screen, attached to your system.

What You'll Do

Start, Update, and View Windows Media Player

Play a Music CD, DVD, or VCD Movie

Control the Volume

Play Media Files and the Playlists

Rip CD Music

Copy Media Files to a CD or Portable Device

Stream Media

Enhance the Media Player Display

View and Play Music Files

Record a Sound File

Associate a Sound with an Event

Use Windows Live Essentials

Starting and Updating Windows Media Player

Before you can use Windows Media Player (WMP), you need to check to make sure you have the latest version (12 or later) installed on your PC computer using the About Windows Media Player command on the Help menu for the current player. If it's not, you can download and install it from the web at *www.microsoft.com/downloads*. You start Windows Media Player like any other Windows program from the Apps screen. After you start Windows Media Player, you should check for software updates on the Internet. Microsoft is continually adding features and fixing problems. You can use the Help menu in Windows Media Player to access the updates.

Start and Update Windows Media Player

1. In the Start screen or Start menu, click or tap **All apps**, and then click or tap **Windows Media Player**.

2. If a setup dialog box appears, click or tap the **Recommended settings** option, and then click or tap **Finish**.

3. Click or tap the **Help** menu, click or tap **Check for updates**, and then follow the instructions to complete the upgrade. To show menus, see the DYK? below.

4. To use the player, click or tap the toolbar button or task tabs. You can use the **Back** and **Forward** button to retrace previous steps.

Did You Know?

You can show and hide the menu bar. To show or hide the menu bar, click or tap the Organize button, point to Layout, and then click or tap Show Menu Bar.

You can automatically check for software updates. Click or tap the Organize button, click or tap Options, click or tap the Player tab, and then click or tap the Once A Day, Once A Week, or Once A Month option.

Viewing the Media Player Window

Now Playing View

Switch to Library

Playback controls

Library View

Search and layout options

Tabs

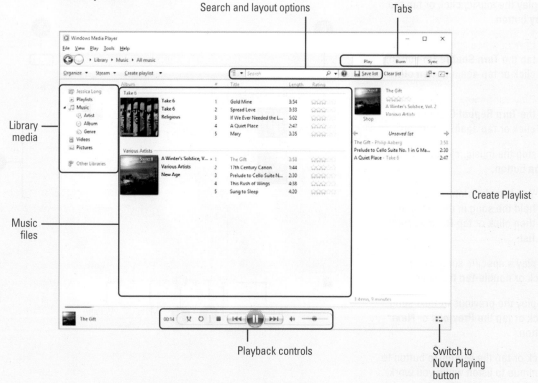

Library media

Music files

Create Playlist

Playback controls

Switch to Now Playing button

Playing Music from CDs

Windows allows you to play music on your PC computer in the background while you work. After you insert a music CD into your CD-ROM drive and the music starts to play, you can minimize Windows Media Player and continue to work with other programs on your computer. If you are connected to the Internet when you play a music CD, Windows Media Player tries to locate information about the CD from the Internet, such as the name of the artist and the songs on the album. If the information is not available, the track number of each song displays instead.

Play a Music CD

1 Insert a music CD into your CD-ROM drive.

2 If the Audio pop-up notification appears, click or tap the pop-up, and then click or tap **Play audio CD** (Windows Media Player).

The Windows Media Player window appears, and the CD starts to play.

3 To play the music, click or tap the **Play** button.

◆ **Play in random order.** Click or tap the **Turn Shuffle On** button; click or tap again to turn off.

◆ **Play continuously.** Click or tap the **Turn Repeat On** button; click or tap again to turn off.

4 To stop the music, click or tap the **Stop** button.

◆ You can also right-click or tap-hold the song in the list, and then click or tap **Remove from list**.

5 To play a specific song, double-click or double-tap the song.

6 To play the previous or next song, click or tap the **Previous** or **Next** button.

7 Click or tap the **Minimize** button to continue to listen while you work, or click or tap the **Close** button (x) to exit.

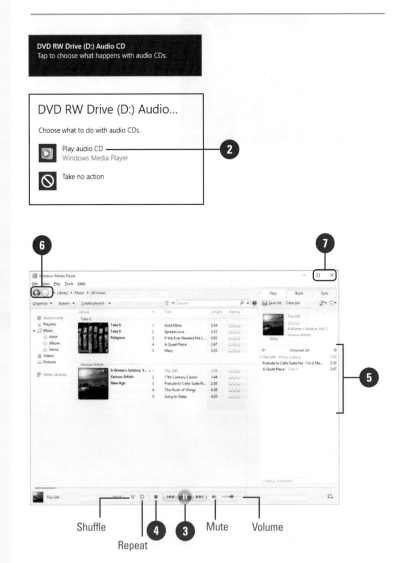

Playing a DVD or VCD Movie

If you have a DVD drive and decoder hardware or software on your PC computer, you can play DVD movies with Windows Media Player. If you don't have a decoder, you can purchase one from a third party manufacturer. If you only have a CD player, you can play VCD movies. A VCD is similar to a DVD, yet the video quality is not as high. When you play a DVD or VCD movie, a list of titles appear with a section of content from the movie. You can use the titles to browse through the contents of the DVD or VCD.

Play a DVD or VCD Movie

1 Insert a DVD into your DVD drive or a VCD into your CD drive.

2 If the Audio pop-up notification appears, click or tap the pop-up, and then click or tap the option to play the DVD or VCD.

The Windows Media Player window appears, and the DVD or VCD starts to play.

3 To expand the contents list of the DVD or VCD click or tap the plus sign (+).

4 To pause the movie, click or tap the **Pause** button.

5 To stop the movie, click or tap the **Stop** button.

6 To play a specific title, double-click or double-tap it in the list.

7 To play the previous or next section of the movie, click or tap the **Previous** or **Next** button.

8 To exit the app, click or tap the **Close** button (x).

Did You Know?

You can display captions and subtitles for a DVD. Click or tap the Play menu, point to Lyrics, Captions, and Subtitles, and then click or tap Off (toggles on and off) or Defaults to select the language you want to use.

Controlling the Volume

Windows comes with master volume controls that allow you to change the volume of all devices and applications on the PC at once. You can increase or decrease the volume, or you can mute (turn off) the sound. The volume control is available on the Settings panel and in the notification area on the taskbar (**New!**). The Volume icon makes it easy to increase or decrease the volume or mute the sound. In addition to changing the master volume on your PC, you can also adjust the volume of specific devices, such as a CD or DVD player, without affecting the volume of other devices.

Change the Volume

1 Click or tap the **Volume** icon in the notification area on the taskbar.

♦ Display volume. Point to the Volume icon in the notification area.

2 Drag the slider to adjust the volume to the level you want.

3 To mute the sound, click or tap the **Mute** button.

4 Press Esc or click or tap off the menu to close the volume controls.

Set Volume Levels for Specific Devices

1 Right-click or tap-hold the **Volume** icon in the notification area on the taskbar, and then click or tap **Open Volume Mixer**.

2 Drag the **Speakers** slider to adjust the settings for the sound level you want.

The volume for the speakers is the main volume control.

3 Drag the other sliders to adjust the settings for the applications you want.

The volume for the speakers is the main volume control.

4 To close the window, click or tap the **Close** button (x).

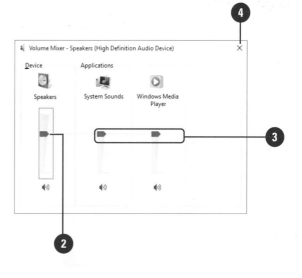

Did You Know?

You can display the Volume icon on the taskbar. In the desktop, right-click or tap-hold the taskbar, click or tap Properties, click or tap Customize, click or tap the Turn System Icons On or Off link, set the Volume Behavior to On, and then click or tap OK.

You can set the recording volume. In the desktop, right-click or tap-hold the Volume icon, click or tap Recording Devices, click or tap a device, click or tap Properties, click or tap the Levels tab, adjust the volume level, and then click or tap OK twice.

Troubleshooting

Testing Your Sound Hardware

If your are having trouble hearing the sound from Windows Media Player, the best place to start is to test your sound hardware. In File Explorer, click or tap This PC in the Navigation pane, click or tap the Control Panel button on the Computer tab, and then click or tap the Sound icon in Small icons or Large icons view. Next, click or tap the Playback tab, select the hardware, click or tap Configure, click or tap Test, click or tap Next, and then follow the instructions to test the hardware. Once you have tested the hardware, click or tap Finish, and then click or tap OK.

Playing Media Files

With Windows Media Player, you can play sound and video files on your PC. You can find and download sound and video files from the Internet or copy media files from a CD or DVD. WMP now supports more audio and video formats, including 3GP, AAC, AVCHD, DivX, MOV, and Xvid. The Library makes it easy to organize your media by category, such as Artist, Album, Genre, Rated Songs, or Year Released. You can quickly search for media by name or you can browse through the Library. If you want to do other things while you listen to media, you can switch to Now Playing view to use a smaller display.

Perform a Quick Search

1 In Windows Media Player, click or tap a media library in the Navigation pane.

2 Click or tap in the **Search** box.

3 Type the text that you want to search by.

> **TIMESAVER** *Click or tap Search Results in the Library list to display it at any time.*

4 To clear the search, click or tap the **Close** button in the Search box (x).

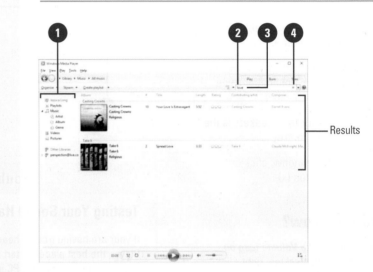

Results

Browse Media Files

1 In Windows Media Player, click or tap a media library in the Navigation pane.

2 Click or tap the **Select a Category** button on the address bar, and then select a category.

3 Select a view of that category in the Navigation pane.

4 To change the view:

◆ **View More**. Click or tap the list arrow next to a button on the address bar, and then select a category.

◆ **View Less**. Click or tap a button on the address bar to the left.

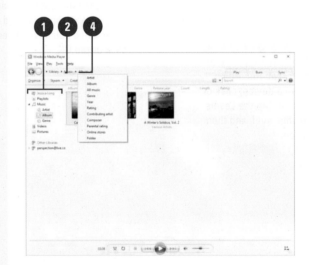

Play Media Files from the Library

1. In Windows Media Player, click or tap a media library in the Navigation pane.

2. Click or tap an arrow next to the category you want to view.

3. Click or tap a category.

4. Double-click or double-tap the media file to play it.

Did You Know?

You can automatically add media files to the Library when played. Click or tap the Organize button, click or tap Options, click or tap the Player tab, select the Add Local Media Files To Library When Played check box, and then click or tap OK.

Play Media Files from a Playlist

1. In Windows Media Player, click or tap a media library in the Navigation pane.

2. Click or tap an arrow next to the **Playlists** category.

3. Double-click or double-tap a playlist to play it.

Did You Know?

You can delete a file from the library. Click or tap a media library in the Navigation pane, right-click or tap-hold the file you want to remove, click or tap Delete, click or tap the Delete from Library Only or Delete From Library And My Computer option, and then click or tap OK.

Playing Media Using a Playlist

Instead of playing digital media files, such as music tracks, video clips, or DVD segments, one at a time or in sequential order from a CD or DVD, you can use Windows Media Player to create a **playlist**. A playlist is a customized list or sequence of digital media that you want to listen to or watch. A playlist allows you to group together media files and specify the order in which you want to play back the media. You can mix and match the media files on your PC computer, a network, a CD, or the Internet, creating a personal juke box. You can create an easy access general playlist called Play list, create one with a specific name, or specify criteria to create an Auto Playlist.

Create Playlist

1. Click or tap a media library in the Navigation pane.

2. Click or tap the **Play** tab.

3. To clear the Play list, click or tap the **Clear list** button.

   ◆ To create a blank new playlist, click or tap the **Create playlist** button, click or tap **Create playlist**, type a name, and then press Enter or tap away.

4. Drag items from the details pane to the Play tab. Use the Ctrl or Shift keys to select multiple items.

   ◆ To rearrange items, drag them up or down the list.

5. To save the list, click or tap the **Save list** button, type a name, specify a location, and then press Enter or tap away.

   ◆ To save a playlist in a another format, click or tap the **List options** button, and then click **Save list as**.

6. To hide the List pane, click or tap the **List options** button, and then click or tap **Hide list**.

7. To add more items to the playlist, drag them to the playlist, or right-click or tap-hold the the media files, point to **Add to**, and then select the playlist name.

Type playlist name

Create an Auto Playlist

1 Click or tap a media library in the Navigation pane.

2 Click or tap the **Create playlist** button, and then click or tap **Create auto playlist**.

3 Type a name for the Auto Playlist.

4 Select the criteria options you want.

5 Click or tap **OK**.

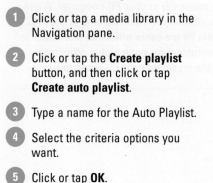

Add Media Files from Your Hard Disk to a Playlist

1 Open the folder window that contains the files or folders you want to add to a playlist.

2 Select the file(s) or folder(s) you want to include in the playlist.

3 Right-click or tap-hold the selection, and then click or tap **Add to Windows Media Player list**.

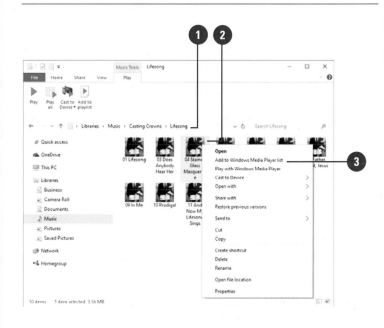

Did You Know?

You can delete a playlist. Right-click or tap-hold the playlist in the Navigation pane, click or tap Delete, click or tap the Delete From Library Only or Delete From Library And My Computer option, and then click or tap OK.

You can edit playlist. Click or tap the playlist in the Navigation pane, drag new items to the list or right-click or tap-hold items in the list, and then click or tap Remove From List.

Ripping CD Music

Windows Media Player (WPM) allows you to **rip**, or copy, one music track or an entire album from a music CD to your PC computer. When you rip music from a CD or download music from the web to your PC computer, Windows copies music by the same artist into one folder in the Music folder and creates subfolders for each album. Windows gives you several ways to play the music on your PC computer.

Rip Tracks from a Music CD

1. Insert your music CD into the CD-ROM drive.

2. If the Autoplay pop-up notification appears, click or tap the pop-up, and then click or tap **Play audio CD** (Windows Media Player) to burn individual tracks, and then click or tap the **Stop** button.

    The WMP window opens, and starts to play the CD.

3. Use default options, or click or tap the **Rip settings** button, point to **Format** or **Audio Quality**, and then select the option you want.

4. Clear the check boxes next to the tracks you don't want to copy.

5. Click or tap **Rip CD** (toggles with Stop Rip).

    The music is copied to the Music folder unless you specify a different location.

6. To stop the copy at any time, click or tap **Stop Rip**.

Toggles to Start **6** **3**

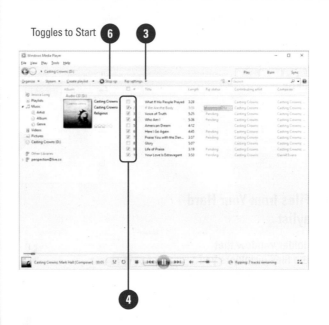

4

Did You Know?

You can use error correction during a copy. Click or tap the Tools menu, click or tap Options, click or tap the Devices tab, select the CD-ROM drive, click or tap Properties, click or tap Digital, select the Use Error Correction check box, and then click or tap OK.

Select Rip Music Settings

1 Click or tap the **Rip settings** button on the toolbar, and then click or tap **More options**.

◆ You can also select Format and Audio Quality options directly from the Rip settings menu.

2 To change the location where Windows Media Player stores ripped music, click or tap **Change**, select a new folder location, and then click or tap **OK**.

3 Select the format and copy setting you want:

◆ **Windows Media Audio** or **Windows Media Audio Pro.** Most common WMA format with widest range of quality and file size.

◆ **Windows Media Audio (Variable Bit Rate).** High quality with variable file size.

◆ **Windows Media Audio Lossless.** Quality closest to the original with high file size.

◆ **MP3.** Common and flexible format.

◆ **WAV (Lossless).** Common alternate format.

4 Drag the slider to adjust audio quality.

5 Click or tap **OK**.

Did You Know?

You can turn off music copy protection. Click or tap the Tools menu, click or tap Options, click or tap the Rip Music tab, clear the Copy Protect Music check box, and then click or tap OK.

For Your Information

Getting a License to Copy Music

Most CD music is secured with a license to prevent illegal distribution. A license is a legal agreement that specifies whether the license expires or how you can use the file. The terms of the license are entirely dependent upon the person or company that provided the file. Windows Media Player cannot play licensed files without a license. When you copy music from a CD with the Acquire Licenses Automatically option selected, Windows Media Player searches the Internet for the license and copies it to your PC computer. If the license is not available, you can still acquire a license by copying the music and selecting the Copy Protect music check box on the Rip Music tab in the Options dialog box. As you copy the music, the licenses are issued. The license allows you to copy the music to your hard disk, a portable device, or a CD. If you want to view the license information for a file, right-click or tap-hold the file, click or tap Properties, and then click or tap the Media Usage Rights tab. If you copy music without a license, you could be violating the music's copyright. You can avoid license problems by backing them up.

Copying Media Files to a CD or Portable Device

Windows Media Player makes it easy to burn (copy) music to a CD using a CD burner or copy the music and video you want to a portable device and keep it in sync. If you have a Portable Digital Media Player, such as an ipod or zune, you can download digital media from an online store and play it on the go. Windows Media Player verifies that there is enough space for the selected files on the portable device and then starts the copying process. As the music copies, the amount of used and free space on the portable device is displayed at the bottom of the Music On Device pane. You can synchronize music, video, and picture files to the device so you can bring your whole library with you. You can choose to automatically or manually sync your digital media between WMP and your device, known as a partnership. Set up sync once, and every time you connect your device to your PC computer, WMP updates the digital media between them, so devices that allow you to rate your music can automatically send them back to WMP.

Copy Music to a CD

1. Insert a blank CD or DVD in your CD recorder.

   If the Autoplay pop-up notification appears, click or tap the pop-up, click or tap **Burn an audio CD**. If the Autoplay dialog box doesn't appear, click or tap the **Burn** tab.

   If you need to erase your disc, right-click or tap-hold the drive in the Navigation pane, and then click or tap **Erase disc**.

2. To select a disc type, click or tap the **Burn options** button, and then click or tap **Audio CD** or **Data CD or DVD**.

3. If you need to clear the List pane, click or tap the **Clear list** button.

4. Drag the files you want to burn from the Details pane to the List pane.

5. To remove a file from the list, right-click or tap-hold the file, and then click or tap **Remove from list**.

6. Drag the files in the list to arrange them in the order you want.

7. Click or tap the **Start burn** button.

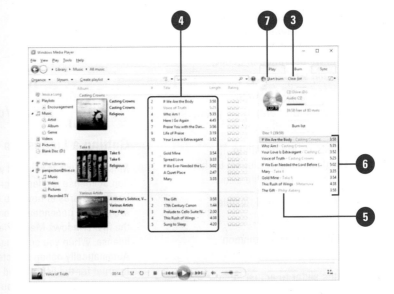

Copy Music to a Portable Device

1. In Windows Media Player, and then connect the portable device to your PC computer.

2. If sync setup is needed for the device, follow the wizard instructions, and then click or tap **Finish**.

3. If you set up Auto Sync, synchronization begins, click or tap **Stop sync**.

4. Click or tap a media library in the Navigation pane.

5. Click or tap the **Sync** tab.

6. If you need to clear the List pane, click or tap the **Clear list** button.

7. Display and drag the media files you want to the sync list.

8. To remove a file from the list, right-click or tap-hold the file, and then click or tap **Remove from list**.

9. To change sync priority order, sync method, and other settings, click or tap the **Sync options** button, and then click or tap **Set up sync**, specify options, and then click or tap **OK**.

10. Click or tap the **Start sync** button.

11. If you want to stop the sync, click or tap **Stop sync**.

    Upon completion, status appears indicating success or failure.

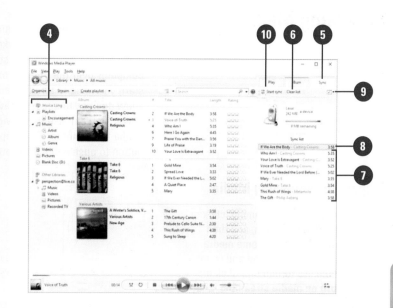

Did You Know?

You can find a list of compatible portable devices. Open your browser, go to *www.windowsmedia.com*, and then click or tap the Music Players link.

For Your Information

Changing the Media Player Look

Windows Media Player gives you the freedom of expression to change the look, known as the **skin**, of the Media Player. Windows Media Player includes several skins from which you can select the one you like the best. When you select a skin, Windows Media Player changes from full mode to skin mode. You can use skins only when Media Player is in skin mode. Skin mode displays a smaller player, which provides more room on the screen for other programs. To apply a skin, click or tap the View menu, click or tap Skin Chooser, click or tap a design, click or tap Apply Skin, and then use the controls to play a media file. To delete a skin, click or tap the Delete Selected Skin button, and then click or tap Yes. Press Shift+F10 to display a shortcut menu of convenient commands in skin mode. To return to the full window, click or tap the Return To Full Mode button. To switch back to skin mode, click or tap the View menu, and then click or tap Skin Mode.

Streaming Media

If you have a home network, you can use Windows Media Player to stream music and video to and from another PC computer and media devices—such as a networked digital stereo receiver, TV, or Xbox 360—in your home. You can also stream your music library from a home PC computer over the Internet to another PC computer. Before you can start, you need to turn on home media streaming and enable options to allow devices to access, play, or control your media. In Windows Media Player, you can use the Navigation pane to access and play streamed media from another PC computer or media device, or use the Play To button to push media to another PC computer or media device.

Prepare for Streaming Media

1. To turn on basic streaming, click or tap the **Stream** button, and then click or tap **Turn on home media streaming**. (If the command is not available, it's turned on.) Click or tap **Turn on media streaming**, and then click or tap **OK**.

2. Click or tap the **Stream** button, and then click or tap **More streaming options.**

3. Click or tap **Allow All** to allow all computers to stream, click or tap **Block All** to block all computers, or select **Allowed** or **Blocked** for each individual computer.

4. Click or tap **OK**.

5. Click or tap the **Stream** button, and then click or tap an option:

   ◆ **Allow Internet access to home media.** Click or tap to establish a link to an Online ID provider, such as Windows Live. Sign in and use your account to share files.

   ◆ **Allow remote control of my Player.** Click or tap to allow or not allow media streaming to another computer.

   ◆ **Automatically allow devices to play my media.** Click or tap to allow or not allow media streaming from another computer.

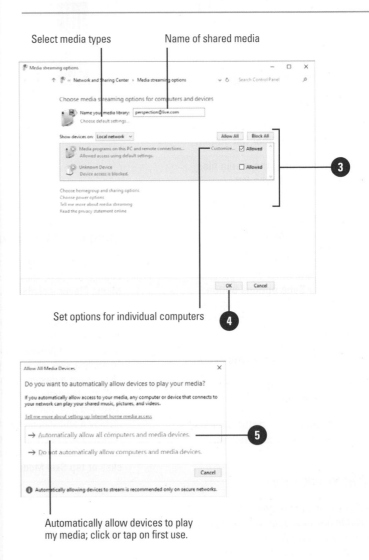

Select media types — Name of shared media

Set options for individual computers

Automatically allow devices to play my media; click or tap on first use.

Play Media Streamed to or from Another PC Computer

1. In Windows Media Player, click or tap a media library in the Navigation pane.

   ◆ **Stream to.** Use your local PC computer under Library.

   ◆ **Stream from.** Use a networked computer under Other Libraries.

2. Click or tap an arrow next to the PC computer you want to view, then click or tap a category.

3. Use either of the following methods.

   ◆ **Stream to.** Click or tap the **Play To** button under the Play tab, then select a networked computer. This opens the Play To window to control the media.

   ◆ **Stream from.** Double-click or double tap the media file to play it.

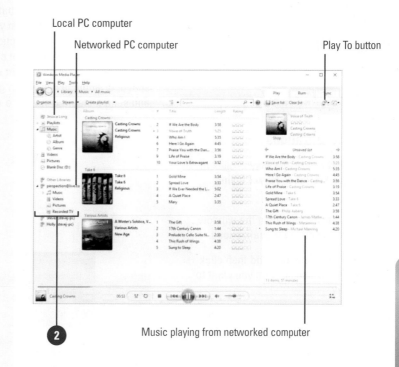

Local PC computer

Networked PC computer

Play To button

2

Music playing from networked computer

Did You Know?

You cannot access or modify the content of a Player library. The people accessing your media are only permitted to use your computer to play the items in your Player library and cannot add, remove, or modify any items.

You may have problems on a public network. If you're on a public network, such as a coffee shop, Windows Firewall might block the streaming process to your Player library. Check your Windows Firewall settings to make sure Windows Media Player is an allowed program. You can also check the Enabled Network Protocols on the Network tab in the Options dialog box. Click or tap the Organize button, and then click or tap Options to open it.

For Your Information

Adding Functionality to Media Player

Windows Media Player allows you to add functionality to the player using plug-ins. Plug-ins add or enhance the media experience with audio and video effects, new rendering types, and visualizations. Before you can use a plug-in, you need to download it from the web and add it to the Media Player. You can find lots of Media Player plug-ins at *www.wmplugins.com*. Before you download a plug-in, read the online information about the plug-in for additional instructions. Click or tap the Organize button, click or tap Options, and then click or tap the Plug-ins tab. Select a plug-in category. Select a plug-in option, if available. To modify a plug-in, click or tap Properties. To remove a plug-in, click or tap Remove. Click or tap OK.

Enhancing the Media Player Display

Visualizations are plug-ins that display geometric shapes and color on the Now Playing mode when you play music. Visualizations are grouped together into collections. You can add and remove visualizations or download additional collections from the web. You can also display special enhancement controls to change video settings, play speed, or audio levels with a graphics equalizer, choose color effects, and send a media link in an e-mail.

Select Visualizations

1. In Windows Media Player, click or tap the **Switch to Now Playing** button.

2. Right-click or tap-hold the window, and then point to **Visualizations**.

3. Point to a category, and then click or tap the visualization you want to display.

4. To go back to the library, click or tap the **Switch to Library** button.

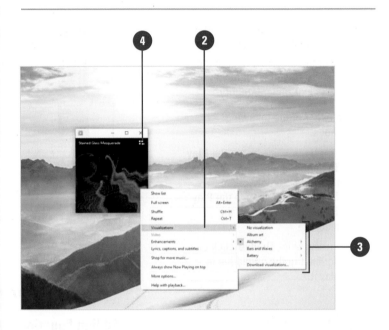

Select Enhancements

1. In Windows Media player, click or tap the **Switch to Now Playing** button.

2. Right-click or tap-hold the window, and then point to **Enhancements**.

3. Click or tap the enhancement you want to display.

4. Adjust the enhancement controls.

5. When you're done, click or tap the **Close** button in the control.

6. To go back to the library, click or tap the **Switch to Library** button.

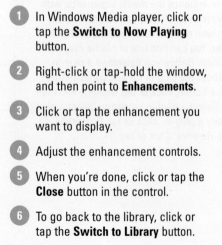

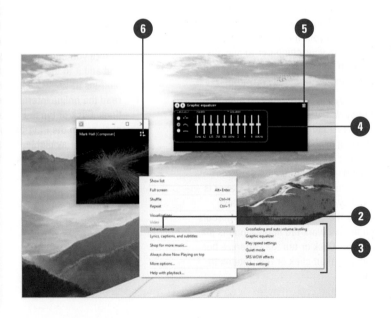

Viewing and Playing Music Files

You can view and play music files with relative ease in the Music folder. The Music folder is a folder specifically designated to play and manage music files. When you copy music files from a CD or download them from the Internet, the files are copied to the Music folder by default unless you specify a different location. The Music folder contains links to specialized music tasks that can help you play the music you store on your PC computer. In the Music folder, you can click or tap Play All or Play on the Play tab or double-click or double-tap an individual music file to open and play the music in Windows Media Player. If you click or tap Play All in the Music folder, Windows Media Player opens and plays all the music in your Music folder and subfolder in random order. If you click or tap Play All in a subfolder within your Music folder, Windows Media Player opens and plays all the music in the folder in consecutive order. In addition to playing music, you can also add music files to a playlist in Windows Media Player.

View and Play Music Files

1 In File Explorer, click or tap **Music** in the Navigation pane.

2 Select the music files or folder you want to play.

3 Click or tap the **Play** tab under Music Tools

4 To add the selected music files to a playlist, click the **Add to playlist** button.

The files are added to a new playlist in Windows Media Player.

5 To play the selected music files or all the music files in the folder, click or tap the **Play** or **Play all** button.

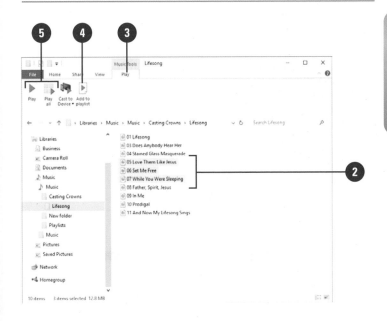

Recording a Sound File

With the Voice Recorder app (**New!**) and a microphone, you can record your own sound files. Voice Recorder creates Windows Media Audio files with the .wma file extension. Before you can use Voice Recorder, you need to have a sound card, speakers, and a microphone installed on your PC computer. When you open the Voice Recorder app for the first time, you're asked to allow or block the use of your microphone. When you record a sound with the app, you can trim the start or end if you like, and play it back. If you don't like the way a sound came out or no longer want it, you can delete it at any time. Sound files are stored in an Sound recordings folder located in the Documents folder, which you can locate in File Explorer.

Use the Voice Recorder App

1. In the Start screen or Start menu, click or tap **All apps**, and then click or tap **Voice Recorder** (**New!**).

2. To select microphone options, click or tap the **More** button, click or tap **Settings**, click or tap the **Microphone Settings** link, click or tap **Yes**, if prompted, to switch apps.

3. Click or tap the **Record** button, and then record the voice or sounds you want.

4. When you're done, click or tap the **Stop Recording** button.

   The recording is automatically saved in the Sound recordings folder (in the Documents folder) with the name Recording, Recording 2, etc. by default.

5. To play or pause the recording, select the recording, and then click or tap the **Play/Pause** button.

   As the sound plays, the play head moves along the progress bar.

   ◆ Playhead. You can drag the playhead to move forward or backward.

6. To exit the app, click or tap the **Close** button (x).

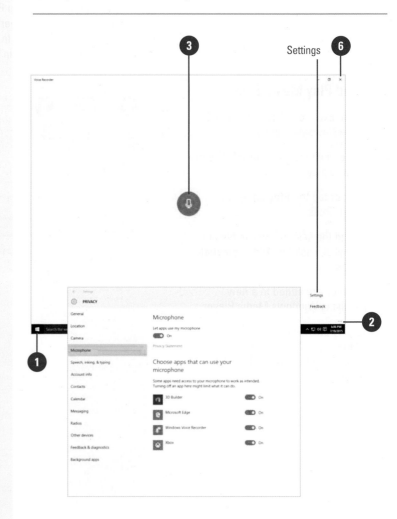

Work with the Voice Recorder App

1. In the Start screen or Start menu, click or tap **All apps**, and then click or tap **Voice Recorder** (**New!**).

2. Select the sound you want to change.

3. To play/pause a sound, select the sound, click or tap the **Play/Pause** button.

   ◆ Playhead. You can drag the playhead to adjust the start position.

4. To rename the sound, click the **Rename** button, enter a name, and then click or tap **Rename**.

5. To trim a sound, click or tap the **Trim** button, drag the start or end trim handles, click or tap **Apply**, and then click or tap **Update original** or **Save a copy**.

6. To delete a sound, select the sound, click or tap the **Delete** button, and then click or tap **OK** to confirm.

7. To exit the app, click or tap the **Close** button (x).

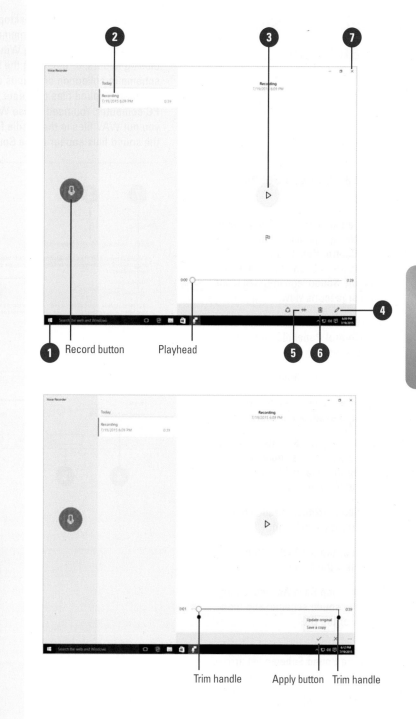

Record button   Playhead

Trim handle   Apply button   Trim handle

Did You Know?

You can share a sound. In the Voice Recorder, select the sound, click or tap the Share button, select the share app you want, and then use the app to send the sound.

You can open file location with the sound files. In the Voice Recorder, select the sound, click or tap the More button, and then click or tap Open File Location.

Associating a Sound with an Event

Besides customizing the desktop appearance of Windows, you can also add sound effects to common Windows commands and functions, such as starting and exiting Windows, printing complete, opening and closing folders, or emptying the Recycle Bin. You can select a sound scheme (a collection of sounds associated with events), or you can mix and match sound files to create your own sound scheme for your PC computer. You need to use Wave files with the .wav file extension. If you put WAV files in the Media folder, located in the Windows folder, the sound files appear in the Sounds list.

Create and Select a Sound Scheme

1. In File Explorer, click **Computer** in the Navigation pane, click or tap the **Control Panel** button on the Computer tab, and then click or tap the **Sound** icon in Small icons or Large icons view.

   ◆ You can also click or tap the **Control Panel** tile on the Apps screen.

2. Click or tap the **Sounds** tab.

3. Click or tap an event to which you want to associate a sound.

4. Click or tap the **Sounds** list arrow, and then select a sound, or click or tap **Browse** and locate the sound file you want to use.

   ◆ Select **(None)** to remove a sound association.

5. Click or tap the **Test** button to preview the sound.

6. Click or tap **Save As**, type a name for the sound scheme, and then click or tap **OK**.

7. To select a sound scheme, click or tap the **Sound Scheme** list arrow, and then select a scheme.

8. Click or tap **OK**.

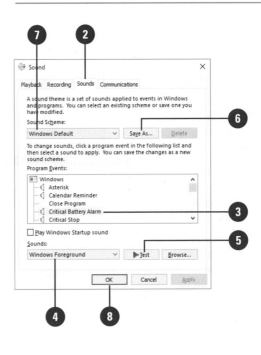

Using Windows Live Essentials

If you want a more full featured program to work with media, you can download and install Windows Live Essentials, which is a set of programs that allows you to create, work with, and share media as well as communicate on the web. The Windows Live programs include Microsoft OneDrive, Mail, Messenger, Photo Gallery, Movie Maker, and Writer. Many of these programs came installed along with Windows Vista, however in Windows 10, you need to download and install them. Installing the programs separately allows you to get and use the latest versions of the software. After you install Windows Live Essentials, you can access the Windows Live programs from the Start screen or menu.

Download and Install Windows Live Essentials

1. In Internet Explorer, visit the Windows Live Essentials web site at the following address:

   http://download.live.com

2. Click or tap **Download now**.

3. Click or tap **Run** or **Save** (if available) to run the setup program or save it to your PC. If you click or tap **Save**, select a location, click or tap **Save**, and then click or tap **Run**.

   If prompted, click or tap **Yes** for authorization to continue.

   The Windows Live setup program starts.

4. Click or tap **Choose the programs you want to install**, and then select the check boxes with the Windows Live programs you want to install.

5. Click or tap **Install**.

6. Follow the on-screen instructions to select additional tools and complete the installation.

7. When you're done, click or tap **Close**.

8. To access the Windows Live programs from the Start or Apps screen.

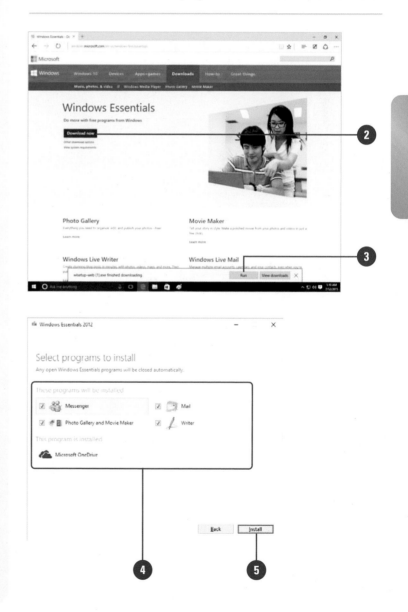

Working with Online Media

Introduction

Windows 10 comes with a host of media related apps that allow you to get specialized information, manage and share files online, capture photos and video, watch movies and tv shows, listen to music, and play games.

If you need information on a specific topic, Windows provides specialized apps, such as News, Money, Sports, Weather, Food & Drink, Health & Fitness, and Maps, with the information you need. For example, if you want to find out the latest sports news, all you need to do is start the Sports app. This reduces the amount of searching you need to perform in order to find what you need. As you browse articles in apps and on the web, you can add them to the Reading List app in order to view later. If you have a PDF or XPS document, you can use the Reader app to view and read it.

In addition to the specialized information apps, you can use OneDrive to work with files stored on a cloud-based file hosting service that you can sync with other devices, such as Windows Phone, iPhone, or Android. With the Camera app, you can use a digital camera, such as a webcam, to capture a still photo or video. After you capture a photo, you can crop it as desired; for a video, you can trim it.

Windows 10 integrates the use of Xbox One for games and plays movies and tv shows, listen to music, and play games (locally or on a connected Xbox One console). With an existing Xbox One or Microsoft account, you can purchase online media content for use in any of these apps.

Windows also comes with Windows apps to help you manage your time and numbers. With the Alarms & Clock app, you can set alarms and world times and use a timer or stopwatch. If you need to make some calculations or convert some numbers, you can use the Calculator app.

What You'll Do

Get News Information

Get Money Updates

Get the Latest Sports News

Get the Latest Weather

Get Food & Drink Information

Get Health & Fitness Information

View Maps and Directions

Create Reading List

Read Documents

Manage and Sync Files with OneDrive

Get Office

Capture a Photo or Video

Watch Movies & TV

Play Games

Listen to Music

Set Alarms & Clock

Calculate Numbers

Getting News Information

The News app that comes with Windows 10 provides a centralized place to focus on news information from around the world. You can view top stories and the latest news in business (US & World), technology, money, entertainment, politics, and sports. If you like to view your news from a specific source, you can select it from an organized list. If you're looking for a specific topic, you can search for it using the News app. The News app provides options—take a tour, customize, add a section—to help you get started as well as organizes information into easy to view and read categories (which you can customize) that you can view directly with the App bar or scroll through to find the information you want.

Use the News App

1. Click or tap the **News** tile on the Start screen or Start menu.

   The My News page appears, displaying categories along the top with the All category by default.

2. Click or tap the **Menu** button on the App bar (if you want), and then click or tap a category:

   ◆ **My News.** Home page with current news articles.

   ◆ **Interests.** Use to customize the news in My News.

   ◆ **Local.** Use to display local news.

   ◆ **Videos.** Use to watch videos.

3. To search for information, enter it in the Search box.

4. To narrow down the news, click or tap a category.

5. To scroll through news, move the pointer to display the scroll bar and then drag the scroll bar or click or tap the arrows, or swipe left or right.

6. Click or tap a topic to view it.

7. To go back to the previous screen, click or tap the **Back** button.

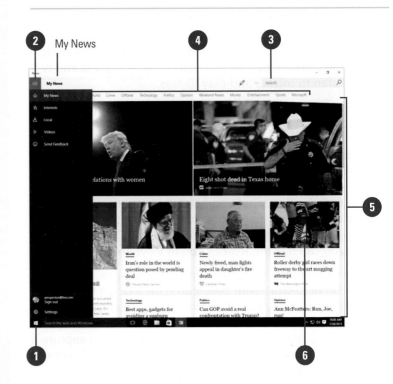

Customize the News App

1 Click or tap the **News** tile on the Start screen or Start menu.

2 Click or tap the **Menu** button on the App bar (if you want), and then click or tap the **Interests** button.

3 Click or tap a category.

◆ My Interests. Displays the main categories in My News.

◆ All Interests. Displays all categories and items.

◆ Other. Displays items in the other categories: Featured, News, Entertainment, Lifestyle, Personal Finance, or Sports.

4 To add an item, click or tap an **Add** button (+).

5 To remove an item, click or tap the **Apply** button (check mark).

6 To reorder items, drag the double-lines in the category to another position.

7 To go back to the previous screen, click or tap the **Back** button.

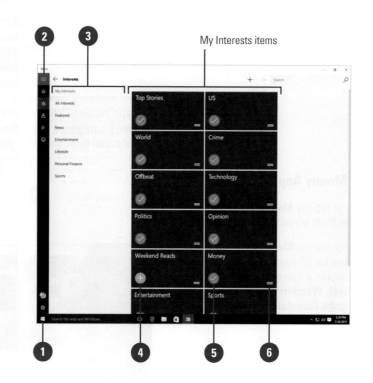

My Interests items

Did You Know?

You can change the language used for the News app and content. In the News app, click or tap the Settings button on the App bar, click or tap General, and then select a language for the app and content under Options.

Getting Money Updates

The Money app (**New!**) that comes with Windows 10 provides a centralized place to focus on financial information from around the world. You can view the latest financial news, industrial averages and indices, world markets, major currencies, stock watch lists and market movers, articles, current rates, and fund returns. The Money also includes a helpful currency converter and mortgage calculator to work with money. The app includes information from financial institutions into easy to view and read categories and videos that you can view directly with the App bar or scroll through to find the information you want.

Use the Money App

1. Click or tap the **Money** tile (**New!**) on the Start screen or Start menu.

2. Click or tap the **Menu** button on the App bar (if you want), and then click or tap a category: **Home**, **Markets**, **Watchlist**, **Currencies**, **Mortgage Calculator**, or **World Markets**.

3. To search for information, enter it in the Search box.

4. To select an option, click or tap a category.

5. To scroll through items, move the pointer to display the scroll bar and then drag the scroll bar or click or tap the arrows, or swipe left or right.

6. Click or tap an item to view it or enter data as requested under Currencies or Mortgage Calculator.

7. To go back to the previous screen, click or tap the **Back** button.

Money Home

Customize the Money App

1 Click or tap the **Money** tile (**New!**) on the Start screen or Start menu.

2 Click or tap the **Menu** button on the App bar (if you want), and then click or tap a category with an add button, such as **Watchlist** or **Currencies**.

◆ Currencies. Click or tap the **Add to Watchlist** button (star).

3 Navigate to the area with the add or tap a category.

4 To add an item to the watchlist, click or tap an **Add** button (+), search for the item, and then select it.

5 To edit the watchlist, click or tap the **Edit** button, make changes, and then click or tap the **Apply** button.

◆ Remove. Click or tap the **Delete** button (x) for the item.

◆ Reorder. Drag the item to another position.

6 To go back to the previous screen, click or tap the **Back** button.

Did You Know?

You can change the language used for the Money app and content. In the Money app, click or tap the Settings button on the App bar, click or tap General, and then select a language for the app and content under Options.

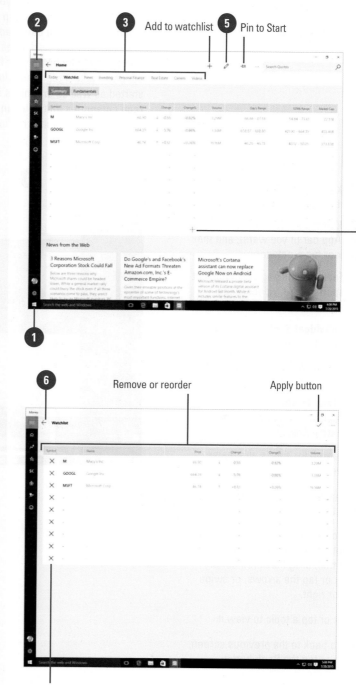

Add to watchlist Pin to Start

Remove or reorder   Apply button

Delete button

Getting the Latest Sports News

If you're a sports nut, then you'll love the Sports app that comes with Windows 10. The Sports app allows you to view the latest news in the world of sports. You can read the top stories, get the latest news, look at schedules, and read magazine articles. You can also customize the Sports app to focus on your favorite teams. The Sports app provides options—take a tour and add your favorite sports—to help you get started as well as organizes sports information into easy to view and read categories that you can view directly with the App bar or scroll through to find the information you want.

Use the Sports App

1. Click or tap the **Sports** tile on the Start screen or Start menu.

2. Click or tap the **Menu** button on the App bar (if you want), and then click or tap a category:

    ◆ **Today.** Home page with current sports score, videos, slide shows and articles.

    ◆ **Individual Sports.** Select a specific sport.

    ◆ **My Favorites.** Use to view, add, and organize your favorites.

    ◆ **More Sports.** Use to add and remove sports from the main categories.

3. To search for sports and teams, enter it in the Search box.

4. To display a category within a sport, click or tap a category.

5. To scroll through news, move the pointer to display the scroll bar and then drag the scroll bar or click or tap the arrows, or swipe left or right.

6. Click or tap a topic to view it.

7. To go back to the previous screen, click or tap the **Back** button.

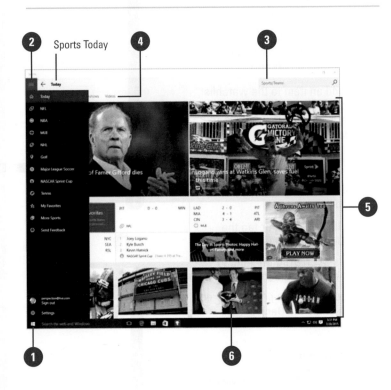

Customize the Sports App for Your Favorite Teams

1. Click or tap the **Sports** tile on the Start screen or Start menu.

2. To customize the sports on the App bar, click or tap the **More Sports** button on the App bar, and then click or tap a **Star** icon to toggle on or off.

3. To quickly add to favorites, enter a search to find the team, and then click or tap the **Add to Favorites** button (star).

4. Click the **My Favorites** button on the App bar.

5. Click or tap the **Add** button (+) under Favorite Teams or Favorite Sports.

6. Type the name of your favorite team or sports. As you type a list of suggestions appears.

7. Click or tap the team or sports you want to add as a favorite.

8. To remove a favorite, click or tap the **Edit** button, click or tap the **Delete** button (x) for the item and then click or tap the **Apply** button.

9. To go back to the previous screen, click or tap the **Back** button.

Did You Know?

You can change the language and auto refresh for the Sports app. In the Sports app, click or tap the Settings button on the App bar, click or tap General, and then select a language for the app and content under Options.

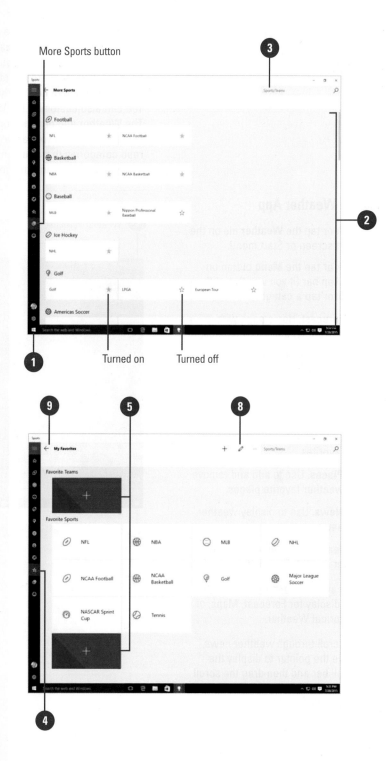

More Sports button

Turned on   Turned off

Getting the Latest Weather

As you get ready to start the day or go on a trip, it's good to know what the weather is like, so you can prepare for it. With the Weather app that comes with Windows 10, you can get all the weather information you need for your local area or other areas that you might be going to visit nationally. You can get hourly forecasts, maps, and historical weather. You can also customize the Weather app to display your local weather. The Weather app provides options—add your favorite places—to help you get started as well as organizes information into easy to view and read categories that you can view directly with the App bar or scroll through to find the information you want.

Use the Weather App

1. Click or tap the **Weather** tile on the Start screen or Start menu.

2. Click or tap the **Menu** button on the App bar (if you want), and then click or tap a category:

   ◆ **Forecast.** Home page with current weather for favorites.

   ◆ **Maps.** Use to display a weather map by temperature, radar, precipitation, satellite, or cloud.

   ◆ **Historical Weather.** Use to display historical weather by temperature or rainfall for favorites.

   ◆ **Places.** Use to add and remove weather favorite places.

   ◆ **News.** Use to display weather news.

3. To search for weather locations, enter it in the Search box.

4. Use available options to change the display for Forecast, Maps, or Historical Weather.

5. To scroll through weather news, move the pointer to display the scroll bar and then drag the scroll bar or click or tap the arrows, or swipe left or right.

6. Click or tap a topic to view it.

7. To go back to the previous screen, click or tap the **Back** button.

Weather Forecast   Add to Favorites

Customize the Weather App

1. Click or tap the **Weather** tile on the Start screen or Start menu.

2. To quickly add to favorites, enter a search to find the team, and then click or tap the **Add to Favorites** button (star).

3. Click or tap the **Places** button on the App bar.

4. Click or tap the **Add** button (+) under Favorite Places.

5. Type the name of your favorite place. As you type a list of suggestions appears.

6. Click or tap the place you want to add as a favorite.

7. To remove a favorite, right-click or tap-hold a favorite, and then click or tap **Remove from Favorites**.

8. To go back to the previous screen, click or tap the **Back** button.

Did You Know?

You can change launch location. In the Weather app, click or tap the Settings button on the App bar, click or tap General, and then click or tap the Always Detect My Location or Default Location option. For the Default Location option, specify a location.

You can view weather in celsius or fahrenheit. In the Weather app, click or tap the Settings button on the App bar, click or tap General, click or tap the Fahrenheit or Celsius option.

Getting Food & Drink Information

The Food & Drink app that comes with Windows 10 provides a convenient place to get information on food & drink. You can find and view recipes, even using hands-free mode by waving your hand in front of a camera. If you like a recipe, you can add it to a collection—like a bookmark—for easy reference in the future or add it to your meal planning for the week. If you have your own tried and true recipes, you can also add them to a collection. If you need ingredients for a recipe, you can add them to a shopping list that you can save or print out.

Use the Food & Drink App

① Click or tap the **Food & Drink** tile on the Start screen or Start menu.

② To search for a recipe, enter search text in the Search box.

③ To navigate around, right-click the screen (on a computer) or swipe up from the bottom edge or down from the top edge of the screen (on a mobile device), and then click or tap a category tile.

◆ To edit or delete, use buttons on the App bar.

④ To browse recipes, scroll, click or tap **Browse Recipes**, or a category, and then click or tap a filter as desired to narrow it down.

◆ To add a recipe, click or tap **Add a recipe**, enter a title, and take a picture or add an image.

⑤ To view a recipe, click or tap it.

⑥ Click or tap any of the following:

◆ **Add to Collections.** Add the recipe to a collection.

◆ **Add to Meal Planner.** Add the recipe a weekly meal planner.

◆ **Hands-Free Mode.** Wave your hand in front a camera to turn recipe pages.

◆ **Add to Shopping List.** Add ingredients to a shopping list.

⑦ To go back to the previous screen, click or tap the **Back** button.

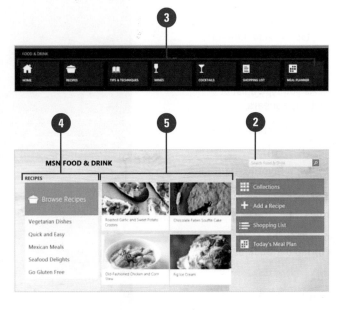

Getting Health & Fitness Information

The Health & Fitness app that comes with Windows 10 provides a convenient place to to get information on health and fitness. You can find and track information on nutrition and calories, exercise, and health, including symptoms, drugs, and conditions. The Health & Fitness app organizes information into easy to view and read categories and videos that you can view directly with the App bar or scroll through to find the information you want. In options, you can specify your own information as a baseline for progress, use information to personalize your experience, and control advertising settings.

Use the Health & Fitness App

1. Click or tap the **Health & Fitness** tile on the Start screen or Start menu.

2. To search for information, enter search text in the Search box.

3. To navigate around, right-click the screen (on a computer) or swipe up from the bottom edge or down from the top edge of the screen (on a mobile device), and then click or tap a category tile.

4. To browse information, scroll, and then click or tap a category, topic, video, or article.

5. Click or tap any of the following:

   ◆ **Diet Tracker.** Track your calorie intake and dietary needs.

   ◆ **Nutrition and Calories.** Look up information.

   ◆ **Exercise Tracker.** Track your exercise program

   ◆ **Health Tracker.** Track your physical health.

   ◆ **Symptoms.** Check symptoms step by step using lists.

   ◆ **Drugs and Conditions.** Look up information.

6. To go back to the previous screen, click or tap the **Back** button.

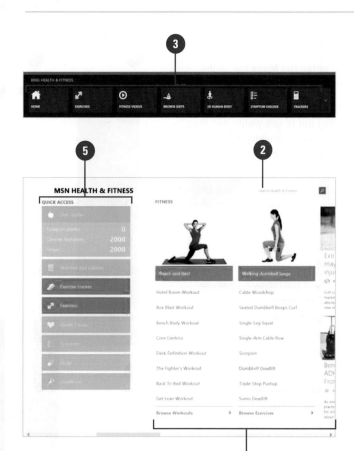

Viewing Maps and Directions

With the Maps app that comes with Windows 10, you can view maps and get directions for any place in the world. The Maps app makes it easy to view maps, either at a high level with a big picture view or at a street level with a details view. When you open the Maps app for the first time, you're asked to allow or block the use of location services, which makes use of your location, a circle on the map. The app organizes information into easy to view and read categories that you can view directly with the App bar or scroll through to find the information you want. You can search for points of interest, such as hotels, coffee, restaurants, shopping, or museums.

View Maps

1. Click or tap the **Maps** tile on the Start screen or Start menu.

2. Click or tap the **Menu** button on the App bar (if you want), and then click or tap a category: **Map**, **Search**, **Directions**, **Favorites**, or **3D Cities**.

3. To search for locations, click or tap the Search box or button on App bar, enter a location or click or tap a category: **Hotels**, **Coffee**, **Restaurants**, **Shopping**, or **Museums**.

4. Use any of the following options on the Map bar.

   ◆ **Rotate Map.** Use to rotate North, counterclockwise or clockwise.

   ◆ **Tilt.** Use to adjust the view tilt.

   ◆ **Show My location.** Shows my location (circle).

   ◆ **Map views.** Displays the map in Road view or Aerial view.

   ◆ **Zoom.** Use to zoom in or out.

   TIMESAVER *Press Ctrl+ + or Ctrl+ - to zoom in or out.*

5. To set app options and preferences, click or tap the **Settings** button on the App bar.

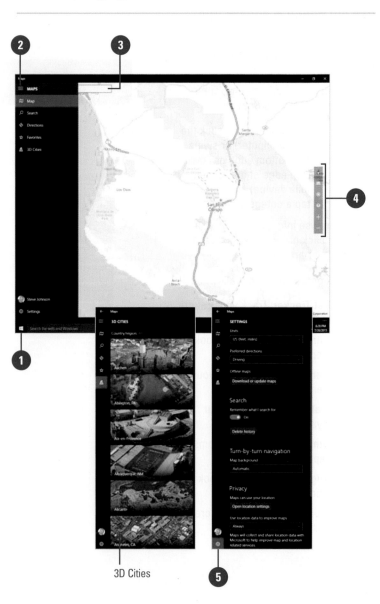

3D Cities

Get Directions with the Maps App

1. Click or tap the **Maps** tile on the Start screen or Start menu.

2. Click or tap the **Directions** button on the App bar.

   TIMESAVER *Press Ctrl+D to get directions.*

3. Click or tap in the **Start** box (A), and then enter a start location.

   ◆ To cancel an entry, click the **Close** button (x) in the box.

4. Click or tap in the **End** box (B), and then enter a end location.

5. To change options, click or tap **Options**, and then select the check boxes settings you want.

6. Click or tap the **Get directions** button.

   ◆ To switch the start and end destination, click or tap the **Get reverse directions** button.

7. Click or tap the travel method (**Car**, **Bus**, or **Walk**).

8. Click or tap the directions on the map, or scroll the top banner or click or tap the **Go** arrow to get step-by-step directions.

9. To go back to the previous screen, click or tap the **Back** button.

Did You Know?

You can set options for offline maps to reduce data charges. Click or tap Settings on the Start screen or menu, click or tap System, click or tap Offline Maps, and then specify options to download maps, metered connections, and map updates.

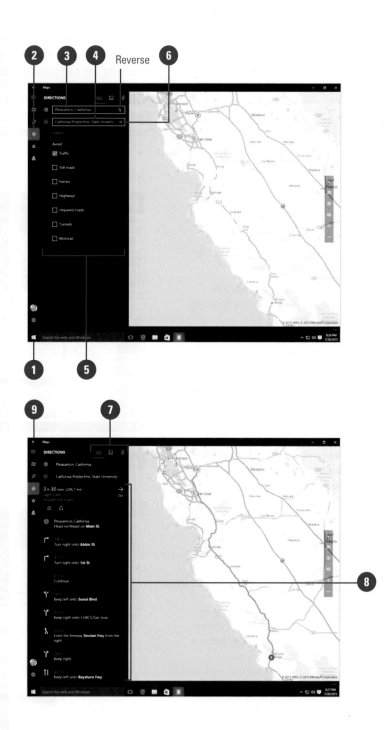

Reverse

Creating Reading Lists

If you don't have time to read an article in an app or on the web, you can add it to your Reading List so you can come back to it later. The Reading List app helps you keep track of and share the articles you want to read. You can quickly add an article to your Reading List by using the Share button. In the Reading List app, you can open and read new articles, or continue reading existing articles in a separate side by side window, or delete articles as you like.

Use the Reading List App

1. To add an article to Reading List, open the app (such as Microsoft Edge) and display the article, click or tap the **Share** button, click or tap **Reading List**, and then click or tap **Add**.

   After you add articles, you can view and read them in the Reading List app.

2. In the Start screen or Start menu, click or tap **All apps**, and then click or tap **Reading List**.

3. To search for an article, click or tap the Search button, and then enter search text.

4. To view an article, click or tap the article or click or tap **Open** or **Continue viewing** for the Spotlight article.

   Your web browser opens in a side by side screen, where you can read the article.

5. Move the point, and then click or tap the **Next** or **Previous** button, or swipe left or right.

6. To close the article in the side by side screen, click or tap the Close button or drag down to the bottom edge of the screen.

7. To delete an article, right-click or tap-hold an article to select it, and then click or tap the **Delete** button on the App bar.

Reading Documents

With the Reader app that comes with Windows 10, you can view PDF and XPS documents. The Reader app allows you to view PDF (Portable Document Format)—instead of using Adobe Reader—as well as view to view Microsoft's XPS (XML Paper Specification). In the Reader app, you can zoom in and out to view the document, search for words and phrases, take notes and fill in forms (with permission and rights), save your changes, and then print or share files with others.

Use the Reader App

1. In the Start screen or Start menu, click or tap **All apps**, and then click or tap **Reader**.

2. Click or tap a recently opened document or click or tap the **Browse** button, select a file, and then click or tap **Open**.

3. Click or tap the **Zoom In** or **Zoom Out** button or pinch in or out.

4. Move the point, and then click or tap the **Next** or **Previous** button, swipe left or right, or use the page controls to navigate pages.

5. Right-click a blank area of the screen or swipe up from the bottom edge or down from the top edge, and then click or tap a button on the App bar.

   ◆ **Find.** Search for text.

   ◆ **One page or Two pages.** Display one or two pages. For two pages, click or tap Coverpage to display page one.

   ◆ **Continuous.** Display one page and continuously scroll.

   ◆ **Save or Print.** Save, Save as, or print the document.

   ◆ **More.** Display a menu with Rotate and Info (document).

6. To highlight or add a note, select text, right-click the selection, and then click or tap **Highlight** or **Add a Note** and type. Click or tap it to remove/delete it.

7. To close a file, click the **Close** button (X) on the Tab bar.

Open File button on Tab bar

Managing Files with OneDrive

OneDrive is a cloud-based file hosting service that allows you to upload files to and download files from an online drive and sync files with other devices, such as Windows Phone, iPhone, or Android. You can use OneDrive in File Explorer (**New!**), a web browser at OneDrive.com, or a mobile device using the OneDrive app to access your online files using your Microsoft account. OneDrive allows you to organize your files so that you can share them with contacts, or make them public, or keep them private. The cloud-based service offers 7 GB (gigabytes) of free storage for new users; however additional storage is available for purchase. OneDrive comes with a default set of folders, Documents, Favorites, Pictures, and some Public (Shared) folders, you can use to store your files. When you store files on OneDrive, it automatically makes them available on other devices without having to sync them. The files you store in the Public (Shared) folder are available for anyone to view and edit.

Use the OneDrive App

1. In the Start screen or Start menu, click or tap **All apps**, and then click or tap **OneDrive**.

   ◆ You can also click the **File Explorer** icon on the taskbar, and then click or tap **OneDrive**.

   File Explorer opens, displaying the OneDrive folder. A check mark next to a folder or file indicates it's synced online.

2. To create a new folder, click or tap the **New folder** button on the Home tab, enter a folder name, and then press Enter.

3. To find a folder or files, click or tap in the Search box, and then enter a name search.

4. To open a folder, click or tap the folder icon.

5. To open a file, double-click or double-tap the file icon to view it.

   If the document is from Microsoft Office, an Office WebApp opens in your web browser where you can view and edit the document.

6. To delete a file, select the file, click or tap the **Delete** button on the Home tab.

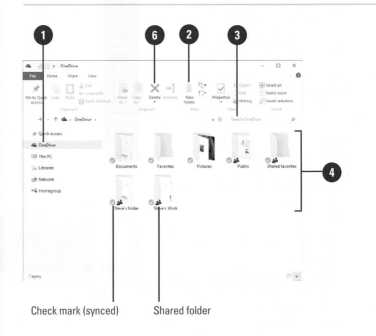

Check mark (synced)   Shared folder

Use OneDrive.com

1. Click or tap the **Microsoft Edge** tile on the Start screen or Start menu, or taskbar button.

2. Enter *www.onedrive.live.com* in the Address box, and the click or tap the **Go** button or press Enter.

   ◆ You can also right-click a folder or file on OneDrive in File Explorer, and then click or tap **View on OneDrive.com**.

3. If prompted, enter your username and password for your Microsoft account to access your OneDrive, and then click or tap **Sign in**.

   The OneDrive web page opens, displaying your files.

4. To open a folder, click or tap **Files**, and then click or tap the folder tile.

5. To open a file, click or tap the file icon to view it.

6. Use any of the following options:

   ◆ **New.** Use to create a new folder or Microsoft Office document.

   ◆ **Upload.** Use to upload files to the OneDrive.

   ◆ **Share.** Use to share OneDrive files using apps.

   ◆ **Download.** Use to download OneDrive files to a local drive.

   ◆ **Move to** or **Copy to.** Use to move or copy files.

   ◆ **More.** Use to rename, create album from folder, or embed.

7. To manage storage or get OneDrive apps (for Windows Phone, iPhone, or Android), click or tap the links.

8. To manage your account, profile, or sign out, click or tap the username (upper-right corner).

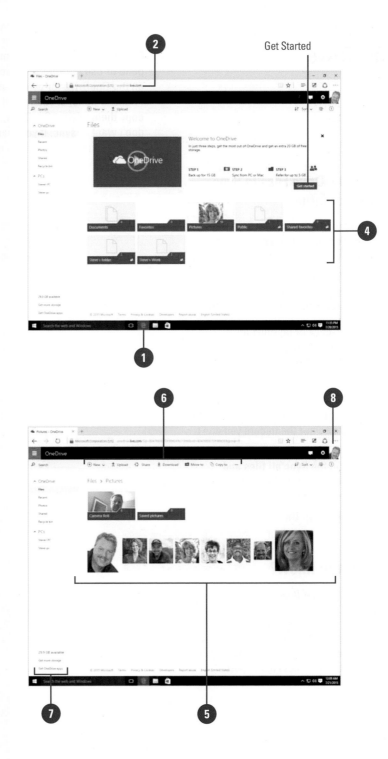

Syncing Files with OneDrive

You can upload (copy) and sync (**New!**) files to your OneDrive using File Explorer or web browser. One way is to select the files in File Explorer, and then copy them to a OneDrive folder in the Navigation pane or use the OneDrive web site. Either way, the files are available on the OneDrive for use on other devices (**New!**), such as Windows Phone, iPhone, or Android. If you don't want to sync files everytime you copy them to your OneDrive, you can specify which folders you do or don't want to sync. If you want to share a folder or file, you can copy (share) a link to paste it in a message or post.

Make OneDrive Files to Sync Online or Offline

1. In the Start screen or Start menu, click or tap **All apps**, and then click or tap **OneDrive**.

   ◆ You can also click the **File Explorer** button on the taskbar, and then click or tap **OneDrive**.

2. Right-click or tap-hold an OneDrive folder, and then click or tap **Choose OneDrive folders to sync**.

3. Click or tap the check boxes to select the folders you want to sync files or clear the folders you don't.

   ◆ All files and folders. Click or tap the **Sync all files and folders in my OneDrive** check box to select it.

4. Click or tap **OK**.

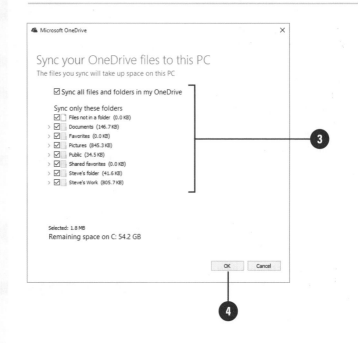

Did You Know?

You can share a OneDrive link. In File Explorer, right-click or tap-hold the folder or file, you want to share, and then click or tap Share a OneDrive link command. The link is copied. Now, you can paste it in a message or post.

Upload Files to the OneDrive

1. In the Start screen or Start menu, click or tap **All apps**, and then click or tap **OneDrive**.

   ◆ You can also click the **File Explorer** button on the taskbar, and then click or tap **OneDrive**.

   File Explorer opens, displaying the OneDrive folder. A check mark next to a folder or file indicates it's synced online.

2. To upload files to OneDrive, drag them to the main OneDrive folder or a subfolder.

   ◆ You can also copy and paste folders or files to OneDrive.

3. To download files from OneDrive, drag them from the the main OneDrive folder or a subfolder to a local drive or folder.

   ◆ You can also copy and paste folders or files from OneDrive to a local drive or folder.

Copy & paste

Getting Office

If you're interested in Microsoft Office 365 (Office in the cloud), you can use the Get Office app (**New!**)—available on the Start screen or menu—to get a free trial for the online Office subscription product. With Office 365, you get full installed Office applications (Word, Excel, PowerPoint, OneNote, Outlook, Publisher, and Access), access to documents across multiple devices, extra storage with OneDrive, and connections with Skype. If you would like to take notes, you can use Microsoft OneNote (**New!**)—which comes with Windows 10—to stay organize and keep them up-to-date on all your devices. OneNote works like a yellow legal pad, where you can create multi-level outlines, draw pictures (using gestures or a mouse), highlight information, scratch out text, insert images, and mark items as done on a To Do list.

Get Microsoft Office 365

1 Click or tap the **Get Office** tile on the Start screen or Start menu.

The Welcome screen opens, displaying links.

2 If you want to try Office 365, click or tap **Try for free**.

Microsoft Edge opens, displaying the Office 365 site, where you get a free trial of Office 365.

3 Read about the details of the subscription, and click or tap any related links.

4 Click or tap the **Close** button (x) to exit Microsoft Edge.

5 To exit the app, click or tap the **Close** button (x).

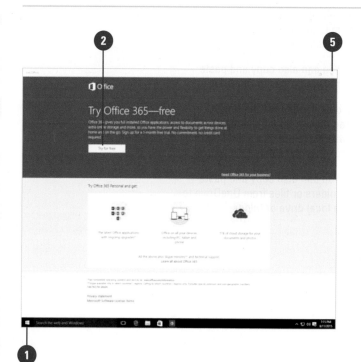

Take Notes with OneNote

1. Click or tap the **OneNote** tile on the Start screen or Start menu.

   ◆ You can also start OneNote from the Action Center. Click or tap the **Action Center** icon on the taskbar, and then click or tap the **Note** button (**New!**).

   The Welcome note opens, displaying OneNote instructions.

2. On first use, click or tap the **Next** or **Previous** button or swipe left or right to take the tour, and then click or tap the **Start using OneNote (read-only)**.

3. To add a note, click or tap the **Add** button (+), enter a title, and then enter notes.

4. To edit a note, select the note, and then change the notes.

5. To work with notes, click or tap a tab.

   ◆ **Home.** Use to format text, and tag an item with a To Do check box.

   ◆ **Insert.** Use to insert a table, file attachment, picture, or link.

   ◆ **Draw.** Use to type text, select objects, select ink, and draw with a marker, highlighter, or mouse/touch gesture,

   ◆ **View.** Use to add rule lines, zoom in and out, and to 100 view.

   Changes to notes are automatically saved.

6. To exit the app, click or tap the **Close** button (x).

Instructions on first use

Existing notes

Capturing a Photo or Video

With the Camera app (**New!**) that comes with Windows 10, you can use a digital camera to capture a still photo or video. When you open the Camera app for the first time, you're asked to allow or block the use of your webcam and microphone. When you capture a photo, you can crop it as desired using the Photos app (**New!**). When you capture a video, you can trim if you like, and play it back in the Photos app (**New!**). After you capture a photo or video, it's automatically saved in a collection folder within the Pictures library folder. If you don't like the way a photo or video came out or no longer want it, you can delete it at any time. You can also view a photo or play a video and manage individual files in the Photos app or in File Explorer. Before you can use the Camera app, you need to have a digital camera such as a webcam, installed on your device.

Use the Camera App

1. In the Start screen or Start menu, click or tap **All apps**, and then click or tap **Camera**.

2. To set the timer, click or tap the **More** button, click or tap **Self timer**, specify a delay time, and then click or tap the **Apply** button (check mark).

   ◆ Continuous photos. Select the **Continue taking photos every 5 seconds until I presss the camera button again** check box.

3. Do either of the following to capture a video or photo:

   ◆ Video. Click or tap the **Video mode** button to select it (if needed), and then click or tap it again to start/stop.

   ◆ Photo. Click or tap the **Photo mode** button to select it (if needed), and then click or tap it again to start/stop.

4. To view photos/videos in Photos, click or tap the **Photos** button.

5. To move between photos/videos in the collection, move the pointer to display buttons, click or tap the **Back** or **Forward** button, or swipe left or right.

Capture a Video

1. In the Start screen or Start menu, click or tap **All apps**, and then click or tap **Camera**.

2. Click or tap the **Video mode** button to select it (enlarges), if needed.

3. Click or tap the **Video mode** button to start the video capture, and then click or tap it again to end it.

4. Click or tap the **Photos** button.

5. Click or tap the **Play/Pause** button or the screen.

6. To trim the video, click or trap the **Trim** button, drag the start or end points, and then click or tap the **Save a copy** button.

7. To delete the video, click or tap the **Delete** button, and then click or tap **Delete** to confirm.

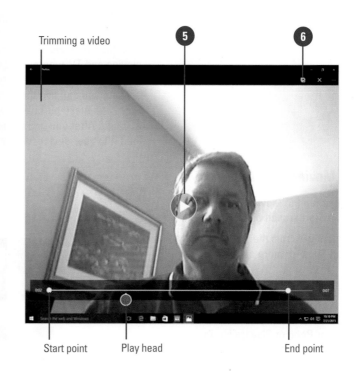

Trimming a video

Start point   Play head   End point

Capture a Photo

1. In the Start screen or Start menu, click or tap **All apps**, and then click or tap **Camera**.

2. Click or tap the **Photo mode** button to select it (enlarges), if needed.

3. Click or tap the **Photo mode** button to capture the still photo.

4. Click or tap the **Photos** button.

5. To crop the photo, click or trap the **Edit** button, click or tap the **Crop** button, drag the corner points, and then click or tap the **Apply** button.

6. To delete the photo, click or tap the **Delete** button, and then click or tap **Delete** to confirm.

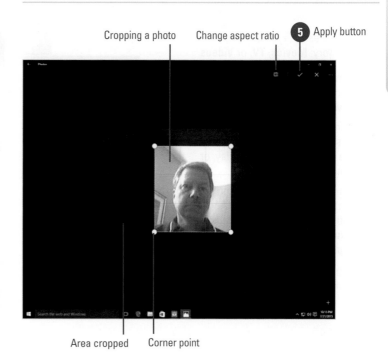

Cropping a photo   Change aspect ratio   Apply button

Area cropped   Corner point

Watching Movies & TV

With the Movies & TV app (**New!**) that comes with Windows 10, you can watch videos located in the Videos library folder or movies & TV from the Windows Store. The Store allows you to rent or buy and watch movies and TV, where you can find them organized by new releases, top-selling, featured, last night's, top rated, and genres. If you can't find a video, you can use the Search button to locate it. In order to use the Store and make purchases, you need to login with an existing Microsoft account. After you find the movie or TV show you want, you can download it to your device, where you can play in in the Movies & TV app.

Use the Movies & TV App

1. Click or tap the **Movies & TV** tile on the Start screen or Start menu.

2. To get media from the Store, click or tap **Shop for more** on the App bar.

   In the Store, browse or search for movies or TV shows. Click or tap a media tile to view it, where you can Buy, Rent, or Play trailer. To return, click or tap **Your video library** under Movies & TV.

   ◆ When prompted to make a purchase, sign in, and then follow the steps to buy, and then download it.

3. In Movies & TV, click or tap a category: **Movies**, **TV**, or **Videos**.

4. Browse or search for media, and then click or tap a media tile to view it.

5. Point to or select a movie or TV episode to display options you can use to get a description, play, or remove it.

6. When you play it, use button controls—**Cast to Device**, **Aspect Ratio**, **Audio menu**, **Play/Pause**, **Volume**, **Full Screen**, and **Repeat**—on the Video bar.

7. To go back to the previous screen, click or tap the **Back** button.

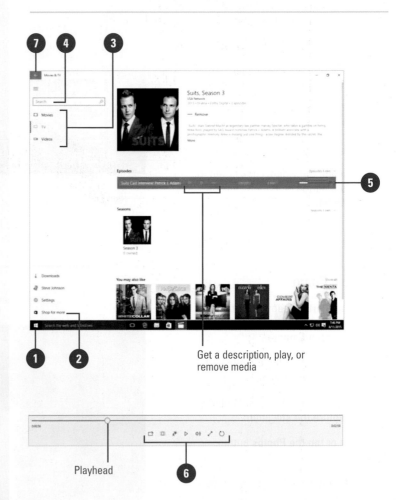

Get a description, play, or remove media

Playhead

Playing Games

With the Xbox app (**New!**) that comes with Windows 10, you can play local or online games, meet up with friends, make new ones, and earn achievements. You don't need Xbox One console to play games, but if you do, you can sign in to your Microsoft account to use your existing achievements, activity, game history, and friends as well as connect to it and stream games—and TV shows and movies with OneGuide. With the Windows Store, you can buy and install games on your PC. As a game player, you can create an avatar—a character that represents you—and profile for use during games, and view your gaming achievements. As you play games, you can messages your friends to add to the action. If you would like to capture your results, you can record or screenshot the action to enjoy it later using Game DVR (**New!**). If you can't find a game, you can use the Search button to locate it.

Use the Xbox App

1. Click or tap the **Xbox** tile on the Start screen or Start menu.

2. To connect to Xbox One, click or tap **Connect** on the App bar, click or tap **Add a device**, select it, and then click or tap **Connect**.

3. To get games from the Store, click or tap **Shop** on the App bar or a tile under Featured on the Home.

   In the Store, browse or search for games. Click or tap a game tile to view it, where you can Buy or get free and download it. To return, click or tap the **Close** button (x).

4. In Xbox, click or tap a category: **Home** or **My games**.

5. On the App bar (as desired), click or tap **Messages** to chat with friends, **Activity alerts** to set them, **Achievements** to view them.

6. Click or tap a game tile to view information—like activity, achievements, and captures—and play it.

7. To capture while you play, click or tap the **Start/Stop Recording** button on the Game bar. Click or tap **Game DVR** on the App bar to access it.

8. To go back to the previous screen, click or tap the **Back** button.

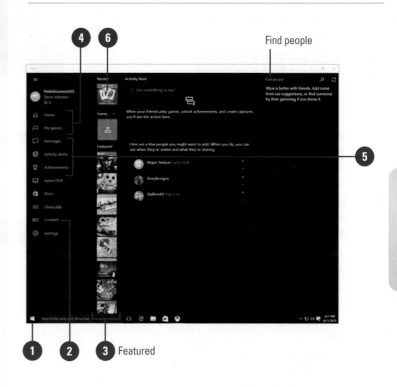

Find people

Featured

Listening to Music

With the Groove Music app (**New!**) that comes with Windows 10, you can listen to music organized by albums, artists, or songs. Groove Music allows you to explorer, buy, and play music from the Windows Store, and create collections of music on your PC (located in the Music library folder) or in the cloud on OneDrive. You can also personalize your music by creating or importing playlists. If you can't find an artist or song, you can use the Search button to locate it. If you like a subscription, you can get a Groove Music Pass to access millions of songs.

Use the Groove Music App

1. Click or tap the **Groove Music** tile on the Start screen or Start menu.

2. To get music from the Store, click or tap **Get music in Store** on the App bar.

   In the Store, browse or search for music. Click or tap a song to view it, where you can buy or get free and download it. To return, click or tap **Your music library**.

   ◆ When prompted to make a purchase, sign in, and then follow the steps to buy, and then download it.

3. In Music, click or tap a category: **Albums**, **Artists**, **Songs**, or **Now playing**.

4. Browse or search for music, and then click or tap a music tile to view it.

5. Select a song to display options you can use to play or add to a playlist.

6. When you play it, use button controls—**Playhead**, **Previous**, **Play/Pause**, **Next**, **Volume**, **Shuffle**, or **Repeat**—on the Music bar.

7. To go back to the previous screen, click or tap the **Back** button.

Settings

Create and Use a Playlist

1. Click or tap the **Groove Music** tile on the Start screen or Start menu.

2. To create a new playlist, click **New playlist** on the App bar, enter a name, and then click or tap **Save**.

   The new playlist appears on the App bar.

3. To add songs to a playlist, navigate to the album or song, click or tap the **Add to** button (+), and then select a playlist on your PC or cloud, or **Now playing**.

4. Click or tap a playlist on the App bar.

5. Click or tap the **Play** button to play the songs on the playlist.

   The current song appears on the App bar for easy access.

6. Use controls—**Playhead**, **Previous**, **Play/ Pause**, **Next**, **Volume**, **Shuffle**, or **Repeat**—on the Music bar.

   The current song appears on the Music bar for easy access.

7. To work with playlists, do any of the following:

   ◆ **Remove song.** Select the song, click or tap the **Remove** button (-) on the Selection bar.

   ◆ **Delete playlist.** Click or tap the **More** button, and then click or tap **Delete**.

8. To go back to the previous screen, click or tap the **Back** button.

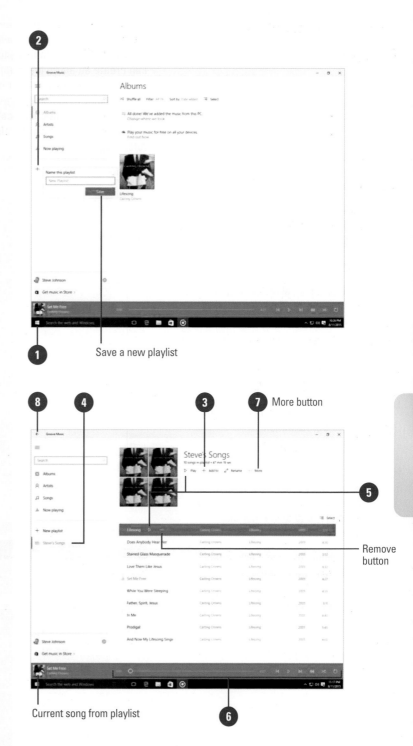

Save a new playlist

More button

Remove button

Current song from playlist

Setting Alarms & Clock

The Alarms & Clock app (**New!**) is useful for those who need to get up in the morning or need a reminder throughout the day. You can create alarms for different things and turn them on when you need them. You can create an alarm that happens only once or repeats on a consistent basis with the sound of your choice. The Alarms & Clock app also provides a timer to countdown and a stopwatch to keep track of time. It's important to note that notifications will only show if the PC is awake. In addition to alarms, you can also set times on a world clock (**New!**) for reference.

Set Alarms and World Clocks

1. In the Start screen or Start menu, click or tap **All apps**, and then click or tap **Alarms & Clock**.

2. Click or tap **Alarm**.

3. Click or tap an alarm to open it or click or tap the **New** button (+) to create one.

4. Specify the alarm time, repeat occurrence (Only once or specific days),a sound, and a snooze time.

5. Click or tap the **Save** button.

   ◆ To delete an alarm, click or tap the **Delete** button.

6. Click or tap the **On/Off** button for the alarm.

7. To use the world clock, click or tap **World Clock**, click or tap the **New** button (+) and then enter and select a location.

   ◆ To compare time, click or tap the **Compare** button.

8. To exit the app, click or tap the **Close** button (x).

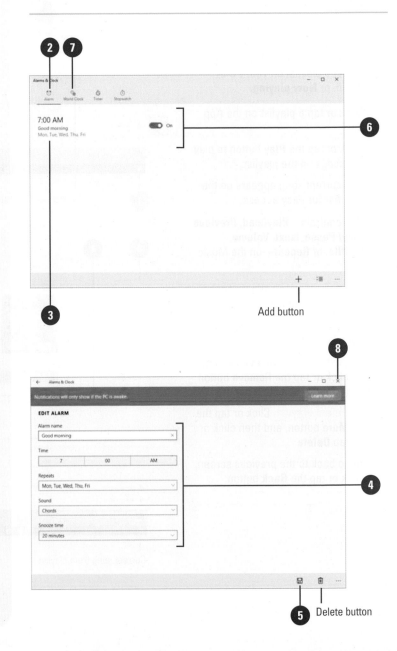

Add button

Delete button

Use a Timer

1. In the Start screen or Start menu, click or tap **All apps**, and then click or tap **Alarms & Clock**.

2. Click or tap **Timer**.

3. Click or tap the **Play/ Pause** button.

4. To add a timer, click or tap the **New** button (+), enter a name, set the time duration, and then click or tap the **Save** button.

5. To delete a timer, click or tap the **Manage** button, click or tap the **Delete** button, and then click or tap **Apply**.

6. To expand/collapse the display, click the **Expand/Collapse** button.

7. To exit the app, click or tap the **Close** button (x).

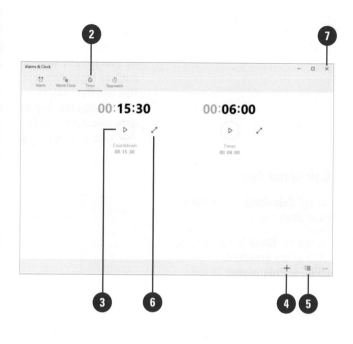

Use a Stopwatch

1. In the Start screen or Start menu, click or tap **All apps**, and then click or tap **Alarms & Clock**.

2. Click or tap **Stopwatch**.

3. Click or tap the **Reset** button (+), if needed.

4. Click or tap the **Play/Pause** button to start/resume the time.

5. To keep track of intervals, click or tap the **Laps/Splits** button (changes to a flag).

6. To expand/collapse the display, click the **Expand/Collapse** button.

7. To exit the app, click or tap the **Close** button (x).

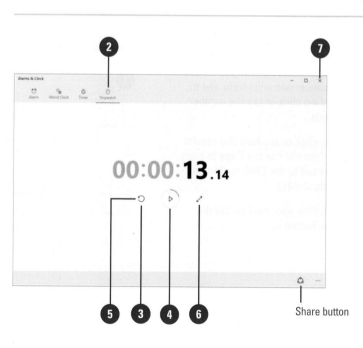

Share button

Calculating Numbers

If you don't have a handheld calculator handy, you can use the Calculator app (**New!**) by Windows 10 to perform standard calculations or even more complex ones. Calculator performs basic arithmetic, such as addition and subtraction, functions found on a scientific calculator, such as logarithms and factorials, programmer conversions, such as Hex and Decimal, as well as functions for statistical analysis. You can also change the display to perform functions, including unit conversion, date calculation, and worksheets, such as mortgage, vehicle lease, or fuel economy (mpg or L/100 km).

Use the Calculator App

1. Click or tap **Calculator** on the Start screen or Start menu.

2. Click or tap the **Menu** button, and then click or tap **Standard**, **Scientific**, or **Programmer** on the App bar.

3. Click or tap the number buttons.

4. Click or tap a function button, and then enter another number.

5. When you've entered all the numbers you want, click or tap the equals (=) button.

6. To use the converter, select a conversion type on the App bar, such as volume or weight, select the conversion units from and to, and then click or tap the number buttons.

7. Right-click or tap-hold the results, and then click or tap **Copy** to copy the result to the Clipboard to paste in a document.

8. To exit the app, click or tap the **Close** button (x).

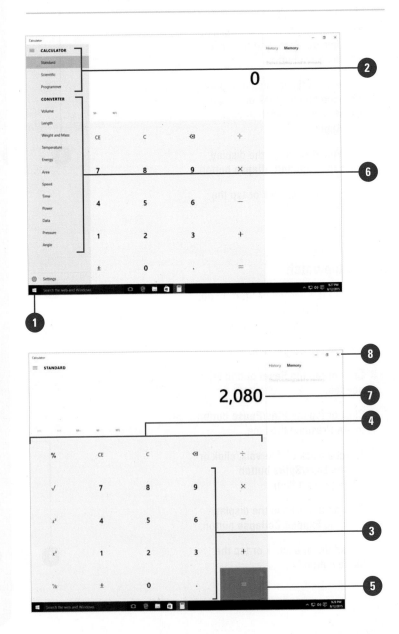

Working with Windows Accessories

11

Introduction

Windows comes with several small programs, called **accessories**, that are extremely useful for completing basic tasks, such as creating a written document. In addition to the accessories, Windows 10 also includes system tools—such as Control Panel and Task Manager—to make it easier to work with Windows.

Windows 10 provides a number of ways for you to resolve some common problems. For example, you can use older programs (designed to run on previous versions of Windows) on your Windows device by changing specific settings. You can run commands from a text-based interface (called a command line), and Windows provides an interface for quitting a program that has stopped responding without turning off your PC computer or mobile device and losing information in other programs.

Using the Windows accessories and system tools allows you to accomplish several tasks:

- ◆ Create and edit documents with WordPad
- ◆ Insert symbols with Character Map
- ◆ Capture screen shots with Snipping Tool
- ◆ Capture a sequence of actions with Steps Recorder
- ◆ Create notes with Sticky Notes
- ◆ Take handwritten notes with Windows Journal
- ◆ Take math notes with Math Input Panel

Starting and Exiting Windows Accessories

The most common way to start a Windows accessory or other system tool is to use the All apps menu, which provides easy access to programs installed on your device. A Windows accessory or system tool is made for use on the desktop, so when you start a Windows accessory or system tool from the All app menu, the program starts and displays a taskbar button. When you're done working with a program, you should exit, or close it, to conserve your PC's resources.

Start a Windows Accessory or System Tool

1. Display the Start menu.

2. Click or tap **All apps** on the menu. The All apps menu appears.

3. Click or tap **Windows Accessories** or **Windows System** to expand the sublist of apps.

4. Click or tap an app under Windows Accessories or Windows System.

   The accessory or system tool opens. A taskbar button appears for the program, which you can pin to the taskbar for easy access later.

Did You Know?

You can open a document and a program at the same time. In File Explorer, double-click or double-tap the document icon. The document opens in the associated program.

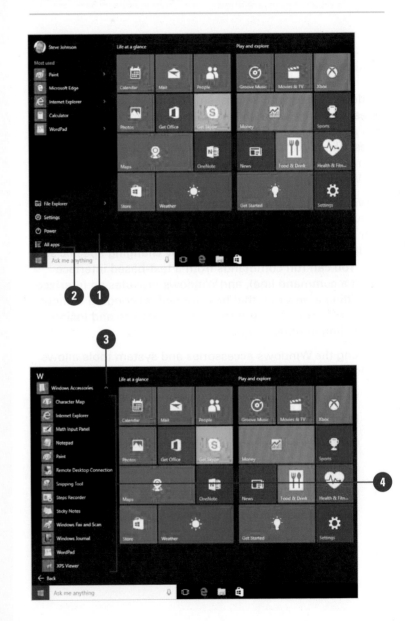

Exit a Windows Accessory or System Tool

Windows provides several ways to exit a Windows accessory or system tool:

◆ Click or tap the **File** tab, and then click or tap **Exit**.

◆ Click or tap the **Close** button on the program's title bar.

◆ Double-click or double-tap the Control-menu on the program's title bar.

◆ Right-click or tap-hold the program's taskbar button, and then click or tap **Close window**.

See Also

See "Using Windows Accessories" on page 273 for information on using Windows built-in programs.

Control menu   Close button

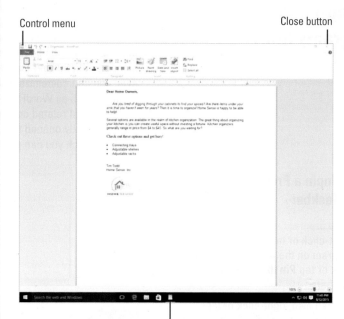

Taskbar button for WordPad

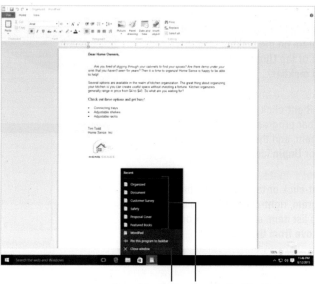

Close WordPad   Jump list for WordPad

Changing the Way Programs Start

In addition to pinning and unpinning programs to the Start screen or Start menu, you can pin and unpin them to the taskbar. The pinned items remain on the Start screen or menu, or taskbar, like a push pin holds paper on a bulletin board, until you unpin them. The default programs pinned to the taskbar include Internet Explorer and File Explorer, however, you can customize it. When you right-click or tap-hold a taskbar button—such as WordPad—on the taskbar, a list of recently opened files or folders and related commands appear for easy access. Windows tracks recently opened files, known as jump lists, to programs on the taskbar, which you can pin or unpin to the list, or click or tap to open.

Pin or Unpin a Program or Items on the Taskbar

◆ **Pin a program on the taskbar.** Right-click or tap-hold an open program on the taskbar, and then click or tap **Pin this program to taskbar**.

You can also, right-click or tap-hold a program on the Start screen or Start menu, and then click or tap **Pin to taskbar**.

◆ **Unpin a program on the taskbar.** Right-click or tap-hold a pinned program on the taskbar, and then click or tap **Unpin this program from taskbar**.

◆ **Pin or unpin an item on a jump list.** Right-click or tap-hold a taskbar program, point to a jump list item, and then click or tap the **Pin** or **Unpin** icon.

◆ **Remove an item on a jump list.** Right-click or tap-hold a taskbar program, right-click or tap-hold a jump list item, and then click or tap **Remove from this list**.

See Also

See "Customizing Apps on the Start Screen" on page 40 for more information on pinning or unpinning an app to the Start screen.

Jump list for WordPad

Click or tap to pin to jump list

Pin WordPad to taskbar

Using Windows Accessories

Windows comes with several accessories, built-in programs that are extremely useful for completing every day tasks.

One of the most useful features Windows offers is the ability to use data created in one file in another file, even if the two files were created in different Windows programs. To work with more than one program or file at a time, you simply need to open them. A pro-

gram button on the taskbar represents any window that is open. When you want to switch from one open window to another, click or tap the program button on the taskbar. If you tile, or arrange open windows on the desktop so that they are visible, you can switch among them simply by click or taping or tapping in the window in which you want to work.

Frequently Used Windows Accessories

Program	Description
Character Map	Identifies and inserts symbols and special characters into documents
Command Prompt	Executes MS-DOS commands
File Explorer	Manages files and folders
Internet Explorer	Displays web (HTML) pages
Math Input Panel	Recognizes handwritten math expressions and inserts them into documents
Notepad	Creates, edits, and displays text only documents
Paint	Creates and edits bitmap pictures
Remote Desktop Connection	Connects to a remote desktop on your network or the Internet
Run	Executes (runs) programs
Snipping Tool	Captures different parts of the screen
Step Recorder	Records a series of actions on your system
Sticky Notes	Creates color notes on the screen
Task Manager	Ends Windows tasks and displays Windows process, performance, app history, startup items, user information, services
Windows Fax and Scan	Sends and receives faxes or scanned pictures and documents
Windows Journal	Creates handwritten notes and drawn pictures to mimic a note pad
Windows Media Player	Plays sound, music, and video
WordPad	Creates, edits, and displays text, Rich Text Format, and Word documents
XPS Viewer	View an XPS document (XML Paper Specification); Microsoft's version of a PDF document

Creating a Document

A **document** is a file you create using a word processing program, such as a letter, memo, or resume. When you start WordPad, a blank document appears in the work area, known as the document window, along with a Ribbon, similar to Microsoft Office 2010, at the top. The Ribbon with two tabs—Home and View—allows you to quickly select document related commands. You can enter information to create a new document and save the result in a file, or you can open an existing file and save the document with changes. As you type, text moves, or **wraps**, to a new line when the previous one is full.

Create a Document

1. In the Start screen or Start menu, click or tap **All apps**, and then click or tap **WordPad** under Windows Accessories.

   If WordPad is already open, click or tap the **File** tab, and then click or tap **New**.

2. Type your text.

3. Press Enter when you want to start a new paragraph.

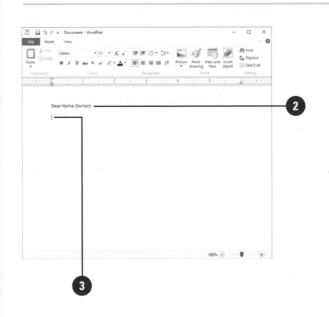

Change the Page Setup

1. Click or tap the **File** tab, and then click or tap **Page setup**.

2. Specify the paper size and source.

3. Specify the page orientation, either portrait or landscape.

4. Specify the page margins.

5. Click or tap **OK**.

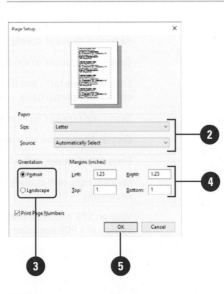

Open an Existing Document from Within a Program

1 Click or tap the **File** tab, and then click or tap **Open**.

2 Click or tap the **Files name** list arrow, and then click or tap the file type you want to open.

3 Use the Navigation pane to navigate to the folder from which you want to open the file.

4 Click or tap the document you want to open.

5 Click or tap **Open**.

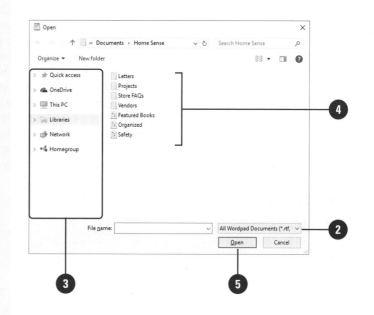

Open a Recent Document from the File Tab or Taskbar

1 Click or tap the **File** tab in the program or right-click or tap the program on the taskbar.

2 Click or tap the recently opened document you want to re-open.

Did You Know?

You can remove recently used documents from a jump list.. Right-click or tap-hold a taskbar program, right-click or tap-hold a jump list item, and then click or tap Remove from this list.

1 File tab

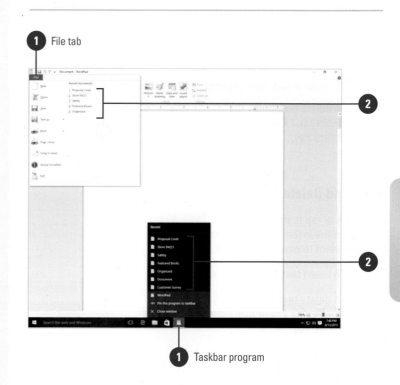

1 Taskbar program

Editing Text

One of the advantages of using a word processing program is that you can edit a document or change the contents without re-creating it. In the WordPad work area, the pointer changes to the I-beam pointer, which you can use to reposition the insertion point (called navigating) and insert, delete, or select text. Before you can edit text, you need to highlight, or select, the text you want to modify. Then you can delete, replace, move (cut), or copy text within one document or between documents even if they're different programs. When you cut or copy an item, it's placed on the Clipboard, which stores only a single piece of information at a time. You can also move or copy selected text without storing it on the Clipboard by using drag-and-drop editing.

Select and Edit Text

1. Move the I-beam pointer to the left or right of the text you want to select.

2. Drag the pointer to highlight the text.

   TIMESAVER *Double-click or tap or double-tap a word to select it; triple-click or tap or triple-tap a paragraph to select it.*

3. Perform any of the following:

   ◆ To replace text, type your text.

   ◆ To delete text, press the Backspace key or the Delete key.

I-beam pointer

Insert and Delete Text

1. Click or tap in the document to place the insertion point where you want to make the change.

   ◆ To insert text, type your text.

   ◆ To delete text, press the Backspace key or the Delete key.

Move or Copy Text

① Select the text you want to move or copy.

② Click or tap the **Cut** button or **Copy** button on the Home tab.

③ Click or tap where you want to insert the text.

④ Click or tap the **Paste** button on the Home tab.

Move or Copy Text Using Drag and Drop

① Select the text you want to move or copy.

② Point to the selected text, and then click or tap and hold the mouse button or finger.

If you want to copy the text to a new location, also press and hold the Ctrl key. A plus sign (+) appears in the pointer box, indicating that you are dragging a copy of the selected text.

③ Drag the selected text to the new location, and then release the mouse button or finger (and the Ctrl key, if necessary).

④ Click or tap anywhere in the document to deselect the text.

Dear Home Owners,

Are you tired of digging through your cabinets to find your spices? Are there items under your sink that you haven't seen for years? Then it is time to organize! Home Sense is happy to be able to help!

Several options are available in the realm of kitchen organization. The great thing about organizing your kitchen is you can create useful space without investing a fortune. Kitchen organizers generally range in price from $4 to $45. So what are you waiting for? Check out these options and get busy!

Tim Todd
Home Sense, Inc.

Dear Home Owners,

Are you tired of digging through your cabinets to find your spices? Are there items under your sink that you haven't seen for years? Then it is time to organize! Home Sense is happy to be able to help!

Several options are available in the realm of kitchen organization. The great thing about organizing your kitchen is you can create useful space without investing a fortune. Kitchen organizers generally range in price from $4 to $45. So what are you waiting for?

Check out these options and get busy!

Tim Todd
Home Sense, Inc.

Formatting Text

You can change the format or the appearance of text and graphics in a document so that the document is easier to read or more attractive. A quick and powerful way to add emphasis to parts of a document is to format text using bold, italics, underline, or color. For special emphasis, you can combine formats, such as bold and italics. In addition, you can change the font style and size. A **font** is a set of characters with the same typeface or design that you can increase or decrease in size. After formatting, you can create lists, and adjust text and line spacing.

Format Text

1. Select the text or click or tap in the paragraph you want to format.

2. Use any of the formatting tools on the Home tab to style text:

   ◆ Font list arrow
   ◆ Font Size list arrow
   ◆ Grow Text
   ◆ Shrink Text
   ◆ Bold button
   ◆ Italic button
   ◆ Underline button
   ◆ Strikethrough button
   ◆ Subscript button
   ◆ Superscript button
   ◆ Text Highlight button
   ◆ Text Color button

3. Use any of the formatting tools on the Home tab to adjust text spacing:

   ◆ Indent buttons
   ◆ List button
   ◆ Line Spacing button
   ◆ Alignment buttons
   ◆ Paragraph button

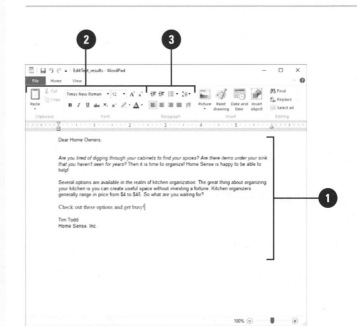

Did You Know?

Font size is measured in points. One point is 1/72 of an inch high.

Setting Paragraph Tabs

Tabs set text or numerical data alignment in relation to the edges of a document. A **tab stop** is a predefined stopping point along the document's typing line. Default tab stops are set every half-inch on the ruler, but you can set multiple tabs per paragraph at any location. Each paragraph in a document contains its own set of tab stops. The default tab stops do not appear on the ruler, but the manual tab stops you set do appear. Once you place a tab stop, you can drag the tab stop to position it where you want. If you want to add or adjust tab stops in multiple paragraphs, simply select the paragraphs first.

Create and Clear a Tab Stop

1. Select the text or click or tap in the paragraph you want to format.

2. Click or tap the ruler where you want to set the tab stop.

   ◆ **View ruler.** Click or tap the **View** tab, and then select the **Ruler** check box.

3. To move a tab, drag the tab stop to position it where you want.

4. To clear a tab stop, drag it off the ruler.

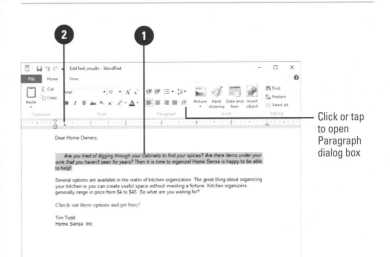

Click or tap to open Paragraph dialog box

Did You Know?

You can insert the date and time in WordPad. Open a document in WordPad, click or tap to place the insertion point, click or tap the Date And Time button on the Home tab, select a format, and then click or tap OK.

See Also

See "Setting Paragraph Indents" on page 280 for information on changing the text alignment.

For Your Information

Changing the Word Wrap Display

As you type a complete line of text, it wraps to the next line. Depending on your preference, you can change the Document window to display text wrapped to the window or ruler. To change word wrap options, click or tap the View tab, click or tap the Word Wrap button, and then click or tap the word wrap option you want. The wrapping options affect only how text appears on your screen. When printed, the document uses the margin settings specified in Page Setup.

Setting Paragraph Indents

When you indent a paragraph, you move its edge in from the left or right margin. You can indent the entire left or right edge of a paragraph or just the first line. The markers on the ruler control the indentation of the current paragraph. The left side of the ruler has three markers. The top triangle, called the **first-line indent marker**, controls where the first line of the paragraph begins. The bottom triangle, called the **hanging indent marker**, controls where the remaining lines of the paragraph begin. The small square under the bottom triangle, called the **left indent marker**, allows you to move the first-line indent marker and the left indent marker simultaneously. When you move the left indent marker, the distance between the hanging indent and the first-line indent remains the same. The triangle on the right side of the ruler, called the **right indent marker**, controls where the right edge of the paragraph ends.

Change Paragraph Indents

Select the text or click or tap in the paragraph you want to format.

◆ To view the ruler, click or tap the **View** tab, and then select the **Ruler** check box.

◆ To change the left indent of the first line, drag the First-Line Indent marker.

◆ To change the indent of the second and subsequent lines, drag the Hanging Indent marker.

◆ To change the left indent for all lines, drag the Left Indent marker.

◆ To change the right indent for all lines, drag the Right Indent marker.

As you drag a marker, the dotted guideline helps you position the indent accurately.

Hanging indent marker

Left indent marker   First-line indent marker   Right indent marker

Did You Know?

You can exact numbers for indents, line spacing, and tabs. Click or tap the Paragraph button on the Home tab, specify the amounts you want, click or tap Tabs if desired, and then click or tap OK.

Previewing and Printing a Document

Before printing, you should verify that the page looks the way you want. You save time, money, and paper by avoiding duplicate printing. Print Preview shows you the exact placement of your text on each printed page. Printing a paper copy is a common way to review and share a document. You can use the Print button on the toolbar to print a copy of your document using the current settings, or you can open the Print dialog box and specify the print options you want.

Preview a Document

1. Click or tap the **File** tab, point to **Print**, and then click or tap **Print preview**.

2. Use the toolbar buttons to preview the document:

   ◆ To change the view size, click or tap the preview screen or **100%**.

   ◆ To view other pages, click or tap **Next Page** or **Prev Page**.

   ◆ To view two pages at a time, click or tap **Two Pages**.

   ◆ To print the document, click or tap **Print**.

3. When you're done, click or tap **Close print preview** button.

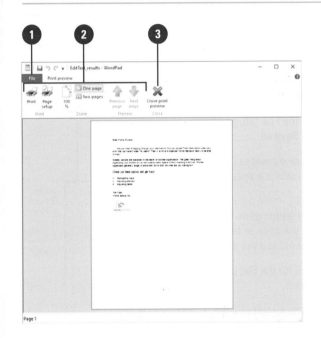

Print All or Part of a Document

1. Click or tap the **File** tab, and then click or tap **Print**.

2. Click or tap a printer.

3. Specify the range of pages you want to print.

4. Specify the number of copies you want to print.

5. Click or tap **Print**.

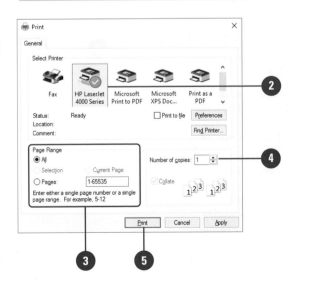

Saving and Closing a Document

Saving your files frequently ensures that you don't lose work during an unexpected power loss. The first time you save, specify a file name and folder in the Save As dialog box. The next time you save, the program saves the file with the same name in the same folder. If you want to change a file's name or location, you can use the Save As dialog box again to create a copy of the original file. To conserve your PC's resources, close any file you are not working on. WordPad saves a document by default in the **Rich Text document (RTF)**. In addition to RTF, you can also save documents in **Office Open XML document (DOCX)**, which is for Microsoft Word 2010 or later, **OpenDocument text (ODT)**, which is for exchanging office documents, and **Plain Text Document (TXT)**, which is for plain text.

Save a Document

1. Click or tap the **File** tab, and then click or tap **Save as**.

   ◆ You can also point to Save as, and then select a specific file format.

2. Use the Navigation pane to navigate to the drive or folder in which you want to save the file.

3. Type a name for the file, or use the suggested one.

4. To change the format of a file, click or tap the **Save as type** list arrow, and then click or tap a file format.

5. Click or tap **Save**.

New folder button

Did You Know?

You can save a file in a new folder. In the Save As dialog box, click or tap the New Folder button, type the new folder name, press Enter, click or tap Open, and then click or tap Save.

You can close a document. Click or tap the Close button in the program window or click or tap the File tab, and then click or tap Close. If necessary, click or tap Yes to save your changes.

Inserting Special Characters

When you need to insert special characters such as ©, ™, or ® that don't appear on your keyboard, you can use a special accessory program called Character Map to do the job. Character Map displays all the characters that are available for each of the fonts on your PC computer or mobile device.

Insert a Special Character

1. In the Start screen or Start menu, click or tap **All apps**, and then click or tap **Character Map** under Windows Accessories.

2. Click or tap the **Font** list arrow, and then click or tap a font.

3. Double-click or double-tap the character you want to insert.

   TIMESAVER *Click or tap a character to see an enlarged view of it.*

4. Click or tap **Copy** to place the character on the Clipboard.

5. To exit the app, click or tap the **Close** button (x).

6. Click or tap in the document to place the insertion point.

7. Click or tap the **Paste** button on the Home tab.

   TIMESAVER *Press Ctrl+V to quickly paste the contents from the Clipboard.*

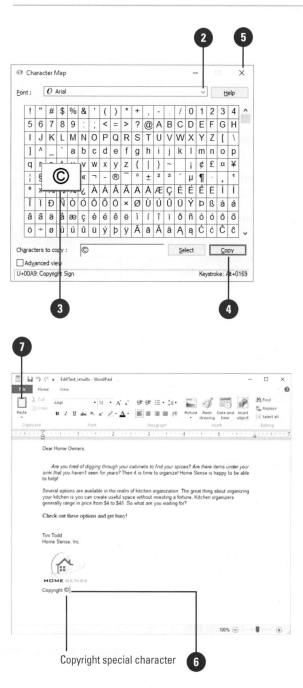

Copyright special character

Inserting and Editing Information

Instead of switching back and forth between programs to copy and paste information, you can insert, or embed, the information. With **embedding**, a copy of the object becomes part of the destination file. If you want to edit the object, you make changes in the destination file, and the original file remains intact. Once you embed data, you can edit it using the menus and toolbars of the source program without leaving the program in which it's embedded (that is, the destination program). For example, you can create a picture in a program, such as Paint, or select an existing picture and insert it into a WordPad document. In WordPad, you can use the Paint drawing button on the Home tab to embed a new Paint object. The inserted picture is an object you can resize.

Embed an Existing Object

1. Click or tap where you want to embed the object.

2. Click or tap the **Insert Object** button on the Home tab.

3. Click or tap the **Create from File** option.

4. Click or tap **Browse**, and then double-click or double-tap the file with the object you want to use.

5. Click or tap **OK**.

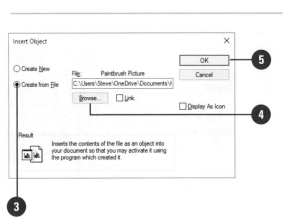

Embed a New Object

1. Click or tap where you want to embed the object.

2. Click or tap the **Insert Object** button on the Home tab.

3. Click or tap the **Create New** option.

4. Double-click or double-tap the type of object you want to create.

5. Enter information in the new object using the menus and toolbars in the source program.

6. Click or tap the **Program** button, and then click or tap **Exit and return to document** to close the object.

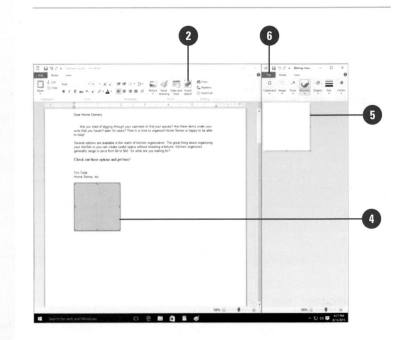

Edit an Object

1. Open the document with the object you want to edit.

2. Double-click or double-tap the object.

3. Edit the object using the menus and toolbars in the source program.

4. Click or tap the **Program** button, and then click or tap **Exit and return to document** to close.

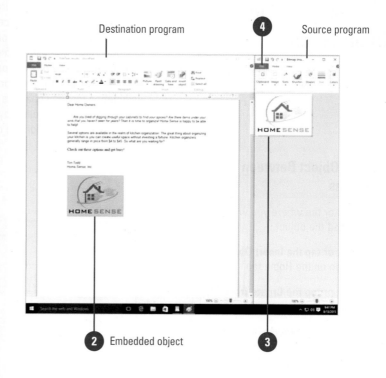

Destination program

④

Source program

② Embedded object

③

Resize an Object

1. Click or tap the object to select it.

2. Drag a sizing handle to change the size of the object.

   ◆ Drag a corner sizing handle to change height and width simultaneously.

   ◆ Drag the top or bottom middle sizing handle to change height.

   ◆ Drag the left or right middle sizing handle to change width.

Drag a sizing handle   ②

Linking and Updating Information

When you want to keep source and destination files in sync with each other, you can link the source file that created the object with the destination file that displays the object. **Linking** displays information stored in one document (the source file) into another (the destination file). You can edit the linked object from either file, although changes are stored in the source file. Only a representation of the object appears in the destination file; any changes made to the object are done in the source file, whether you access it by double-clicking or double-tapping the object in the destination file or by opening it in the source program.

Link an Object Between Programs

1. Click or tap where you want to embed the object.

2. Click or tap the **Insert Object** button on the Home tab.

3. Click or tap the **Create from File** option.

4. Click or tap **Browse**, and then double-click or double-tap the file with the object you want to link.

5. Select the **Link** check box.

6. Click or tap **OK**.

Did You Know?

You can use Paste Special to link part of a file. Select and copy the information, click or tap where you want to link the copied information, click or tap the Edit menu, click or tap Paste Special, click or tap the Paste Link option to link, select a format, and then click or tap OK.

Linked object

Update a Linked File

1. Open the file with the source program.

2. Edit the file using the source program's commands.

3. Click or tap the **Save** button on the toolbar.

4. Click or tap the **Close** button (x) to exit the source program.

5. Open the linked file with the destination program.

   The object automatically updates.

6. Click or tap the **Save** button on the toolbar.

7. Click or tap the **Close** button (x) to exit the destination program.

Destination program   Source program

Did You Know?

You can share information among programs with OLE. With OLE (Object Linking and Embedding), you can work with a document in WordPad and at the same time take advantage of the specialized tools in another program, such as Paint or Microsoft Excel. By using OLE, you'll be able to access features from other programs, edit data easily, update to the latest information, and save space.

You can change a link to update manually. In the destination program, right-click or tap-hold the linked object, click or tap Links, click or tap the Manual option button, and then click or tap Close.

For Your Information

Finding, Changing, and Breaking a Linked Object

Instead of opening a linked object from the source file to make changes, you can open a linked object from the destination file using the Open Source button in the Links dialog box. The Open Source button finds the source file containing the linked object and opens that file. After making changes, you exit and return to the destination file. The Links dialog box keeps track of the source file location. You can change the linked source to a different file by using the Change Source button. If you want to disregard a link and change it to an embedded object, select the linked object in the destination file, right-click or tap-hold the object, click or tap Object Properties, click or tap the Link tab, click or tap Break Link, click or tap Yes in the message box, and then click or tap OK. On the Link tab in the Object Properties dialog box, you can also open or change the source file, change update options, and update the source for the selected object.

Running Commands

Besides running Windows programs, you can also enter commands and run programs written in MS-DOS. **MS-DOS** stands for Microsoft Disk Operating System. MS-DOS, or DOS, employs a **command-line interface** through which you must type commands at a **command prompt** to run different tasks. A character such as a > or $ appears at the beginning of a command prompt. Each DOS command has a strict set of rules called a **command syntax** that you must follow when expressing a command. Many commands allow you to include switches and parameters that give you additional control of the command.

Run a Command

1. In the Start screen or Start menu, click or tap **All apps**, and then click or tap **Command Prompt** under Windows System.

   ◆ You can also right-click or tap-hold the lower-left corner, and then click or tap **Command Prompt**.

2. At the prompt, type a command including any parameters, and then press Enter.

3. When you're done, click or tap the **Close** button (x), or type **exit**, and then press Enter.

Find a Command

1. In the Start screen or Start menu, click or tap **All apps**, and then click or tap **Command Prompt** under Windows System.

2. At the prompt, type **help**, and then press Enter.

3. Read the list of commands. Use the scroll bar or scroll arrows to display additional information.

4. When you're done, click or tap the **Close** button (x), or type **exit**, and then press Enter.

Prompt

Get Information About a Command

1 In the Start screen or Start menu, click or tap **All apps**, and then click or tap **Command Prompt** under Windows System.

2 At the prompt, type a command followed by a space and **/?**, and then press Enter.

3 Read the information about the command. Use the scroll bar or scroll arrows to display additional information.

4 When you're done, click or tap the **Close** button (x), or type **exit**, and then press Enter.

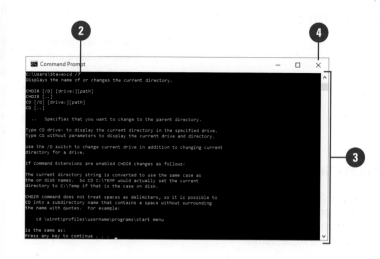

Did You Know?

You can use a wildcard character to change more than one file. An asterisk is a wildcard and represents any number of characters. For example, the command *dir at*.doc* matches atback.doc, ati.doc, and atlm.doc.

You can change the appearance of the Command Prompt window. Right-click or tap-hold the Command Prompt window title bar, and then click or tap Properties.

You can ping a connection to make sure it works and find out an IP address. Ping is a diagnostic network tool that verifies whether an IP address is accessible. To test a connection, type **ping *IP address*** at the command prompt, and then press Enter. To find an IP address, type **ipconfig /?** or type **ipconfig /all**, and then press Enter. To get a new IP address, type **ipconfig/release**, press Enter, type **ipconfig/renew**, and then press Enter.

Common DOS Commands

Command	Purpose
cd *foldername*	Changes to the specified folder
cls	Clears the screen
copy	Copies the specified files or folder
dir	Lists the contents of the current folder
c: (where c is a drive)	Switches to the specified drive
exit	Closes the Command Prompt window
rename	Renames the specified file or files
more *file name*	Displays the contents of a file, one screen of output at a time
type *file name.txt*	Displays the contents of the text file

Snipping the Screen

The Snipping Tool allows you to capture a screen shot of anything currently on your screen as an image file. If you want to delay the capture, you can use the delay (**New!**). After you capture the image, you can annotate, save and share it with others in an e-mail. You can capture the screen in different ways: draw a free-form shape around an object, draw a rectangle around an object, select a window, or take the entire screen. If you want to use a keyboard shortcut in any app, you can press Win+PrtScn (Print Screen) to take a screenshot and automatically save it in the Pictures folder as a PNG file.

Use the Snipping Tool

1. In the Start screen or Start menu, click or tap **All apps**, and then click or tap **Snipping Tool** under Windows Accessories.

2. To change snipping options, click or tap the **Options** button, select the options you want, and then click or tap **OK**.

   ◆ **Delay.** Use to select a delay in seconds for the capture (**New!**).

3. To capture a screen, click or tap the **New Snip** button arrow, and then select a capture option: **Free-form Snip**, **Rectangle Snip**, **Window Snip**, or **Full-screen Snip.**

4. Drag a free-form or rectangle shape, or click or tap a window.

5. To annotate the image, use the **Pen**, **Highlighter**, and **Eraser** tools.

6. To share the image, use the **Send Snip** button.

7. Click or tap the **Save** button, select a save location, and then select a file format (PNG, GIF, JPEG, or MHT). MHT is for a single page web page.

8. To copy it to the Clipboard to paste in a document, click or tap the **Copy** button.

9. To exit the app, click or tap the **Close** button (x).

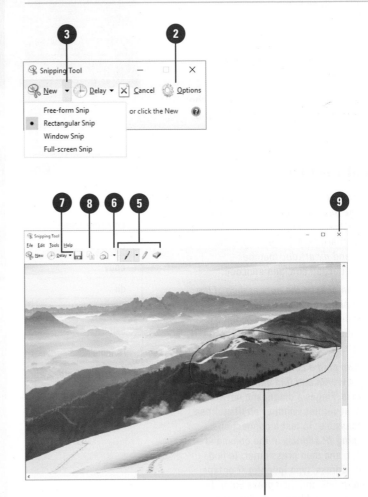

Annotation

Recording Steps

Using Steps Recorder, you can record a series of actions you take on your system, including a text description of your steps and a picture of the screen during each step. After you capture the steps you want to take, you can save them in a ZIP file that you can use later or send to others in an email message. There are a few important notes to be aware of before you get started. You cannot record anything you enter and some full screen apps might not capture the entire screen. If you use two monitors, Steps Recorder will capture both screens, so you should adjustments as needed.

Record a Series of Actions

1. In the Start screen or Start menu, click or tap **All apps**, and then click or tap **Steps Recorder** under Windows Accessories.

2. Click or tap the **Start Record** button, and then execute the steps you want.

3. When you're done, click or tap the **Stop Record** button.

   The Steps Recorder window opens, displaying a text description of your steps and a picture of the screen during each step,

4. Click or tap the **Save** button.

5. Select a folder, type a name for the file, and then click or tap **Save**.

   The recorded steps are saved in a ZIP file.

   ◆ **Email.** Click or tap to send the recorded steps as a file attachment in your default email program.

6. To exit the app, click or tap the **Close** button (x).

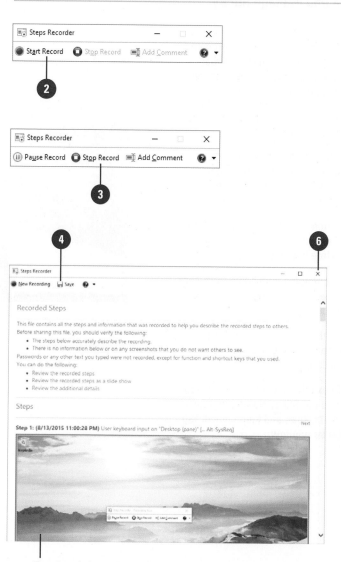

Text description and screen shots of the recorded steps

Creating Sticky Notes

A sticky note is an electronic postem note. With Sticky Notes, you always have a not pad handy for jotting down things you want to remember or keep handy when you need them. When you start the Sticky Notes program, a new sticky note appears on the desktop along with the Sticky Notes button on the taskbar. You can add more notes or remove the ones you no longer need. The notes appear in yellow by default, however, you can change them to another color to make them easier to identify.

Create and Manage Sticky Notes

1. In the Start screen or Start menu, click or tap **All apps**, and then click or tap **Sticky Notes** under Windows Accessories.

2. If a new sticky note appears, type the text you want in it.

3. To create a new sticky note in Sticky Notes, point to a notes, and then click or tap the **Add** button (+).

4. To delete a sticky notes, point to a notes, and then click or tap the **Delete** button (x).

5. To change a note color, right-click or tap-hold a note, and then select a color.

6. To move a note, drag the top of the note to another location on the desktop.

7. To exit the app, right-click or tap-hold the Sticky Notes program on the taskbar, and then click or tap **Close window**.

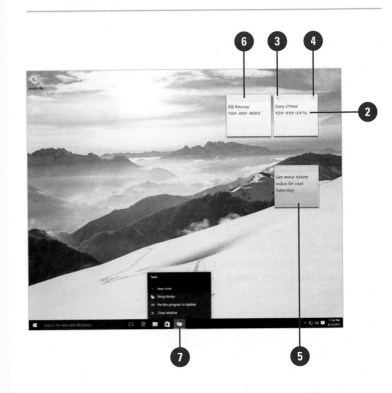

Handwriting Journal Entries

With Windows Journal, you can handwrite notes and draw pictures to mimic a notebook pad. Since Windows 10 is designed for use with tablets and mobile devices, you can use a pen or finger to take hand-written notes. The program is available on a standard PC and you can use them with a mouse, but not as effectively. Windows Journal provides a toolbar with easy to use buttons that allow you to select a pen, highlighter, or eraser to create and save notes.

Handwrite Journal Entries

1 In the Start screen or Start menu, click or tap **All apps**, and then click or tap **Windows Journal** under Windows Accessories.

 ◆ **Of first use.** Click or tap **Install** or **Cancel** to install the Journal Note Writer printer driver, which captures an image of the document.

2 Click or tap the **Pen** button arrow on the toolbar, and then select a pen style.

3 Handwrite notes or make a drawing.

4 To make corrections, click or tap the **Erase** button arrow, select an eraser size, and then drag to erase on the page.

5 Use many of the common tools on the toolbar and menus to create a handwritten document.

6 When you're done, click or tap the **Save** button on the toolbar, type a name, specify a location, and then click or tap **Save**.

7 Click or tap the **File** menu, and then click or tap **Exit**.

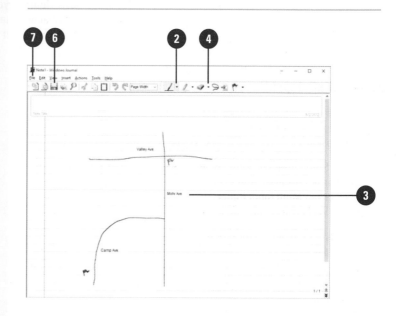

Using the Math Input Panel

If you use Windows to take notes in math or you work in an engineering or scientific profession, then you need the Math Input Panel. The Math Input Panel recognizes handwritten math expressions and inserts them into other programs. The program needs to support Mathematical Markup Language (MathML). Just open the document in which you want to insert your math expressions, start Math Input Panel, handwrite your math expression, and then click or tap Insert. If you take notes in Windows Journal, you can convert your handwritten math expression to normal text that you can use in a word processing program. Simply drag the select expression directly into the Math Input Panel.

Use the Math Input Panel

1. Open the document in which you want to insert the math expression.

2. In the Start screen or Start menu, click or tap **All apps**, and then click or tap **Math Input Panel** under Windows Accessories.

3. Handwrite the math expression you want.

   As you write, the expression appears in the recognition box. The **Write** button is selected by default.

4. To correct a letter, click or tap the **Select and Correct** button, select a part of the expression, and then select a correction from the menu.

5. To erase the expression, click or tap the **Erase** button, and then drag to erase it.

6. To clear the expression and start over, click or tap the **Clear** button.

7. To undo or redo, click or tap the **Undo** or **Redo** button.

8. Click or tap **Insert** to place it in the open document.

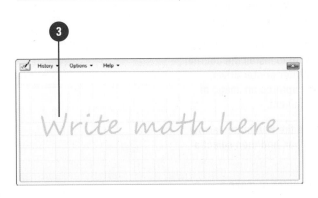

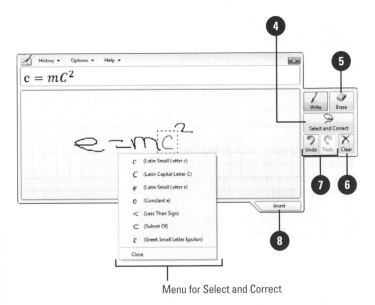

Menu for Select and Correct

Running Older Programs

Some older programs are designed to run on earlier versions of Windows and don't work properly on Windows 10. You can set the compatibility of Windows 10 to act like an earlier version of Windows to run an older program. In addition, you can also set display resolution and color settings, and user privilege levels to provide the best level of compatibility for the program and the Windows 10 operating system. You set options in the Compatibility tab in the program's Properties dialog box.

Set Compatibility for an Older Program

1. Click or tap the **File Explorer** icon on the taskbar, and then locate the older program.

2. Right-click or tap-hold the program you want to run, and then click or tap **Properties**.

3. Click or tap the **Compatibility** tab.

4. Select the **Run this program in compatibility mode for** check box.

5. Click or tap the list arrow, and then click or tap the version of Windows in which the program was designed.

6. Select the check boxes for applying the appropriate settings to the display, based on the program's documentation.

7. Click or tap **OK**.

Did You Know?

You can test your program using the Program Compatibility troubleshooter. In the Control Panel (under Windows System on All apps), click or tap the Troubleshooting icon in Small icons or Large icons view, and then click or tap the Run Programs Made For Previous Versions Of Windows link to start the Program Compatibility troubleshooter. Follow the on-screen instructions.

Quitting a Program Not Responding

If a program stops responding while you work or freezes up, Windows provides you with the option to end the task. When you end a task, you'll probably lose any unsaved work in the problem program. If the problem persists, you might need to reinstall the program or contact product support to fix the problem. Pressing Ctrl+Alt+Delete or click or tapping the Close button closes the non responsive program and opens the Task Manager, where you can stop the program. You can also use the Task Manager to view system performance and log off users.

End a Task Not Responding

1. Right-click or tap-hold the taskbar, and then click or tap **Task Manager**.

   If Windows doesn't respond, press Ctrl+Shift+Esc or press Ctrl+Alt+Delete, and then click or tap **Task Manager**.

2. Click or tap the **More details** or **Fewer details** to display more or less information.

3. Select the program not responding (on the Processor tab in More details view).

4. Click or tap **End task**. If you're asked to wait, click or tap **End now**.

End a Program Not Responding

1. If a program is not responding, click or tap the **Close** button on the program's title bar. Click or tap several times, if necessary.

2. If you see a dialog box telling you the program is not responding, click or tap **End Now**.

3. When a message appears, click or tap **Send Information** to send information about the error over the Internet to Microsoft, or click or tap **Cancel** to continue.

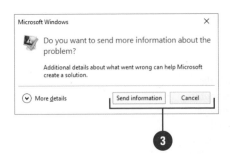

More details   Fewer details

Customizing Windows

Introduction

Windows 10 gives you the ability to customize your work environment to suit your personal needs and preferences. You can customize Windows 10 by using Settings or by using the Control Panel. Settings provide the options you need for using Windows in full-screen view with Windows apps, while the Control Panel provides the options you need for customizing the desktop and other advanced Windows settings. Some options overlap between Settings and Control Panel.

You can change the main Windows features through Settings, which displays a list of categories, including System, Devices, Network & Internet, Personalization, Accounts, Time & language, Ease of Access, Privacy, and Update & security, where you can specify the options you want. For example, you can personalize the Lock screen, Start screen or menu, and account picture, and specify general options to set the time, app switching, spelling, and language. You can also set options to refresh, remove, or reinstall Windows 10.

You can adjust some Windows features through the Control Panel, a central location for changing Windows settings. From the Control Panel you access the individual programs for changing the properties, or characteristics, of a specific element, such as the desktop or the taskbar. The Control Panel displays utilities in two different views: Category and Small or Large Icons. Control Panel Category view displays utilities in functional categories based on tasks with some direct links, while Small or Large Icons view displays an icon for each utility program. Each icon in the Control Panel represents an aspect of Windows that you can change to fit your own working habits and personal needs. Some Control Panel settings are vital to how you work (such as the Date and Time or the Language settings) and others are purely aesthetic (such as the background picture).

What You'll Do

View Windows Settings

Personalize the Lock and Start Screen

Change the Start Appearance

Customize the Start Screen

Change System Settings

Change Time and Language Settings

Sync Options on Other Devices

View the Control Panel

Customize the Desktop

Use a Screen Saver

Change Text Size on the Screen

Change the Screen Display

Set the Date and Time

Change Regional and Language Options

Work with Fonts

Display and Arrange Toolbars

Customize the Taskbar & Notifications

Change the Way a Disc or Device Starts

Use the Ease of Access Tools & Center

Listen to Your System

Recognize Your Speech

Set Ease of Access Options

Viewing Windows Settings

With Settings, you can customize the use of Windows 10. You can access Settings from the Start menu, which displays a list of main categories (**New!**), including System, Devices, Network & Internet, Personalization, Accounts, Time & Language, Ease of Access, Privacy, and Update & security, where you can specify the options you want. When you select a main category, a navigation pane appears with subcategories, where you can specify specific options, such as add devices and accounts, personalize the display, check for Windows update, set spelling correction, time, and language. You can also set options to refresh, remove, or reinstall Windows 10. If you're not sure where an option is located, you can search for it using the Search box on the taskbar (**New!**) or in Settings.

View and Change Windows Settings

1. Click or tap the **Settings** button on the Start screen or Start menu.

   The Settings window appears with easy access links.

2. To search for a setting, enter it in the Search box.

3. Click or tap a main category under Settings.

4. Click or tap a subcategory under a category.

5. Specify the options you want.

6. Click or tap the **Back** button to go back to the main categories.

7. To close the window, click or tap the **Close** button (x) or drag the title bar down to the bottom edge of the screen.

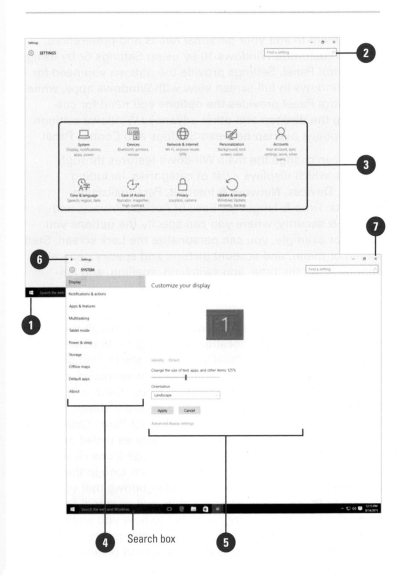

Search box

Personalizing the Lock Screen

The Lock screen appears when you start Windows 10, switch users, or put Windows to sleep. It's a security feature that helps prevent other from accessing your device. You can customize (**New!**) the Lock screen by changing it's picture, displaying status information, showing alarms, playing a slide show, or using a camera. You can select up to seven apps to run in the background and show quick status and notification on the Lock screen, and select one app to display detailed status and one app to show and set alarms.

Personalize the Lock Screen

① Click or tap the **Settings** button on the Start screen or Start menu.

② Click or tap **Personalization**.

> **TIMESAVER** *Right-click or tap-hold a blank area of the desktop, and then click or tap Personalize.*

③ Click or tap **Lock screen** under Personalization.

④ Specify the options you want for use on the Lock screen.

- ◆ **Background.** Select a background type: **Picture** or **Slideshow**.

- ◆ **For Slide Show.** Select a folder and advanced settings.

- ◆ **For Picture.** Click or tap **Browse** to select a picture.

- ◆ **Lock screen apps.** Select an app to show detailed status and show quick status. Click or tap the **Add** icon (+) to add an app for status or click or tap an icon to change or remove it.

- ◆ **Advanced.** Click or tap the **Screen timeout settings** or **Screen saver settings** links to set advanced settings.

⑤ To close the window, click or tap the **Close** button (x).

Personalizing the Start Screen

The Start screen or Start menu provides a central place to access apps, utilities, files, and device settings. The Start screen or menu display app tiles in groups with information and notifications. You can customize (**New!**) the Start screen or menu with a background design (from a picture or a collection of pictures as a slideshow) and colors. The colors change the background, menu, and selection color in Windows 10. To apply a coordinated set of colors, you can change themes.

Personalize the Start Screen or Menu

1. Click or tap the **Settings** button on the Start screen or Start menu.

2. Click or tap **Personalization**.

3. Click or tap **Background** under Personalization.

4. Specify the options you want for use on the Lock screen.

   ◆ **Background.** Select a background type: **Picture**, **Solid color**, or **Slideshow**, and then choose options to select a picture, color, or folder (with images).

   ◆ **Choose a Fit.** Select how to fill the screen: **Fill**, **Fit**, **Stretch**, **Tile**, **Center**, or **Span**.

5. Click or tap **Colors** under Personalization.

6. Drag to turn on or off the following options:

   ◆ **Automatically pick an accent color from my background.** When turned off, select a color tile.

   ◆ **Show color on Start, taskbar, and action center.**

   ◆ **Make Start, Taskbar, and action center transparent.**

7. To close the window, click or tap the **Close** button (x).

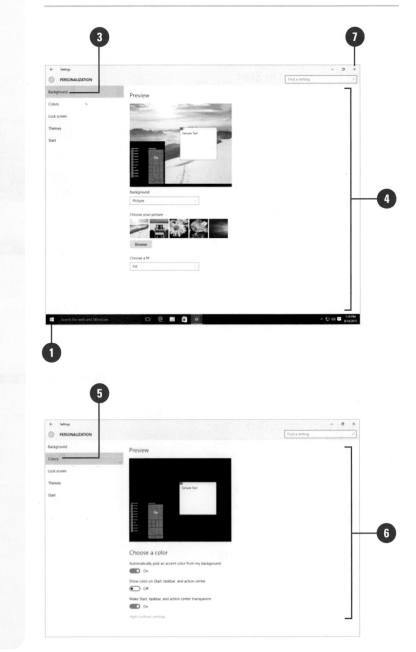

Changing the Start Appearance

You can change the entire appearance of the Start screen and desktop by using themes. A **theme** changes the background, screen saver, pointers, sounds, icons, and fonts based on a set theme, such as Lines and color or Flowers. You can use one of the predefined desktop themes (Windows Default or High Contrast), a synced theme, or create and save your own. If a theme isn't exactly what you want, you can change the appearance of colors, fonts, and sizes used for major window elements such as title bars, icons, menus, borders, and the desktop itself. The theme options differ depending on the theme type, either Windows or high contrast. High contrast is helpful for those who need Ease of Access tools, which you can set in Settings.

Change the Theme for the Start Screen

1. Click or tap the **Settings** button on the Start screen or Start menu.

2. Click or tap **Personalization**.

3. Click or tap **Themes** under Personalization, and then click or tap the **Theme settings** link.

4. Click or tap a theme in the list under My Themes, Windows Default Themes, or High Contrast Themes.

   ◆ **Get more themes.** In the Theme list, click or tap the **Get more themes online** link, and then follow the on-screen instructions to download the themes.

5. To save a theme, click or tap **Save theme** (under My Themes), name the theme, specify a location, and then click or tap **Save**.

6. To close the window, click or tap the **Close** button (x).

Customizing the Start Screen

When you start windows 10, the default is set to display the Start screen in with desktop; however, if you like using the full Start screen (for tablet) instead, you can set options to by-pass the desktop and go straight to the Start screen in full screen. You can specify which apps (most used or recently added apps) and folders appear on the Start screen or menu (**New!**) as well as whether to show items in Jump Lists (**New!**). This customization allows you to personalize the way the Start screen works in addition to how it looks.

Set Start Options

1. Click or tap the **Settings** button on the Start screen or Start menu.

2. Click or tap **Personalization**.

3. Click or tap **Start** under Personalization.

4. Drag to turn on or off the following options:

    ◆ **Show most used apps.**

    ◆ **Show recently added apps.**

    ◆ **Use Start full screen.**

    ◆ **Show recently opened items in Jump Lists on Start or the taskbar.**

5. Click or tap the **Choose which folder appear on Start** link.

6. Drag to turn on or off the folder you want to appear on Start: **File Explorer, Settings, Documents, Downloads, Music, Pictures, Videos, HomeGroup, Network, or Personal folder.**

7. To go back to the previous screen, click or tap the **Back** button.

8. To close the window, click or tap the **Close** button (x).

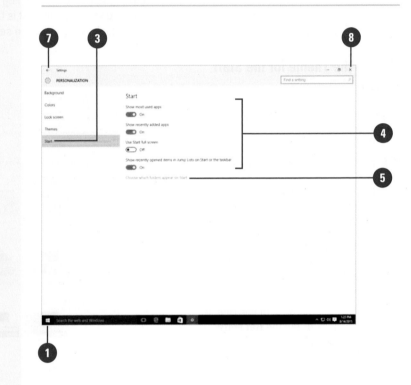

Changing System Settings

In Settings, there are an array of options for general PC use, including changing the display (size and orientation), notifications & actions (**New!**), power & sleep, multitasking between apps, using full screen Tablet mode (**New!**), and specifying default apps. If you need more space, you can uninstall or move apps, view file storage (**New!**) sizes to know what to delete, and remove all downloaded maps (**New!**). If you need to find out about your Windows version, PC name, and system information, you can locate what you need under About (**New!**).

Change System Settings

1. Click or tap the **Settings** button on the Start screen or Start menu.

2. Click or tap **System**.

3. Click or tap **Apps & features** under System.

4. Search, sort, and filter apps by drive, select the one you want, and then click or tap **Move** or **Uninstall**.

5. Click or tap **Storage** under System.

6. Specify the options you want:

   ◆ **Storage.** Click or tap a drive to see what's taking up space.

   ◆ **Save locations.** Click or tap a list arrow to specify a default location for types of files.

7. Click or tap **Offline maps** under System.

8. Specify the options you want:

   ◆ **Maps.** Click or tap the **Add** button(+) to download maps around the world. Click or tap **Delete all maps** to remove them.

   ◆ **Metered connections.** Drag on or off to only download maps on free Wi-Fi.

   ◆ **Map updates.** Drag on or off to automatically update maps.

9. To close the window, click or tap the **Close** button (x).

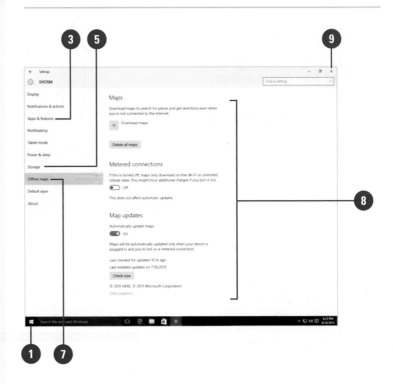

Changing Time and Language Settings

In Settings, you can specify time and language setting to customize they Windows works in your area of the world. For example you can specify date and time for your time zone and the language you prefer as you type or speak (**New!**). For date & time, you can specify the date and time in your area, formats, and whether to automatically adjust for daylight saving time. For region & language, you can specify your country or region and the language you read and type. For speech, you can specify the language you speak, default voice for apps and preview the voice, and set up your mic for speech recognition.

Change Date & Time Options

① Click or tap the **Settings** button on the Start screen or Start menu.

② Click or tap **Time & language**.

③ Click or tap **Date & time** under Time & Language.

> **TIMESAVER** *Click or tap the time & date on the taskbar, and then click or tap the Date and time settings link.*

④ Specify the options you want:

◆ **Set time automatically.** Drag the Slider on or off. Click or tap **Change** when off, specify a manual date and time, and then click or tap **Change**.

◆ **Time zone.** Select a time zone.

◆ **Adjust for daylight saving time automatically.** Drag the Slider on or off.

◆ **Formats.** Click or tap the **Change date and time formats** link to set format options (First day of week, short & long date, and short & long time).

◆ **Adjust for daylight saving time automatically.** Click or tap **Browse** to select a picture.

⑤ To close the window, click or tap the **Close** button (x).

Click or tap to display time and date settings

Set a date and time manually

Set Region & Language Options

1. Click or tap the **Settings** button on the Start screen or Start menu.

2. Click or tap **Time & language** under System.

3. Click or tap **Region & language** under Time & language.

4. Specify the options you want:

   ◆ Country or region. Select a country or region.

   ◆ Languages. Click or tap **Add a language** to select a language. Click or tap an existing icon to set as primary, change options, or remove it.

5. To close the window, click or tap the **Close** button (x).

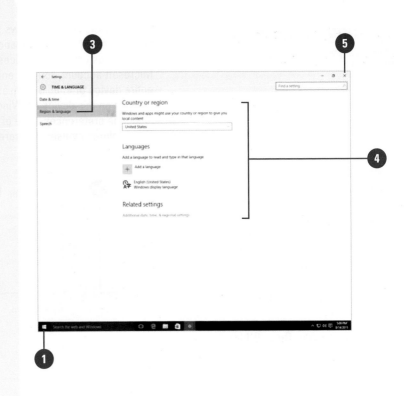

Set Speech Options

1. Click or tap the **Settings** button on the Start screen or Start menu.

2. Click or tap **Time & language** under System.

3. Click or tap **Speech** under Time & language.

4. Specify the options you want:

   ◆ Speech language. Select a language you speak.

   ◆ Text-to-speech. Select a default voice app and speed, and preview the voice.

   ◆ Microphone. Use to set up your mic for speech recognition.

5. To close the window, click or tap the **Close** button (x).

Syncing Settings on Other Devices

When you sign in to Windows 10 with a Microsoft account, you can enable the system to automatically synchronize your system and some app settings with other devices that also sign in with the same Microsoft account. You can enable or disable sync settings for the entire device or enable or disable individual settings. You can sync your settings on this device for Windows theme, web browser, passwords, language preferences, Ease of Access, and other Windows settings (File Explorer, mouse, and more).

Sync Settings with Other Devices

1. Click or tap the **Settings** button on the Start screen or Start menu.

2. Click or tap **Time & language**.

3. Click or tap **Sync settings** under Accounts.

4. Drag the slider **On** or **Off** for Sync settings.

5. Drag the sliders **On** or **Off** individual sync settings (when Step 4 is turned on):

   ◆ **Theme.**

   ◆ **Web browser settings.**

   ◆ **Passwords.**

   ◆ **Language preferences.**

   ◆ **Ease of Access.**

   ◆ **Other Windows settings.**

6. To close the window, click or tap the **Close** button (x).

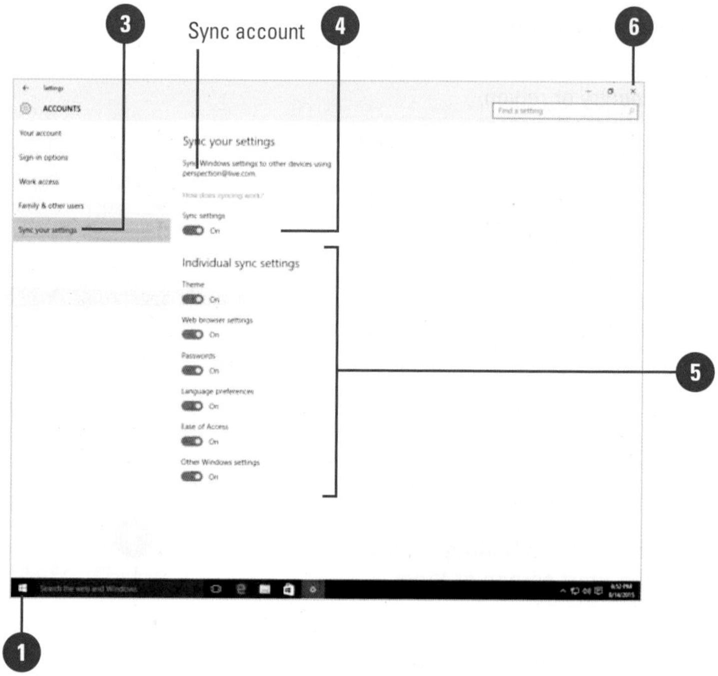

Sync account

Viewing the Control Panel

The Control Panel is a collection of advanced utility programs that determine how Windows looks and works on your PC. The Control Panel displays utilities in two different views: Category and Small or Large Icons. Control Panel Category view displays utilities in functional categories based on tasks with some direct links, while Small or Large Icons view displays an icon for each utility program as in previous versions of Windows. You can change views by using the View by button in the Control Panel. If you're not sure where an option is located, you can search for it by using the Search box in the Control Panel.

View the Control Panel

1. In the Start screen or Start menu, click or tap **All apps**, and then click or tap **Control Panel** under Windows System.

   ◆ You can also right-click or tap-hold the **Start** button, and then click or tap **Control Panel**.

2. Click or tap the **View by** button, and then click or tap a view: **Category**, **Small icons**, or **Large icons**.

3. Click or tap a Control Panel link or icon.

4. Click or tap the **Back** button on the toolbar to return to the previous Control Panel screen.

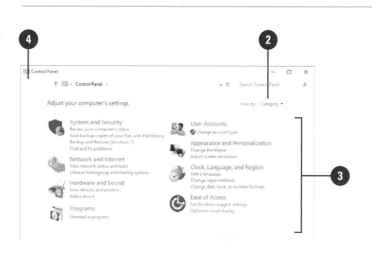

Search for Options in the Control Panel

1. In the Start screen or Start menu, click or tap **All apps**, and then click or tap **Control Panel**.

2. Click or tap in the Search box.

3. Type a word or phrase related to the option you want.

4. Click or tap a Control Panel link or icon in the list of results.

5. Click or tap the **Back** button (when available) on the toolbar or click or tap the **Close** button (x) in the Search box.

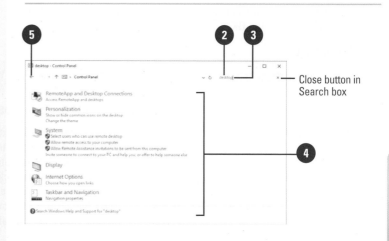

Close button in Search box

Customizing the Desktop

The icons on the desktop provide easy access to programs, folders, and system related shortcuts. If your desktop is getting cluttered, you can quickly show or hide the desktop icons. In addition, you can customize the desktop to show or hide the familiar icons: Computer, User's Files, Network, Recycle Bin, or Control Panel. You can also quickly sort, resize, and rearrange desktop icons by right-clicking or tap-holding the desktop, and then using commands on the View and Sort By submenus. In addition to customizing the desktop, you can also group apps into virtual desktops (**New!**), so you can work and multitask with apps on multiple desktops. In Task View (**New!**), you can create desktop, switch between desktops, and remove one.

Display or Hide Desktop Icons

1. Right-click or tap-hold a blank area on the desktop, and then click or tap **Personalize**.

   TIMESAVER *To show or hide all desktop icons, right-click or tap-hold the desktop, point to View, and then click or tap Show Desktop Icons.*

2. Click or tap **Themes**, and then click or tap the **Desktop icon settings** link.

3. Select or clear the check boxes to show or hide desktop icons.

4. To change the appearance of an icon, select the icon, click or tap **Change Icon**, select an icon, and then click or tap or tap **OK**.

5. Click or tap **OK**.

6. Click or tap the **Close** button.

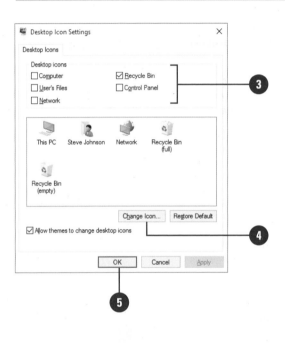

For Your Information

Previewing the Desktop with Peek Options

Peek with the Show Desktop button on the taskbar allows you to quickly preview the desktop when you have a lot open windows and apps. To change Peek options, right-click or tap-hold a blank area on the taskbar, and then click or tap Properties. On the Taskbar tab, select or clear the Use Peek To Preview The Desktop When You Move Your Mouse To Show Desktop Button At The End Of The Taskbar check box to enable or disable the option, and then click or tap OK.

Customize the Desktop Appearance

- ◆ **Resize desktop icons.** Right-click or tap-hold a blank area on the desktop, point to **View**, and then click or tap **Large Icons**, **Medium Icons**, or **Small Icons**.

- ◆ **Auto arrange icons.** The Auto arrange icons option keeps icons organized so they don't overlap each other. Right-click or tap-hold a blank area on the desktop, point to **View**, and then click or tap **Auto arrange icons**. (the option toggles on and off)

- ◆ **Align icons to grid.** The Align icons to grid option aligns icons in a window according an invisible grid to keep them organized. Right-click or tap-hold a blank area on the desktop, point to **View**, and then click or tap **Auto arrange icons**. (the option toggles on and off)

- ◆ **Show or hide desktop icons.** Right-click or tap-hold a blank area on the desktop, point to **View**, and then click or tap **Show desktop icons**. (the option toggles on and off)

- ◆ **Sort desktop items.** Right-click or tap-hold a blank area on the desktop, point to **Sort by**, and then select an option.

- ◆ **Switch between desktops.** Click or tap the **Task View** button (**New!**) on the taskbar, create a desktop (if desired), and then click or tap a desktop thumbnail to select it.

Desktop view options

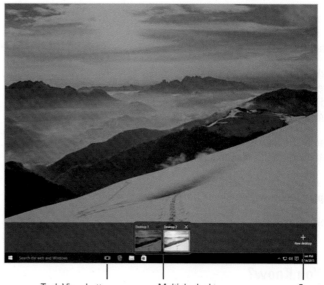

Task View button   Multiple desktop   Create desktop

Using a Screen Saver

In the past, you needed a screen saver, a continually moving display, to protect your monitor from burn in, which occurs when the same display remains on the screen for extended periods of time and becomes part of the screen. Those days are gone with the emergence of new display technology. Screen savers are more for entertainment than anything else. When you leave your system idle for a specified wait time, a screen saver displays a continuous scene, such as an aquarium, until you move your mouse or drag your finger to stop it.

Select a Screen Saver

1. Right-click or tap-hold a blank area on the desktop, and then click or tap **Personalize**.

2. Click or tap **Lock screen**, and then click the **Screen saver settings** link.

3. Click or tap the list arrow, and then click or tap a screen saver.

4. Click or tap **Settings**.

5. Select the options you want for the screen saver, and then click or tap **OK**.

6. Click or tap **Preview** to see the screen saver in full-screen view, and then move your mouse or drag your finger to end the preview.

7. Specify the time to wait until your system starts the screen saver.

8. Select or clear the **On resume, display logon screen** check box.

9. Click or tap **OK**.

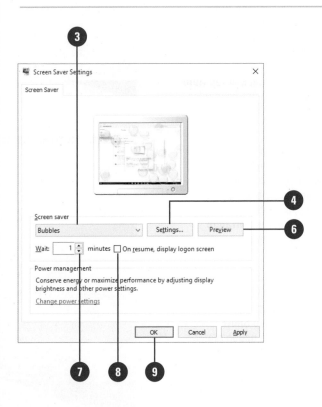

Did You Know?

You can turn off a screen saver. On the Screen Saver tab, click or tap (None) from the Screen Saver list arrow.

Changing Text Size on the Screen

If text and other items, such as icons, on the screen are not large enough for you to comfortably view, you can customize the screen to display items larger. Windows 10 allows you to increase the screen scaling option, known as the Dots Per Inch (DPI) scale, which is the number of dots that a device can display or print per linear inch. The greater the number, of dots per inch, the better the resolution. DPI is a standard measurement used to specify screen and printer resolution. After you change the screen scale option, you need to log off and restart Windows to see the change.

Change the Screen Scaling Options

1. Right-click or tap-hold a blank area on the desktop, and then click or tap **Display settings**.

2. Drag the Slider to change the size of text, apps, and other items.

3. Click or tap **Apply**.

    To set advanced settings, continue, otherwise you can stop.

4. Click or tap the **Advanced display settings** link.

5. Click or tap the **Advanced sizing of text and other items** link.

6. Specify the options you want to change the size of items or only the text size.

    NOTE *Some options are only available for displays that support it.*

7. Click or tap **Apply**.

    To see the changes, close all your programs, and log off Windows.

8. If a message alert appears, click or tap **Log off now** or **Log off later** to log off now or later.

9. To close the open windows, click or tap the **Close** button (x).

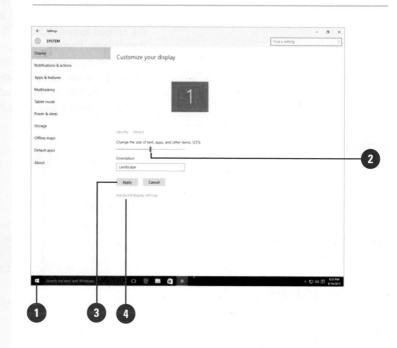

For Your Information

What's ClearType

ClearType is a font technology that improves the display on a monitor. ClearType makes on-screen text more clear, smooth, and detailed, which can reduce eye strain. ClearType is turned on by default in Windows. This is useful and most effective when you use LCD (Liquid Crystal Displays) devices, including flat-panel monitors, mobile PCs, and smaller hand-held devices. To set the ClearType setting, open Settings, click or tap Display, click or tap the Advanced display settings link, click or tap Clear Type text link, select the Turn On ClearType check box, click or tap Next, and then follow the on-screen instructions to complete it.

Changing the Screen Display

If you find yourself frequently scrolling within windows as you work or squinting to read small text, you might want to change the size of the desktop on your monitor. A monitor displays pictures by dividing the display screen into thousands or millions of dots, or pixels, arranged in rows and columns. The pixels are so close together that they appear connected. The **screen resolution** refers to the number of pixels on the entire screen, which determines the amount of information your monitor displays. A low screen resolution setting, such as 640 by 480 pixels (width by height), displays less information on the screen, but the items on the screen appear relatively large, while a high setting, such as 1024 by 768 pixels, displays more information on the screen, but the items on the screen appear smaller. You can also change the screen orientation (Landscape, Portrait, or flipped), brightness, and color quality. The higher the color quality, the more colors the monitor displays, which requires greater system memory. The most common color quality settings are as follows: 16-bit, which displays 768 colors, and 24-bit and 32-bit, both of which display 16.7 million colors.

Change the Display Size

1. In the Start screen or Start menu, click or tap **All apps**, and then click or tap **Control Panel** under Windows System.

2. Click or tap the **Adjust screen resolution** link.

3. Click or tap the **Display** button, and then click or tap a display.

4. Click or tap the **Resolution** button, and then click or tap a screen size.

5. Click or tap the **Orientation** list arrow, and then click or tap an orientation option.

6. To change color quality, click or tap the **Advanced settings** link, click or tap the **Monitor** tab, select a color setting, and then click or tap **OK**.

7. Click or tap **OK**.

8. If a message alert appears, click or tap **Keep changes** or **Revert** to accept or decline the settings.

Change Display Options in Settings

1. Right-click or tap-hold a blank area on the desktop, and then click or tap **Display settings**.

   ◆ You can also click or tap **Settings** on the Start screen or Start menu, click or tap **System**, and then click or tap **Display**.

2. Click or tap the **Orientation** list arrow, and then click or tap an orientation option: **Landscape**, **Portrait**, **Landscape (flipped)**, or **Portrait (flipped)**.

3. If available, drag the Slider to adjust brightness.

4. Click or tap **Apply**.

5. Click or tap the **Advanced display settings** link.

6. Click or tap the **Resolution** list arrow, and then click or tap a screen size.

7. Click or tap **Apply**.

8. To close the open windows, click or tap the **Close** button (x).

See Also

See "Adding a Secondary Monitor" on page 394 for more information on using a second display adapter.

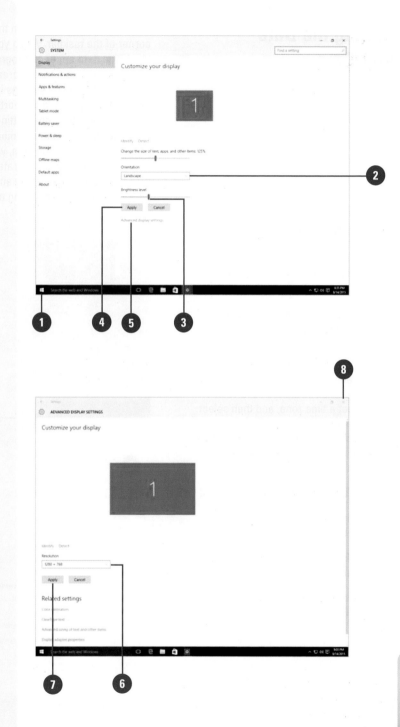

Setting the Date and Time

The date and time you set in the Control Panel appear in the lower-right corner of the taskbar. When you click or tap or hover over the taskbar clock, the data appears. Programs use the date and time to establish when files and folders are created and modified. To change the date and time, you modify settings in the Date and Time dialog box. When you modify the time, it's important to also verify or update the time zone setting in the Time Zone Settings dialog box, which is used to accurately display creation and modification dates in a different time zone. With an Internet connection, you can set options on the Internet tab to make sure the time is accurate. If you need to know the time in other time zones, you can display additional clocks, which you can display by clicking, tapping, or hovering over the taskbar clock.

Change the Date or Time

1. Click or tap the time on the taskbar in the notification area, and then click or tap **Date and time settings**.

2. Click or tap the **Add clocks for different time zones** link.

3. Click or tap the **Date and Time** tab.

4. If needed, click or tap **Change time zone**, click or tap the list arrow, select a time zone, and then select or clear the **Automatically adjust clock for Daylight Saving Changes** check box, and then click or tap **OK**.

5. Click or tap **Change date and time**.

6. Click or tap the date arrows to select the month and year.

7. Click or tap a day, and then specify a time.

8. Click or tap **OK**, and then click or tap **OK** again.

See Also

See "Changing Time and Language Settings" on page 304 for information on setting date and time options in Settings.

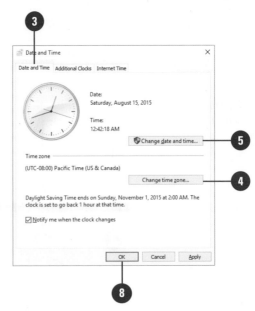

Keep the Time Accurate

1. Click or tap the time on the taskbar in the notification area, and then click or tap **Date and time settings**.

2. Click or tap the **Add clocks for different time zones** link.

3. Click or tap the **Internet Time** tab.

4. Click or tap **Change settings**.

5. Select the **Synchronize with an Internet time server** check box.

6. Click or tap the **Server** list arrow, and then click or tap a time server.

7. Click or tap **Update now**, and then wait for the time to update.

8. Click or tap **OK**, and then click or tap **OK** again.

Add Clocks

1. Click or tap the time on the taskbar in the notification area, and then click or tap **Date and time settings**.

2. Click or tap the **Add clocks for different time zones** link.

   The Additional Clocks tab appears on the Date and Time dialog box.

3. Select the **Show this clock** check box.

4. Click or tap the **Select time zone** list arrow, and then select a time zone.

5. Type a name.

6. If you want another clock, perform steps 3 through 5 for Clock 2.

7. Click or tap **OK**.

Changing Language Options

You can also install multiple input languages on your system and easily switch between them. An **input language** is the language in which you enter and display text. When you install additional languages on your device, the language for the operating system doesn't change, only the characters you type on the screen. Each language uses its own keyboard layout, which rearranges the letters that appear when you press keys. You can set options to switch the input method, including the use of the Language bar, which appears on your desktop and in the Toolbars menu. Text services are text-related add-on programs for a second keyboard layout, handwriting recognition, speech recognition, and an Input Method Editor (IME), which is a system that lets you input Asian language characters with a standard 101-keyboard. You can switch between different language keyboard layouts using the Language bar or keyboard shortcuts.

Add or Change Languages

1. In the Control Panel, click or tap the **Language** icon in Small icons or Large icons view.

2. To add a language, click or tap **Add a language**, select the language you want from the list, and then click or tap **Open**. If there are dialects, select one, and then click or tap **Add**.

3. To move language in the list, select a language, and click or tap **Move** up or **Move down**. The language at the top is the primary language.

4. To change language options, select the language, click or tap the **Options** link, specify the options you want, and then click or tap **Save**.

   ◆ **Add an input method.** Use to add a touch keyboard layout.

   ◆ **Personalize handwriting recognition.** Use to teach the recognizer your handwriting style.

5. To remove a language, select it, and then click or tap **Remove**.

6. Click or tap the **Close** button.

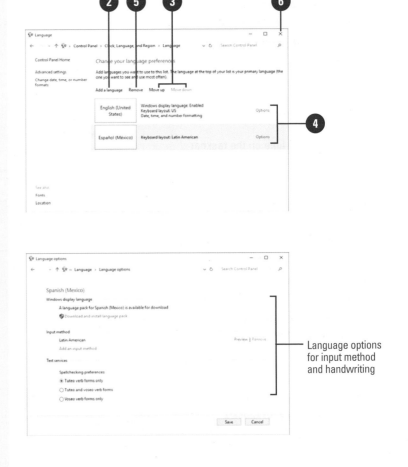

Language options for input method and handwriting

Change the Advanced Options

1 In the Control Panel, click or tap the **Language** icon in Small icons or Large icons view.

2 Click or tap the **Advanced settings** link.

3 Select the options you want:

◆ **Override the display language or input method.** Select an override language.

◆ **Switch input methods.** Select options to set different options for different apps and use the Language bar.

◆ **Use personalization data.** Select to use or not automatic learning for improved handwriting recognition.

4 Click or tap **Save**.

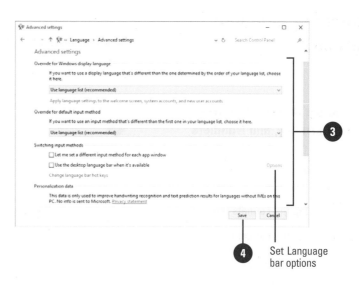

Set Language bar options

Use the Language Bar

◆ To switch languages, click or tap the **Language bar** icon, and then click or tap a language.

> **IMPORTANT** *If the Language bar icon doesn't appear, turn on Input Indicator in Settings under Notifications & actions within Turn system icons on or off.*

◆ To change Language bar settings, click or tap the **Options** button (small white arrow) or right-click or tap-hold the **Language bar**, and then click or tap an option, such as transparency, vertical (orientation), and minimize.

◆ To change Text Services and Input Languages, right-click or tap-hold the **Language bar** icon, and then click or tap **Settings**.

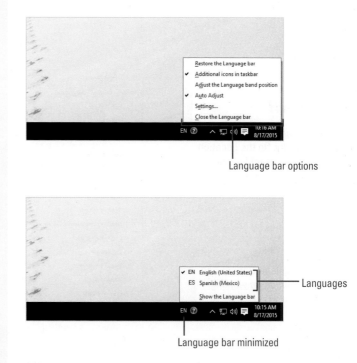

Language bar options

Language bar minimized

Languages

Changing Regional Options

For those who work in international circles, you can change the format of the date, time, currency, and number into almost any form. For example, you can change the decimal symbol and list separator, the format used for negative numbers and leading zeros, and the measurement system (U.S. or metric).

Change the Display for Dates, Times, Currency, and Numbers

1. In the Control Panel, click or tap the **Region** icon in Small icons or Large icons view.

2. Click or tap the **Formats** tab.

3. Click or tap the **Format** list arrow, and then click or tap a locale with the settings you want.

4. Click or tap the buttons to select the date and time formats you want.

5. Click or tap **Additional settings** to change individual settings.

6. Select the format options you want on the different tabs.

7. Click or tap **OK**.

8. Click or tap **OK**.

Did You Know?

You can change regional format by language and country. On the Location tab, click or tap the Current language list arrow, and then click or tap a language.

See Also

See "Changing Language Options" on page 316 for information on working with different languages.

Working with Fonts

Everything you type appears in a **font**, or typeface, a particular design set of letters, numbers, and other characters. The height of characters in a font is measured in points, each point being approximately 1/72 inch, while the width is measured by **pitch**, which refers to how many characters can fit in an inch. You might have heard common font names, such as Times New Roman, Arial, Courier, or Symbol. Windows comes with a variety of fonts for displaying text and printing documents. Using the Fonts window, you can view these fonts, see a sample of how a font appears when printed, and even install new fonts.

View or Install Fonts

1. In the Control Panel, click or tap the **Fonts** icon in Small icons or Large icons view.

   The installed fonts appear in the Fonts window.

2. To install a font, drag the font into the Fonts window in the Control panel.

   ◆ You can also right-click or tap-hold the font, and then click or tap **Install**.

3. To delete a font, select the font, and then click or tap the **Delete** button on the toolbar.

   ◆ Use the Ctrl key to select more than one font.

4. To hide or show a font in your programs, select the font, and then click or tap the **Hide** or **Show** button on the toolbar.

5. To show and hide fonts based on language settings, install fonts using a shortcut, or restore default font settings, click or tap **Font settings** in the left pane.

6. To group fonts by font style, type, category, etc., right-click or tap-hold a blank area, point to **Group by**, and then select an option or click or tap **More**.

7. To close the window, click or tap the **Close** button (x).

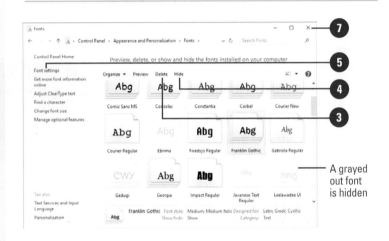

A grayed out font is hidden

For Your Information

What's the Difference Between the Fonts?

Everything you type appears in a font, a particular typeface design and size for letters, numbers, and other characters. Usually, each typeface, such as Times New Roman, is made available in four variations: normal, bold, italic, and bold italic. There are two basic types of fonts: scalable and bitmapped. A **scalable font** (also known as **outline font**) is based on a mathematical equation that creates character outlines to form letters and numbers of any size. The two major scalable fonts are Adobe's Type 1 PostScript and Apple/Microsoft's TrueType or OpenType. Scalable fonts are generated in any point size on the fly and require only four variations for each typeface. A **bitmapped font** consists of a set of dot patterns for each letter and number in a typeface for a specified type size. Bitmapped fonts are created or prepackaged ahead of time and require four variations for each point size used in each typeface. Although a bitmapped font designed for a particular font size will always look the best, scalable fonts eliminate storing hundreds of different sizes of fonts on a disk.

Displaying and Arranging Toolbars

Toolbars provide easy access to commonly used tasks. Windows comes with a set of toolbars you can use to access programs, folders, documents, and web pages right from the taskbar. You can quickly show or hide toolbars—such as Cortana/Search (**New!**)—and buttons (**New!**)—such as Task View and Touch Keyboard—on the taskbar to use them when you want. In addition, you can rearrange, resize, and move the toolbars to compliment your working style.

Show or Hide a Toolbar

1 In the desktop, right-click or tap-hold a blank area on the taskbar.

2 Select any of the options to show or hide toolbars or buttons:

◆ Point to **Toolbars**, and then click or tap a toolbar without a check mark.

◆ Point to **Cortana** or **Search** (**New!**), and then click or tap an option: **Hidden**, **Show Cortana icon**, or **Show search box**.

◆ **Show Task View button** (**New!**) or **Show touch keyboard button** (**New!**).

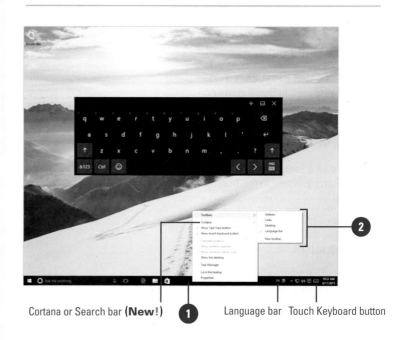

Cortana or Search bar (**New!**) 1   Language bar   Touch Keyboard button

Did You Know?

You can also show or hide toolbars using the Taskbar Properties dialog box. In the desktop, right-click or tap-hold the taskbar, click or tap Properties, click or tap the Toolbars tab, select or clear the toolbar check boxes, and then click or tap OK.

See Also

See "Using the Taskbar" on page 12 for information on using the taskbar, including showing/hiding toolbars and button on the Start screen or desktop.

Toolbars on the Taskbar

Toolbar	Description
Cortana/Search	Displays the Cortana or Search bar (**New!**)
Address	Opens web pages, networks, files, and folders using the Address bar from Intenet Explorer
Links	Opens the Links toolbar from Internet Explorer
Touch Keyboard button (**New!**)	Displays the Touch Keyboard button to open the touch keyboard as an input device
Desktop	Opens windows to files, folders, and shortcuts on the desktop
Language bar	Opens the Language bar toolbar to switch between languages (needs to be enabled in Advanced Language options in the Control Panel)
New Toolbar	Adds a new toolbar to Windows

Unlock or Lock the Taskbar

① In the desktop, right-click or tap-hold a blank area on the taskbar.

② Click or tap **Lock the taskbar**.

◆ Toolbars on the taskbar are locked when a check mark is displayed.

◆ Toolbars on the taskbar are unlocked when a check mark isn't displayed.

Move a Toolbar

① In the desktop, right-click or tap-hold a blank area on the taskbar, and then click or tap **Lock the taskbar** to remove the check mark, if necessary.

② Point to the double-line bar or name of the toolbar, and then drag it to a new location on the desktop docked to the side or floating in the middle.

Did You Know?

You can resize a toolbar. Unlock the taskbar, and then drag the small vertical bar at the beginning of the toolbar.

You can expand or collapse a toolbar. Unlock the taskbar, and then double-click or tap the small vertical bar at the beginning of the toolbar.

Double-line bar indicates taskbar is unlocked.

Customizing the Taskbar and Notifications

The taskbar is initially located at the bottom of the desktop and is most often used to switch from one program to another. As with other Windows elements, you can customize the taskbar; for example, you can change its size and location, customize its display, add or remove toolbars, or show and hide notifications (**New!**). If you need more room on the screen to display a window, Auto-hide can be used to hide the taskbar when it's not in use. If icons in the notification area are hidden when you want to see them, you can customize the notification area to always show the icons and notifications you want to use. In addition, you can choose whether to show or hide common system icons, including Clock, Volume, Network, Power, Input Indicator (**New!**), Location (**New!**), and Action Center. And as a bonus, you can even show tips about Windows (**New!**) as notifications.

Customize the Taskbar

1. In the desktop, right-click or tap-hold a blank area on the taskbar, and then click or tap **Properties**.

2. Click or tap the **Taskbar** tab.

3. Select the **Auto-hide the taskbar** check box to hide the taskbar when you're not using it.

   The taskbar appears when you move the pointer to where the taskbar would appear.

4. Select the **Use small taskbar button** check box to display small button icons on the taskbar.

5. Click or tap the **Taskbar location on screen** button, and then select a taskbar location: **Bottom**, **Left**, **Right**, or **Top**.

   ◆ You can also drag a taskbar. Unlock the taskbar, and then drag a blank area on the taskbar to a new location on any side of the desktop.

6. Click or tap the **Taskbar buttons** button, and then select a combine option: **Always combine, hide labels** (default), **Combine when taskbar is full**, or **Never combine**.

7. Click or tap **OK**.

For Your Information

Showing and Hiding Icons in Notification Area

You can show and hide icons by dragging them in the notification. To show hidden icons, click or tap the Show Hidden Icons button in the notification area, drag a hidden icon to the notification area. To hide an icon, drag an icon to the Show Hidden Icons button, and then to the top of the menu.

Customize the Notification Area

① In the desktop, right-click or tap-hold a blank area on the taskbar, and then click or tap **Properties**.

② Click or tap the **Taskbar** tab, and then click or tap **Customize**.

◆ You can also click or tap the **Settings** on the Start screen or menu, click or tap **System**, and then click or tap **Notifications & actions** (**New!**).

③ To show or hide icons on the notification area, click or tap the **Turn system icons on or off** or **Select which icons appear on the taskbar** link, select **On** or **Off** for the icons, and then click or tap the **Back** button.

④ Specify the notification options you want:

◆ **Show me tips about Windows.** Displays tips as a notification on a periodic basis (**New!**).

◆ **Show app notifications.**

◆ **Show notifications on the lock screen.**

◆ **Show alarms, reminders and incoming VOIP calls on the lock screen.** Show or hide notifications for internet phone calls (**New!**).

◆ **Hide notifications while presenting.** Show or hide notifications while making presentations (**New!**).

⑤ To show or hide notifications for apps, select **On** or **Off** for the individual apps.

⑥ To close the window, click or tap the **Close** button (x).

⑦ Click or tap **OK** to close the dialog box.

Notifications & actions in Settings

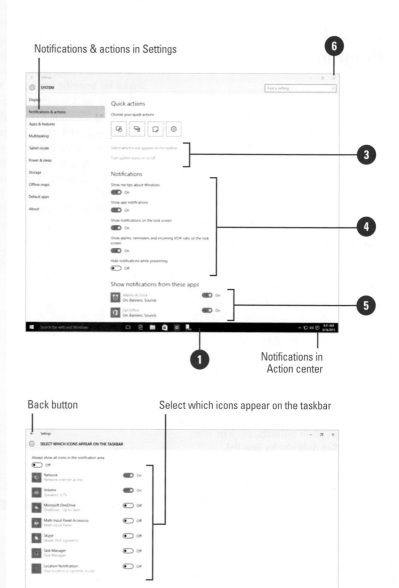

Notifications in Action center

Back button

Select which icons appear on the taskbar

Show hidden icons

System icons on the taskbar

Setting Default Programs

When you double-click or double-tap an audio or video file, or click or tap a web link, a default program associated with that file type automatically starts and opens the file. Default Programs in Settings (**New!**) or the Control Panel provide an easy way to change the default program used for specific file types. You can change file types, such as .bmp or .jpg, and set file associations for common activities, such as web browsing, sending e-mail, playing audio and video files, sending instant messaging, and using a search application, either Windows Search Explorer or a third-party one, such as Google Desktop Search. You can also specify which programs are available from the Start screen or menu, the desktop, and other locations. To change default options, you need to have administrator privileges for your system. The options you set apply to all users on your PC computer or mobile device.

Set Your Default Programs

1. In the Start screen or Start menu, click or tap te **All apps**, and then click or tap **Default Programs** (Settings) under Windows System.

2. Click or tap the **Add** button (+) to choose a default or an existing app icon to change a default.

   Continue to set other defaults or skip to step 8.

3. To set other defaults, click or tap the **Set defaults by app** link.

   ◆ To access in the Control Panel, click or tap **Default Programs** (Control Panel) on the All apps menu under Windows System, and then click or tap **Set your default programs**.

4. Select a program.

5. Click or tap **Set this program as default**, or **Choose defaults for this program**.

6. If you select Choose defaults for this program, select the extension you want this program to open by default, and then click or tap **Save**.

7. To close the window, click or tap the **Close** button (x).

8. Click or tap the **Close** button (x).

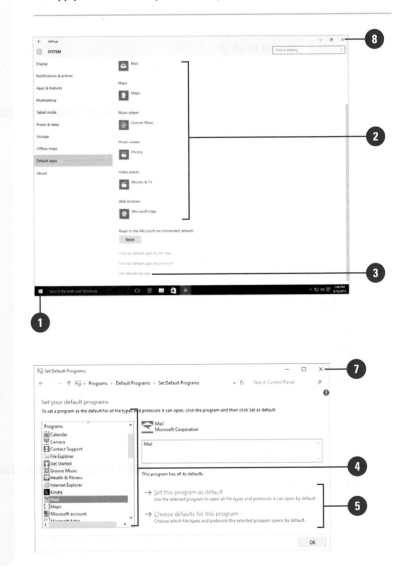

Set Program Access and Computer Defaults

1. In the Start screen or Start menu, click or tap te **All apps**, and then click or tap **Default Programs** (Control Panel) under Windows System.

2. Click or tap **Set program access and computer defaults**, and then enter administrator permissions, if requested.

3. Click or tap the option for the type of program you want to set: **Computer Manufacturer** (if available), **Microsoft Windows**, **Non-Microsoft**, or **Custom**.

4. Click or tap the option or select from a list the defaults you want to set.

5. Click or tap **OK**.

6. Click or tap the **Close** button (x).

Change File Type or Protocol Association with a Program

1. In the Start screen or Start menu, click or tap te **All apps**, and then click or tap **Default Programs** (Settings) under Windows System.

2. Click or tap the **Choose default apps by file type** or **Choose default apps by protocol** link.

3. Click or tap the **Add** button (+) to choose a default or an existing app icon to select a file type or protocol.

4. Click or tap the **Close** button (x).

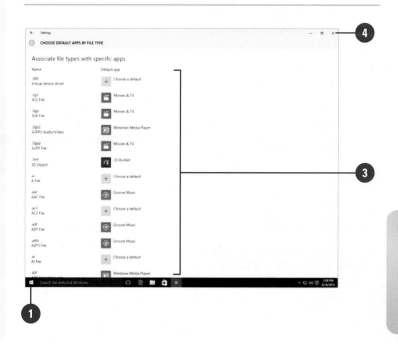

Changing the Way a Disc or Device Starts

When you insert a CD or DVD disc into your drive or attach devices, such as digital cameras with a memory card or removable drives, you can specify how you want Windows to respond. You can have Windows detect the type of content on the disc and automatically start, or prompt you each time to choose an action. If you have CDs or DVDs with music files, pictures, video files, or mixed content, you can change the action Windows takes when it detects the content on the disc. You can have Windows play or rip a CD or DVD using Windows Media Player, open the first folder to view files using File Explorer, or take no action. Windows allows you to set AutoPlay options for a wide-variety of CDs and DVDs, including an audio or enhanced audio CD, DVD or enhanced DVD movie, Software and games, pictures, video and audio files, blank CD or DVD, mixed content, HD DVD or Blu-ray Disc movie, Video or Super Video CD. In Settings, you can turn on or off AutoPlay and choose defaults for removable drives and memory cards.

Set AutoPlay Options

1. Click or tap the **Settings** button on the Start screen or Start menu.

2. Click or tap **Devices**.

3. Click or tap **AutoPlay** under Devices.

4. To display the AutoPlay pop-up when you use media or device, drag the Slider **On** for Use Auto-Play for all media and devices.

5. For each item, click or tap the list arrow, and then select a default action; options vary depending on the type of disc or device.

   ◆ To turn off AutoPlay for a specific media type, click or tap **Take no action**.

6. Click or tap the Close button (x).

Set default app options

Did You Know?

You can stop Windows from performing an action on a CD or DVD. Hold down the Shift key while you insert the CD or DVD.

Using Ease of Access Tools

If you have difficulty using a mouse or typing, have slightly impaired vision, or are deaf or hard of hearing, you can adjust the appearance and behavior of Windows 10 to make your system easier to use. The Ease of Access Center helps you configure Windows for your vision, hearing, and mobility needs. You can also answer a few questions about your daily PC use that can help Windows recommend accessibility settings and programs for you. To open the Ease of Access Center, press Win+U, or click or Ease of Access in Settings (**New!**) or the Control Panel. To use the Ease of Access questionnaire, click or tap Get recommendations (Control Panel) to make your PC easier to use. The Ease of Access Center provides utilities to adjust the way your keyboard, display, and mouse function to suit various vision and motor abilities. Some of the accessibility tools available include Magnifier, On-Screen Keyboard, Narrator, High Contrast, and Closed captions (**New!**). You can also set accessibility options, such as StickyKeys, FilterKeys, ToggleKeys, Sound-Sentry, ShowSounds, and MouseKeys, that automatically turn off accessibility features, provide warning sounds, and determine when to apply the settings. The accessibility tools in Windows are intended to provide a low level of functionality for those with special needs. If these tools do not meet your daily needs, you might need to purchase a more advanced accessibility program.

Ease of Access Center Tools

Option	Description
Magnifier	Displays a separate window with a magnified portion of the screen; this is designed to make the screen easier to read for users who have impaired vision. In Windows, you can use full-screen and lens modes for added functionality.
On-Screen Keyboard	Displays an on-screen keyboard; this is designed to use the PC computer without the mouse or keyboard.
Narrator	Use the PC without a display; this is a text-to-speech utility program designed for users who are blind or have impaired vision.
High Contrast	Sets the desktop appearance to high contrast to make the monitor easier to see; this is designed to make the screen easier to read for users who have impaired vision.
StickyKeys	Enables simultaneous keystrokes while pressing one key at a time, such as Ctrl+Alt+Del.
FilterKeys	Adjusts the response of your keyboard; ignores repeated characters or fast key presses.
ToggleKeys	Emits sounds when you press certain locking keys, such as Caps Lock, Num Lock, or Scroll Lock.
SoundSentry	Provides visual warnings for system sounds.
ShowSounds	Instructs programs to provide captions.
MouseKeys	Enables the numeric keypad to perform mouse functions.

Using the Ease of Access Center

The Ease of Access Center allows you to check the status of and start or stop the Magnifier, Narrator, and On-Screen Keyboard accessibility programs. Magnifier is a utility that enlarges the full screen, the mouse area, or an area of the screen. Narrator is a text-to-speech utility that gives users who are blind or have impaired vision access to the PC. On-Screen Keyboard is a utility that displays a keyboard on the screen where users with mobility impairments can type using a mouse, joystick, or other pointing device. If you have administrator access, you can specify how the accessibility programs start when you log on, lock the desktop, or start the Ease of Access Center.

Use the Ease of Access Center

1. Press Win+U to start the Ease of Access Center.

   ◆ In the Control Panel, you can also click or tap the **Ease of Access** icon in Small icons or Large icons view.

2. To get recommendations on what to use, click or tap **Get recommendations to make your computer easier to use**, and then follow the instructions.

3. To provide quick access to common tools, select the **Always read this section aloud** and **Always scan this section** check boxes.

4. Click or tap the utility program or the settings you want to manage.

5. Select or clear the check boxes you want to specify how you want the selected program to start or a setting to be applied.

6. Click or tap **Save** or exit the window.

7. To close the window, click or tap the **Close** button (x).

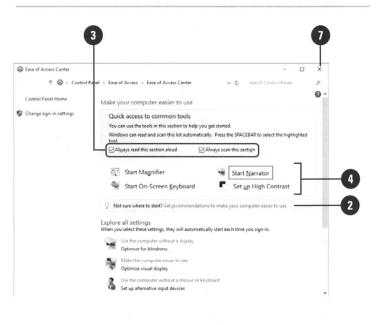

For Your Information

Using Ease of Access from the Sign in Screen

When you start your system, the Sign in screen appears, where you can log into Windows 10. If you want to use Ease of Access features, you can quickly start or enable them with the Ease of Access button. When you click or tap the Ease of Access button, a menu appears where you can start Narrator, Magnifier, or On-Screen Keyboard, and turn on or off High Contrast, Sticky Keys, and Filter Keys.

Use the Magnifier

1. In the Start screen or Start menu, click or tap **All apps**, and then click or tap **Magnifier** under Windows Ease of Access.

2. Click or tap the **Views** button, and then select a view: **Full screen**, **Lens**, or **Docked**.

3. Click or tap the **Options** button.

4. Drag the **Zooming** slider to adjust the view level.

5. Select or clear the **Turn on color inversion** check box.

6. Select or clear the check boxes with the tracking options to follow the mouse pointer or keyboard focus, or have Magnifier follow the text insertion point.

7. Click or tap **OK** to use the Magnifier program. When you're done, click or tap the **Close** button (x) to close the program.

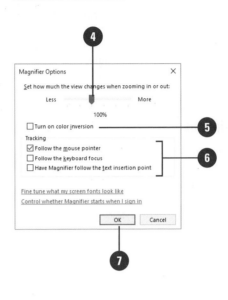

Use the On-Screen Keyboard

1. Open the program in which you want to type.

2. In the Start screen or Start menu, click or tap **All apps**, and then click or tap **On-Screen Keyboard** under Windows Ease of Access.

3. Position the cursor, if necessary.

4. Type the text you want, or type keyboard commands.

5. To close the window, click or tap the **Close** button (x).

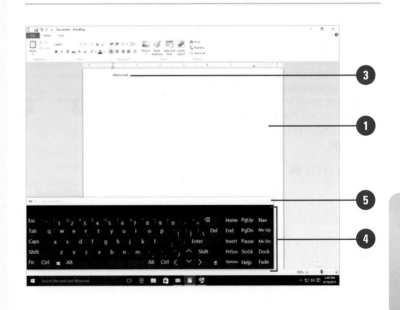

Listening to Your System

Windows 8 comes with an accessibility tool called Narrator that reads aloud what appears on your screen, such as window items, menu options, and typed characters. Windows uses Text-to-Speech (TTS) technology to recognize text and play it back as spoken words using a synthesized voice, which is chosen from several pre-generated voices. Narrator is designed for those who are blind or have impaired vision and works with the Windows desktop and setup, Control Panel, Notepad, WordPad, and Internet Explorer. Narrator supports only the English language and might not read words aloud correctly in other programs. You can adjust the speed, volume, or pitch of the voice in Narrator and change other Text-to-Speech options using Speech properties in the Control Panel.

Change Text-To-Speech Options

1. In the Control Panel, click or tap the **Speech Recognition** icon in Small icons or Large icons view.

2. In the left pane, click or tap **Text to Speech**.

3. Click or tap the **Voice selection** list arrow, and then select a voice.

4. Drag the **Voice speed** slider to adjust the speed of the voice.

5. Click or tap **Preview Voice**.

6. To set a preferred audio device as output for TTS playback, click or tap **Advanced**, make a selection, and then click or tap **OK**.

7. To adjust settings for your audio output devices, click or tap **Audio Output**, specify the options you want on the Playback, Recording, or Sounds tabs, and then click or tap **OK**.

8. Click or tap **OK**.

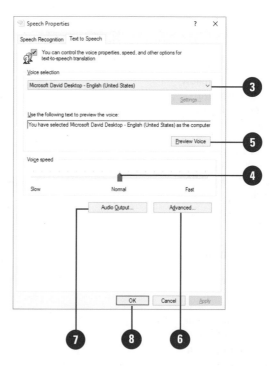

See Also

See "Recognizing Your Speech" on page 332 for information on speech capabilities.

Use the Narrator

① In the Start screen or Start menu, click or tap **All apps**, and then click or tap **Narrator** under Windows Ease of Access.

TIMESAVER *Press Win+Enter to start Narrator.*

② Select the Narrator options you want:

◆ **General.** Select options to change how Narrator stars and other standard settings.

◆ **Navigation.** Select options to change how you interact with your PC using Narrator.

◆ **Voice.** Select options to change the speed, pitch, or volume of the current voice or choose a new voice.

◆ **Commands.** Select options to create your own keyboard shortcuts.

③ Click or tap **Save changes** or **Discard changes**.

④ Click or tap **Minimize** to use the Narrator program or click or tap **Exit** to close the program; restore the Narrator window, if necessary; and then click or tap **Yes**, if necessary.

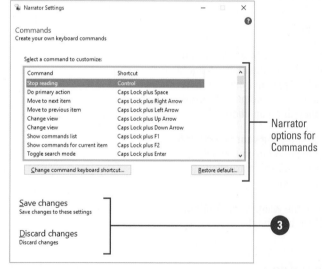

Narrator options for Commands

Recognizing Your Speech

If you have a speech-enabled program, you can initialize and customize speech recognition options using Speech properties in the Control Panel. **Speech recognition** is the ability to convert a spoken voice into electronic text. Windows adapts to your speech, and speech recognition increases over time. You can use the speech recognition properties to select a language, create a profile to accommodate your speaking style and environment, and train your PC computer in as little as ten minutes to recognize and adapt to the sound of your voice, word pronunciation, accent, speaking manner, and new or distinctive words. Some programs use speech differently, so you need to check the speech-enabled program for details. Speech Recognition is not available in all languages.

Set Up Speech Recognition

1. In the Control Panel, click or tap the **Speech Recognition** icon in Small icons or Large icons view.

2. Click or tap **Set up microphone**, and then follow the wizard instructions to adjust the microphone.

3. Click or tap **Take Speech Tutorial**, and then follow the instructions to take the 30 minute training tutorial to teach you the commands used with speech recognition.

4. Click or tap **Train your computer to better understand you**, and then follow the wizard instructions to train your voice.

5. To close the window, click or tap the **Close** button (x).

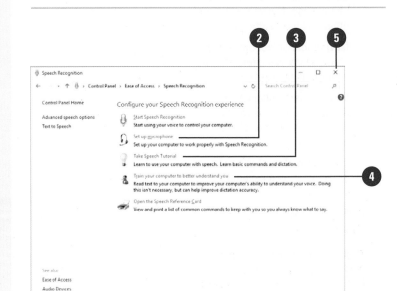

Did You Know?

You can view and print a Speech Recognition reference card. In the Control Panel (desktop), click or tap the Speech Recognition icon in Small icons or Large icons view, and then click or tap Open and Speech Reference Card.

Set Speech Recognition Options

1. In the Control Panel, click or tap the **Speech Recognition** icon in Small icons or Large icons view.

2. In the left pane, click or tap **Advanced speech options**.

3. Click or tap the **Speech Recognition** tab.

4. Click or tap the list arrow, and then select a language.

5. To start the Profile Wizard, click or tap **New**, type your name, click or tap **OK**, follow the wizard instructions to create a profile, adjust the microphone, and train your voice, and then click or tap **Finish**.

6. Select or clear the User Settings check boxes you do or don't want.

7. Click or tap **OK**.

Speech Recognition options

Start Speech Recognition

1. In the Start screen or Start menu, click or tap **All apps**, and then click or tap **Windows Speech Recognition** under Windows Ease of Access.

2. If requested, follow the wizard instructions to create a profile, adjust the microphone, and train your voice, and then click or tap **Finish**.

3. Click or tap the **Speech Recognition** button to toggle between Sleeping/Listening mode.

   TIMESAVER *Right-click or tap-hold the Speech Recognition button to select command options.*

4. To close the window, click or tap the **Close** button (x).

Setting Ease of Access Options

With Settings, you can set options to use Ease of Access. You can set options in the following areas: Narrator, Magnifier, High contrast, Closed captions (**New!**), Keyboard, Mouse, and Other, which includes settings to play animations, show background, show notifications, or for cursor thickness. You can turn features (Narrator, Magnifier, or On-Screen Keyboard) and individual options on or off or customize them to fit your needs. For example, you can use the High contrast color scheme or Closed captions (**New!**) to format the text to make it easier to see.

Set Ease of Access Options

1. Click or tap the **Settings** button on the Start screen or Start menu.

2. Click or tap **Ease of Use**.

3. Click or tap the following under Ease of Access:

   ◆ **Narrator**. Set options for Hear text and controls, Voice, Sounds you hear, or Cursor and keys.

   ◆ **Magnifier**. Set options for Magnify things on the screen or Tracking.

   ◆ **High contrast**. Choose a theme, customize, and apply.

   ◆ **Closed captions**. Set font, background, and window formatting for captions (**New!**). If needed, you can restore defaults.

   ◆ **Keyboard**. Set options for On-Screen Keyboard and Useful keys.

   ◆ **Mouse**. Set options for Pointer size & color and Mouse keys.

   ◆ **Other options**. Set options to play animations, show background, show notifications, or for cursor thickness.

4. To close the window, click or tap the **Close** button (x).

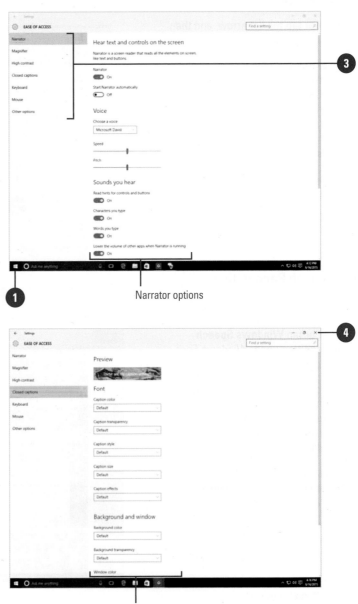

Narrator options

Setting for Closed captions

Setting Up Accounts and Maintaining Security

13

Introduction

With user accounts, you can customize and personalize Windows for each user on your system. Each user can have their own Documents folder and list of web favorites, customize system preferences, and protect private files. When you set up a new user account, the account appears on the Sign-in screen, where the new user can log on. You can use Accounts in Settings or User Accounts in the Control Panel to add or delete user accounts, change a user's group or account type, change the way Windows starts, change the account picture, and set, change, and reset an account password.

Keeping your system safe and secure is a continuing battle. With the Action Center and security and maintenance options, you can manage system security from one place. In the Action Center, you can check your security status, and quickly get support from Microsoft for a security-related issue.

While you're browsing the Internet or working in your email program, you need to be aware of viruses and other harmful attacks so you can protect your system from being infected by one. Internet Options include security enhancements to help you make your system more secure. In Internet Options, you can create security zones to designate trusted web sites, set web site ratings to restrict user access, clean up Internet files and information, and manage cookies to protect your personal identity from unauthorized access. If you're tired of closing unwanted pop-up ads, you can use Pop-up Blocker in Internet Options to prevent most pop-up windows from appearing.

What You'll Do

Explore Windows Security

Change User Account Settings

Add and Delete User Accounts

Connect to Work or School

Change a User Account Type

Change an Account Picture

Set, Change, and Reset a Password

Lock the Screen

Manage Security in One Place

Defend Against Malicious Software

Set Family Safety Controls

Encrypt Files for Safety & BitLocker

Avoid Viruses and Other Harmful Attacks

Understand Security on the Internet

Create Security Zones and Set Ratings

Protect Internet Privacy and Identity

Block Content with Tracking Protection

Manage Add-Ons

Protect Privacy with Edge

Exploring Windows Security

Windows 10 provides several ways to secure your PC computer or mobile device.

Create User Accounts

For a shared or workgroup system, there are four main types of user accounts: administrator and standard for general usage and child or adult for family usage. For a domain network system, different account types (administrator, standard user, and restricted user) provide similar permissions as the ones on a shared or workgroup system.

The **administrator** account is for the person who needs to make changes to anything on the system as well as manage user accounts. An administrator account can install programs and hardware, make system-wide changes, access and read all non private files, create and delete user accounts, change other people's accounts, change your own account name, type and picture, and create, change, or remove your own password.

The **standard** account is for the person who needs to manage personal files and run

programs. This account cannot install software or hardware, or change most system settings.

The **child** account is for a family person that you want to manage and limit PC use with Family Safety. When you add a child account, it turns on Family Safety, which you can manage in the Control Panel.

The **adult** account is for a family adult person that you want to manage one or more child accounts for the family.

Use Action Center

Use the Action Center to check your security settings, view security alerts, take actions about security and maintenance issues with and learn how to improve the security of your system.

If an option displays the Security icon next to it, you need to enter the administrator password or provide confirmation when prompted by the **User Account Control (UAC)**. This adds an additional level of security to

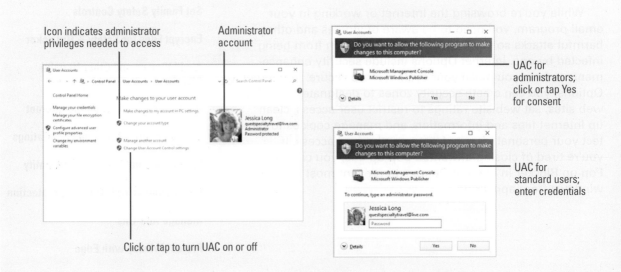

Icon indicates administrator privileges needed to access

Administrator account

UAC for administrators; click or tap Yes for consent

UAC for standard users; enter credentials

Click or tap to turn UAC on or off

keep your system secure. If you don't need the security (not recommended), you can turn it off in User Accounts.

Enable Windows Firewall

Windows Firewall is a security system that creates a protective barrier between your PC or network and others on the Internet. Windows Firewall monitors all communication between your system and the Internet and prevents unsolicited inbound traffic from the Internet from entering your system. For more information on Windows Firewall, see "Connecting to the Internet" on page 133 and "Setting Up Windows Firewall" on page 134.

Enable Automatic Updates

Windows Automatic Updates allows you to keep your system up-to-date with the latest system software and security updates over the Internet. For more information, see "Updating and Refreshing Windows" on page 380.

Enable Internet Security Options

Internet Explorer provides security zones to browse secure web sites and a rating system to screen content, protects personal information and your privacy on the Internet, blocks pop-up ads, and displays information to help you make security decisions. For more information, see "Understanding Security on the Internet" on page 362.

Enable Email Security Options

Email programs, such as Windows Live Mail, provide security zones to help you determine whether or not to run potentially harmful content from inside an email, prevents your email program from sending mail with your email address to your contacts (which is a common way to propagate a virus), and stops pictures and other content from automatically downloading inside and email to your system (which is a common way spammers confirm your email address to send more spam). For more information, see "Sending and Retrieving a File" on page 170, "Reading and Replying to Email" on page 168, or "Using Windows Live Essentials" on page 237.

Protect Files and Folders

Another way to protect the files on your system is to use the built-in security provided by the NTFS file system. The NTFS file system is available for Windows NT-based systems, which doesn't include pre-Windows XP. You can select your hard disk in the Computer window and display Details view to determine whether your PC uses the NTFS file system.

The NTFS file system provides additional security for your files and folders. You can make a folder private, use the advanced Encrypting File System (EFS) to protect sensitive data files on your system. If someone tries to gain access to encrypted files or a folder on your system, a unique file encryption key prevents that person from viewing it. While these security options are more advanced, they could be helpful for securing very sensitive information. For more information, see "Encrypting Files for Safety" on page 358.

Understand the Enemy

Knowing your enemy (harmful intruders) can help you make safe computing decisions that lead to a secure system rather than unsafe ones that lead to potential disaster. For information, see "Avoiding Viruses and Other Harmful Attacks" on page 360.

Changing User Account Settings

In Settings, you can change your account, sign in, and other user account settings. An account can be local using a username and password (no email) or online using your Microsoft email account. When you sign in with a Microsoft account, your account settings are maintained online. You can access and manage your Microsoft account online from Settings. You can change online account options, including personal info, password and security info, aliases (other connected email addresses), notifications, permissions, billing, and even close the account. You can sign in and switch between local and online accounts by using links in Your account under Accounts in Settings. If you have multiple accounts—like Office 365 or other business services from Microsoft (**New!**)—that you use, you can link them together.

View User Account Settings

1. Click or tap the **Settings** button on the Start screen or Start menu.

2. Click or tap **Accounts**.

3. Click or tap **Your account** under Accounts.

4. Use any of the following options:

   ◆ Verify Identity. Click or tap the **Verify** link to specify or change a security code to verify your identity.

   ◆ Local account. Click or tap the **Sign in with a local account instead** link to create or sign in to a local account.

   ◆ Online account. Click or tap the **Sign in with my Microsoft account instead** link to sign in to your online account.

   ◆ Your Picture. Click or tap **Browse** to select a picture or **Camera** to take your picture.

   ◆ Add accounts. Click or tap the **Add a Microsoft** or **Add a work or school account** link to link an account to your Microsoft account, Office 365, or other business services from Microsoft (**New!**).

5. To close the window, click or tap the **Close** button (x).

Change User Account Online Settings

1. Click or tap the **Settings** button on the Start screen or Start menu.

2. Click or tap **Accounts**.

3. Click or tap **Your account** under Accounts.

4. Click or tap the **Manage my Microsoft account** link.

   Your default web browser opens, displaying your Microsoft account.

5. Specify the options you want.

   ◆ **Home.** View and edit basic account information.

       ◆ **Edit name.** Edit your first and last name.

       ◆ **Change password.** Change your password.

   ◆ **Your info.** Edit account, personal, and profile information.

   ◆ **Services & subscriptions.** View and manage OneDrive, and other services, like Office 365 and Xbox Live.

   ◆ **Payment & billing.** View and change billing and purchase information.

   ◆ **Devices.** View and change devices attached to your account.

   ◆ **Family.** Add and manage kids accounts.

   ◆ **Security & privacy.** View recent account activity, change passwords, and other settings.

6. Click or tap the **Close** button (x) in your browser.

7. To close the window, click or tap the **Close** button (x).

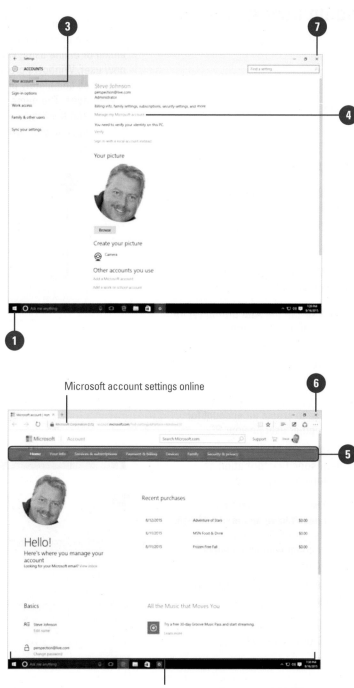

Microsoft account settings online

Home page option; yours might differ

Adding User Accounts

If you have an administrator account, you can create a new user account, either standard or family (child)—needed to turn on Family Safety. An account can be local using a username and password (no email) or online using your Microsoft email account. When you add a new user, Windows creates a separate identity, allowing the user to keep files completely private and customize the system with personal preferences. The name you assign to the user appears on the Sign in screen and the Start screen or menu. The steps to add user accounts differ, depending on whether your system is part of a domain network.

Add an Account

1. Click or tap the **Settings** button on the Start screen or Start menu.

2. Click or tap **Accounts**.

3. Click or tap **Family & other users** under Accounts.

4. Click or tap the **Add** button (+) for either of the following:

   ◆ Add a family member. Use to create an account for a child or adult account on your PC.

   ◆ Add someone else to this PC. Use to create an account for another user on your PC.

5. Click or tap **Next** to continue and then specify information or options as requested.

   ◆ **The person I want to add doesn't have an email address.** Use this link to create an account without an email address.

6. When you're done, click or tap **Finish**.

7. To close the window, click or tap the **Close** button (x).

Add someone else to this PC

Add a family member

Add an Account on a Domain Network

1. Click or tap the **Settings** button on the Start screen or Start menu.

2. Click or tap **Accounts**.

3. Click or tap **Work access** under Accounts.

4. Click or tap the **Join or leave a domain** link.

5. Click or tap the **Join a domain** button.

6. Type a domain name, and then click or tap **Next** to continue.

7. Specify the requested information, including username, and user access level option: Standard user, Administrator, or Other.

8. When you're done, click or tap **Finish**.

9. To close the window, click or tap the **Close** button (x).

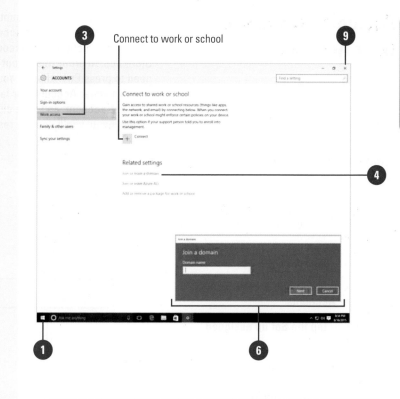

Connect to work or school

Did You Know?

You may need administrator access to make security changes. If a security option displays the Action Center icon next to it, you need to enter the administrator password or provide confirmation when prompted to make a change.

You can turn User Account Control on or off. In the Control Panel, click or tap User Accounts, click or tap User Accounts again, and then click or tap Change User Account Control Settings link. Click or tap Turn User Account Control on or off, select or clear the User Account Control (UAC) To Help Protect Your Computer check box, click or tap OK, and then click or tap the Close button.

For Your Information

Domain vs Workgroup

A domain network and a workgroup are different. A domain network is a group of PCs connected together to share and manage resources by an administrator from a central PC called a domain controller. A workgroup is a network of PCs connected together to share resources, but each PC is maintained and shared separately. You can join a domain in Settings under System in About. You can also use the Control Panel. In the Control Panel, click or tap System, and then click or tap the Change settings link. In the dialog box, click or tap Network ID to join a domain or workgroup, or click or tap Change a domain or workgroup.

Assigning Access to User Accounts

If you want to limit an account to use only one Windows Store app, you can make it assigned access. An account for assigned access allows you to choose an account to have access to only one Windows Store app. In order to sign out of an assigned access account, you need to press Ctrl+Alt+Del. You can assign access to an account in Settings under Accounts for family & other users. To unassign access, click the account, and then click the Don't use assigned access link on the menu; you'll need to restart your PC to apply the changes.

Limit an Account with Assigned Access

1. Click or tap the **Settings** button on the Start screen or Start menu.

2. Click or tap **Accounts**.

3. Click or tap **Family & other users** under Accounts.

4. Click or tap the **Set up assigned access** link.

5. Click or tap the **Add** button (+) for Choose which account will have assigned access, and then select an account.

6. Click or tap the **Add** button (+) for Choose which app this account can access, and then select an app.

7. Click or tap the **Back** button to return to the previous screen.

8. To unassign access, click the account, and then click the **Don't use assigned access** link on the menu; you'll need to restart your PC to apply the changes.

9. To close the window, click or tap the **Close** button (x).

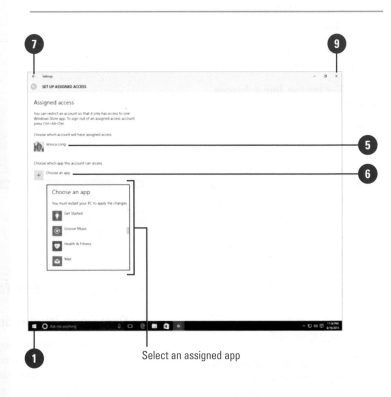

Select an assigned app

Connecting to Work or School

If you have a separate account for work or school, you can connect to it in order to gain access to shared resources, such as apps, the network, and email). When you connect, your work or school might enforce policies on your device as well as collect information about you. In addition, it might also install or remove apps, change settings or disable features, delete content, or reset your PC. Every work or school handles these things differently, so talk to your support person to learn more about your specific situation.

Connect to Work or School

1. Click or tap the **Settings** button on the Start screen or Start menu.

2. Click or tap **Accounts**.

3. Click or tap **Work access** under Accounts.

4. Click or tap the **Add** button (+) for Connect.

5. Enter an email address for your work or school.

6. Click or tap **Continue** to continue and then specify information or options as requested.

7. To close the window, click or tap the **Close** button (x).

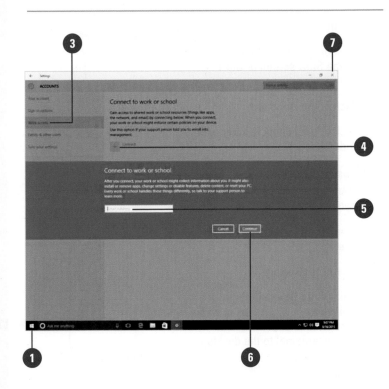

Did You Know?

You can add or remove a package for work or school. Packages help you set up your device for work or school. In Settings under Accounts in Work access, click or tap the Add Or Remove A Package For Work Or School link, click or tap the Add button (+) for Add a package, and then specify information or options as requested.

Deleting User Accounts

If you have an administrator account or are a member of the Administrators group, you can delete an existing one. When you delete an account, you have the choice to delete the contents of the account or keep it. When you keep the contents, Windows automatically saves the content of the User's desktop and Documents, Favorites, Music, Pictures, and video folders to a new folder (named the same as the user) on your desktop. The steps to delete user accounts differ, depending on whether your system is part of a domain network.

Delete an Account

1. Click or tap the **Settings** button on the Start screen or Start menu.

2. Click or tap **Accounts**.

3. Click or tap **Family & other users** under Accounts.

   IMPORTANT *Before you can delete an account, you need to sign out first.*

4. Select the account you want to delete.

5. Click or tap **Remove**.

6. Click or tap **Delete Files** to remove all account files or **Keep Files** to save account folder (with username) to the desktop.

7. Click or tap **Delete Account**.

8. To close the window, click or tap the **Close** button (x).

Did You Know?

You can delete a user account in the Control Panel. In the Control Panel, click or tap User Accounts , click or tap Remove User Accounts, click or tap the account you want to delete, click or tap Delete The Account, click or tap Delete Files or Keep Files, and then click or tap Delete Account.

Delete an Account on a Domain Network

1. Click or tap the **Settings** button on the Start screen or Start menu.

2. Click or tap **Accounts**.

3. Click or tap **Work access** under Accounts.

4. Click or tap the **Join or leave a domain** link.

5. Click or tap the **Leave a domain** button.

6. Select the user you want to delete.

7. Click or tap **Remove**, and then click or tap **Yes** to confirm the deletion.

8. To close the window, click or tap the **Close** button (x).

Changing a User Account Type

If you have an administrator account or are a member of the Administrators group, you can change a user's account type (Administrator or Standard) or user group on a domain network. A user account or group grants permissions to a user to perform certain types of tasks based on the account type or user group (domain network). You can change a user account type in Settings under Accounts in family & other users.

Change a User Account Type

1 Click or tap the **Settings** button on the Start screen or Start menu.

2 Click or tap **Accounts**.

3 Click or tap **Family & other users** under Accounts.

4 Select the account you want to change.

5 Click or tap **Change account type**.

6 Click or tap the **Account type** list arrow, and then click or tap **Standard User** or **Administrator**.

7 Click or tap **OK**.

8 To close the window, click or tap the **Close** button (x).

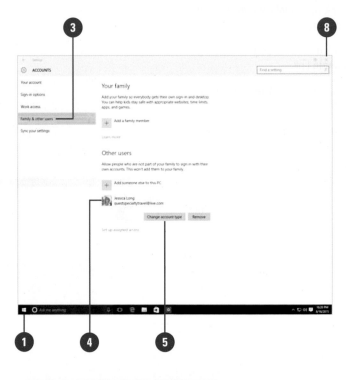

Changing an Account Picture

When you start Windows, the Sign in screen appears, displaying a list of user accounts with a picture next to each one. When you complete the sign in process, the picture associated with your account appears at the top of the Start menu along with your username. This identifies you as the current user of the system. You can change the picture to suit your own personality using an existing file or installed camera. You can even add more than one.

Change an Account Picture

1 Click or tap the **Settings** button on the Start screen or Start menu.

2 Click or tap **Accounts**.

3 Click or tap **Your account** under Accounts.

> **TIMESAVER** *In the Start menu, click or tap the user account, and then click or tap Change account settings.*

4 Use any of the following methods:

◆ **Use an Existing Picture.** Click or tap **Browse**, select the file, and then click or tap **Choose picture**.

◆ **Use a Camera to Take a Picture.** Click or tap **Camera**. In the Camera app, click or tap the **Photo** button to take a picture, resize the crop corners, and then click or tap the **Apply** button.

◆ If prompted, click or tap **Yes** or **No** to let Windows Camera access your location.

5 To close the window, click or tap the **Close** button (x).

Changing a Password

A password controls who has access to your device and all the files and information on it. When you add an account, you specify a password, however you can change it at any time. When you specify a password, enter one that is easy for you to remember, yet difficult for others to guess. In Windows, you can use multiple security passwords or codes, such as text or picture, and Windows Hello (**New!**) with face or fingerprint recognition. In Settings under Accounts in Sign-in options, you can change your account password, create a picture password with gestures, or create a 4-digit PIN (Personal Identification Number) code. If you want to work with multiple accounts at the same time, you can use the Credential Manager in the Control Panel to edit or remove an account's username and password. You can also back up and restore credentials for protection and security.

Change a Password and Sign In

1 Click or tap the **Settings** button on the Start screen or Start menu.

2 Click or tap **Accounts**.

3 Click or tap **Sign-in options** under Accounts.

4 Click or tap the **Require sign-in** list arrow, and then select an option: **When PC wakes up from sleep** or **Never**.

5 Specify the options you want.

◆ Password. Click or tap **Change** to change your password. You'll need to sign in to your Microsoft account, if prompted.

◆ PIN. Click or tap **Add** to create a 4-digit PIN (Personal Identification Number) code. You'll need to sign in to your Microsoft account, if prompted.

◆ Picture password. Click or tap **Add** to create or **Change** to edit a picture password. Click or tap **Remove** to delete it.

◆ Windows Hello. Set options for face, fingerprint, or iris (**New!**), if supported with hardware.

6 To close the window, click or tap the **Close** button (x).

Edit or Remove Username and Password

1 In the Start screen or Start menu, click or tap **All apps**, and then click or tap **Control Panel** under Windows System.

2 Click or tap the **User Accounts** icon in Small icons or Large icons view, and then click or tap **Manage Windows Credentials**.

3 Click or tap the **Expand arrow** to display an account.

4 To edit account credentials, click or tap the **Edit** link, edit the credentials, and then click or tap **Save**.

5 To remove account credentials, click the **Remove** link, and then click or tap **Yes** to confirm..

6 To close the window, click or tap the **Close** button (x).

Backup or restore credentials

Did You Know?

What's a good password. Good passwords are typically at least seven characters and include letters (uppercase and lowercase), numbers, and symbols.

The Windows password is case-sensitive. Windows makes a distinction between uppercase and lowercase letters. Your password should be at least seven characters, the optimal length for encryption, which logically scrambles and secures the data.

You can back up or restore credentials. In the Credentials Manager dialog box, click or tap Back Up Credentials to specify a backup file or click or tap Restore Credentials to use a backup file to restore credentials.

Security Alert

Working Smarter as the Administrator

If you are an administrator, it's recommended that you log out and use another account for general work to avoid harmful damage to your system by a virus or malicious user. For example, if a hacker received access to your system with administrator privileges, the attacker could reformat your hard drive, delete files, or create a new administrator account.

Resetting a Password

If you have ever forgotten your password, you understand how important it is to write it down. However, writing down a password is not very secure. If you forget your password, you can reset it. For a Microsoft account, you can reset it online at *account.live.com/password/reset*. In Settings, you can use the Forgot My Password wizard to help you reset your password using an alternate email address that you specified during your Windows installation or when you created an account. Using the alternate email, Windows sends you a code that you enter during the wizard process. Resetting your password also erases any security credentials and certificates on your system.

Reset Your Password

1. Click or tap the **Settings** button on the Start screen or Start menu.

2. Click or tap **Accounts**.

3. Click or tap **Sign-in options** under Accounts.

4. Click or tap **Change**.

   A dialog box opens, asking you to sign in with your Microsoft account.

5. Click or tap the **Forgot my password** link.

6. Follow the instructions in the Forgot My Password wizard to create a password reset disk.

7. To close the window, click or tap the **Close** button (x).

Did You Know?

You can reset a password for an online account. Open your browser, go to *account.live.com/password/reset*, and then follow the on-screen instructions to reset your password for your Microsoft account

Locking the Screen

If you are working on sensitive material and need to leave your PC unattended for a while, you can lock it so that no one can use it without your permission. While your PC is locked, all your programs continue to run. When you return to your PC, you can access it in the same way you started Windows, which is by selecting your account and entering your password. The Lock screen is a full screen image with the time, date and notification icons (with app status). When your screen locks, you can still access some apps without having to unlock your PC. When you display the Lock screen, you can answer Skype calls, take photos or see a slide show of your photos without having to unlock it first. In the Start screen or menu, click or tap the User Account, and then click or tap Lock to manually lock your PC. With a simple drag of a mouse, press of a key, or movement of your finger, you can dismiss the Lock screen to display the Sign in screen.

Lock and Unlock the Screen

1. Display the Start screen or Start menu for the account you want to change.

2. Click or tap the **User Account** (username and picture).

3. Click or tap **Lock** on the menu.

   TIMESAVER *Press Win+L to lock the system.*

   ◆ You can also press Ctrl+Alt+ Del, and then click or tap **Lock**.

4. When the Lock screen appears, drag your mouse anywhere on the screen, move your finger sideways from the edge, or press a key to dismiss it.

5. At the Sign in screen, click or tap your username or picture (if prompted), type your password, and then click or tap the **Submit arrow** or press Enter.

See Also

See "Personalizing the Lock Screen" on page 299 for information on customizing the Lock screen.

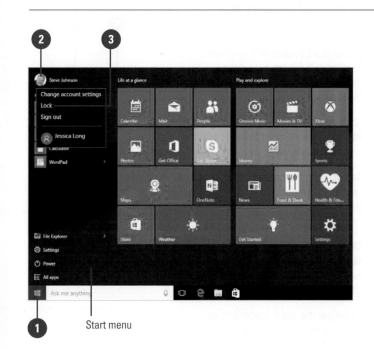

Start menu

Managing Security in One Place

Security and Maintenance in the Control Panel provides a place to view alerts and take actions about security and maintenance issues with your PC. It displays important and recommended alerts that need your attention to help protect your PC and keep Windows running smoothly. It also provides links to important information about the latest virus or other security threat, or to get customer support from Microsoft for a security related issue. As you work, Windows uses security alerts and icons in the notification area on the taskbar to help you recognize potential security risks, such as a new virus, out of date antivirus software or an important security option is turned off, and choose appropriate settings. If Windows requires your attention, a notification alert appears in the Action Center (**New!**). Click or tap the Action Center icon (**New!**) on the taskbar to view alerts and suggested fixes.

View Essential Security and Maintenance Settings

1. In the Start screen or Start menu, click or tap **All apps**, and then click or tap **Control Panel** under Windows System.

2. Click or tap the **Security and Maintenance** icon in Small icons or Large icons view.

3. To find out information on a security area, click or tap the down arrow next to it.

4. To set settings, click or tap the **Change Security and Maintenance settings** link, select or clear check boxes to turn alert messages on or off, and then click or tap **OK**.

5. To adjust the notification setting for preventing harmful programs from making changes, click or tap the **Change User Account Control settings** link, drag the slider, and then click or tap **OK**.

6. To close the window, click or tap the **Close** button (x).

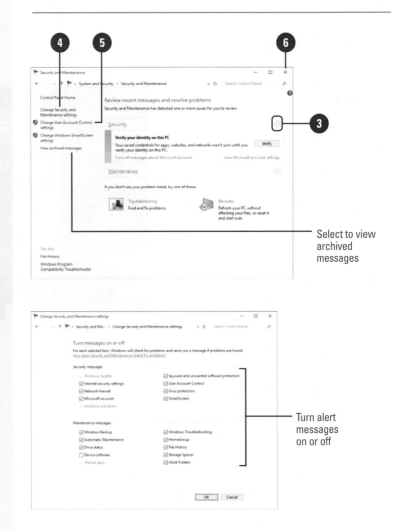

Select to view archived messages

Turn alert messages on or off

Act Upon Security Alerts in the Action Center

1 If Windows requires your attention, click or tap the **Action Center** icon on the taskbar in the notification area, and then click or tap an issue.

◆ If the Action Center detects that your PC needs enhanced security, it displays an alert (if enabled) in the notification area, read the security alert, and then click or tap it..

2 To find out information on a security notification, click or tap the down arrow next to it.

3 To find out how to address the problem, click or tap the security notification, and then follow the instructions.

4 To clear a notification, click or tap the **Close** button (x) for the item.

5 To close the Action Center, click or tap off the panel or click or tap the **Action Center** icon on the taskbar.

Clear all notifications

Quick action to easily toggle on and off

Defending Against Malicious Software

Windows Defender helps you protect your system from spyware and other potentially harmful software that attempts to install itself or run on your system. Spyware is software that tries to collect information about you or change Settings without your consent. Windows Defender alerts you in real-time when unwanted software tries to run on your PC. Windows Defender uses definitions to determine potential problems. Since software dangers continually change, it's important to have up-to-date definitions, which you can get online. You can change Windows Defender options in Settings (**New!**) help stop malware from installing or running on your PC as well as send security information to Microsoft to help them better protect our system.

Use Windows Defender

1. If a real-time alert appears with an attempt to:

   ◆ **Install software.** Click or tap **Ignore**, **Quarantine**, **Remove**, or **Always Allow**.

   ◆ **Change Windows settings.** Click or tap **Permit** or **Deny**.

2. In the Start screen or Start menu, click or tap **All apps**, and then click or tap **Windows Defender under Windows System**.

   ◆ In the Control Panel, you can also click or tap the **Windows Defender** icon in Small icons or Large icons view.

3. To get updates, click or tap the **Update** tab, and then click or tap the **Update** button.

4. To perform a scan, click or tap the **Home** tab, click or tap the **Quick Scan** or **Full Scan** option, and then click or tap **Scan now**.

5. To view or clear history, click or tap the **History** tab, select an option, click or tap **View details**, and then click or tap an item to view history. Use the **Remove all**, **Remove**, or **Restore** buttons as needed.

6. When you're done, click or tap the **Close** button (x).

Update tab

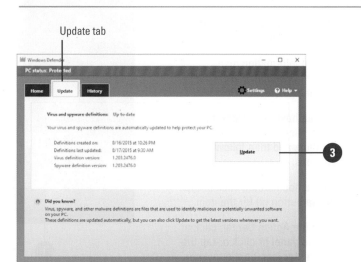

Home tab

Change Windows Defender Options

1 Click or tap the **Settings** button on the Start screen or Start menu.

2 Click or tap **Update & security**.

3 Click or tap **Windows Defender** (**New!**) under Update & security.

4 Drag the Slider **On** or **Off** for the the options you want to change.

◆ **Real-time protection.** Enable the option to get protection alerts against malicious attacks.

◆ **Cloud-based Protection.** Enable the option to send Microsoft information about security problems you encounter.

◆ **Sample submission.** Enable the option to send Microsoft malware samples to learn and catch security problems.

5 To exclude files, folders, file types, or processes to speed up scans, click or tap the **Add an exclusion** link, click or tap the Add button (+) to select items, and then click or tap the **Back** button.

6 To open Windows Defender, click or tap the **Use Windows Defender** link.

7 To close the window, click or tap the **Close** button (x).

Setting Family Safety Controls

Family accounts (**New!**) can help you manage how your children use the PC. Family accounts allows you to set limits on your children's web access, the amount of time spent logged on the system, and which games and programs they can use. You can set different settings for each user account on your PC, so you can adjust the level you want for each child. You can also review activity reports on a periodic basis to see what your children are doing on the PC. You can manage Family accounts on this device in Settings and on the Microsoft account web site. To allow a Family account, you need to create a child or adult account; to block it, change the account to Standard or remove it (**New!**).

Block or Allow Family Accounts

1. Click or tap the **Settings** button on the Start screen or Start menu.

2. Click or tap **Accounts**.

3. Click or tap **Family & other users** under Accounts.

4. Click or tap the family account you want to change.

5. To block use of the family account, click or tap **Block**, and then click or tap **Block** to confirm.

6. To allow use of the family account, click or tap **Allow**, and then click or tap **Allow** to confirm.

7. To close the window, click or tap the **Close** button (x).

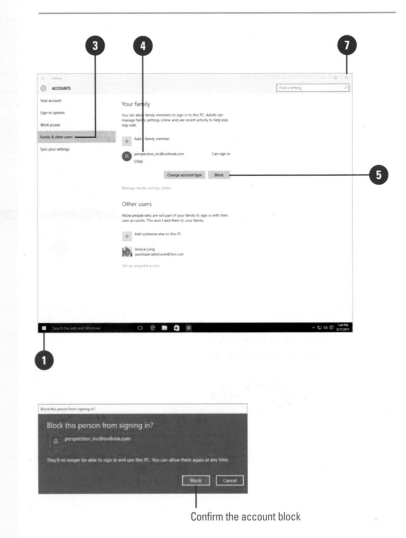

Confirm the account block

Set Family Account Controls

1. Click or tap the **Settings** button on the Start screen or Start menu.

2. Click or tap **Accounts**.

3. Click or tap **Family & other users** under Accounts.

4. Click or tap the **Manage family settings online** link.

5. To add or remove a family account, click or tap the **Add** or **Remove** link.

6. Click or tap the family account for which you want to set controls.

7. Drag the Slider **On** or **Off** for **Activity reporting** and **Email weekly reports to me**.

8. Click or tap the links to the Windows settings you want to change (use the **Back** button to go previous screens):

    ◆ **Web browsing.** Select options to block or allow web sites based on ratings and content or specific ones.

    ◆ **Screen time.** Select options to set time allowance and curfew time to set the hours you want to block or allow for device usage.

    ◆ **Apps & games.** Select options to block or allow Windows Store apps and games based on ratings or specific ones.

9. Click or tap the **Close** button (x) to exit your browser.

10. To close the window, click or tap the **Close** button (x).

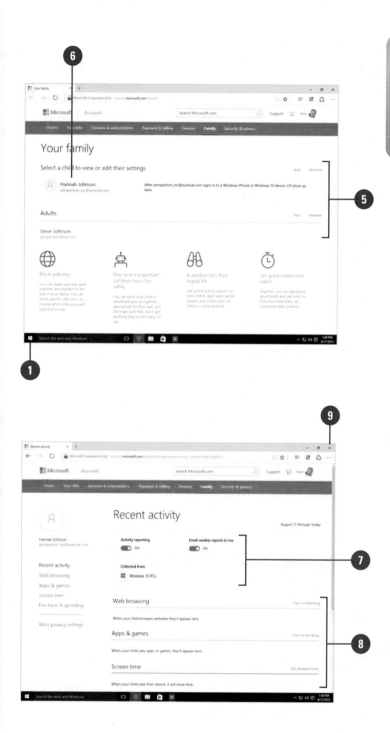

Encrypting Files for Safety

If your PC uses NTFS, you can use the advanced Encrypting File System (EFS) to protect sensitive data files on your PC. If someone tries to gain access to encrypted files or a folder on your PC, a unique file encryption key prevents that person from viewing it. When you encrypt a file, you also need to decide whether you want to encrypt the folder, too. When you encrypt a folder, you need to decide whether you want to encrypt all files and subfolders within it. After you encrypt your files, you can use the Backup using File History in Settings under Update & Security to back them up for safe keeping.

Encrypt or Decrypt a File or Folder

1. In File Explorer, select the file or folder you want to encrypt.

2. Click or tap the **Properties** button on the Home tab.

3. Click or tap the **General** tab.

4. Click or tap **Advanced**.

5. Select the **Encrypt contents to secure data** check box to encrypt the file or folder or clear the check box to decrypt it.

6. Click or tap **OK**.

7. Click or tap **OK**.

8. If necessary, click or tap an option to apply changes to this folder only or to this folder, subfolders, and files.

9. Click or tap **OK**.

Did You Know?

You can compress files and folders with NTFS. In File Explorer, select the file or folder, click or tap the Properties button on the Home tab, click or tap the General tab, click or tap Advanced, select the Compress Contents To Save Disk Space check box, and then click or tap OK twice.

For Your Information

Managing and Backing Up Encryption Certificate

When you encrypt a file or folder, Windows uses information from your Encrypting File system certificate. A certificate is a digital document that verifies the identify of a person, which is issued by a trusted Certification Authority. If you lost the certificate or it becomes corrupted, you will not be able to recover an encrypted file or folder. To avoid this problem, you should back up your Encrypting File System (EFS) certificate. To manage and back up your EFS certificate, open the Control Panel, click or tap the User Accounts icon in the Small icons or Large icons view, click or tap Manage Your File Encryption Certificates, and then follow the Encrypting File System wizard.

Encrypting Files Using BitLocker

BitLocker helps protect your system and blocks hackers from accessing sensitive information behind the scenes. For internal drives and volumes, you can use BitLocker to encrypt it. With BitLocker To Go, you can apply the same protection to portable storage devices, such as USB flash drives and external hard drives. BitLocker provides the most protection when used with a compatible Trusted Platform Module (TPM) (version 1.2) microchip and BIOS. However, it's not required. When you turn on BitLocker, it uses a password and recovery key (which gets backed up) for security. When you add files to your PC, BitLocker automatically encrypts them. When you copy files to another location, the files are decrypted. If a problem occurs at startup or someone tries to illegally access your system, Windows switches into recovery mode until you supply the recovery password.

Use BitLocker to Encrypt Files

1. In the Start screen or Start menu, click or tap **All apps**, and then click or tap **Control Panel** under Windows System.

2. Click or tap the **BitLocker Drive Encryption** icon in Small icons or Large icons view.

   ◆ You can also select a drive in Computers in File Explorer, and then use **BitLocker** button arrow on the Manage tab.

3. Click or tap **Turn On BitLocker** on the volume you want.

4. Follow the wizard to specify a password, recovery key, and encrypt options, click or tap **Start encrypting**, wait for BitLocker to encrypt the volume upon restart, and then click or tap **Close**.

   If a problem occurs or someone tries to illegally access the drive, your PC switches into recovery mode until you supply the recovery password.

5. To turn off BitLocker, click or tap **Turn Off BitLocker**, and then click or tap **Decrypt Drive**. To change or remove a password, save or print a recovery key, or automatically unlock a drive, click or tap a link.

Avoiding Viruses and Other Harmful Attacks

Understanding Harmful Attacks

Using the Internet can expose your PC to a wide variety of harmful attacks, such as viruses, worms, and Trojan Horses. These attacks can come through email, file transferring, and even possibly through Java and ActiveX, which are both programming languages used to enhance web pages.

A **virus** is an executable program whose functions range from just being annoying to causing havoc to your PC. A virus may display an innocuous warning on a particular day, such as Friday the 13th, or it may cause a more serious problem, such as wiping out your entire hard disk. Viruses are found in executable (.exe and .com) files, along with Microsoft Word and Microsoft Excel macro files. A **worm** is like a virus, but it can spread without human action across networks. For example, a worm might send email copies of itself to everyone in your email contacts. A worm can consume memory causing your PC to stop responding or even take it over. A **Trojan Horse**, like its mythological counterpart, is a program that appears to be useful and comes from a legitimate source, but actually causes problems.

Spreading Harmful Infections

Many viruses and other harmful attacks spread through file downloads and attachments in email messages. Virus writers capitalize on people's curiosity and willingness to accept files from people they know or work with, in order to transmit malicious files disguised as or attached to benign files. When you start downloading files to your PC, you must be aware of the potential for catching a PC virus, worm, or Trojan Horse. Typically, you can't catch one from just reading a mail message or downloading a file, but you can catch one from opening or running an infected program, such as a file attached to an email message, or one you download for free. And even though most viruses and other harmful attacks take the form of executable programs, data files that have macros or Visual Basic code attached to them, such as Word or Excel files, can also be infected with viruses.

Avoiding Harmful Attacks

There are a few things you can do to keep your system safe from the infiltration of viruses and other harmful attacks.

1) Make sure Windows Firewall is turned on. Windows Firewall helps block viruses and worms from reaching your PC, but it doesn't detect or disable them if they are already on your PC or come through email. Windows Firewall doesn't block unsolicited email or stop you from opening email with harmful attachments. For more information on Windows Firewall, see "Connecting to the Internet" on page 133 and "Setting Up Windows Firewall" on page 134.

2) Make sure Automatic Updates is turned on. Windows Automatic Updates regularly checks the Windows Update web site for important updates that your PC needs, such as security updates, critical updates, and service packs. Each file that you download using Automatic Update has a digital signature from Microsoft to ensure its authenticity and security. For more information, see "Updating and Refreshing Windows" on page 380.

3) Make sure you are using the most up-to-date antivirus software. New viruses and more virulent strains of existing viruses are discovered every day. Unless you update your virus checking software, new viruses can easily bypass outdated virus checking software.

Companies such as McAfee and Symantec offer shareware virus checking programs available for download directly from their web sites. These programs monitor your system, checking each time a file is added to make sure it's not in some way trying to change or damage valuable system files.

4) Be very careful of the sites from which you download files. Major file repository sites, such as FileZ, Download.com, or TuCows, regularly check the files they receive for viruses before posting them to their web sites. Don't download files from web sites unless you are certain that the sites check their files for viruses. Internet Explorer monitors downloads and warns you about potentially harmful files and gives you the option to block them. For more information, see "Downloading Files from the Web" on page 130.

5) Be very careful of file attachments in email you open. As you receive email, don't open or run an attached file unless you know who sent it and what it contains. If you're not sure, you should delete it. To protect your PC from harmful attacks, see "Sending and Retrieving a File" on page 170, "Reading and Replying to Email" on page 168, and "Using Windows Live Essentials" on page 237.

6) Make sure you activate macro virus checking protection in both Word and Excel. To do so in Office 2010 or 2013, select the File tab, select Options, select Trust Center, select Trust Center Settings, select Macro Settings, select the Disable all macros with notification option, and then click or tap OK. And always elect not to run macros when opening a Word or Excel file that you received from someone who might not be using proper virus protection.

Avoiding Other Intruders

Spyware is software that collects personal information without your knowledge or permission. Typically, spyware is downloaded and installed on your PC along with free software, such as freeware, games, or music file-sharing programs. Spyware is often associated with **Adware** software that displays advertisements, such as a pop-up ad. Examples of spyware and unauthorized adware include programs that change your home page or search page without your permission. To avoid spyware and adware, read the fine print in license agreements when you install software, scan your PC for spyware and adware with detection and removal software (such as Ad-aware from Lavasoft), and turn on Pop-up Blocker. For details, see "Blocking Pop-Up Ads" on page 369.

Spam is unsolicited email, which is often annoying and time-consuming to get rid of. Spammers harvest email addresses from web pages and unsolicited email. To avoid spam, use multiple email addresses (one for web forms and another for private email), opt-out and remove yourself from email lists, and turn on the Block Images And Other External Content In HTML Email option.

Phishing is an email scam that tries to steal your identity by sending deceptive email asking you for bank and credit card information online. Don't be fooled by spoofed web site that look like the official site. Never respond to requests for personal information via email; call the institution to investigate and report it.

Understanding Security on the Internet

No other web browser offers as many customizable features as Internet Explorer does, particularly advanced security features that are built into the program. To understand all the Internet Explorer security features, you first have to learn about security on the Internet in general.

When you send information from your PC to another PC, the two PCs are not linked directly together. Your data may travel through multiple networks as it works its way across the Internet. Since your data is broadcast to the Internet, any PC on any of these networks could be listening in and capturing your data. (They typically aren't, but they could be.)

In addition, on the Internet it's possible to masquerade as someone else. Email addresses can be forged, domain names of sites can easily be misleading, and so on. You need some way to protect not only the data you send, but also yourself from sending data to the wrong place.

Furthermore, there is always the potential that someone (referred to as a "hacker") or something, such as a virus or worm, could infiltrate your PC systems. Once infiltrated, a hacker or virus can delete, rename, or even copy valuable information from your PC without your knowledge.

Security Zones

Through the use of **security zones**, you can easily tell Internet Explorer which sites you trust to not damage your PC and which sites you simply don't trust. In your company's intranet you would most likely trust all the information supplied on web pages through your company's network, but on the Internet you may want to be warned first of potential dangers a site could cause your system. You can set up different levels of security based on different zones.

Certificates

When shopping on the Internet, you want to do business with only those companies that offer a certain level of security and promise to protect your buying information. In turn, those companies want to do business with legitimate customers only. A **certificate** or **digital ID** provides both the browser and the company with a kind of guarantee confirming that you are who you say you are and that the site is secure and genuine, not a fraud or scam. When you send an email message, it also verifies your identity to your recipients.

A digital ID is made up of a public key, a private key, and a digital signature. When you digitally sign an email, email programs, like Windows Live Mail, add your public key and digital signature (the two together is the certificate) to the message. When your recipients receive the email, your digital signature verifies your identity and your public key is stored in their contacts so they can send you encrypted messages, which only you can open with your private key.

An independent company, called a **credentials agency**, issues three types of certificates: personal, authority, and publisher. A **personal certificate** identifies you so that you can access web sites that require positive identification, such as banks that allow online transactions. You can obtain a personal certificate from a credentials agency called VeriSign using the Content tab of the Internet Options dialog box. An **authority certificate** ensures that the web site you are visiting is not a fraud. Internet Explorer automatically checks site certificates to make sure that they're valid. A **publisher certificate** enables you to trust software that you download, such as ActiveX controls. Internet Explorer maintains a list of software companies whose certificates are valid and trustworthy. You can view your certificate settings on the Content tab of the Internet Options dialog box.

Cookies

When you browse the Internet, you can access and gather information from web sites, but web sites can also gather information about you without your knowledge unless you set up Internet security on your PC. You can set Internet privacy options to protect your personal identity from unauthorized access. When you visit a web site, the site creates a **cookie** file, known as a **first-party**

cookie, which stores information on your PC, such as your web site preferences or personal identifiable information, including your name and email address. Not all cookies are harmful; many first-party-cookies save you time re-entering information on a return visit to a web site. However, there are also **third-party cookies**, such as advertising banners, which are created by web sites you are not currently viewing. Once a cookie is saved on your PC, only the web site that created it can read it. The privacy options allow you to block or permit cookies for web sites in the Internet zone; however, when you block cookies, you might not be able to access all the features of a web site. When a web site violates your cookie policy, a red icon appears on the Status bar.

Security zones

Certificates

Creating Security Zones

Internet Explorer lets you create security zones based on where information comes from. For example, you might want to restrict access to web pages that can be viewed from the Internet, but not to those sites within your company's intranet. You can specify the level of security for each of the four available security zones: Local Intranet, Trusted Sites, Restricted Sites, and Internet. When you access a web page or download content from the site, Internet Explorer checks its security settings and determines the web site's zone. Internet Explorer displays a padlock icon in the status bar to indicate the web site is secure. All Internet web sites are assigned to the Internet zone until you assign individual web sites to other zones.

Select a Security Zone and Its Security Level

1. In the Start screen or Start menu, click or tap **All apps**, and then click or tap **Control Panel** under Windows System.

2. Click or tap the **Internet Options** icon in Small icons or Large icons view.

3. Click or tap the **Security** tab.

4. Click or tap the zone to which you want to assign security options.

5. If you want, click or tap **Default level** to reset the settings to Microsoft's suggested level.

6. Move the slider to the level of security you want to apply.

   TROUBLE? *If the slider is not available, click or tap Default Level to change the security level to Medium and display the slider.*

7. If you want to specify individual security options, click or tap **Custom level**.

8. Scroll to a settings area, and then click or tap the **Enable**, **Prompt**, or **Disable** option button.

9. Click or tap **OK**.

10. Click or tap **OK**.

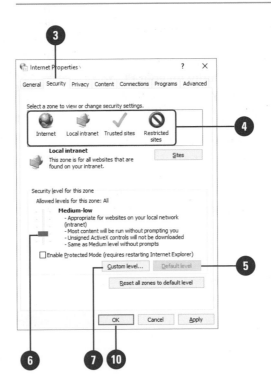

Add Sites to Your Restricted Sites Zone

1 In the Start screen or Start menu, click or tap **All apps**, and then click or tap **Control Panel** under Windows System.

2 Click or tap the **Internet Options** icon in Small icons or Large icons view.

3 Click or tap the **Security** tab.

4 Click or tap **Restricted Sites**.

5 Click or tap **Sites**.

6 Type the full URL for the site.

7 Click or tap **Add**.

8 Click or tap **Close**, and then click or tap **OK**.

Did You Know?

You can reset default settings for security options. To return each option to its default settings for a specified security level, click or tap the Reset Custom Settings list arrow, select a level, and then click or tap Reset.

You can remove a site from your Restricted Sites zone. In the Internet Properties dialog box, click or tap the Security tab, click or tap Restricted Sites, and then click or tap the Sites button. In the Web Sites box, click or tap the site you want to remove, click or tap Remove, and then click or tap OK. Click or tap OK to close the Internet Options dialog box.

You can enable Internet Explorer protection mode in Internet Properties. In the Internet Properties dialog box, click or tap the Security tab, select the Enable Protected Mode (required restarting Internet Explorer) check box, and then click or tap OK.

Security Zones

Zone	Description
Internet	Contains all web sites that are not assigned to any other zone; default is Medium
Local intranet	Contains all web sites that are on your organization's intranet and don't require a proxy server; default is Medium
Trusted sites	Contains web sites that you trust not to threaten the security of your PC; default is Low (allows all cookies)
Restricted sites	Contains web sites that you believe threaten the security of your PC; default is High (blocks all cookies)

Cleaning Up Internet Files and Information

As you browse the web, Internet Explorer stores information relating to what you have provided to web sites when you log on (passwords) or fill out a form, the location of web sites you have visited (history), and preference information used by web sites (cookies). When you visit a web site, Internet Explorer saves web pages, images, media (temporary Internet files), and InPrivate filtering information for faster viewing and protection in the future. You can clean up the Internet files and information, which will also improve your PC performance. You can save web page data (cookies and temporary files) from your trusted favorites, so you don't have to restore them.

Delete Internet Files and Information

1 In the Start screen or Start menu, click or tap te **All apps**, and then click or tap **Control Panel** under Windows System.

2 Click or tap the **Internet Options** icon in Small icons or Large icons view.

3 Click or tap the **General** tab.

4 Click or tap **Delete**.

5 Click or tap the check boxes you want to clean up your PC:

- ◆ **Preserve Favorites website data.** Keeps cookies and temporary files from your trusted favorites.

- ◆ **Temporary files.** Deletes files created while browsing.

- ◆ **Cookies.** Deletes information gathered by using web sites.

- ◆ **History.** Deletes list of web sites you have visited.

- ◆ **Form data.** Deletes saved information entered into forms.

- ◆ **Passwords.** Deletes password used for site automatic logon.

- ◆ **ActiveX Filtering and Tracking Protection Data.** Deletes saved Tracking Protection data.

6 Click or tap **Delete**.

7 Click or tap **OK**.

3 Select to delete browsing history on exit in IE

Protecting Internet Privacy

You can set Internet privacy options to protect your personal identity from unauthorized access. The privacy options allow you to block or permit cookies for web sites; however, when you block cookies, you might not be able to access all the features of a web site. When a web site violates your cookie policy, a red icon appears on the status bar. To find out if the web site you are viewing in Internet Explorer contains third-party cookies or whether any cookies have been restricted, you can get a privacy report. The privacy report lists all the web sites with content on the current Web page and shows how all the web sites handle cookies.

Control the Use of Cookies

1. In the Start screen or Start menu, click or tap **All apps**, and then click or tap **Control Panel** under Windows System.

2. Click or tap the **Internet Options** icon in Small icons or Large icons view.

3. Click or tap the **Privacy** tab.

4. Click or tap **Sites**, specify the web sites you want to always or never allow to use cookies, and then click or tap **OK**.

5. Click or tap **Advanced**, select options how cookies are hangled, and then click or tap **OK**.

6. Click or tap **OK**.

Did You Know?

You can delete all cookies. In the Internet Properties dialog box, click or tap the General tab, click or tap Delete, select the Cookies check box, click or tap Delete, and then click or tap OK.

You can get a privacy report in Internet Explorer. Open the web page you want to view a privacy report, click or tap the Tools button on the toolbar, point to Safety, then click or tap Webpage Privacy Policy.

For Your Information

Denying Location Request from Web Sites

As you visit web sites, they can request physical location information behind the scenes. If you don't want sites to do this, you can deny their requests. In the Internet Properties dialog box, click or tap the Privacy tab, and then select the Never Allow Websites To Request Your Physical Location check box. To clear a list of sites requesting location information, click or tap Clear Sites.

Protecting an Internet Identity

To further protect your privacy, you can use certificates to verify your identity and protect important information, such as your credit card number, on the Internet. A **certificate** is a statement verifying the identity of a person or the security of a web site. You can obtain your personal security certification from an independent Certification Authority (CA). A personal certificate verifies your identity to a secure web site that requires a certificate, while a web site certificate verifies its security to you before you send it information. When you visit a secure web site (one whose address may start with "https" instead of "http"), the site automatically sends you its certificate, and Internet Explorer displays a lock icon on the status bar. A certificate is also known as a Digital ID in other programs, such as Windows Live Mail.

Import a Certificate

1. In the Start screen or Start menu, click or tap **All apps**, and then click or tap **Control Panel** under Windows System.

2. Click or tap the **Internet Options** icon in Small icons or Large icons view.

3. Click or tap the **Content** tab.

4. Click or tap **Certificates**.

5. Click or tap the tab with the type of certificate you want.

6. Click or tap **Import**.

7. Follow the instructions in the Certificate Import Wizard to import a certificate.

8. Click or tap **Close**.

9. Click or tap **OK**.

Click or tap to find out about site certificate problems

Blocking Pop-Up Ads

The Pop-up Blocker prevents most unwanted pop-up windows from appearing. When Internet Explorer blocks an ad, a new window appears with an alert message. Blocked items are replaced in the window with a red "x". The Notification bar in Internet Explorer lets you temporarily or permanently open pop-ups, change Pop-up Blocker settings, and get help. With the Pop-up Blocker Settings dialog box, you can allow or disallow pop-ups from specific sites, play a sound or show the Notification bar when a pop-up is blocked, and set a filter level to block pop-ups.

Set Options to Pop-Up Blocker

1 In the Start screen or Start menu, click or tap **All apps**, and then click or tap **Control Panel** under Windows System.

2 Click or tap the **Internet Options** icon in Small icons or Large icons view.

3 Click or tap the **Privacy** tab.

4 Select the **Turn on Pop-up Blocker** check box.

5 Click or tap **Settings**.

6 To add a pop-up exception, enter a web site address, then click or tap **Add**.

7 Select or clear check boxes to play sound or show on Notification bar when an pop-up is blocked.

8 Click or tap the **Filter level** list arrow, then click or tap a pop-up filter: **High**, **Medium**, **Low**.

9 Click or tap **Close**.

10 Click or tap **OK**.

Protecting Against Phishing

Phishing is a technique people use to trick PC users into revealing personal for financial information. Typically, a phishing scam starts with an email message that appears to come from a trusted source, such as a bank or credit card company, but actually directs recipients to provide information to a fraudulent web site. Windows and Internet Explorer provide the SmartScreen Filtering to increase security to help protect you from phishing schemes. You can set SmartScreen filtering options on the Safety menu in Internet Explorer. You can check web sites for phishing and report them to Microsoft if you think they are fraudulent.

Protect or Unprotect Against Phishing

1. In Internet Explorer, click or tap the **Tools** button on the toolbar, and then point to **Safety**.

2. Click or tap **Turn On SmartScreen Filter** or **Turn Off SmartScreen Filter** on the menu.

3. Click or tap the **Turn on SmartScreen Filter (recommended)**, or **Turn off SmartScreen Filter** option.

4. Click or tap **OK**.

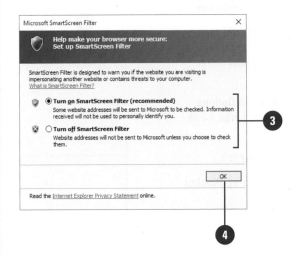

For Your Information

Blocking Sites with Do No Track

The Do Not Track option blocks requests from websites and advertising platforms from collecting user data. In Internet Explorer, click or tap the Tools button on the toolbar, and then point to Safety, click or tap Turn On Do Not Track Requests or Turn Off Do Not Track Requests on the menu, and then click or tap Turn On or Turn Off. You'll need to restart Internet Explorer to enable or disable Do No Track.

Check and Report a Web Site for Phishing

1. In Internet Explorer, click or tap the **Tools** button on the toolbar, and then point to **Safety**.

2. Click or tap the command you want to perform:

   ◆ **Check This Website.** Click or tap **Check This Website**, click or tap **OK**, and then respond to the alerts as needed.

   ◆ **Report Unsafe Website.** Click or tap **Report Unsafe Website**, specify the website language, select the **I think this is a phishing website** check box, and then click or tap **Submit**.

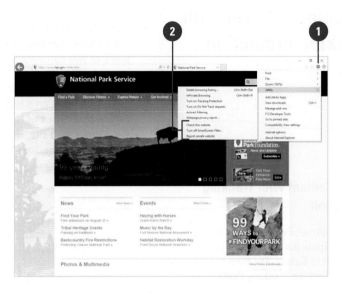

Results of check this web site

Web site to submit a possible phishing site

Did You Know?

You can display security information in the Security Status bar. While you browse the web, Internet Explorer automatically checks for valid web site certificates and any irregularities that might indicated a possible phishing site or any unwanted or malicious programs. If Internet Explorer detects a potential problem, it displays a color warning in the Address bar with text in the Security Status bar on the right indicating the problem type. The Address bar displays red for certificate errors and known phishing sites, green for sites with high security (connected to the certificate), and yellow for suspected phishing sites. You can click or tap the security icon in the Security Status bar to find out more information and possible solutions.

Blocking Content with Tracking Protection

Tracking Protection Lists (TPL) provide enhanced privacy by preventing web sites you visit from automatically sending details about your visit to the content providers. You can create a personalized list of sites to block or you can install a TPL add-on that will do it for you. When you install a TPL, a Do Not Track signal is sent to web sites and content providers not already blocked by the TPL. When Tracking Protecting is filtering content on a web site, a blue Do Not Track icon appears in the Address bar. Click or tap on the icon to turn off Tracking Protection for the current web site. If content is blocked, some portions of a web site may not be available.

Block Content with Tracking Protection

1. In Internet Explorer, click or tap the **Tools** button on the toolbar, point to **Safety**, and then click or tap **Turn on Tracking Protection**.

2. If prompted to install a TPL, click or tap **Get a Tracking Protection List online**, click or tap **Add** for the TPL you want, and then click or tap **Add List**.

3. Click or tap **Tracking Protection**.

4. To enable or disable, or remove an installed TPL add-on, select the TPL add-on, and then click or tap **Enable**, **Disable**, or **Remove**.

5. To use your personal list, select **Your Personalized List**, do any of the following:

   ◆ **Enable** or **Disable**. Enables or disables the use of your personalized list.

   ◆ **Settings.** Allows you to select options to automatically block or choose content to block or allow. Select the options you want, and then click or tap OK.

6. Click or tap **Close**.

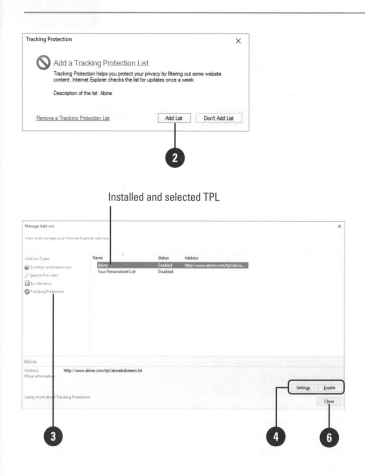

Installed and selected TPL

Managing Add-Ons

Add-ons are programs that extend the functionality of Internet Explorer to perform a unique task, such as provide search toolbars or display Flash content. In most cases, add-ons are useful, but sometimes poorly built or old ones can slow down your PC, cause system crashes, or invade your privacy (such as Spyware or Adware that are sometimes deceptively installed). To help you work with add-ons, Internet Explorer includes the Add-on Manager, which provides a list of add-ons currently loaded or used by Internet Explorer. they are grouped into types: Toolbars and Extensions, Search Providers, Accelerators, and Tracking Protection. You can use the Add-on Manager to individually enable, disable, or update add-ons. The Add-on Manager can also detect add-ons related crashes in Internet Explorer and displays an option to disable it.

Manage Browser Add-Ons

1. In the Start screen or Start menu, click or tap **All apps,** and then click or tap **Control Panel** under Windows System.

2. Click or tap the **Internet Options** icon in Small icons or Large icons view.

3. Click or tap the **Programs** tab.

4. Click or tap **Manage add-ons**.

   TIMESAVER *In Internet Explorer, click or tap the Tools button on the toolbar, and then click or tap Manage add-ons.*

5. Click or tap the type of add-ons you want to display.

6. Click or tap the **Show** list arrow, and then click or tap the option with the type of add-ons you want to display.

7. Click or tap the add-on you want to manage.

8. Click or tap **Enable** or **Disable**.

9. Click or tap **Close**.

10. Click or tap **OK**.

Protecting Privacy with Edge

Before you start browsing with Edge (**New!**) and searching the web, you should take a look at the privacy settings and make any changes to make sure your personal data is protected. You set options to block content from services that could track your browsing, send Do Not Track requests to sites, block third-party cookies, and let sites ask for my physical location. Web services allow you to improve your browsing experience by sharing information with Microsoft. You set options to flip ahead with page prediction (share history), suggestions as I type, protect my PC from malware and phishing sites with SmartScreen and play protected media with downloaded licenses, identifiers, and data.

Change Edge Privacy Settings

1. Click or tap **Edge** on the Start screen or Start menu.

2. Click the **More** button (. . .), and then click or tap **Settings**.

3. Click or tap the **View advanced settings** button on the Settings panel.

4. Drag the Slider **On** or **Off** for the following options:

   ◆ Offer to save passwords. When On, click or tap the **Manage my saved passwords** link.

   ◆ Save form entries.

   ◆ Send Do Not Track Requests.

   ◆ Have Cortana assist me in Microsoft Edge.

   ◆ Search in the address bar with. Add or select a search engine from the list.

   ◆ Show search suggestions as I type.

   ◆ Cookies. Select an option: **Block all cookies, Block only third party cookies**, or Don't block cookies.

   ◆ Let sites save protected media licenses on my devices.

   ◆ Help protect me from malicious sites and downloads with SmartScreen Filter.

5. Click or tap a blank area of the screen to exit the panel.

Back button to Settings panel

Managing Windows

Introduction

Windows 10 offers a number of useful tools for managing and maintaining routine tasks on your PC. Windows 10 comes with File History that allows you to back up and restore drives and files on your system. Keeping your PC up-to-date is a way to keep your PC in good working condition and protect it against new and ongoing attacks over the Internet. Windows Update scans your PC for any software components or fixes (including security and high priority updates) that need to be installed and automatically or manually downloads them from the Internet.

A **hardware device** is any physical device that you plug into and is controlled by your PC or mobile device. This device can be a mouse or keyboard card that you install inside your system. It can be a printer or a scanner that you plug into the outside of the system. When you plug or insert a hardware device into the appropriate port or expansion slot, Windows attempts to recognize the device and configure it for you using plug-and-play technology. Plug-and-play technology will recognize most any kind of hardware device, such as a mouse, modem, keyboard, game controller, laptop battery, or secondary monitor just to name a few. All hardware devices can be managed or removed from Settings or the Control Panel.

Windows 10 comes with many tools for managing files and folders across multiple PCs and devices. A **network** is a system of two or more PC computers and other mobile devices connected together to share resources. It consists of at least one host and one client. Using the Network icon and Settings, you can view the entire network (hosts and clients) and create and manage your network connections.

Keeping a File History

File History (**New!**) allows you to make back up copies of files that are in your libraries, favorites, OneDrive, and your desktop to an external drive or network location. If you have files or folders in other locations, you can include them in an existing library or create a new one. In Settings or the Control Panel, you can specify advanced settings to specify how often to save copies and how long to keep them. You can quickly restore a folder or individual file to the version you want.

Back Up Using File History

1. Click or tap the **Settings** button on the Start screen or Start menu.

2. Click or tap **Update & security**.

3. Click or tap **Backup** under Update & security (**New!**).

4. If available, click or tap the **Add** button (+) to select a backup location.

   It means a back up drive has not been selected.

5. Drag the Slider **On** or **Off** to enable or disable automatic back ups.

6. To close the window, click or tap the **Close** button (x).

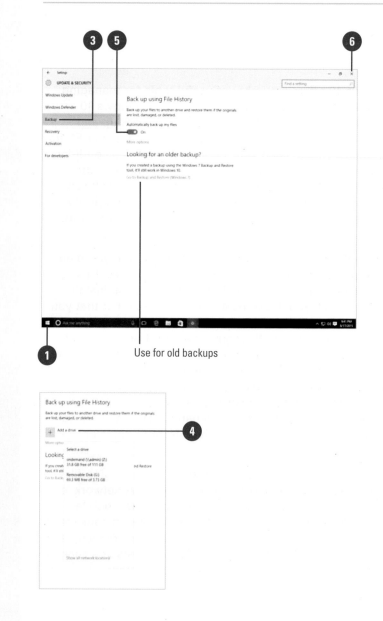

Use for old backups

Did You Know?

You can set advanced settings in the Control Panel. In Setting under Update & Security in Backup, click or tap More Options link, click or tap the See Advanced Settings link, and then set options in Control Panel.

You can restore files from a current backup in the Control Panel. In Setting under Update & Security in Backup, click or tap More Options link, click or tap the Restore Files From A Current Backup link, and then set options in Control Panel.

Set Up File History Options

1 Click or tap the **Settings** button on the Start screen or Start menu.

2 Click or tap **Update & security**.

3 Click or tap **Backup** under Update & security.

4 Click or tap the **More options** link (**New!**).

5 Click or tap the list arrow, and then select an option:

◆ **Back up my files.** Specify an interval.

◆ **Keep my backups.** Specify when to get rid of backups.

6 To add a folder, click or tap the **Add** button (+), and then select a folder.

7 To remove a folder, select the folder, and then click or tap **Remove**.

8 To exclude a folder, click or tap the **Add** button (+), and then select a folder.

9 To change the current backup drive, click or tap **Stop using drive**, click the **Back** button, and then click or tap the **Add** button (+), and then select a drive.

10 To perform a manual back up, click or tap **Back up now**.

11 To close the window, click or tap the **Close** button (x).

Restoring a File History

When you use File History to make back up copies of files that are in your libraries, favorites, OneDrive, and your desktop to an external drive or network location, you can quickly restore a folder or individual file to the version you want. If you have files or folders in other locations, you can include them in an existing library or create a new one. You can specify advanced settings to specify how often to save copies and how long to keep them. When you restore files, you can replace the original in the same location or keep both versions. If you not sure about a file version, you can open it directly in File History to view it.

Restore a File or Folder Using File History

1. Click or tap the **Settings** button on the Start screen or Start menu.

2. Click or tap **Update & security**.

3. Click or tap **Backup** under Update & security.

4. Click or tap the **More options** link, and then click or tap the **Restore files from a current backup** link.

5. Navigate to the file or folder that you want to restore.

6. To open a file, double-click or double-tap the file icon.

   ◆ Use the **Back** and **Forward** buttons to move back and forth between folders and files.

   A document preview appears, where you can review versions.

7. Click or tap the **Previous version** or **Next version** button to view them.

8. To restore a version, click or tap the **Restore to original location** button.

9. Click or tap **Replace the file in the destination**, **Skip this file**, or **Compare info for both files**.

10. Click or tap the **Close** button (x).

Back and Forward buttons

Getting Information About Windows

If you're not sure what version of Windows your PC is running, what system requirements your PC includes, or what name is assigned to your PC, you can display that information in About in Settings under System. If your version of Windows is not yet activated, you can active the software as well as upgrade it if you want. In addition to displaying information, you can also join a domain (like a work or school network) or join Azure AD (Active Directory). If you need to change the name of your PC, you can do it here; although I suggest you don't do it unless requested by an Administrator.

Get Windows About Windows and Your PC

1. Click or tap the **Settings** button on the Start screen or Start menu.

2. Click or tap **System**.

3. Click or tap **About** under System.

4. View the information about Windows and your PC.

5. To change the product key or update Windows, click or tap the **Change product key or upgrade your edition of Windows** link.

6. To rename your PC, click or tap **Rename PC**, and then specify the requested information.

7. To join a domain or Azure AD (server), click or tap **Join a Domain** or **Join Azure AD**, and then specify the requested information.

8. To close the window, click or tap the **Close** button (x).

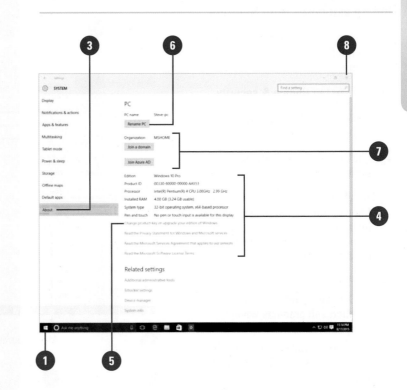

Did You Know?

You can activate Windows. In Settings, click or tap Update & Security, click or tap Activation, and then activate windows or change the product key.

Updating and Refreshing Windows

In Settings under Update & Security, you can set options to update windows with the latest fixes, patches, and Windows apps as well as refresh (reinstall), reset (new install), or restart the Windows 10 operating system. You can set automatic updates or schedule or defer (**New!**) them for later. If your system is not running very well, you can refresh the Windows software without affecting your personal files. You can also start up from a device such as a USB or DVD, change Windows startup settings, or restore Windows from a system image (.iso).

Update Windows with Settings

① Click or tap the **Settings** button on the Start screen or Start menu.

② Click or tap **Update & security**.

③ Click or tap **Windows Update** under Update & security.

④ Click or tap the **Advanced options** link.

⑤ To set update options, click the **Choose how updates are installed** list arrow, and then select **Automatic (recommended)** or **Notify to schedule restart**.

⑥ Select or clear check boxes.

◆ **Give me updates for other Microsoft products when I update Window.**

◆ **Defer upgrades.** Download and install upgrades later (**New!**).

⑦ Click or tap links.

◆ **View your update history.** View or uninstall updates.

◆ **Choose how updates are delivered.** Set options (**New!**) to specify how to get updates.

⑧ Click or tap the **Back** button to return to the previous screen.

⑨ Click or tap **Check now**; if available, click or tap the **View details** link and then click or tap **Download** or **Install**.

⑩ To close the window, click or tap the **Close** button (x).

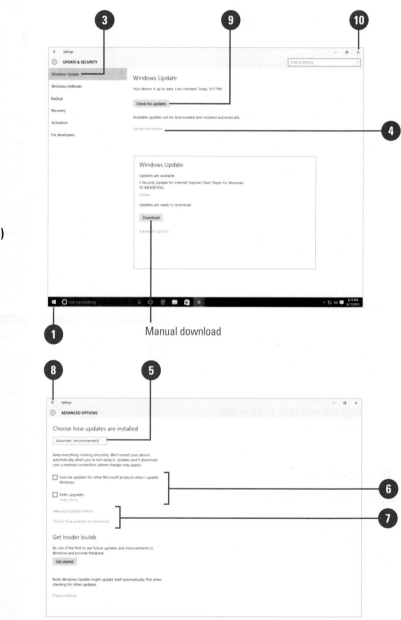

Manual download

Refresh, Remove, or Startup Windows in Settings

1. Click or tap the **Settings** button on the Start screen or Start menu.

2. Click or tap **Update & security**.

3. Click or tap **Recovery** under Update & security.

4. Specify the options you want:

   ◆ Reset this PC (keep file or remove them). Click or tap **Get started**, and then follow the wizard instructions to reinstall Windows and keep your files or remove your files.

   ◆ Advanced startup. Click or tap **Restart now** to restart up from a device or disc. Choose an option from the Restart screen: **Continue**, **Troubleshoot**, or **Turn off your PC**.

      ◆ For Troubleshoot, choose an option: **Refresh your PC**, **Reset your PC**, or **Advanced options**.

      ◆ For Advanced options, choose an option: **System Restore**, **System Image Recovery**, **Startup Repair**, **Command Prompt**, or **Startup Settings**.

Reset option for this PC

Viewing Hardware Devices

If you connect an external device—typically those you plug into a USB port or add wirelessly—to your system, Windows 10 detects and installs it using plug and play. After a device is installed, it appears in the Devices and Printers folder, Devices panel and in Settings. The Devices and Printers folder and Settings are two places where you can check and manage all devices connected to your system—such as a USB hard drives, flash drives, webcams, Bluetooth, scanners, keyboards, or mice. Devices installed inside your system—such as internal hard drives, disc drives, sound cards, video cards, RAM, and older devices—do not appear in the Devices and Printers folder; you can find these devices in the Device Manager. In the Devices and Printers folder, you can add a new wireless or network device or printer to your system. If there is a problem with a device (indicated by a yellow warning icon), you can also start the troubleshooter to help you detect and fix the problem.

View Hardware Devices

1. In the Start screen or Start menu, click or tap **All apps**, and then click or tap **Control Panel** under Windows System.

2. Click or tap the **Devices and Printers** icon in Small icons or Large icons view.

3. Click or tap the **down** or **up** arrow to expand or collapse the Devices or Printers and Faxes section.

4. Click or tap a hardware device.

5. View hardware details in the Details pane.

6. For more information about a hardware device, double-click or double-tap the device icon.

7. View the hardware properties.

8. Click or tap **OK**.

9. If you see a yellow warning icon for a hardware device, click or tap the device, click or tap the **Troubleshoot** button on the toolbar, and then follow the instructions to detect and fix the problem.

10. Click or tap the **Close** button (x).

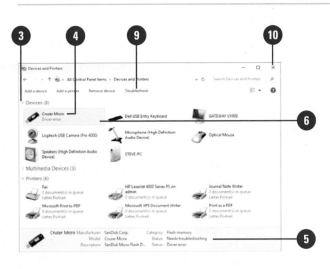

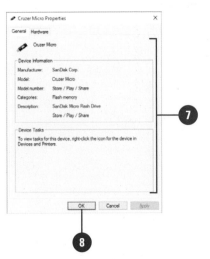

Work with Devices in Settings

1. Click or tap the **Settings** button on the Start screen or Start menu.

2. Click or tap **Devices**.

3. Click or tap **Printers & scanners** or **Connected devices** under Devices.

4. Specify the options you want for the category.

    ◆ Add a device. Click or tap the **Add** button (+), select the device, and then follow the on-screen instructions.

    ◆ Remove a device. Select the device, and then click or tap the **Remove device** button.

5. Drag the Slider **On** or **Off** to allow or prevent metered connections to download and install devices.

6. To view devices and printer in the Control Panel or the Device Manager, click or tap the links.

7. To close the window, click or tap the **Close** button (x).

Did You Know?

You can quickly delete a printer. In the Devices and Printers window, select the printer icon you want to delete, and then click or tap Remove Device, and then click or tap Yes.

See Also

See "Installing Hardware Devices and Printers" on page 384 for more information on installing devices using a wizard in the Control Panel.

Add button

4

5

6

3

Printers & scanners

Remove device button

Installing Hardware Devices and Printers

Before you install a new hardware device, be sure to carefully read the product installation guide provided by the manufacturer. If the hardware device comes with an installation disc, it is recommended that you use the manufacturer's disc and related instructions to install the hardware. If the product documentation instructs you to perform a typical plug and play installation, turn off your system, physically connect your hardware to your system, and then turn on your system again. In most cases, Windows detects your new hardware device and installs it or starts the Add a device or Add a printer wizard. The wizard installs hardware devices by asking you a series of questions to set up the necessary software for the new hardware device. If Windows doesn't detect the new hardware, you can start the wizard in the Devices and Printers folder and select the new hardware device to install it. You might need to be logged on as an administrator in order to install a hardware device.

Install a Hardware Device or Printer Using a Wizard

1 If necessary, attach the hardware device or printer you want to install according the manufacturers directions.

If Windows doesn't detect and install it, use the Add a device or Add a printer wizard to complete the installation.

2 In the Start screen or Start menu, click or tap **All apps**, and then click or tap **Control Panel** under Windows System.

3 Click or tap the **Devices and Printers** icon in Small icons or Large icons view.

4 Click or tap the **Add a device** or **Add a printer** button on the toolbar.

5 Select the discovered device you want to install.

6 Click or tap **Next** to continue.

7 Follow the wizard instructions to complete the installation; steps vary depending on the hardware device.

For Your Information

More About Plug and Play Hardware

Windows includes plug and play support for hardware, making it easy to install and uninstall devices quickly. With plug and play support, you simply plug the device in, and Windows sets the device to work with your existing hardware and resolves any system conflicts. When you install a hardware device, Windows installs related software, known as a **driver**, that allows the hardware to communicate with Windows and other software applications. Plug and play tells the device drivers where to find the hardware devices. Plug and play matches up physical hardware devices with the software device drivers that operate them and establish channels of communication between each physical device and its driver.

Removing Hardware Devices

Most plug and play hardware devices, such as a USB Flash or external drive, can be removed and unplugged at anytime as long as the system is not using it. If the Safely Remove Hardware icon appears in the notification area on the taskbar, you can use it to quickly and safely remove the hardware. If you no longer use a hardware device (not plug and play), such as a sound or modem card, or if you have an older hardware device that you want to upgrade, you need to remove the hardware device drivers and related software before you remove the physical hardware device, which you can do with the Device Manager.

Remove or Eject a Plug and Play Hardware Device Safely

1. In the desktop, click or tap the **Safely Remove Hardware and Eject Media** icon in the notification area on the taskbar, and then select a device.

   TIMESAVER *Right-click or tap-hold the device in the Computer window, and then click or tap Safely Remove.*

2. If prompted, click or tap **OK** to confirm the removal.

3. Unplug or eject the device.

Eject media 1

Remove a Hardware Device

1. In the Start screen or Start menu, click or tap **All apps**, and then click or tap **Control Panel** under Windows System.

2. Click or tap the **Device Manager** icon in Small icons or Large icons view.

3. Click or tap the white arrow next to the hardware category you want to expand.

4. Click or tap the device you want to remove.

5. Click or tap the **Uninstall** button, and then click or tap **OK**.

6. Click or tap the **Close** button (x).

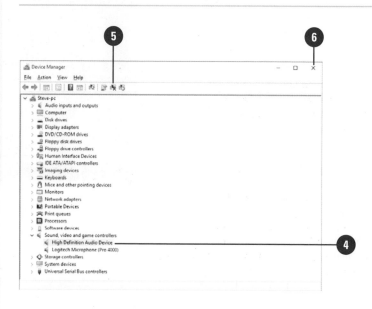

Connecting to Networks

You can have multiple network connections on your device. For example, with a laptop PC, you can have a wireless (Wi-Fi) connection, ethernet broadband connection with a cable, or VPN (Virtual Private Network) secure connection between your PC computer and the network. Windows also supports Bluetooth-enabled hardware devices, allowing you to use wireless devices, including wireless keyboards, mice, printers, and connections with cell phones and other devices, like speakers. You can view all your connections with the Network icon on the taskbar or in Settings. In Settings under Update & Security (**New!**), you can specify options to set up network connections.

Connect and Disconnect Networks

◆ **Wi-Fi Network.** Click or tap the **Wi-Fi Network** icon on the taskbar, select the network, click or tap **Connect** (or **Disconnect**), and then enter the password and instructions.

 ◆ **Connect automatically.** Select the check box to enable it.

◆ **Cellular Network.** Click or tap the **Network** icon on the taskbar, select the cellular network. This is available if you have a SIM card like you do on a cell phone.

◆ **VPN Network.** Click or tap the **Action Center** icon on the taskbar, click or tap **VPN**, and then select a network in Settings.

◆ **Bluetooth Network.** Click or tap the **Action Center** icon on the taskbar, click or tap **Connect** (or **Disconnect**), and then select a device.

Did You Know?

You can set Airplane mode options. In Settings, click or tap Devices, click or tap Airplane mode, and then drag the Slider On or Off to stop all wireless communications or Wireless Network Connection.

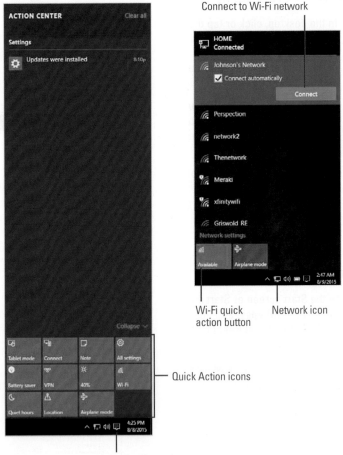

Connect to Wi-Fi network

Wi-Fi quick action button

Network icon

Quick Action icons

Action Center icon

Set Up Network Connections

1 Click or tap the **Settings** button on the Start screen or Start menu.

2 Click or tap **Network & Internet**.

> **TIMESAVER** *Click or tap the Network icon on the taskbar, and then click or tap the Network Settings link.*

3 Click or tap **Data usage** under Network & Internet.

4 View data usage or click or tap the **Usage details** link to find out app specific usage.

- ◆ **View storage.** Click or tap the **Storage settings** link to view drive and app size usage.

5 Click or tap a category under Network & Internet.

6 Select links or options to specify connection settings:

- ◆ **Wi-Fi.** Use to enable or disable Wi-Fi and select networks.

- ◆ **Airplane mode.** Use to enable or disable all wireless: Wi-Fi, cellular, Bluetooth, and GPS.

- ◆ **VPN.** Click or tap the **Add** button (+), and then connect to and select a network.

- ◆ **DirectAccess.** Use to connect to a workplace entry point in an enterprise network.

- ◆ **Dial-up.** Click or tap the **Set up a new connection** link.

- ◆ **Ethernet.** Use to connect to or change ethernet settings.

- ◆ **Proxy.** Use for Ethernet or Wi-Fi connections as needed by ISP.

7 To close the window, click or tap the **Close** button (x).

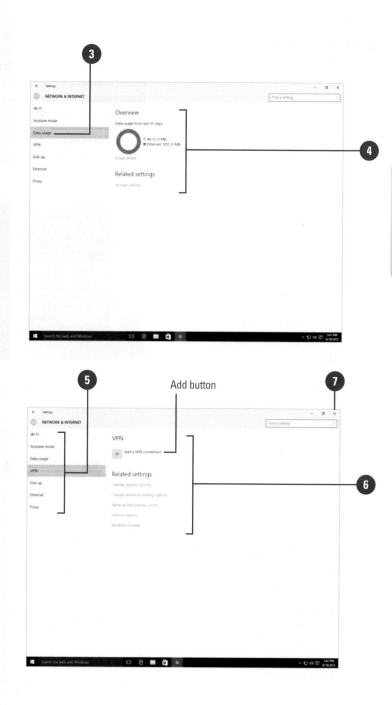

Add button

Using Quick Actions

Quick actions (**New!**) appear on the Action Center panel as buttons for easy access. The quick action buttons take you to Settings or turn on or off options or apps. The typical quick action buttons include Tablet mode, Connect, Note, All Settings, Battery saver, VPN, Brightness, Wi-Fi, Quiet Hours (not disturbed by any notifications from the system or apps), Location (GPS your location), and Airplane mode (transmit all mobile device data). However, options might vary depending on your device and connections. In addition, you can customize your top four quick actions in Settings, which you can collapse in the Action Center panel.

Use Quick Actions

1. Click or tap the **Action Center** icon on the taskbar, swipe in from the right edge, or press Win+A.

2. Click or tap a quick action icon on the Action Center panel to turn on or off a setting or app.

   The icons vary depending on your device and connections.

3. To close the panel, click or tap off of the panel or press Esc.

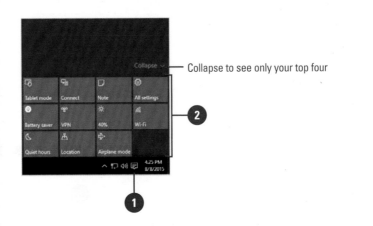

Collapse to see only your top four

Customize Quick Actions

1. Click or tap the **Settings** button on the Start screen or Start menu.

2. Click or tap **System**.

3. Click or tap **Notifications & actions** under System.

4. Click or tap a quick action icon, and then select an available action; options vary depending on your device options.

5. To close the window, click or tap the **Close** button (x).

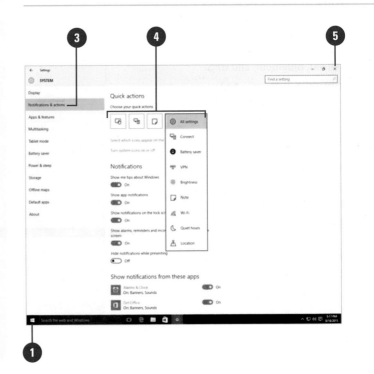

Using Tablet Mode

If you have a tablet or 2-in-1 PC, tablet mode (**New!**) makes it easier to use your device with a touch screen. In Settings, you can set options to make it easier for you to quickly switch into tablet mode when you want it. A helpful option allows you to specify what mode you want when you sign in to Windows and how you want to switch. To make it easy to turn table mode on and off, you can use Table mode button on the Action Center (**New!**).

Use Tablet Mode

1. Click or tap the **Settings** button on the Start screen or Start menu.

2. Click or tap **System**.

3. Click or tap **Tablet mode** under System.

4. Drag the Slider **On** or **Off** to enable or disable Make Windows more touch-friendly when using your device as a tablet.

   TIMESAVER *Click the Action Center icon on the taskbar, and then click or tap the Tablet mode button to toggle on or off.*

5. Click or tap the **When I sign in** list arrow, and then select an option: **Automatically switch to tablet mode**, **Go to the desktop**, or **Remember what I used last**.

6. Click or tap the **When this device automatically switches tablet mode on or off** list arrow, and then select an option: **Always ask me before switching** or **Don't ask me and always switch**.

7. Drag the Slider **On** or **Off** to enable or disable Hide app icons on the taskbar in tablet mode.

8. To close the window, click or tap the **Close** button (x).

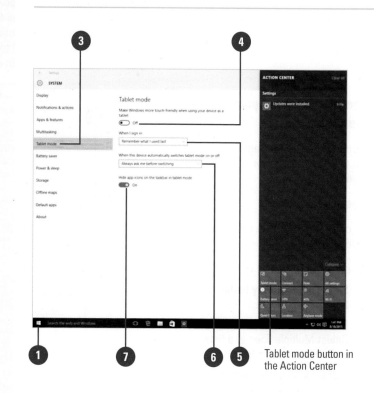

Tablet mode button in the Action Center

Changing Mouse and Touchpad Settings

A mouse does not require adjustments after you plug it in and start Windows. However, you can use Mouse and touchpad options in Settings or Mouse properties in the Control Panel to change the way your mouse or touchpad works and the way the pointer looks and behaves. For the mouse, you can switch the role of the buttons, or you can change the double-click or taping speed. For the mouse pointer, you can modify its appearance using a pointer scheme, change its speed, improve its visibility with a pointer trail, or set it to be hidden when you are typing. If your button has a wheel, roll the wheel with your forefinger to move up or down in a document or on a web page. If you have a tablet pen (**New!**) attached to your touchscreen device, you can set options to use and write with the pen like a mouse.

Change Mouse, Touchpad, or Pen Settings

1. Click or tap the **Settings** button on the Start screen or Start menu.

2. Click or tap **Devices**.

3. Click or tap **Mouse & touchpad** under Devices.

4. Specify the following options:

   ◆ **Select your primary button.** Select Left or Right.

   ◆ **Roll the mouse wheel to scroll.** Select Multiple lines at a time or One screen at a time.

   ◆ **Choose how many lines to scroll each time.** Drag to set the number of lines.

   ◆ **Scroll inactive windows when I hover over them.** Drag the Slider On or Off (**New!**).

5. If you have a touchpad, select a delay option before clicks work.

6. To change more options in the Control Panel, click or tap the **Additional mouse options** link.

7. If you have an attached pen, click or tap **Pen**, and then specify pen options (**New!**).

8. To close the window, click or tap the **Close** button (x).

Button options in the Control Panel

Change Pointer Appearance

1. In the Start screen or Start menu, click or tap **All apps**, and then click or tap **Control Panel** under Windows System.

2. Click or tap the **Mouse** icon in Small icons or Large icons view.

3. Click or tap the **Pointers** tab.

4. Click or tap the **Scheme** list arrow, and then select a pointer scheme.

5. Click or tap **OK**.

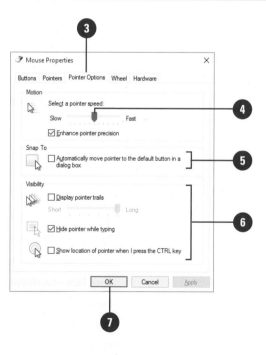

Change Pointer Options

1. In the Start screen or Start menu, click or tap **All apps**, and then click or tap **Control Panel** under Windows System.

2. Click or tap the **Mouse** icon in Small icons or Large icons view.

3. Click or tap the **Pointer Options** tab.

4. To adjust the pointer speed, drag the **Motion** slider.

5. To snap the pointer to a button, select the **Automatically move pointer to the default button in a dialog box** check box.

6. To display a trail after the pointer, hide the pointer while you type, or show the pointer location, select the visibility check box you want.

7. Click or tap **OK**.

Changing Keyboard Settings

While your keyboard should just work when you start up your system, you can use Keyboard properties in the Control Panel to adjust the rate at which a character is repeated when you hold down a key, and the time delay before it starts repeating. You can also adjust the blink rate of the insertion point.

Change Keyboard Settings

1. In the Start screen or Start menu, click or tap **All apps**, and then click or tap **Control Panel** under Windows System.

2. Click or tap the **Keyboard** icon in Small icons or Large icons view.

3. Click or tap the **Speed** tab.

4. To adjust the character repeat delay, drag the slider.

5. To adjust the character repeat rate, drag the slider.

6. Click or tap **OK**.

Common Keyboard Shortcuts	
Action	**Result**
Open or close Start (**New!**)	Win
Lock your PC	Win+L
Open Settings	Win+I
Open Action Center (**New!**)	Win+A
Open search (**New!**)	Win+S
Open Cortana in listening mode (**New!**)	Win+C
Open Task view (**New!**)	Win+Tab
Show or hide the desktop	Win+D
Add a virtual desktop (**New!**)	Win+Ctrl+D
Close the virtual desktop (**New!**)	Win+Ctrl+F4

Changing Typing Settings

In Settings, you can set options to misspelling as you type (**New!**). There are two available options. One option highlights misspelled words to make them easier to recognize when there is a problem. The other option is to AutoCorrect misspelled words as you type. The options are simple, however every effective as you type in a word processing or email app.

Change Typing Settings

1 Click or tap the **Settings** button on the Start screen or Start menu.

2 Click or tap **Devices**.

3 Click or tap **Typing** under Devices.

4 Drag the Slider **On** or **Off** to enable or disable Autocorrect misspelled words (**New!**) or Highlight misspelled words (**New!**).

5 To close the window, click or tap the **Close** button (x).

Adding a Secondary Monitor

If you need more space on your desktop to work, you can add a secondary monitor to your system. This allows you to view and work with more than one full size window on the screen at the same time. Before you can use more than one monitor, you need another **display adapter**—a hardware device that allows a system to communicate with its monitor—on your system, or use a built-in one that supports multiple monitor ports. One monitor serves as the primary display while the other serves as the secondary display. You can set the multiple displays to duplicate the displays on both monitors, extend the displays over two monitors, and show desktop only on one or the other. In addition, you can set different screen resolutions and orientation settings for each monitor.

Set Secondary Monitor Options

1. Right-click or tap-hold a blank area on the desktop, and then click or tap **Display settings**.

   ◆ You can also, click or tap **Settings** on the Start screen or Start menu, click or tap **System**, and then click or tap **Display**.

2. If the secondary monitor doesn't appear, click or tap **Detect**.

3. Click or tap the **Multiple displays** list arrow, and then select an option:

   ◆ **Duplicate these displays.**

   ◆ **Extend these displays.**

   ◆ **Show desktop only on 1.**

   ◆ **Show desktop only on 2.**

4. Select a monitor icon or drag an icon to represent how you want to move items between monitors.

5. To change the primary display, select a non primary monitor, and then select the **Make this my main display** check box.

6. Click or tap **Apply**.

7. To close the open window, click or tap the **Close** button (x).

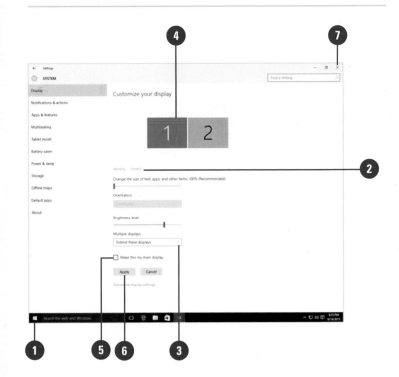

Saving Battery Life

If you have a mobile device—such as a laptop, 2-in-1, tablet, or phone—with a battery, you can use the Battery icon on the taskbar to quickly determine your battery life in percentages. You can also use Settings to enable or disable battery saver (**New!**) or specify when it automatically turns on, and how you want to use the battery for optimum use. For example, you can lower screen brightness while in battery saver and allow notifications from apps while in battery saver.

Change Battery Saver Settings

1. Click or tap the **Settings** button on the Start screen or Start menu.

2. Click or tap **System**.

3. Click or tap **Battery saver** under System.

4. To find out how your system and apps use battery, click or tap the **Batter use** link, and then view information.

   ◆ To return to the main screen, click or tap the **Back** button.

5. Drag the Slider **On** or **Off** to enable or display Battery saver.

6. To set Battery saver options, click or tap the **Batter saver settings** link.

7. Specify the following options:

   ◆ **Turn batter saver on automatically if my battery falls below.** Drag the Slider to the percentage you want.

   ◆ **Allow push notification from any app while in battery saver.**

   ◆ **Lower screen brightness while in battery saver.**

   ◆ Always allowed. Click or tap the **Add** button (+) to specify apps allows to use battery in the background.

   To return to the main screen, click or tap the **Back** button.

8. To close the window, click or tap the **Close** button (x).

Quick action buttons   Battery icon

Controlling Power Options

Windows 10 works more efficiently for longer battery life including less power use for DVD playback, automatic screen dimming, power off unused ports, and more accurate battery life. You can change power options properties for a laptop, notebook, or tablet to reduce power consumption and maximize battery life. For example, if you often leave your system for a short time while working, you can set your system to go into **sleep**, a state in which your system saves everything in memory and turns off your monitor and hard disks after being idle for a set time. If you are often away from your system for an extended time, you can set it to go into **hibernate**, a state in which your system saves everything in memory and to your hard disk, and then shuts down. To help you set power options, you can choose one of the power plans, modify one to suit your needs, or create your own. A **power plan** is a predefined collection of power usage settings (dim display, turn off display, put to sleep, and adjust brightness). If you want more options, you can set advanced options to define the power button (sleep, hibernate, or shut down) or other settings, such as **hybrid sleep**, which adds saving to your hard disk to sleep mode.

Select and Modify a Power Plan

① Click or tap the **Settings** button on the Start screen or Start menu.

② Click or tap **System**.

③ Click or tap **Power & sleep** under System.

④ Click or tap the list arrows to select a screen or sleep option.

⑤ Click or tap the **Additional power settings** link.

⑥ Click or tap the power plan option you want: **Balanced**, or **Power saver**, **High performance**.

⑦ Click or tap **Change plan settings** below the selected option.

⑧ Select an amount of time to: **Dim the display**, **Turn off the display**, **Put the computer to sleep**, or **Adjust plan brightness**.

⑨ To restore defaults, click or tap **Restore default settings for this plan**, and then click or tap **Yes**.

⑩ Click or tap **Save changes**.

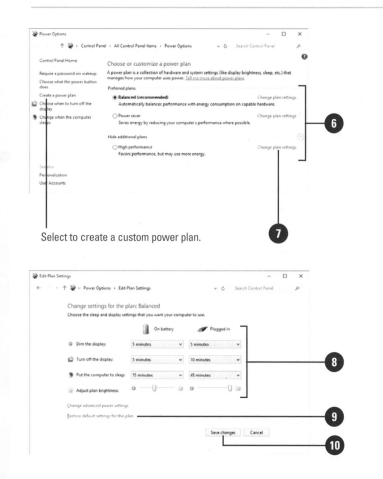

Select to create a custom power plan.

Define Power Button and Set Password Protection

① Click or tap the **Power** icon in the notification area, and then click or tap **More power options**.

- In the Control Panel, you can also click or tap the **Power Options** icon in the Small or Large icons view.

② Click or tap **Choose what the power buttons does**.

③ Specify the options you want when you press the power or sleep button, or when you close the lid.

④ Select the **Require a password (recommended)** or **Don't require a password** option.

⑤ Click or tap **Save changes**.

Set Advanced Options

① Click or tap the **Power** icon in the notification area, and then click or tap **More power options**.

- In the Control Panel, you can also click or tap the **Power Options** icon in the Small or Large icons view.

② Click or tap **Change plan settings** below the selected power plan.

③ Click or tap **Change advanced power settings**.

④ Click or tap the plus sign (+) and minus sign (-) icons to display the option you want to change.

⑤ Click or tap the option list arrow, and then select a setting.

⑥ Click or tap **OK**.

⑦ Click or tap **Save changes**.

Managing Storage Spaces

If you're running out of disk space on your device, you can see what's taking up space in Settings. If you have multiple drives, you can specify where to save apps, documents, and other files to save space. If you need more space, you can uninstall or move apps, view file storage (**New!**) sizes to know what to delete. If you have more than one drive attached to your system, you can also use Storage Spaces to group drives together in a storage pool. This allows Windows to save files on multiple drives. If there is a failure with a drive, your files are still protected. If you add more drives later, you can include them in the pool. You can use different types of internal and external drives, including USB, SATA, and SAS drives. Storage spaces are virtual drives that you can use in File Explorer.

Manage Storage

1. Click or tap the **Settings** button on the Start screen or Start menu.

2. Click or tap **System**.

3. Click or tap **Storage** under System.

4. To see what's taking up space, click or tap a drive to see what's taking up space.

   ◆ **Folders and Files.** Click or tap to view folders with files to remove items to free up space.

   ◆ **Apps.** Click or tap to open Apps & feature settings, where you can view space usage and remove apps to free up space.

   To return to the previous screen, click or tap the **Back** button.

5. To specify a save location for your apps, documents, music, pictures, and videos, click the list arrow, and then select a drive.

6. To close the window, click or tap the **Close** button (x).

Manage Storage Spaces

1 In the Start screen or Start menu, click or tap **All apps**, and then click or tap **Control Panel** under Windows System.

2 Click or tap the **Storage Spaces** icon in Small icons or Large icons view.

3 To set Storage Spaces, click or tap **Create a new pool and storage space**, select the drives, click or tap **Create pool**, enter a name and letter, select a layout, enter the max size, and then click or tap **Create storage space**.

4 To manage Storage Spaces, select from the following options.

- ◆ **Rename pool.** Renames the storage pool of drives.

- ◆ **Create a space.** Creates a new space.

- ◆ **Add drives.** Adds one or more drives to the pool.

- ◆ **View files.** View files in the pool.

- ◆ **Rename or Delete space.** Rename or delete a space.

- ◆ **Rename drive.** Renames a drive in the pool.

5 Click or tap the **Close** button (x).

Options to create a new pool and storage space

Did You Know?

You can clean up a drive to free up space. In File Explorer, select the drive in This PC, click or tap the Manage tab, click or tap the Cleanup button, select items to delete, (click or tap Clean Up System Files for only system files), and then click or tap OK.

Syncing with a Phone

If you have a Windows, Android, iPhone, or iPad, you can connect it to your PC or device and sync information between the two devices. With a Windows phone, it's a perfect pair with Windows 10; you can share information with Cortana, photos, music, OneNote, Skype, Office and Outlook and no setup is required. With an Android, iPhone, or iPad, you can sync content, however, there is some setup and apps required, such as OneDrive. You can get more information and get started from the Phone Companion app (**New!**). You'll need to sign in to your Microsoft account to make a connection.

Connect and Sync a Phone

1. In the Start screen or Start menu, and then click or tap **Phone Companion**.

2. View the information, and then click or tap a phone type to get more information.

3. Click or tap the content you want to sync.

4. Click or tap **Yes, this is me!** to sign in to your Microsoft account.

5. Follow the on-screen instructions to complete the connection and sign in to an app, as needed.

   ◆ To return to the main screen, click or tap the **Back** button.

6. When you're finished, click or tap **Done**.

7. To close the window, click or tap the **Close** button (x).

See Also

See "Syncing Files wtih OneDrive" on page 256 for more information on syncing content with your phone using OneDrive.

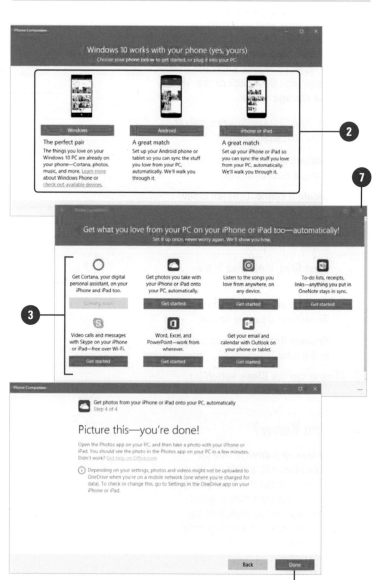

New! Features

Microsoft Windows 10

Microsoft Windows 10 comes with new features that make your PC computer or mobile device significantly easier and faster to use than earlier versions of Windows. Windows 10 makes it easier to use the Start screen, Start menu, Cortana (personal assistant), Action center and notifications, and accomplish other common tasks, such as browse the Internet, find and view photos, play music and videos, and change more settings. Windows 10 enhances the metro user experience with new apps, including Microsoft Edge, Get Started, Groove Music, Movies & TV, Money, Get Office, OneNote, and Phone Companion.

Only New Features

If you're already familiar with Microsoft Windows 8, you can access and download all the tasks in this book with Microsoft Windows 10 New Features to help make your transition to the new version simple and smooth. The Microsoft Windows 10 New Features, as well as other Windows 8 to 8 transition helpers, are available on the web at *www.perspection.com.*

What's New

If you're searching for what's new in Windows 10, just look for the icon: New!. The new icon appears in the table of contents and throughout this book so you can quickly and easily identify a new or improved feature in Windows 10. The following is a brief description of each new feature, and it's location in this book.

Windows 10

- ◆ **Windows Editions (p. 2)** Windows 10 comes with new editions, including Education and IoT Core.

- ◆ **Tablet mode (p. 2, 4, 7, 388-389)** You can optimize your experience for a PC computer with a mouse or mobile device with a touch screen or pad by turning Tablet mode on or off (available in the Actions center on the taskbar).

- ◆ **Windows Hello (p. 3, 20-21, 348)** Windows Hello changes how you sign in; it allows you to use your face or fingerprint instead of a password and still get enterprise-grade security. It's not available on all devices.

- **Get Started (p. 3, 18, 28)** You can get a welcome to Windows 10, find out what's new, and get general help on common topics of interest.

- **Desktop (p. 3, 8-9)** The desktop is no longer an app and goes back to the functionality of Windows 7 with some enhancements in Windows 10.

- **Start menu (p. 3, 6-7, 10, 23-25, 29-30)** The Start menu is back and includes easy access to all apps (frequently used in a list and pinned as tiles) and options to customize it. The Start menu is also added to the Start screen.

- **Gestures (p. 4-5)** Windows 10 comes with some new gestures to make it easier to navigation with touch.

- **Start screen (p. 6-7, 300, 302)** The Start screen includes the Start menu and taskbar.

- **Task View (p. 6, 12-15, 32-33, 320)** Task view allows you to switch among open programs and work directly with multiple desktops by using the Task View button on the taskbar. In Task view, you can create a new desktop (known as a virtual desktop) or switch between desktops and open windows. Pressing Alt+Tab still rotates among all running windows.

- **Taskbar (p. 6, 12-13, 220, 322-323)** The taskbar from Windows 7 returns to Windows 10 with some added features, including Search/Cortana, Task View button, and Action Center & notifications.

- **Search box (p. 6, 11, 12-13, 26-27, 44, 302)** The Search box appears on the taskbar where you can quickly search for content on your PC or the web. The Search box is integrated with Cortana.

- **Action Center (p. 6, 44, 322-323, 352-353, 386-389)** The Action Center allows you easier access to notifications and Quick Action buttons from the taskbar.

- **Microsoft Edge (p. 9, 28, 94-104, 108-112, 124-126, 374)** Edge is the first browser that lets you take notes, write, doodle, and highlight directly on webpages. Use the reading list to save your favorite articles for later, and then read them in reading view. Cortana is built in to Edge to help you do things faster and easier.

- **Cortana (p. 11, 18-19, 26-27, 44, 95, 104, 320)** Cortana is a digital personal assistant on your desktop that allows you to set up a meeting or send an email to a friend. Simply, select the Search box on the taskbar, type what you want Cortana to do, or just select the microphone to say it.

- **Virtual desktops (p. 14-15, 32-33, 308-309)** You can create and work with multiple desktops to help you manage and work with apps.

- **Power button (p. 22)** The Power button is available on the Sign in screen on the Start and Lock screen.

- **Touchpad gestures (p. 27)** (1) Swipe three fingers up to open Task view and see all your open apps, (2) Swipe three fingers down to show the desktop, and (3) Swipe three fingers either left or right to switch between your open apps. Slide fingers slowly across the touchpad to flip through them all.

◆ **New and improved apps** (p. 28, 136, 148-149, 158, 178, 192-193, 242, 254-257, 258-268, 290) Windows 10 comes with some new apps, including Microsoft Edge, Get Started, Groove Music, Movies & TV, Money, Get Office, OneNote, and Phone Companion. Windows 10 also improved some apps, including People, Contacts, Calendar, Mail, Photos, OneDrive, Get Skype, Camera, Xbox, Alarms & Clock, Calculator, and Snipping Tool.

◆ **Privacy options** (p. 46) The Privacy options in Settings include Speech, inking, & typing, Account info, Contacts, Calendar, Messaging, Radios, Feedback & diagnostics, and Background apps.

◆ **Quick access** (p. 48, 54, 60, 62, 81-82) In File Explorer, Quick access shows frequently used folders and recently used files alongside pinned items in the Navigation pane. Quick access has replaced Favorites.

◆ **Share Files** (p. 88) In File Explorer, you can share files using the Share button on the Share tab.

◆ **Write instead of type** (p. 258-259) In addition to Microsoft Edge, there are other apps, such as OneNote, where you can use a stylist pen, finger, or mouse to write everywhere you could type before.

◆ **Voice Recorder** (p. 234-235) You can record your own sound files. Voice Recorder creates Windows Media Audio files with the .wma file extension.

◆ **Settings** (p. 298-300, 302-304, 354-355, 356-357, 376-378, 393, 295, 398) You can access Settings from the Start menu, which displays a list of main categories, including System, Devices, Network & Internet, Personalization, Accounts, Time & Language, Ease of Access, Privacy, and Update & Security, where you can specify the options you want.

◆ **Ease of Access** (p. 327, 334) In Settings for Ease of Access, you can set formatting for closed captioning text.

◆ **Windows Backup and Restore** (p. 376-378) The old Windows 7 backup and restore programs, File History and the Windows 7 Backup and Restore tool, are available in Settings.

◆ **Quick Actions** (p. 388) Quick Actions appear on the Action Center panel as buttons for easy access. The Quick Action buttons take you to Settings or turn on or off options or apps.

◆ **Pen Device (p. 390)** With a touchscreen device, you can use a pen to write with like a mouse. In Settings for Mouse & Touchpad, you can specify options to use the pen.

◆ **Keyboard Shortcuts (p. 392)** Windows 10 comes with some new keyboard shortcuts to make it easier to perform commands and navigation around Windows.

◆ **AutoCorrect (p. 393)** In Settings for Typing, you can enable or disable options to highlight and correct misspellings as you type.

◆ **Battery Saver (p. 395)** In Settings for Battery Saver, you can enable or disable battery saver or specify when it automatically turns on, and how you want to use the battery for optimum use.

◆ **Phone Companion (p. 400)** If you have a Windows phone, Android, iPhone, or iPad, you can connect it to your PC or device and sync information between the two devices.

What Happen To ...

◆ **Charm bar** The Charm bar has been replaced by the redesigned Start menu.

◆ **Start bar** The Start bar has been replaced by the redesigned Start menu.

◆ **Windows Media Center** Windows Media Center has been removed, although Microsoft provides a free DVD player for Media Center previous owners.

◆ **Apps View button** The Apps View button has been replaced by the redesigned Start menu.

◆ **Finance app** The Finance app has been replaced by the Money app.

◆ **Help+Tips app** The Help+Tips app has been replaced by the Get Started app.

◆ **SkyDrive** SkyDrive has been replaced by OneDrive.

◆ **Video app** The Video app has been replaced by the Movies & TV app.

◆ **Favorites** In File Explorer, favorites in the Navigation pane has been replaced by Quick access, which shows frequently used folders and recently used files along with pinned items.

◆ **Travel** The Travel app have been removed from the product.

◆ **Sound Recorder** The Sound Recorder app has been replaced by the Voice Recorder app.

Index